All Things in the

Bible

All Things in the Bible

An Encyclopedia of the Biblical World

Volume 2

M–Z

Nancy M. Tischler

Ellen Johnston McHenry, Illustrator

Greenwood Press
Westport, Connecticut • London

Library of Congress Cataloging-in-Publication Data

Tischler, Nancy Marie Patterson.
    All things in the Bible / by Nancy M. Tischler ; Ellen Johnston McHenry, illustrator.
      p.   cm.
    Includes bibliographical references and index.
    ISBN: 0–313–33082–4 (set: alk. paper)—ISBN 0–313–33083–2 (Vol. 1: alk. paper)—
ISBN 0–313–33084–0 (Vol. 2: alk. paper)
    1. Bible—Encyclopedias.   I. Title.
  BS440.T57   2006
  220.3—dc22   2005034355

British Library Cataloguing in Publication Data is available.

Library of Congress Catalog Card Number: 2005034355
ISBN: 0–313–33082–4 (set)
     0–313–33083–2 (Vol. 1)
     0–313–33084–0 (Vol. 2)
ISSN:

First published in 2006

Greenwood Press, 88 Post Road West, Westport, CT 06881
An imprint of Greenwood Publishing Group, Inc.
www.greenwood.com

Printed in the United States of America

The paper used in this book complies with the
Permanent Paper Standard issued by the National
Information Standards Organization (Z39.48–1984).

10 9 8 7 6 5 4 3 2 1

For Merle

Contents

Alphabetical List of Entries

Guide to Related Topics

Agriculture

Agriculture
Chaff
Goad
Grains
Insects
Olives, Olive Oil, Olive Trees
Olive Press
Ox, Oxen
Plagues
Plants
Plow
Sheepfold
Threshing, Threshing Floor
Trees
Vineyards
Watchtower
Winepress, Wine-making
Yoke

Animals

Animals
Behemoth, Leviathan
Birds
Blood
Camel

Dogs
Donkey, Ass
Fish
Goats
Horse
Hunting
Ox, oxen
Serpent
Sheep
Swine, Pigs

Arts and Crafts

Art: Christian
Art: Jewish
Cosmetics, Ornamentation
Dance
Gemstones
Ivory
Jewelry
Leather
Metal and Mines
Metal: Copper and Bronze
Metal: Gold
Metal: Iron
Metal: Silver
Music

Abbreviations

2 Chronicles	2 Chron.
Ezra	Ezra
Nehemiah	Neh.
Esther	Esther
Job	Job
Psalms	Ps. (*pl.* Pss.)
Proverbs	Prov.
Ecclesiastes	Eccles.
Song of Solomon	Song of Sol.
Isaiah	Isa.
Jeremiah	Jer.
Lamentations	Lam.
Ezekiel	Ezek.
Daniel	Dan.
Hosea	Hos.
Joel	Joel
Amos	Amos
Obadiah	Obad.
Jonah	Jon.
Micah	Mic.
Nahum	Nah.
Habakkuk	Hab.
Zephaniah	Zeph.
Haggai	Hag.
Zechariah	Zech.
Malachi	Mal.

New Testament

Matthew	Matt.
Mark	Mark
Luke	Luke
John	John
Acts of the Apostles	Acts
Romans	Rom.
1 Corinthians	1 Cor.
2 Corinthians	2 Cor.
Galatians	Gal.

Ephesians	Eph.
Philippians	Phil.
Colossians	Col.
1 Thessalonians	1 Thess.
2 Thessalonians	2 Thess.
1 Timothy	1 Tim.
2 Timothy	2 Tim.
Titus	Titus
Philemon	Philem.
Hebrews	Heb.
James	James
1 Peter	1 Pet.
2 Peter	2 Pet.
1 John	1 John
2 John	2 John
3 John	3 John
Jude	Jude
Revelation	Rev.
or Apocalypse	Apoc.

Apocrypha

1 Esdras	1 Esd.
2 Esdras	2 Esd.
Tobit	Tob.
Judith	Jth.
The Rest of Esther	Rest of Esther
The Wisdom of Solomon	Wisd of Sol.
Ecclesiasticus	Ecclus.
Baruch	Bar.
The Song of the Three Holy Children	Song of Three Children
Susanna	Sus.
Bel and the Dragon	Bel and Dragon
Prayer of Manasses *or* Manasseh	Pr. of Man.
1 Maccabees	1 Macc.
2 Maccabees	2 Macc.

Magic

(Gen. 30:27; Exod. 7:5–13, 20:3; Deut.18:10, 18:14; 2 Kings 17: 8–17) Magic is the use of occult practices to determine the future or to influence the behavior of others. The ancients, when interpreting omens and divination, were usually seeking to read the future, not to alter it. Witchcraft and sorcery, on the other hand, involved practices that sought to cast **curses** or bring **blessings** on people or to alter the course of events. In Scripture, occult practices are strictly forbidden, largely because they imply allegiance to a pagan god or an **idol**. This relates to the first commandment, in which the Israelites were forbidden to "have any gods before me" (Exod. 20:3).

In the early stories of Genesis, the practice of divination by Laban (and possibly by other people of Padam Aran, the homeland of the Hebrews) suggests that this was part of the heritage of Abraham's family. Laban discovered through divination that he was blessed because of Jacob (Gen. 30:27). Shortly after this, Jacob used poplar branches to breed spotted cattle, apparently also using magic for his own purposes, although there are various interpretations of this action (Gen. 30:37). His wife Rebekah seems also to have believed in pagan practices, using mandrake roots to help her conceive (Gen. 30:14). Her subsequent theft of the household gods (small images probably made of clay) and her duplicity in hiding them under her clothes indicate that she believed they would bring her luck (Gen. 31:19ff).

Although this practice of idolatry is not apparent in the rest of the stories of the patriarchs, Joseph did display a talent for reading **dreams**, a form of divination much admired by the **Egyptians**. He alienated his own family by his offensive display of this talent but won the attention of the Pharaoh. His abilities apparently went beyond the benign practice of interpretation of dreams: the cup that he placed in Benjamin's sack is the one his servants identify as "the cup my master drinks from and also uses for divination" (Gen. 44:5). This sounds a bit like the modern reading of tea leaves, a practice that has ancient roots.

In **Egypt**, which was famous for its magicians, Moses found himself forced to prove his god's power to be greater than the power of local deities through magical contests. This would seem to have been the motive behind the scene when he turned the rods into snakes. The court magicians also found the means to make their rods come alive—through "secret arts." Moses and Aaron proved the superior power of God over the demonic powers of the "wise men" and "magicians" by commanding snakes to devour the others (Exod. 7:5–13). The following plagues reinforced this early message of the magic trick, becoming increasing fierce, signaling the overwhelming superiority of the God of Moses.

Probably because the Hebrews were infected by Egyptian thinking through their years of residence in this country, the **law** of Moses explicitly forbade sorcery, divination, idolatry, and witchcraft (Deut. 18:10; 18:14). Even with this forthright prohibition, as they grew accustomed to their new neighbors in **Canaan**, the Hebrews were once again tempted by idolatry and even human **sacrifice**. By the days of the kingdom, they were admonished to avoid the sacrifice of their sons and daughters in the fire. "The Israelites secretly did things against the Lord their God.... they were stiff-necked.... They followed worthless idols.... They imitated the nations around them.... They sacrificed their sons and daughters in the fire. They practiced divination and sorcery and sold themselves to do evil in the eyes of the Lord, provoking him to anger" (2 Kings 17:8–17). Manasseh, the King of Judah, became an example of the most heinous of pagan practices, sacrificing his own son in the fire, practicing sorcery and divination, and consulting mediums and spiritists (2 Kings 21:6). The Psalmist also notes the use of sorcery—the "whispering" of charms, the use of magical waters—a "noxious thing poured" on the singer (Theodore Gaster 1969, 752; Ps. 41:7–9).

Among the earlier **prophets**, notably Elisha, some of his miraculous works verge on magic: the waving of his hands over the body of Naaman mimics a common feature of magical procedures, an attempt to diffuse the otherworldly quality by which the magic is worked (Theodore Gaster 1969, 520). The later prophets clearly condemned any magical practices among the people: Isaiah noted that the children of the house of Jacob were "full of superstitions from the East," practicing divination "like the **Philistines**" (Isa. 2:6). Ezekiel warned against "false visions" and "divination" (Ezek. 13:23). And Micah told of a day when all visions would cease: "The sun will set for the prophets, and the day will go dark for them" (Mic. 3:6).

The Magi, wise men from the East, probably were influenced by pervasive eastern interest in stars and prophesy. Some believe their interest in the Jewish messiah may have been a vestigial sign of lingering memories of Hebrew prophesies in **Babylon;** others that they are simply practitioners of astrology.

In the early days of the **Christian Church**, sorcery again became a problem. Among those attracted to the faith was a man named Simon, who practiced sorcery and "amazed all the people of Samaria." Realizing the **Disciples'** greater power to perform miracles, Simon followed Philip. Later, when he saw the spirit that came with the "laying on of hands" empowering the **apostles**, he sought to buy this power. Peter admonished him for seeking to purchase the power of the **Holy Spirit**, and Simon repented (Acts 8:9, 18–24). Even so, his name is still associated with buying and selling of spiritual gifts—a sin called "simony."

Later, Paul was tormented by a **slave** girl who could predict the future. Her spirit possession led her to follow him and Silas shouting, "These men are servants of the Most High God." Finally, Paul commanded the spirit to come out of her, leaving her free of the spirits that her masters had found very lucrative. This exorcism triggered Paul's arrest (Acts 16:16–18). This spirit-possessed slave girl sounds like the oracle at Delphi. Her "python" spirit, or demonic spirit that allowed her to predict the future, was worshipped at Delphi. This voice that spoke through her was described as "ventriloquism" (NIV notes, 1681).

Finally, in Revelation, a curse was pronounced on all those "who practice magic arts, the idolaters and all liars—their place will be in the fiery lake of burning sulfur" (Rev. 21:8). This firm prohibition returns believers to the clarity of the Mosaic law, with the further reminder that they face the peril of eternal perdition.

Nevertheless, the interest in magic was then and is still widespread. In the medieval world, occult knowledge and practice were soundly condemned by the Church, but survived nonetheless. Dr. Faustus and his magical arts were popular as folk stories and later inspired tragic dramas by Marlowe and Goethe. In return for such forbidden knowledge, the brilliant doctor sold his soul to the Devil. Many of the early "scientists" were alchemists, in search of the sorcerer's stone. They dreamed of the key to changing baser metals into gold.

The obsession with witchcraft in the sixteenth and seventeenth centuries in Europe and America was closely related to the practice of black magic. The wave of witch hunts in Europe and to a more limited extent in New England grew out of this obsession. Some of this was inspired by ecclesiastical documents from the late Middle Ages enumerating the "signs" of a witch. Women were especially noted for their "secret knowledge" of spells and potions, which had been passed from generation to generation in an oral tradition. As the primary caregivers who often used blends of herbs, as medicine, they were suspected of being in league with the Devil in their activities (Barbara G. Walker 1983, 1082).

In America, some of the witchcraft and voodoo derived from relations with African cultures, encounters with cults of sorcery and the casting of spells, especially among the slaves who were taken to islands in the Caribbean. The abused and illiterate slaves in these French colonies, with little of the Christian influence that was more typical of those in the English colonies, proved a rich incubator for occult practices. Arthur Miller makes effective use of this in *The Crucible,* a play about the Salem witch trials, in which the nurse is an emigrant from Barbados. In her midnight gatherings with the young girls in the woods, dancing and casting spells, and her reading of tea leaves, she ignited their imaginations and led to much of the hysteria. New Orleans became the home of a number of these slaves from French colonies who brought their magic potions and spells with them. That city still has shops full of occult paraphernalia.

In modern times, the revival of interest in witchcraft is associated with feminism and the veneration of the Great Goddess. This enthusiasm has generated both serious and comic works, from the practice of the religion of Wicca to the tales of Harry Potter. Some churches take these activities as passing fads or as fun for children, but others see them as a threat to their faith.

In some churches, Halloween has become especially troubling. Its bizarre revelry, its mock-celebration of witchcraft, and its trivialization of black magic have led some Christians to reject any participation in the activities connected with "All Hallows Eve," the day originally intended to honor the saints who have died and entered eternal glory. Another revival of the occult has come with the feminist interest in "Mother Earth," Sophia (or Wisdom), and an ecumenical spirit that embraces practices drawn from Native American and Far Eastern religions.

Religion, so full of prophesy, visions, dreams, miracles, and mystical moments, has a close kinship with magic and a justifiable suspicion of it. *See also* Blessing; Curse; Dreams; Witchcraft, Witches.

Further Reading

Gaster, Theodor H. *Myth, Legend, and Custom in the Old Testament*. New York: Harper and Row, 1969. Kee, Howard Clark. "Magic and Divination," in *The Oxford Companion to the Bible*. New York: Oxford University Press, 1993. Miller, Madeleine S. and J. Lane Miller. "Magic and Divination," in *Harper's Bible Dictionary*. New York: Harper and Row, 1961. Walker, Barbara G. *The Woman's Encyclopedia of Myths and Secrets*. San Francisco: HarperSanFrancisco, 1983.

Manna

(Exod. 16:1–4, 12, 15, 22, 31; Num. 11:7–8; Deut. 8:3; Neh. 9:15, 20; Ps. 78:24; John 6:31; Heb. 9:4; Rev. 2:17) The name *manna* is thought to derive from the question the Israelites asked when they first saw it: "What is it?" This miraculous food, "bread which the Lord" gave to his people during their 40 years in the wilderness, has puzzled historians for years.

Manna is described as a small round thing, like hoar frost on the ground, or the coriander seed, the color of bdellium resin. It is sticky, quickly solidified, and perishable. If it is not picked early in the morning, it disappears. If it is not eaten or placed in a tightly sealed jar, "worms" eat it. It can be baked into wafers or cakes and tastes like "fresh oil" (Exod. 16:1–31; Num. 11:7–8).

Since the nineteenth century, biblical scholars have linked this miraculous food with a secretion exuded by the tamarisk trees and bushes that are found in Sinai. In the twentieth century, an "organized manna expedition" set out to study the theory scientifically. Friederich Simon Bodenheimer and Oskar Theodor from the Hebrew University in Jerusalem investigated the dry water courses and oases in the region around Mt. Sinai before reporting their findings and providing photographs establishing the factual basis for the biblical experience. They found that bedouins pick the "Mann es-Samà" or "manna from heaven" before 8:30 A.M. to keep the ants from consuming it. The sealing of the containers is also protection from these insects. Bedouins can collect four pounds per head in a morning that they kneed into a purée; it keeps indefinitely and is sweet and nutritious (Werner Keller 1982, 123–125). Chemical analysis shows the presence of three basic sugars with pectin—a real delicacy for nomadic people who have no dates, beets, or sugar cane (Madeleine S. Miller and J. Lane Miller 1961, 417).

God instructed the Israelites to place an omer of manna in the **Ark of the Covenant** as a reminder of his infinite goodness to them, preserving manna during their long sojourn in the wilderness. When Jesus was challenged to prove his ministry with a sign comparable to that of the manna, he explained that he was the "true bread from heaven" (John 6:32–35). *See also* Bread; Last Supper.

Further Reading

Bechtel, F. "Manna," http://www.newadvent.org (accessed January 10, 2005). Cook, James I. "Manna," in *The Oxford Companion to the Bible*. New York: Oxford University Press, 1980. Keller, Werner. *The Bible as History*. New York: Bantam Books, 1982. Miller, Madeleine S. and J. Lane Miller. "Manna," in *Harper's Bible Dictionary*. New York: Harper and Row, 1961.

Marriage

(Gen. 2:22–24; Exod. 34:11–16; Deut. 7:1–5; Matt. 22: 23–30) Marriage is taken to mean the legal and binding relationship of a husband and wife. The word *marriage* denotes "the action, contract, formality, or ceremony by which the conjugal union is formed or the union itself as an enduring condition.... It is usually defined as the legitimate union between husband and wife. 'Legitimate' indicates the sanction of some kind of law, natural, evangelical, or civil, while the phrase, 'husband and wife' implies mutual rights of sexual intercourse, life in common, and an enduring union" (John Ryan 2005).

Marriage in the Creation Narrative

After God had taken the rib from man and made a woman and brought her to the man, "Adam said, This is now bone of my bones, and flesh of my flesh: she shall be called Woman because she was taken out of Man. Therefore shall a man leave his father and his mother, and shall cleave unto his wife: and they shall be one flesh" (Gen. 2:22–24). This **creation** story sets the pattern for marriage—between one man and one woman. It also implies that the man, not the woman, will leave home and that the bond is intrinsic and permanent.

Later in the Genesis story, after the Fall, we find additional details of the marriage relationship. God told the woman, "I will greatly multiply thy sorrow and thy conception; in sorrow thou shalt bring forth children; and thy desire shall be to thy husband, and he shall rule over thee" (Gen. 3:16). This prophetic utterance became the basis of the concept of *paterfamilias*, the idea that the man was the head of the household, the final authority in the family. It also established woman's role as childbearing and her position as a subordinate to her husband.

Hebrew Marriage Customs

Hebrew customs conformed only partially to these ideas: even the patriarchs often took more than one wife, not to mention the maidservants and concubines who also bore them children. The marriages may have been matrilocal (that is tied to the family of the wife) in the early days. That is suggested in Abraham's concern that his son's wife be brought to him rather than have Isaac go to Paddan Aram, where his relatives still lived, to seek her. Isaac would probably have been tempted to settle back in his ancient homeland rather than making his home in the Promised Land.

The following generation had the same pull toward the wife's family. Laban, Jacob's father-in-law, apparently assumed that Jacob's wives and children—in fact all his possessions—were still his. As the father of both of Jacob's wives, Laban considered himself the head of the family. Jacob's escape to **Canaan** (Gen. 29:16–32:1) marked a dramatic change, altering the custom so that the husband's family became the center of the family, changing marriage from matrilocal to patrilocal (tied to the home of the father). In fact, the ideal was that brothers would live together under their father's roof, even after the father died. As late as the story of Gideon, some families expected sons-in-law to reside with the wife's clan or to leave the new wife among her own people, visiting her occasionally (Judg. 8:30–31, 9:1–3). Samson's troubled marriage indicates a similar pattern (Judg. 14–15), suggesting that foreigners continued the matrilocal custom long after it was discarded by the Hebrews (Ze-ev W. Falk 2001, 124–126).

For most of history, the bride was "given" in marriage by her father and "taken" by her husband. Women generally married very young, sometimes in their early teens, and men were encouraged to marry before they were 20, although men often waited until they were in their twenties or thirties before marrying. The age differences between Abraham and Sarah, and Isaac and Rebekah suggest this was the custom from early patriarchal times. Marriage was less a matter of romance than economics: the goal of the marriage was to have and raise children, especially boys (King and Stager 2001, 54).

Polygyny—marriage of a man to more than one woman—was an accepted practice as early as the days of Lamech (Gen. 4:19). Laban actually tricked Jacob into marrying both of his daughters, although he then insisted that he marry no other women. Laban also understood the practice of "concubinage, which may be regarded as a higher form of polygamy" various peoples, including the Hebrews (John A. Ryan 2005). It was with this understanding that Jacob took the maidservants of his wives as concubines, having several "legitimate" sons by each of them with the apparent approval of his wives.

Powerful men were known to marry multiple wives, sometimes for lust, sometimes to produce more sons, sometimes to cement relations with other leaders, tribes, or nations. David took Saul's daughter in marriage, along with numerous other women. His choice of Bathsheba was based entirely on desire. His son Solomon had a vast harem, which began with marriage to the pharaoh's daughter. This practice was discouraged by the law (Deut. 17:17), which proved prophetic in its message that multiple political marriages should be avoided. They caused the **king**'s heart to "turn away" from God. Monogamy was probably the rule for the high **priest** (Lev. 21:13) and for most common folk.

The Choice of a Bride

In arranging for marriages, a dowry or bride price was often involved. These arrangements were controlled by Hebrew **law**, indicating in the case of the bride price that the wife was a possession of the husband. This wifely status is signaled in much of Mosaic law, which speaks of coveting the wife along with other possessions, and excludes the wife from the list of potential heirs who might inherit the husband's estate, as she was part of that estate.

Because the family unit was so basic a part of Hebrew society and the production of male children so essential for their heritage, the choice of the proper wife was a matter of great concern for the whole family. Romantic love only occasionally was a determining factor in the choice of the mate; husbands and wives often met for the first time at the wedding. Their families arranged the marriage, preferably with someone from the same kinship group. This meant that relatives often married one another—cousins in the case of Jacob and Laban's daughters and half-brother and half-sister in the case of Abraham and Sarah. Unlike the **Egyptians**, this early custom of marriage of near-kin was discouraged even before the codification of the law. In Hebrew tribal law, there were rules against incest—sexual relations between ascendants and descendants, maternal brothers and sisters (Ze'ev W. Falk 2001, 130).

The period of the **Judges**, when the **Hebrews** were "settling" the land already inhabited by indigenous peoples, more marriages were contracted outside of this kinship group. This was followed by the usual problems of marrying foreigners who worshipped foreign gods. Mosaic law was strongly in favor of close marriage ties and avoidance of outsiders (Exod. 34:11–16; Deut. 7:1–5). An outsider who wished to marry a Hebrew woman was expected to become "bridegroom of blood" (Exod. 4:25–26), probably suggesting that he be circumcised. This may have been the process involved in the early story of the rape of Dinah, when all the men of Shechem were circumcised in anticipation of the wedding, only to be slaughtered while they were still recovering from the surgery (Gen. 34). The problems of intermarriage outside of the near kinship group increased as the Israelites settled into Canaan. As the men fought in more wars and brought home captive women whom they took as wives, the bloodline of the Hebrews became diluted. By the time of Ezra and Nehemiah, the intermarriages had become a major threat to the perseverance of the faith. A strong message from Ezra to avoid taking foreign wives and to divorce those already taken was seen as a "holy war" to preserve the purity of Abraham's seed (Ezra 9; Neh. 10:31, 13:23–28). Even today, intermarriage with people of other faiths and traditions is seen as a major threat to the preservation of Judaism. Among Christians as well, "unequal yoking"—marriage to a non-Christian—was discouraged. In this case, the bloodline was less significant than the heritage of faith.

The tight kinship ties also led to the rules of levirate marriage, where the **inheritance** was preserved within the male line by having a brother marry his dead brother's wife. This complex set of family relationships became the basis for the Sadducees' question to Jesus regarding the resurrection (Matt. 22:23ff). They asked about seven brothers who, in turn, married the same woman, who had been the wife of the first brother. Rather than stating which of the brothers was her husband in the resurrection, Jesus explained, "in the resurrection they neither marry, nor are given in marriage, but are as **angels** of God in **heaven**" (Matt. 22:30).

Symbolism of Marriage

Among the prophets, especially Hosea, marriage became the symbol of Israel's union with God. Isaiah is also full of wedding symbolism, again related to this union. This carries over into the New Testament, where Christ and his **Church** are seen as married, with parallel relationships to those known on earth between husband and wife. The metaphor of marriage carries over into Paul's letters and into the Revelation of John, which ends with the wedding feast of the lamb.

In **Christian** Church history, the concept of marriage has changed in some aspects. The Roman Catholic Church consider it a sacrament, akin the mystical union of Christ and the believer. The vow made is for life: "until death do us part." "The spouses who exchange their vows before God and in front of the priest who represents him—and who blesses the couple in his role as a sacramental witness, according to the ancient rules which were codified in the sixteenth century by the Council of Trent—participate in the fullness of this holy unity" (Dom Robert LeGall 2000, 60). The investiture in holy orders involves much the same symbolism. Nuns wear the gold ring that signifies they have become the brides of Christ.

For most Protestants, wedding vows are sacred, but marriage is not a sacrament. Most Protestant churches consider sacraments those sacred activities in which Christ himself participated and which he specifically ordained. Both **baptism** and **communion** are therefore accepted because Jesus was baptized and did partake in the breaking of **bread** and the drinking of wine at the **Last Supper**, but Jesus himself did not marry. He did attend the **wedding** at Cana, where he changed the water into **wine**. The solemn nature of marriage has encouraged Protestants to have clergy perform their wedding ceremonies, but even the Puritans often had the weddings in private homes. Church weddings gradually became popular in America as they grew increasingly royal in tone, with large wedding parties, elegant apparel, and grand music. Civil ceremonies, officiated over by a justice of the peace, are becoming increasingly common with modern couples.

Marriage is currently being redefined. Many young couples (and old ones) reject formal weddings, preferring cohabitation; some marry and remain childless; some indulge in serial monogamy through a series of divorces; others opt for "open marriages," in which adultery is considered acceptable. The most heated debate in recent years has involved the marriage of same-sex couples. The legitimacy and morality of such unions have caused extensive controversy within several of the Protestant denominations. It is clear that the whole concept of marriage is undergoing scrutiny. And yet, at the same time, millions of couples continue to make the traditional trip to the altar to say their vows and exchange their rings "before God and this company." *See also* Betrothal; Divorce; Husband and Wife; Weddings.

Further Reading

Falk, Ze'ev. *Hebrew Law in Biblical Times*. Provo, Utah: Brigham Young University Press, 2001. King, Philip J. and Lawrence E. Stager. *Life in Biblical Israel*. Louisville, Ky.: Westminster John Knox Press, 2001. LeGall, Dom Robert. *Symbols of Catholicism*. New York: Assouline Publishing, 2000. Ryan, John A. "History of Marriage," http://www.newadvent.org (accessed January 5, 2005).

Meals

(Matt. 9:10; John 21:4–19) In biblical times, workers began their day very early, taking only snacks with them for breakfast. **Olives**, raisins, flat **bread**, or **goat**'s cheese (John 21:4–19) would have been portable and satisfying (Madeleine Miller and J. Lane Miller 1961, 429). The remainders of this would serve as the noontime meal, which they would have eaten with fellow workers at their place of labor, as Ruth did in the fields with Boaz.

The main meal of the day was eaten in the evening after sunset, with the whole family present. This was called supper, feast, or "sitting at meat" (Matt. 9:10). For most families, the meal was a one-pot stew served in a large bowl. A thick porridge or blend of vegetables, on special occasions containing meat, was the usual fare (Philip J. King and Lawrence E. Stager 2001, 67–68). For celebrations and **feasts**, meat might be boiled and cut up, with vegetables stewed in the juices served over the meat. Or the meat might be roasted over a spit. Cakes of figs or special breads made with honey might provide a special treat.

Typical meal during Greek and Roman eras, with the diners reclining around the table, as at the Last Supper.

Because tables and chairs were rare, most ancient peoples gathered around the **cooking** or serving utensils, sitting on mats or stools on the ground or floor, and reaching out to serve themselves. Guests were frequent at evening meals and often ate until they were exhausted and rolled over into sleep (Madeleine S. Miller and J. Lane Miller 1961, 429).

By Roman times, and in wealthier homes, the diners stretched out on couches (*triclinia*), which were arranged in sets of three, around a table on a pedestal. Certain locations were designated as the "highest" and "lowest," leading the **Disciples** to argue about their placement in relationship to Jesus (Luke 14:9–112). They would lean on the left elbow as they reached out with the other hand. Only wealthy people would have had separate dishes for each of the diners. Virtually no one would have used spoons or forks; instead he or she had large griddle cakes or bent brown bread. They used these to scoop out bites of the main dish, which was usually served in a large **pottery** bowl. When they had finished the meal, they wiped out the dishes with their bread. Crumbs might have been tossed to the **dogs**.

At special events celebrating **weddings**, birthdays, the return of the prodigal, or a welcome for special visitors, the meal was enhanced by invitations issued in advance, by entertainment such as **music** and **dancing**, and by posing riddles (as at Samson's wedding). Wedding feasts were managed by stewards or "rulers" (John 2:9), who served as masters of ceremonies and also regulated the distribution of food and drink. The rooms were apparently visible to the public, perhaps separated from the street only by a curtain. The **Pharisees** were well aware of where Jesus was eating his meals, and with whom. At such celebratory events, guests would have been treated with the whole ritual of **hospitality**.

For more informal meals, such as the meals one might pack for a journey, a flask of **water** and some bread with raisins, olives, and fig cakes would be sufficient. By contrast, the great **palace** meals during the reign of **King** Solomon were elaborate and ceremonious. Solomon had

Tableware from the first century (artifacts found in a cave): wood bowls and wooden utensil, a bronze pitcher, and a knife with a wood handle and blade.

foods and spices brought from all over the known world and undoubtedly had his food served on beautiful platters. In one ancient depiction, some servants are handing goblets of wine to guests of Queen Shubad (ca. 2500 B.C.?) while others fan the guests and play the harp for their entertainment (Madeleine S. Miller and J. Lane Miller 1961, 430).

The meals were very different among the varied peoples with whom the Israelites intermingled: the **Egyptians** ate lavish meals, had palace bakers, golden cups, and a wide variety of foods. Their wall paintings show roast beef, chicken, pigeon, vegetables, barley beer, and elaborate condiments, with huge jars of **wine** from which the guests drank using glass tubes, like straws. The Assyrians enjoyed date palms and were noted for their drunken feasts; the Persians sometimes feasted for as much as 180 days. In the days of the Greco-**Roman** Empire, although some orgies continued, many feasts became intellectual feasts as well. At the end of these meals, small tables with nuts and dried fruit were placed among the guests, who talked on into the night. *See also* Cooking, Cooking Utensils; Festivals; Food; Furnishings, Household.

Further Reading

King, Philip J. and Lawrence E. Stager. *Life in Biblical Israel.* Louisville, Ky.: Westminster John Knox Press, 2001. Miller, Madeleine S. and J. Lane Miller. "Meals," in *Harper's Bible Dictionary.* New York: Harper and Row, 1961.

Measures

(Lev. 19:35–36; 1 Chron. 23:29) The ancient Hebrews were not particularly interested in mathematics, precise reckoning, or the general study of metrology (the science of measuring). They referred to time in large general terms and measured space by their own bodies or the distance they might walk in a day. It is therefore no surprise that, at least in their earliest history, their weights and measures varied from place to place, with no universal standard of measurement available. Although the Chronicler indicates that the Levites had the official responsibility for "all manner of measure and size" (1 Chron. 23:29), that does not prove any uniformity. This flexibility was to remain until the **kings** sought to levy **taxes**, making some standards essential for fairness (E. W. Heaton 1956 , 189).

Some believe that 2 Sam 8:1 indicates that the Philistines had a "standard cubit," but this is a debatable interpretation. Swindlers apparently used the flexibility available to them to give short measure, so that they could overcharge (Amos 8:5). There was so much variation that weights were called "heavy" or "light" (Deut. 25:13). Many complained of short bushels and faked weights (Mic. 6:10–11; Prov. 20:10).

The law (Lev. 19:35–36) did prescribe "just" weights and measures, but these were apparently estimates, not official standards (deVaux 1961, 195). DeVaux notes that even in modern Palestine, merchants may estimate most measurements, using ropes or outstretched arms for size, a stone or horseshoe for weight, and a jam pot for volume. He suggests that readers of Scripture should allow for approximation rather than insisting on an exact science for biblical metrology (196).

Measurements were also influenced by foreign control or contact. Because the **Babylonians** used a numerical system based on six, and the **Egyptians** used one based on ten, the Israelites sometimes found themselves using either or both. (So do most of us, who still use the decimal system for money and sixes for measures of weight and distance.) In addition, in the marketplace and in the home, they held onto their old barter system and their homemade measurements. Just as modern Americans are reluctant to give up inches and bushels for the metric system, so the ancients kept those measurements they found most handy and comfortable.

As a result, the numerical equivalents cited in the charts are estimates based on the best evidence available. Translators over the years have wrestled with the problem of selecting terms that readers will understand, although the meaning is not exact. Thus, British terms such as "farthing" or "penny" appear in some versions of Scripture. Their concern, like that of their readers, is that the general meaning be clear.

Measures—Capacity

The measuring of volume—for such things as corn, oil, and **wine**, which were sold or taken for taxes by volume—like weight, demanded standard measurements over time. The standard became the "royal bath," a liquid measure for which a particular jar was used. Eventually, the other measures also fell into a regular pattern, which we can only estimate, based on the discoveries of archaeologists:

DRY	LIQUID
1 omer = 1 gallon (2.3 litres)	1 hin = 5/6 gallon (3.8 litres)
10 omers = 1 ephah = 5 gallons	6 hins = 1 bath = 5 gallons
10 ephahs = 1 homer = 50 gallons	10 baths = 1 kor = 50 gallons
kor = 1 homer = 50 gallons	kor = 1 bath = (5 gallons?)

The *homer* was the most commonly used measure in the entire region in the second millennium B.C. and thereafter served as the measure for cereals. The *omer*, "a small bowl" occurs only in the collection of manna (Exod. 16:18, 32–33). The *kor* was a large dry measure equal to the homer (Ezek. 45:14), which was used for fine flour, meal, wheat, and barley (1 Kings 4:22, 2 Chron. 2:10). It also seems to be the same measure as a *bath* (D.J. Wiseman 1980, 1367–9). The *bath* is the liquid equivalent of the *ephah* (Ezek. 45:11) and was used to measure **water**, **wine**, and oil (1 Kings 7:26, Isa. 5:10, 2 Chron. 2:10). Because we do not know the exact volume of a bath, these other measures that depend on the bath are also estimates at best.

Translators have had some difficulty in dealing with most of these terms, as they generally referred to the actual receptacles, which have long since disappeared, that contained provisions—just as we use the term *bushel* because of the basket's size. Thus the *homer* was an "ass-load" and the *epah* was a "large receptacle, closed with a lid and large enough to hold a woman" (Roland deVaux 1961, 199). Obviously, these measurements would vary with the size of the **donkey** and of the woman.

Measures—Linear

Linear measurements were based on limbs of the human body, finally standardized for greater precision. The *span* was based on spreading the hand out and measuring from the tip of the thumb to the tip of the little finger, the *cubit* from the elbow to the tip of the second finger.

1 finger = 3/4 inch (Jer. 52:21)
4 fingers = 1 palm = 3 inches
3 palms = 1 span = 9 inches (Judg. 3:16)
2 spans = 1 cubit = 18 inches

The *rod,* which Ezekiel used in his description of the **Temple**, was not a general unit of measurement. He had a rod of six "great cubits" (Ezek. 40:3) and a flaxen cord, which is the "measuring cord" also mentioned in Amos 7:17 and Zechariah 1:16; 2:1, but these may or may not have been standardized, like the Babylonian cord (Roland deVaux 1961, 196).

Herodotus indicates that Mesopotamia also had a "royal cubit," which measured 27 fingers, as opposed to the 24 that would be considered usual. The Egyptians had a "royal cubit" that was 28 fingers. This suggests that the term *royal* may be interpreted as a generous measurement.

Distance was measured only by paces or by time—the days of marching or the steps between two places. An "acre" was the amount of land two **oxen** could plow in a day (E.W. Heaton 1956, 191). There are really no uniform measures in Hebrew for area. Usually, even the size of a farm was measured by the amount of **grain** needed to sow it (cf. 1 Kings 18:32; Roland deVaux 1961, 198). Thus, a field valued at 50 shekels would be a vast area, and the amount mentioned refers to the grain to be harvested, not the monetary value of the land itself (Lev. 27:16).

"A **Sabbath** day's journey" (the maximum distance a person was allowed to travel on the Sabbath, according to Jewish **law**) was estimated at 2,000 cubits or 1,000 yards, 914 meters. This became important as the Sabbath laws were elaborated. The Pharisees based their judgment against Jesus and his disciples on such regulations.

The **Greeks** and the **Romans** added fresh terms that were not precise, but had approximate meanings:

> fathom or orgyle = 6 feet or 1.85 meters
> stadion or furlong = 202 yards or 185 meters (2 Macc. 12:9, 10, 16, 17, 29)

A "stadion" (pl. *stadia*) was a Greek unit of measure used in Palestine during Hellenistic and Roman periods (Pat Alexander 1978, 246).

Measures—Weight

The term *shekel* means "to weigh" and points to the scales in the marketplace. The shekel was, in fact, the basic unit of weight, common to all ancient Semitic systems of measurement (Roland deVaux 1961, 203). Stone weights were used to establish the value of precious **metal**—usually silver and gold. These limestone balls, sometimes shaped like **animals**, have been found by archaeologists excavating the ancient tells. They were often inscribed with indicators of their weight. The multiples of the shekel are the *mina* and the *talent*, with the mina a rare and late measurement (1 Kings 10:17, Neh. 7:70); however, it was frequently mentioned in Mesopotamian texts (Roland deVaux 1961, 204).

Generally, the following measures parallel our standards:

> 1 shekel = 2/5 ounce (11.4 grams)
> 50 shekels = 1 mina = 20 ounces (511 grams)
> 60 minas = 1 talent = 75 pounds (34,000 grams) (Heaton 1956, 190)

This was the manner in which Abraham paid for the **cave** of Machpelah, by weighing out 400 shekels of silver (Gen. 23:16). The seller mentioned in this passage would have officiated at the weighing of the ingots or jewelry used in the payment. It is also the way that Joseph's brothers would have planned to pay for the grain they bought in Egypt.

The stones used for weighing produce were not uniform in size and weight. Scripture notes that traders used two types of stones, large and small ones (Deut. 25:13; Prov. 20:23). There were also "royal" weights, guaranteed by monarchs, which were double the value of "ordinary" weights. The "shekel of the sanctuary" (Exod. 30:13) was the official standard, or perhaps heavier (deVaux, 1961, 203). By and large, the measurements were gross standards, refined over time by merchants and monarchs who had much to gain or lose by more precise calculation.

Money

The accompanying table lists, in roughly chronological order, the coins used by the Hebrews that are referred to in Scripture. The weights are approximate and variable.

Coin	Weight/Value	Metal	Period/Scripture
Shekel (s)	11.4 gm/1 stater	silver	Persian—7th C B.C. OT
Shekel (g)	15 silver shekels	gold	OT/NT
Mina (s)	561 mg/50 shekels	silver	Neh. 7:71–72; Luke 19:11–27
Mina (g)	631 mg (light)	gold	OT/NT
Talent (s)	336 kg/60 minas	silver	OT/NT
Talent (g)	370 kg (light)	gold	OT/NT
Daric (dram)	130 gm = Gr. stater	gold	Persian—400 B.C., Ezra 8:27; 1 Chron 29:7
Lepton	smallest unit	bronze	Greek/Roman Mark 12:42; Luke 12:59
Drachma	day's pay	silver	Greek, Luke 15:8–9
Didrachma	2 drachmas/1/2 shekel	silver	Greek, Matt. 17:24–27
Stater	4 drachmas (tetradrachma)		Greek, Matt. 17:27
Quadrans	penny—1/2 as		Roman, Matt. 5:26; Mark 12:42
As	4 quadrans	bronze	Roman, Matt. 10:29
Denarius	16 as (day's pay)	silver	Roman, Matt. 18:28; Mark 6:37; Rev. 6:6
Aureus		gold	Roman, NT

Payment was not necessarily in the form of money. Often barter or trade satisfied both parties, rendering money unnecessary—the exchange of goods in kind. Even as late as the New Testament, Jesus could speak in his parable of the unjust steward (Luke 16:5–7) of men who paid their debts in oil and wheat.

The earliest "money" was not coinage but simply precious metal. From the time of Abraham, the Hebrews used gold, silver, and brass to buy or sell land, grain, and **slaves**. The payment Abraham offered for the land where he buried Sarah, and where he and his descendants were buried, cost 400 shekels (Gen. 23:16). When Joseph's brothers sold their brother to the Midianites, they received 20 "pieces of silver" (Gen. 37:28).

Archaeologists have discovered weights that were used as far back as the time of King Gudea (about 2500 B.C.). A series of these stones, of different sizes and shapes, would have been used to measure the silver and gold. The Hebrews undoubtedly saw the Egyptians melting precious metals into bars or ingots for easier management. The heated metal was poured into a clay receptacle. When the jar became full, the clay was broken off, leaving a shape of precious metal. A merchant could cut off as much of the ingot as he needed to pay a bill. The Hebrews also used **jewelry** as a means of exchange. Some used rings or bracelets, which were weighed before they were shaped and used as a handy and attractive form of money. After they escaped from Egypt, taking "jewelry" with them, the Israelites continued to use precious metals for exchange in **Canaan**. In fact, the word for silver (*kesef*) was used as a general term for money (Exod. 21:11).

It was Croesus, the King of Lydia (some time around the seventh century B.C.) who was credited with first using coins. The abundant gold that he found in his country made him famous; the enormously rich are still referred to as being "as rich as Croesus." The concept of the coin was to produce a standardized disk of metal, with the weight guaranteed by the king, whose name or

Coins from various periods, marking bits of history: silver stater minted at Antioch, showing head of Augustus Caesar (time of Christ); Babylonian coin (300 B.C.); silver denarius with head of Tiberius (time of Christ); silver shekel minted in Sidon (400 B.C.); shekel minted 66–70 A.D.; Vespasian's coin "Judea Capta" that marked the end of the Jewish revolt (70 A.D.).

image appeared on it. The amount of its worth was also indicated by an inscription. For archaeologists and historians, the thousands of tiny coins discovered in various places have provided extensive information regarding these monarchs, as well as commerce and other historical data.

Even when the Hebrews knew of coins, they did not appear to use them. It was not until after the Exile that the Scriptures refer to coinage—the *daric,* named after Darius I (522–485 B.C.). The Gold daric is mentioned as the "adarkonim" in Ezra 8:27, 1 Chronicles 29:7. The "darkemonim" in Ezra 2:69 and Nehemiah 7:70 is used in connection with royal gifts and contributions to the Temple treasury. These terms appear to be synonymous (Joseph Jacobs and Théodore Reinach 2004). The speculation is that the Persian government also struck some special coins for the Palestinian and Phoenician coast to pay sailors, double shekels of Phoenician standards, which were attributed to the mint of Sidon. Until the second century B.C., Phoenician money standards prevailed among the Jews. The Temple tax was a Phoenician half-shekel.

Hebrews did not have their own coinage until the time of the Maccabees, and perhaps not even then. Briefly after the collapse of the Persian Empire, Judea became a Macedonian province, thus ending the use of Phoenician silver as well as Persian darics. The new coins were Macedonian, of gold and silver, and using the Attic system of weights. The silver tetradrachm of about 17 grams and a gold stater of 8.60 grams did not easily change the old customs, but the Phoenicians adopted the tetradrachm and stater as their own standards. During those periods when the Attic standard prevailed (330–300 B.C., 200–150 B.C.), taxpayers were often unable to procure the old Phoenician coins and therefore had to change their money when they came to the Temple. For the public's convenience and their own profit, **money changers** set up their booths in the precincts of the Temple (Joseph Jacobs and Thèodore Reinach 2004).

The Seleucids and Ptolemies were jealous of their right to strike money and therefore reserved this privilege to themselves. They had an absolute monopoly on gold and silver and even controlled the minting of copper. During the period of the Hasmoneans, during the second century B.C., a weakened empire began to allow local municipalities to mint their own coins.

The Jewish priest-state was granted permission for its own coinage along with considerable autonomy (1 Macc. 15:1–9). This permission was quickly revoked (1 Macc. 15:27). They may, in fact, have been reluctant to issue coinage because of the Mosaic prohibition against graven images. Eventually, they appear to have used some simple coins for Temple tax and for local exchange. Some believe that Jewish silver shekels and half-shekels found in Jerusalem and in Jericho may date from this brief era. Small Hasmonean brass coins have also been discovered. These conform to Jewish law: they have no representation of an **animal**, but were issued in the name of the reigning prince, some of them in Hebrew and some bilingual.

In 63 B.C., Pompey took Jerusalem by storm, becoming the dominant force for some years. The Roman denarius became the dominant coin, with elaborate celebrations of heroes and events pictured on them. The Herodians and the local Roman governors (such as Pontius Pilate) were allowed to strike brass and copper coins, but not silver or gold. (The *lepton*—Mark 12:42—was such a coin.) These might be inscribed with a palm, a wreath, a cornucopia, a tripod, a helmet, a caduceus, or other image, but not a living creature. When the Roman Emperor Titus conquered Jerusalem in 70 A.D., he issued a commemorative coin that bore on its face *Judaea capta* or "Judea captured," and the figure of a standing man and a weeping woman beneath a palm tree—the woman, seated and despondent, representing the Jewish population of the rebellious Judea (Wright 1974, 23).

For the most part, the Jews used the legal tender of their various conquerors. This explains the manner in which Jesus responded to the question about paying taxes. When questioned about paying tribute, Jesus asked for a coin. He then inquired: Whose is this image and superscription?" (Matt. 22:19–20).

The shekel was a common unit of value, equivalent to four Greek drachmas or four Roman denari. The minted coin was slightly larger than the American half-dollar. There were two standards, light and heavy (Madeleine S. Miller and J. Lane Miller 1961, 455). This appears to derive from various customs. The gold coin was worth approximately twice the value of the silver. In addition (as noted earlier), the "royal" weight was often heavier than the average. And finally, there was the question of *honest weight:* merchants were known to carry two sets of weights with them to measure money. One set, used in selling, weighed about half of the others, which were used in buying, thus ensuring a tidy profit.

As with other measurements, so also with money: it is difficult to determine precise values, in part because it is so difficult to determine precise weights. A further complication is the change in the calculation of weights and denominations: the sexagesimal (multiples of 6) system used in Babylon was combined with the purely decimal (multiples of 10) system used in Egypt. Thus, the talent might be reckoned as 60 minas, but the mina at 50 shekels. In addition, the shekel was divided into halves, quarters, and twentieths. The whole process forced the Temple officials to deposit a set of standard weights there for more standardized measurement, the so-called "holy shekel" referred to in the Priestly Code (Exod. 30:23, Joseph Jacobs and Théodore Reinach 2004).

The scriptural attitude toward money is typical of the view of all possessions: they belong to God and are lent to us for the time being. This explains Jesus's admonition to "Render unto Caesar that which is Caesar's." Money—or the love of it—was identified as the root of evil (1 Tim. 6:10). Haggai reminded the Jews that silver and gold belong to God (2:8), but humans were encouraged to be good stewards of their money (Luke 14:28–30;

Mal.3:8–10) and fair in paying their workers. The emphasis throughout Scripture is to avoid allowing money to become an **idol** for worship, for no one can "serve God and money," or Mammon (Matt. 6:24). *See also* Metal: Gold; Metal: Silver; Time.

Further Reading

Alexander, Pat, ed. *Eerdmans' Family Encyclopedia of the Bible.* Grand Rapids, Mich.: William B. Eerdmans Publishing Company, 1978. DeVaux, Roland. *Ancient Israel: Its Life and Institutions.* Grand Rapids, Mich.: William B. Eerdmans Publishing Company, 1961. Heaton, E.W. *Everyday Life in Old Testament Times.* New York: Charles Scribner's Sons, 1956. Jacobs, Joseph and Théodore Reinach, "Numismatics," http:// www.jewishencyclopedia. com (accessed November 10, 2004). S. Miller, Madeleine S. and J. Lane Miller. "Money," in *Harper's Bible Dictionary.* New York: Harper and Row, 1961. Wight, Fred Hartley. *Manners and Customs of Bible Lands.* Chicago: Moody Press, 1953. Wiseman, D. J. "Weights and Measures, in *The Illustrated Bible Dictionary.* Sydney, Australia: Tyndale House Publishers, 1980. Wright, G. Ernest, ed. *Great People of the Bible and How They Lived.* Pleasantville, N.Y.: The Reader's Digest Association, Inc., 1974.

Messiah

(Gen. 49:10; Deut. 18:15; Hos. 1:11, 3:5; Amos 9:11–15; Ps. 110:4; Isa. 2:2–4, 11:1–2, 49:1–9; Dan. 7:13–14; Matt. 16:16; Mark 8:29; Luke 1:11; Rev. 3:21) The dream of a Messiah or "anointed one" who would reign over his people in a Messianic Age of peace and tranquility recurs through Scripture. The Greek form, *Messias,* is a transliteration of the Hebrew, *Messiah,* "the **anointed**." The word appears only twice in the Old Testament as a prediction of the promised prince (Daniel 9:26; Psalm 2:2) (L.W. Geddes 2005). In the New Testament, the Greek form, *Christos,* is used for the same concept, appearing in English translations as "Christ."

The idea of the "anointed one" was probably meant only as a reference to a **priest** or **king** in its earliest usage, as in David's reluctance to kill Saul, because he has been anointed. On some later occasions, a pagan monarch— Cyrus, the king of Persia—was addressed as "the anointed," probably because of his role in the redemption of God's people (Isa. 45:11–13). The concept itself, however, was far larger than this secular ruler. Especially during the difficult days of the Exile and afterwards, the **prophets** proclaimed a time when the world would be set right by a benevolent and godly Prince. In post-exilic times, the Messiah was the vision of the king who would reign over all created things, resorting in his rule the lost innocence of Eden, redeeming humankind from the curse for sin. In his person would meet the roles of the prophet, priest, and king.

The **Psalms** are full of imagery about the anointed conqueror, the triumphant prince, the redeemer king. The Royal Psalms, some of which may have been written to celebrate specific coronations, echo this Messianic hope. These prophesies resonated with the Jews, promising that God had a firm hold on their history and plans for their future redemption. Sometimes in the Hebrew Scriptures the reference is to the king, sometimes to the high priest, and sometimes to Israel as a people. The idea of a "personal Messiah runs through the Old Testament. It is the natural outcome of the prophetic future hope. The first prophet to give a detailed picture of the future ideal king was Isaiah" (Is. 9:1–6, 11:1–10, 32:1–5, Joseph Jacobs and Moses Buttenwieser 2005).

Isaiah outlined the conditions of the Savior's birth, his lineage, his hope for Israel, his role as "Immanuel"—the "possessor," a world ruler and yet a servant willing to be led to his death like a lamb to slaughter for the sins of the many. The image of this Prince of Peace is most powerfully expressed in Isaiah:

> he shall grow up before him as a tender plant, and as a root out of the dry ground. . . . He is despised and rejected of men; a man of sorrows, and acquainted with grief. . . . and we esteemed him not. . . . But he was wounded for our transgressions. . . . and with his stripes we are healed. . . . he is brought as a lamb to the slaughter. . . . his life an offering for sin. (Isa. 53:1–10)

These famous words, set to music in Handel's "Messiah"(1742), reverberate through much of Hebrew prophecy.

The actual term *The Messiah* (with the article and not in apposition with another word) is, however, "not an Old Testament expression, but occurs for the first time in apocalyptic literature" (Joseph Jacobs and Moses Buttenwieser 2005; c.f., Book of Jubilees, the Testament of the Twelve Patriarchs, and the Vision of Weeks of Enoch.). In the period between the Testaments, Jewish writings not included in the Bible preached that the Messianic kingdom would be associated with the **"Day of the Lord,"** a time of dreadful conflict followed by a general **resurrection**. In some of the writings, the Messiah himself becomes the leader of the armies of **Heaven;** sometimes he is the **judge** (Edwin Lewis 1961, 441; cf., the Psalms of Solomon, written probably about 40 B.C. and Ecclesiasticus).

Some came to believe that Alexander the Great might be the promised ruler but were disappointed. "Not until after the fall of the Maccabean dynasty, when the despotic government of Herod the Great and his family, and the increasing tyranny of the Roman empire had made their condition ever more unbearable, did the Jews seek refuge in the hope of a personal Messiah. They yearned for the promised deliverer of the house of David, who would free them from the **yoke** of the hated foreign usurper, would put an end to the impious Roman rule, and would establish His own reign of peace and justice in its place. In this way their hopes became gradually centered in the Messiah" (Joseph Jacobs and Moses Buttenwieser 2005).

Much of the New Testament echoes these contemporary ideas, relating them to the person of Jesus, called "the Christ," understood by his followers to be the promised Messiah. Matthew, in particular, quotes a large number of the prophetic utterances, revealing how Christ fulfilled them in his lineage, his birth, his life, and his death. The welcome Jesus received in Jerusalem on Palm Sunday demonstrates the eagerness of the crowds to believe that he was the promised deliverer. The inscription over Jesus at the time of the **Crucifixion**, "King of the Jews," (Matt. 2:4, 26:28, 27:17, 22; Mark 12:35, 15:32; Luke 23:2) links this sacrificial death to the Jewish prophetic tradition.

Jesus was reluctant to apply the title *christos* to himself, using it only with the Samaritan woman (Mark 9:41; Matt. 23:10; John 4:25f.) He neither explicitly claimed that he was the Messiah nor denied it, but did constantly stress his fulfillment of the Old Testament hopes in his own ministry. When John the Baptist asked if he was the "coming one," Jesus replied by pointing to his fulfillment of Isaiah 35:5f. and 61:1. (John's question may be testimony to the numerous charismatic leaders during this period who were thought briefly to be the Messiah, each eventually disappointing his followers. Some even thought that John himself would prove to be the "anointed one." The Zealots especially dreamed of a Messiah leading them to political independence.) At Nazareth, Jesus declared that the prophesy was fulfilled "today" (Luke 4:18ff.; R. T. France 1980, 994). More frequently, he used the term the *Son of Man*, a title referring back to Daniel 7:13f.

In the Jewish tradition, some applied the term to the revolutionary hero Simon Bar Kokhba (d. 135 A.D.), the seventeenth-century mystic Shabbetai Zevi and other "false messiahs" (John F. A. Sawyer 1993, 513). Although the hope has dimmed over the ages, Jews still hold out a hope for the coming of the Messiah. Jews who convert to Christianity are usually referred to as "messianic Jews," a commentary on their recognition of Jesus as the Christ.

Among the early Christians, the messiahship of Jesus was central. This proclamation that he was "the Christ" was based on his resurrection from the dead and his promise to come again. The image of Christ, exalted to the right hand of God, enthroned as the Messianic King (Ps. 110:1; Dan. 7; Acts 2:34–36) is vividly presented in Hebrews and in the Revelation of John. Like Melchizedek, in his risen state, Christ combines the roles of priest and king (Heb. 5:5–10, 7:1–28).

For Christians, the Second Coming of the Messiah, which is foretold in Scripture (Matt. 19:28–30, 20:20–23), is the great eschatological hope—the Millennium, the thousand years at the end of the present age, when Christ will reign over mankind. *See also* Anointing; Day of Judgment, Day of the Lord; Kings; Priest, High Priest; Throne.

Further Reading

Brumble, H. David and David L. Jeffrey, "Messiah," in *A Dictionary of the Biblical Tradition in English Literature*. Grand Rapids, Mich.: William B. Eerdmans Publishing Company, 1992. France, R. T. "Messiah," in *The Illustrated Bible Dictionary*. Sydney, Australia: Tyndale House Publishers, 1980. Geddes, L. W. "Messiah," http://www.newadvent.org (accessed January 11, 2005); Jacobs, Joseph and Moses Buttenwieser. "Messiah," http://www.jewishen-cyclopedia.com (accessed January 11, 2005). Lewis, Edwin. "Messiah," in *Harper's Bible Dictionary*. New York: Harper and Row, 1961. Sawyer, John F. A. "Messiah," in *The Oxford Companion to the Bible*. New York: Oxford University Press, 1993.

Metal and Mines

(Gen. 4:22; Deut. 8:9; Num. 31:22; Job 28:4, 7, 8; Dan. 2:32–33)
Moses promised the Israelites a land that would be rich—not only with milk and honey, but also: "Its rocks have iron in them, and from its hills you can mine copper" (Deut. 8:9). These are, in fact, the only two metals native to Israel. The Israelites were obliged to import gold, silver, tin, and lead (Pat Alexander 1978, 234). This famous passage may refer specifically to Bashan, the present Hauran, where the rocks contain as much as 20 percent iron. The Hebrews themselves knew nothing of mining, but learned the techniques in **Egypt**, where the people had engaged in mining on the Sinai Peninsula from earliest times. "The existence of these mines in Sinai may account for the fact that the Jerusalem Pentateuch Targum translates "'the wilderness of Zin' (Num. 23:21;34:3, 4) by 'mountain of iron'" (Joseph Jacobs and Samuel Krauss 2004).

Mines and Mining in Scripture

Moses appeared to have been speaking metaphorically, meaning only that "the stones were like iron in hardness. Here and there, however, superficial deposits of iron ore, such as pea ore or meadow ore, are to be found. In the Wadi Ajlun there are even thin deposits of red iron ore, but whether these were perhaps worked in some primitive manner is unknown. Traces of iron mines and ancient copper works are found in the Lebanon. Possibly the words in Deuteronomy refer to this territory, although it was never inhabited by the Israelites"(Emil G. Hirsch 2004).

The archaeologist Nelson Glueck and others have discovered rich Iron Age mines in the modern Kingdom of Jordan, in the "deep cleft in of the Jordan Valley and the Arabah, as far as Aquabah" (Madeleine S. Miller and J. Lane Miller 1961, 446). This would have been a good region for mines and refining ore because it had plenty of water and abundant charcoal fuel from the forests of Gilead and Edom. Glueck also describes slag heaps that are "still green with copper not fully refined out" that provide evidence of a lively copper industry in the region. (Nelson Glueck, *The Other Side of the Jordan,* cf. Madeleine S. Miller and J. Lane Miller 1961, 446). There is even a fortress erected in the era of the kings of Israel and Judah to guard the approach to mines and furnaces.

Having no deposits of precious metals in **Canaan**, the Hebrews sought their gold at Havilah, Ophir, and Uphaz. When Solomon was **king**, he sent his ships to these districts (I Kings 9: 28). The markets of Tyre also had quantities of imported silver, iron, tin, and lead for purchase (Ezek. 27:12), probably brought by traders from Tarshish. Two other unidentified ancient cities, Betah and Berothai, were conquered by David. From them he "took exceeding much brass" (2 Sam. 8:8; in 1 Chron.18:8 these cities are Tibhath and Chun). Copper utensils came from *Javan* (which here probably means Cyprus), Tubal, and Meshech (Ezek. 2713) (Joseph Jacobs and Samuel Krauss 2004).

It is the author of Job, however, who reveals a more exact knowledge of mining. In Job 28:4, 7, 8, "he refers to the passages and galleries which run crosswise with many sharp turns, following the labyrinthine course of the vein of ore. Verse 3 refers to the miner's light, which, according to Diodorus (iii.11), the workers in **Egyptian** mines used to wear fastened to their foreheads." In verse 5, the writer "refers to the process of breaking the stone by making it intensely hot and then pouring water on it. This process also is mentioned by Diodorus." In verse 10, he "refers to the cleaving of a rock in which a vein of ore ran through it in a fissure. Water burst from the fissure, and the flow was stopped by closing up the gap. The writer's knowledge of the subject came from Egyptian sources" (Emil G. Hirsch 2004).

Mining was not carried on by regular miners, but by **slaves**, convicts, and prisoners of **war**. Perhaps among the slaves who worked in these mines were Israelites, even ancestors of Job, providing the writer of this book with such vivid detail of the work of the miner. Conscripted labor also seems to have worked King Solomon's mines, the source for the lavish decorations in the **Temple** and in his many royal constructions.

The Egyptians apparently did not smelt iron until ca.1300 B.C. Their copper works on the Sinai Peninsula, which the Pharaoh's forces guarded, left traces for archaeologists, who have discovered evidence of extensive mining operations "the wadis Maghara and Nas'b, in the heaps of rubbish, the piles of slag, and the ruined passages. The inscriptions found on the rocks there intimate that the ore was excavated even before the time of Cheops (the builder of the great pyramid), under King Snefru" (Emil Hirsch 2004). Also discovered here were six-foot saws, chisels, and drills; drain pipes; and evidence of temple ornamentation (Madeleine S. Miller and J. Lane Miller 1961, 446).

In **Canaan**, it was the **Philistines** who had the iron supply and technology. Gerar, a Philistine coastal city, may have imported much of its metal. The archaeologist Flinders Petrie discovered there four large iron furnaces and a sword factory. Scripture testifies to the Philistine monopoly over iron works until the time of David. Some speculate that certain regions derived their names from the metals they produced—for example, "Zarephat" (1 Kings 17:9) and "Misrephoth" (Josh.11:8, 13:6).

The reference to Tubal-Cain, who became the first smith or miner (Gen. 4:22) suggests that the Israelites were aware of metallurgy from an early time but saw it as a work of cursed people. The wealth of the **patriarchs** in gold and silver is often emphasized (Gen. 12:2, 24:22). There is a legend that Abraham built himself a high iron tower, and Scripture clearly states that the Israelites took articles of silver and gold with them out of Egypt (Exod. 11:2, 12:35). The Midrash on this passage asserts that they melted the **idols** of the Egyptians into lumps of metal. The golden calf and the Tabernacle furnishings would have required large quantities of this precious metal. Many fabulous stories are told of the wealth of Joseph, David, and Solomon. Solomon's **throne** was especially costly (1 Kings 10:18). Some of the later Jewish kings, especially after the looting of the Temple for tribute, were so poor that they were reduced to using copper instead of gold (Joseph Jacobs and Samuel Krauss 2004).

One of the more interesting portrayals of metal in Scripture is in Daniel— the vision of the great Man: "This image's head was of fine gold, his breast and his arms of silver, his belly and his thighs of brass, His legs of iron, his feet part of iron and part of clay" (Dan. 2:32–33). Nebuchadnezzar's dream has been interpreted multiple ways over the years, but clearly indicates in descending order the value of the minerals named, reflecting the same pattern as in the quotation from Numbers.

Uses of Metal

Common uses of metals include metal mirrors, crowns, helmets, lances, and other weapons; armor such as greaves and cuirass; and jewelry such as necklaces, nose-rings, finger-rings, metal threads, etc. The Jews also had swords, knives, daggers, sickles, scissors, and hair curlers. Mortars were usually made of copper, probably for sanitary reasons, because copper does not rust; the pestle would have been of iron. There was also the hoe, the cutting-knife, the metal funnel, as well as the furnace and hearth of metal.

Until they became a monarchy, the Hebrews had little need for sophisticated knowledge of metals or access to them. In fact, there is no general name for "metal" in the Bible, only references to gold, silver, copper, iron, tin, lead, antimony or stibium, and electrum. The only passage in the Bible that contains an almost complete list of the metals gives their order of value is as follows: gold, silver, copper, iron, tin, and lead (Num. 31: 22).

Generally, however, in the Bible, as also on the Egyptian monuments, silver is named before gold, although gold was the preferred metal. It was more difficult to obtain and thus rarer. In estimating Solomon's wealth, however, it is said of silver that "it was nothing accounted of." Consequently, even at that early time, gold must have been known at its true value (1 Kings 10: 21).

Rather than interest in the metals themselves, the Scripture references are usually to the objects produced: the **jewelry**, tables, bowls, **altars**, **lamp** stands, pillars, shovels, or **chariots**. For the most part, the splendid armor or architecture were subjects of celebration, as in the case of the building of the Temple or the display of golden shields. Or they might be objects of remorse, when that same wealth was stolen. When Nebuchadnezzar, king of Babylon, took the whole royal family captive, he also "carried out thence all the treasures of the house of the Lord, and the treasures of the king's house, and cut in pieces all the vessels of gold which Solomon king of Israel had made in the temple of the Lord" (2 Kings 24:13). Antiochus IV also stole much gold and silver from the Second Temple, and Herod the Great enriched himself by plundering the graves of the kings. The favorite target of invaders was the metalwork on display in Jerusalem, in palaces, or in tombs.

It is not surprising that wealth became a symbol of life's short-lived delights, easily stolen or destroyed. Jesus constantly warned about placing too much trust in such treasures—whether the threats from thieves or the temptation to allow it to become a barrier to salvation. John presents his vision of the Heavenly City as full of the lavish display of precious metals, echoing the vision of Ezekiel: "And the building of the wall of it was of jasper: and the city was pure gold, like unto glass" (Rev. 21:18). *See also* Jewelry; Metal: Copper and Bronze; Metal: Gold; Metal: Iron; Metal: Silver; Tabernacle; Temple; Throne.

Further Reading

Alexander, Pat. "Mining and Metalwork," in *Eerdmans' Family Encyclopedia of the Bible*. Grand Rapids, Mich.: William B. Eerdmans Publishing Co.,1978. Glueck, Nelson. *The Other Side of Jordan*. Winona Lake, Ind.: Eisenbraums, Inc., 1970. Hirsch, Emil G. "Mines and Mining," http://www.jewishencyclopedia.com (accessed December 21, 2004). Miller, Madeleine S. and J. Lane Miller. "Mines," in *Harper's Bible Dictionary*. New York: Harper and Row, 1961. Jacobs, Joseph and Samuel Krauss. "Metals," http://www.jewishencyclopedia.com (accessed December 20, 2004).

Metal: Copper and Bronze

(Job 28:2–10; Ezek. 22:20–30) Copper is a beautiful **metal**, although not as strong as **iron** nor as precious as gold and silver. Deposits of it are found around **Canaan** (as Moses promised his people) and in the Sinai peninsula and in Arabah, the desert area between the Dead Sea and the Gulf of Aqaba.

Archaeologists have discovered the remains of great mines where shafts were dug for as much as 15 miles. Job describes the miners at work : "Iron is taken from the earth, and copper is smelted from ore. Man puts an end to the darkness; he searches the farthest recesses for ore in the blackest darkness. Far from where people dwell he cuts a shaft, in places forgotten by the foot of man; far from men he dangles and sways.... Man's hand assaults the flinty rock, and lays bare the roots of mountains. He tunnels through the rock" (Job 28:2–10). Some suggest that Moses may have learned the craft of copper mining while he was among the Midianites.

Processing Metals

Copper can be extracted by heating the ore, and shaping it by cold hammering. In early times, the smiths would take the ore, melt it in a clay pot over a charcoal stove, and then shape the article. Around 2000 B.C., workers discovered that the addition of up to four percent of tin would make the metal harder and stronger, producing bronze. This new, improved metal also had a lower melting point. This meant it could be poured into molds of stone or other materials and cast into various shapes. There were copper furnaces during the time of the **judges**. Additional furnaces, which were used for both copper and iron, have also been discovered, dating from Solomon's era.

Since the Hebrews probably knew copper only in its natural state, and not as bronze, the biblical-Hebraic word for "brass" or "bronze" may mean simply "copper." The scholars suspect that the "bronze sea," for example, may be really a copper basin. Also, the "bronze serpent" (Num. 21: 9; 2 Kings 18:4) was also thought to be copper, rather than bronze (Joseph Jacobs, Samuel Krauss 2004).

More often, however, Scripture refers to bronze specifically, even in the first reference to Tubal-Cain in Genesis. It is listed among the offerings to be brought to God, among the details of the **Tabernacle**: the clasps (Exod. 26:11), the overlay of the **altar** and its grating (Exod. 27:2), the pots to remove the ashes, sprinkling bowls, shovels, meat forks, and fire pans (Exod. 27:3) to be used for the sacrifices. It was even used for an overlay for the poles to hold the **Ark of the Covenant**. Perhaps because it could be scoured and purified, it was considered a better material for sacramental vessels than clay or even more precious metals. Levitical law notes that a clay pot in which meat has been cooked "must be broken, but if it is cooked in a bronze pot, the pot is to be scoured and rinsed with water (Lev. 6:28). Ezekiel's image of the burning pot suggests that it was heated to a fiery glow to purify it.

Bronze Products

Bronze could be ornamental and cast in different shapes, including the bronze serpent of Moses (Num. 21:9) or the capitals with pomegranate designs in Solomon's **Temple**. It could be engraved in decorative ways and shined (burnished) to a mirror polish. It was good for coins and for household items such as **lamps**. It was also used in city **gates**, along with iron and wood. Several mentions are also made of **musical instruments** of bronze, including bronze cymbals (1 Chron. 15:19). The "main products were for the army and home use: arrowheads, lances and spear-tips, swords, daggers, axes, plough-points, adzes, chisels, needles, safety pins, tweezers, bracelets, bowls and pails" (Pat Alexander 1978, 235). In the New Testament, copper coins, "worth only a fraction of a penny" are mentioned in connection with the poor widow, as her "mite" (Mark 12:42; Luke 21:2). Matthew refers to copper money as well in Christ's admonition to take no "gold or silver or copper in your belts" when traveling as evangelists (Matt. 10:9).

Bronze and copper are regularly mentioned with the other metals as treasures belonging to the Lord, or as booty stolen by invaders. They represented the wealth of the city. The **Philistines** used bronze shackles on Samson (Judg. 16:21) and later the **Babylonians** used bronze shackles on Zedekiah, once again a blinded captive of a foreign people (Jer. 39:7). Goliath, the Philistine warrior, had a bronze helmet, "scale armor," greaves, and javelin (1 Sam. 17:5–6). David, by contrast was offered only Saul's bronze helmet, which he refused, preferring to use his wits instead of bronze coverings in battle with the giant foe. Nonetheless, David was later eager to accept bronze tributes from other **kings** and to accumulate them in Jerusalem, as was his son Solomon (2 Sam. 8:8).

In the building of the Temple and his other construction projects, Solomon used foreign craftsmen—in this case Huram, a man of Tyre "and a craftsman in bronze.... highly skilled and experienced in all kinds of bronze work" (1 Kings 7:14). He cast the bronze pillars and their capitals, which had bronze pomegranates decorating them all around; the movable stands, the basins, the pots, shovels, and sprinkling bowls—all of "burnished bronze." The listing, including the famous bronze bulls holding the giant "sea," concludes with this summary: "Solomon left all these things unweighed, because there were so many; the weight of the bronze was not determined" (1 Kings: 7:15–47). The enormous altar, covered with copper that did not melt, although fire was continually burning on it, was the crowning glory of the Temple (2 Chron. 4:1).

Over time, the bronze became the tribute paid to threatening or invading armies. Some surmise that Ahaz, who "took away the side panels and removed the basins from the movable stands.... removed the Sea from the bronze bulls that supported it" (2 Kings 17:16) needed the bronze to mollify Tiglath-Pileser III. In a more deliberate destruction, when Hezekiah, King of Judah, "broke into pieces the bronze snake Moses had made" it was because "up to that time the Israelites had been burning incense to it" (2 Kings 18:4). The "graven images" that were formed of bronze, were thus broken even when originally designed for worship of God. What still remained was broken up and taken away by the Babylonians, including many of the coverings of pillars and all of the enumerated instruments of sacrifice and worship (2 Kings 25:13–14). Many of these were returned after the Exile for the new Temple.

Poetic Usage of Bronze Imagery

The beauty of bronze and its value led **prophets** and poets to refer to it with some frequency. For Ezekiel, the stunning appearance of the bronze enhanced the vision "I saw a man whose appearance was like bronze; he was standing in the gateway with a linen cord and a measuring rod in his hand" (Ezek. 40:3). For Daniel, bronze was the material constituting the belly and thighs of the giant figure of his vision (Dan. 2:32). Daniel also mentioned the gods shaped of metals, including bronze, which the Babylonians worshiped (5:4). Jeremiah pointed to the strength of the metal, using the image of a bronze wall for protection, referring to the people as "hardened rebels" "bronze and iron" (Jer. 1:18, 6:28). Micah referred to the "hoofs of bronze" that will break to pieces many nations" (Micah 4:13). Zechariah had a powerful image: he looked up to see four **chariots** coming out from between "two mountains—mountains of bronze" (Zech. 6:1). And John used the image of "feet of bronze glowing in the furnace" and the Son of God, "whose eyes are like blazing fire and whose feet are like burnished bronze" (Rev. 1:15, 2:18). The religious usages of the metal and its strength in the fire reverberate in these passages.

As with the other metals, the usual imagery involves the furnace and the fire that refines, with the dross representing the useless remnants. Ezekiel is especially eloquent and vivid: "Son of man, the house of Israel has become dross to me; all of them are the copper, tin, iron and lead left inside a furnace" (Ezek. 22:18); or "As men gather silver, copper, iron, lead and tin into a furnace to melt it with a fiery blast, so will I gather you in my anger and my wrath and put you inside the city and melt you" (Ezek. 22:20); or an example of a vessel that must be purified before it may be used again "Then set the empty pot on the coals till it becomes hot and its copper glows so its impurities may be melted and its deposit burned away" (Ezek. 24:11). *See also* Metal and Mines; Tabernacle; Temple.

Further Reading

Alexander, Pat. *Eerdmans' Family Encyclopedia of the Bible.* Grand Rapids, Mich.: William B. Eerdmans Publishing Company, 1978. Jacobs, Joseph and Samuel

Krauss, "Metals," http://www.jewishencyclopedia.com (accessed December 10, 2004).

Metal: Gold

(Gen. 2:10–12; Exod. 32:4; 1 Kings 10:11–24; Zech. 13:9; Prov. 17:3; 1 Cor. 3:12–16) The **Garden of Eden** itself had a river named Pison, which encompassed "Havilah, where there is gold; And the gold of that land is good: there is bdellium and onyx stone" (Gen. 2:10–12). This early reference suggests that Abraham's forebears knew where to find gold deposits and how to extract and use this lovely metal. It served by weight as money even before there was coinage. Genesis notes that Abram was very wealthy in livestock, silver, and gold (13:2).

The **patriarchs** used gold jewelry for bridal gifts whether or not they had any skill in manipulating the metal themselves. The first evidence of the Hebrews themselves working with gold is the story of the Golden Calf, when Aaron took the people's **jewelry** and melted the gold down to shape a calf that they might worship (Exod. 32:4). Directions for the **Tabernacle** also make extensive reference to using gold—sometimes "pure gold," sometimes "fine gold," and other times "choice gold"—perhaps different qualities or colors.

When looting the cities of **Canaan**, the Israelites found **silver** and gold, which they took as spoils of war. Even during this period—Joshua and Judges—Scripture makes no reference to mining or to metal crafts. In fact, when the monarchy, under Solomon, called for elaborate gold work in the **Temple**, with other metals as well in the brazen sea (the great bronze basin) and candlesticks, the **king** imported craftsmen from Phoenicia and gold from Omir. In his lavish decorations, he is said to have made silver as common in Jerusalem as **stone**.

The process for refining gold or silver, melting it to separate off impurities—the refiner's fire—became a standard symbol in the Old Testament (Exod. 11:2; Josh. 6:19; Judg. 17:1–4; Isa. 2:20, 40:19; Hos. 8:4; 2 Chron. 2:7; 1 Kings 10:1–27; Zech. 13:9; Mal. 3:2–3). Peter also used it (1 Pet. 1:7). When gold is softened by heat, it can be poured into molds or cooled and shaped into various forms. It may also be beaten into thin sheets that can be used to cover objects. This malleability as well as beauty has made it the world's most precious metal.

Scripture mentions gold hundreds of times, frequently distinguishing varieties of the metal and the process used to refine it. 1 Kings 10:11–24 has this famous listing of Solomon's gold:

And the navy also of Hiram that brought gold from Ophir.... Now the weight of gold that came to Solomon in one year was six hundred threescore and six talents of gold.... And king Solomon made two hundred targets of beaten gold: six hundred shekels of gold went to one target. And he made three hundred shields of beaten gold; three pounds of gold went to one shield: and the king put them in the house of the forest of Lebanon. Moreover the king made a great throne of ivory, and overlaid it with the best gold.... And all king Solomon's drinking vessels were of gold, and all the vessels of the house of the forest of Lebanon were of pure gold. For the king had at sea a navy of Tarshish with the navy of Hiram: once in three years came the navy of Tarshish, bringing gold, and silver, ivory, and apes, and peacocks. So king Solomon exceeded all the kings of the earth for riches and for wisdom.

Some of these terms designate the color or the degree of purity. For example, "good gold," which Solomon imported from Ophir, may be "pure gold," which can be put into the fire without losing weight. Some terms may mean unalloyed gold or spun gold, as flexible as wax. On occasion, it was shaped so thin it formed threads and was woven into fabrics. Different regions produced different colors and qualities of gold, so the location of its origin was considered important in testifying to its value (Joseph Jacobs and Samuel Krauss 2004).

The symbolic meanings of gold are clear in Scripture—in **Proverbs**, **Psalms**, and in the prophetic books. Revelation sums up the most popular usages of gold imagery as a sign of wealth and power (as in the case of Solomon's court), as a sign of God's glory and the magnificence of his earthly and heavenly Temple (in the descriptions of the furnishings of the Tabernacle and the Temple, Exodus 25), as the stuff of pagan **idols** (the Golden Calf the Israelites worshipped in the wilderness), and as a symbol of human vanity. The splendid color and great value of the metal caused it to become the very symbol of God's glory, probably the reason that medieval art was so full of beaten gold backgrounds, golden thrones and crowns, and golden haloes.

Even in more recent history, the lure of gold brought many explorers to America, especially to Central America, where gold was thought to be abundant. In the nineteenth century, the Gold Rush in California was followed by discoveries of gold in Alaska and in Australia, when people rushed to distant places in hopes of striking it rich. And the "gold standard" remains the ideal today for wedding rings, bracelets, and other fine jewelry. *See also* Ark of the Covenant; Idols, Idolatry; Jewelry; Metals and Mines; Tabernacle; Temple.

Further Reading

Jacobs, Joseph and Samuel Krauss. "Metal," http://www.jewishencyclopedia.com (accessed October 15, 2004). Jeffrey, David Lyle. "Gold," in *A Dictionary of Biblical Tradition in English Literature*. Grand Rapids, Mich.: William B. Eerdmans Publishing Company, 1992.

Metal: Iron

(Deut. 8:9; Josh. 17:16; 1 Sam. 13:19–22; 1 Chron. 22:3) Iron, a hard, enduring **metal**, has been the perennial symbol of strength and power. This metal can cut deep into the earth or into the human body, plowing up a field or severing a limb. It was especially precious to the Hebrews because it was so useful and so rare. Moses promised the Israelites a land that would be rich, not only with milk and honey: "Its rocks have iron in them, and from its hills you can mine copper" (Deut. 8:9). These are, in fact, the only two metals native to Israel. "Gold, silver, tin and lead had to be imported" (Pat Alexander 1978 , 234).

When they settled **Canaan**, the Israelites found that the Canaanites already had iron weapons and tools, much like those used by the **Egyptians**. In the face of the **Philistines' chariots** with iron wheels and their iron weapons, the Hebrews' wagons with wooden wheels and slingshots were primitive indeed. In Judges (4:3), Deborah noted that Jabin, a king of Canaan, whose army was commanded by Sisera, had 900 iron chariots "and had cruelly oppressed the Israelites for twenty years." Ironically, she used the land and the flooding river against the enemy, causing them to sink in the mire while the Israelites slaughtered their **warriors**.

The Philistines, recognizing that their monopoly gave them strategic supremacy over the Israelites, refused to allow their neighbors even to have blacksmiths of their own. The Hebrews were reduced to going to the Philistines to have their copper tools sharpened or repaired. As a result, David saw the need to gather great stores of iron "for making nails and clamps" as well as for weaponry, thereby breaking the Philistine monopoly (Josh. 17:16; 1 Sam. 13:19–22; 1 Chron. 22:3). King David was the first leader to have access to large supplies of iron, perhaps because of his conquest of Edom.

In the building of the **Temple**, reference is made to iron coins, 100,000 talents of iron (1 Chron. 29:7). For the most part, iron was used for agricultural implements, sickles, axes, plows (Deut. 19:5; 2 Kings 6:5), threshing carts and threshing boards (Amos 1:3; 1 Sam. 8:20), or weapons, swords, hatchets, knives, and spears (1 Sam. 17:7). It was also used for bolts, chains and fetters, nails, hooks, and hilts (Jer. 17:1; Job 19:24).

Iron is usually mentioned in connection with furnaces, and in crafts, although the work with iron is quite different from that of silver or gold. Job, in fact, mentions that an iron tool was used to inscribe on lead or engrave in rock (Job 19:24). To forge and harden iron, the blacksmith must put it red-hot into cold water. Iron was heated on coal; and there were regulations for doing this. Iron, as well as lead, was used on the **yokes** of animals. The rabbis were also acquainted with the magnetic stone that attracts iron (Joseph Jacobs and Samuel Krauss 2004).

Common terms for iron were those meaning "lumps" or "plates." Plates of iron were warmed for the high **priest;** iron plates and "hard iron" are other terms, including perhaps even references to the Sanctuary of the Temple, in which the **lamp** of the sanctuary might be made of *eshet* as well as of gold, an unidentified metal that is classed above silver. The term, which may mean iron, may instead refer to another hard metal that was more valued than silver or even than gold because of its rarity. The metal must also have cast a reflection when it was used for lamps. Therefore, the plates, whether of iron, silver, or gold, must have been highly polished, somewhat like the ancient mirrors.

Yet iron apparently was seen as a contaminated metal and one that contaminated things it touched. The stone masons were careful to use "only blocks dressed at the quarry ... and no hammer, chisel or any other iron tool was heard at the temple site while it was being built" (1 Kings 6:7). This may also be an indication of the care to avoid excessive noise in the building. Altars were sometimes constructed of natural stones, untouched by iron tools.

As for its symbolic usage, one of the more curious references to iron is in 2 Chron 18:10, when Zedekiah "had made iron horns," apparently as a visual aid, declaring, "This is what the Lord says: 'With these you will gore the Armeaans until they are destroyed.'" Iron is mentioned only four times in the first four books of Moses. The Torah notes that a teacher of the **law** must be as hard as iron. A "yoke of iron"(Jer. 28:13) was considered a terrible burden. Iron shackles (Ps. 105:18) also became the symbol of the vicious treatment of the Lord's **anointed;** and an "iron sceptre" (Ps. 2:9) represented the power of the King of Israel over God's enemies, an image repeated in Revelation, where the **Messiah** was to reign with an iron scepter (Rev. 12:5; 19:15).

Precious iron tools of ancient Israel, often made by Philistines, who guarded their craft: mattock, plow points, adze, and ox goad. Isaiah 2:4 notes that these tools could be melted down and turned into instruments of war. In peacetime, the spears would once again be beaten into pruning hooks.

The author of Proverbs notes that "iron sharpens iron, so one man sharpens another" (Prov. 27:17). Most often, iron simply meant strength or toughness, as in the neck with sinews of iron (Isa. 48:4) or Daniel's fourth kingdom, with large iron teeth, like the pieces of iron in sledges used to thresh wheat (Dan. 7:7). Another example is the fabulous Man in Daniel, whose legs were of iron (2:33–34). Daniel goes on to explain Nebuchadnezzar's vision: "Finally, there will be a fourth kingdom, strong as iron —for iron breaks and smashes everything—and as **iron** breaks things to pieces, so it will crush and break all the others" (Dan. 2:40).

We also have the hardened rebels Jeremiah speaks of as being "bronze and iron" (Jer. 6:28). The strength in construction of fortified cities with their iron reinforcement—and the superior strength of their destroyers—is noted in the breaking of the "bars of iron" along with the gates of bronze in Isaiah's prophesy (Isa. 45:21). Only Elisha used iron in his miracles, when he made the iron axhead float in the water (2 Kings 6:5–6).

As with the other metals, the image of the furnace and the refiner's fire is used powerfully with iron: "Son of man, the house of Israel has become dross to me; all of them are the copper, tin, iron and lead left inside the furnace" (Ezek. 22:18). *See also* Agriculture; Carpenters, Carpentry; Chariots; Measures; Metals and Mines; Temple.

Further Reading

Alexander, Pat. "Mining and Metalwork," in *Eerdmans' Family Encyclopedia of the Bible*. Grand Rapids, Mich.: William B. Eerdmans Publishing Company, 1978. Hirsch, Emil G. and Wilhelm Nowack. "Iron," http://www.jewishencyclopedia.com (accessed October 15, 2004). Jacobs, Joseph and Samuel Krauss. "Metals," http://www.jewishencyclopedia.com (accessed October 18, 2004).

Metal: Silver

(Job 22:25, 28:1; 2 Chron. 2:7; Proverbs 17:3, 25:4; Rev. 18:12) The precious metal silver derives its name from its color; it means "make pale." The word used in Job 22:25 seems to suggest something shining. Job 28:1 mentions veins of silver. Unlike gold, it is not found on the surface, nor in riverbeds; "but it must be taken with hard labor from the depths of the mountain" (Joseph Jacobs and Samuel Krauss 2004).

In Scripture, it usually is mentioned along with gold, as a sign of wealth and occurs in most of the same listings. It was used in some of the first coins and as a result is frequently a synonym for money. Silver coins were exchanged for Joseph, when he was sold into slavery. And Judas was paid 30 silver pieces for the betrayal of Christ—the price of a slave. The metal was also used for decorations, much like gold, and therefore occurs frequently in the words of King Solomon: "Send me, therefore a man skilled to work in gold and silver, bronze and iron, and in purple, crimson and blue yarn" (2 Chron. 2:7).

The author of Proverbs (17:3) does differentiate between the lesser and greater metals in their value: "The crucible for silver and the furnace for gold, but the Lord tests the heart." The purification was important in much the same way it was for the gold, "Remove the dross from the silver, and out comes material for the silversmith" (Prov. 25:4). This refining process increasingly becomes the image of God's cleansing fury—the refiner's fire at work on God's imperfect people: "As silver is melted in a furnace, so you will be melted inside her, and you will know that I the Lord have poured out my wrath upon you" (Ezek. 22:22); or "He will sit as a refiner and purifier of silver; he will purify the Levites and refine them like gold and silver" (Mal 3:3).

One of the more memorable references to silver thread is in Ecclesiastes, when death is spoken of in these lyrical terms, "before the silver cord is severed, or the golden bowl is broken" (Eccles. 12:6). References to statues covered with silver and the use of "hammered silver" from Tarshish (Jer. 10:9) are parallel to the gold references, to idols of "gold or silver or stone, an image made by man's design and skill" (Acts 17:29). This combination of wealth and craftsmanship is reinforced by the story of the silversmith Demetrius, "who made silver shrines of Artemis" and was horrified that the Christians were costing him business (Acts 19:24).

The **Christians** in the early **Church** were encouraged to follow the penniless path of Christ, choosing not wealth but salvation. "Peter said, 'Silver or gold have I none; but such as I have give I to thee'" (Acts 3:6). Paul also indicated that he did not covet any man's silver and suggested to Timothy that silver, like anything, may be used for noble or ignoble purposes (2 Tim. 2:20). James noted, in a more fiery tone, that the man greedy for wealth will find in the last days that his gold and silver "are corroded. Their corrosion will testify against you and eat your flesh with fire" (James 5:3). John's Revelation used silver, like gold and precious stones, to signal both the idols (9:20) and the cargoes on their way to Babylon, the Great Harlot (Rev. 18:12).

As another term for wealth, silver became the very image of corruption without the redeeming quality of glory, which we see in gold. Nonetheless, because of its whiteness and its preciousness and its testing by fire, it became for medieval writers and painters the symbol of purity and chastity (George Ferguson 1966, 44). *See also* Measures; Metals and Mines.

Further Reading

Ferguson, George. *Signs and Symbols in Christian Art*. New York: Oxford University Press, 1966. Jacobs Joseph and Samuel Krauss. "Metals," http://www. jewishencyclopedia.com (accessed October 18, 2004).

Metalsmiths

(Gen. 4:22; Jer. 9:7; Zech. 13:9; Mal. 3:3) Miners were usually **slaves**, but metalsmiths, the men who refined and shaped the metal, were free men who were considered craftsmen. Smelters and gold workers in general were called "refiners" (Neh. 3:32). Scripture also mentions ironsmiths (2 Chron. 24:12) and coppersmiths (1 Kings 7:14).

Although Abraham undoubtedly had seen much sophisticated metal work in Sumer in his youth, he was in no position to encourage or develop this craft when he set out for the Promised Land. He and his descendants were a semi-migratory people, without skills in metallurgy and without a need for elaborate decorations. The **jewelry** and agricultural items they treasured were made by craftsmen from Sumer or **Egypt**. They even considered Tubal-Cain, the progenitor of all metalworkers, a descendant of the cursed Cain, "an instructor of every artificer in brass and iron" (Gen. 4:22), quite alien to their own culture.

Refining silver, gold, or other metals was a special process: To rid the cast of slag, the metal was refined a second time in the fire. To aid the process of melting, the workers threw a kind of soap (Isa.1: 25) into the furnace. Note references to "unrefined silver" (Ezek. 22:18) and "refined silver" (1 Chron. 29:4; Ps. 12:7). After the metal-smith purified the metal, the workers tested it. Copper could be worked in various ways; there were shining copper or "yellow bronze" (Ezra 8:27), polished copper (Ezek. 1:7, Dan. 10:6), and perhaps gilded copper also (Emil G. Hirsch and Wilhelm Nowack 2004).

The first Hebrew smiths probably used charcoal furnaces, leaning over them, holding bits of metal with tongs, encouraging the flame with hand bellows. When they removed the hot metal from the furnace, they beat it on an anvil with a hammer, fashioning teraphim, **idols**, or simple household hardware (Isa. 44:12). The tools used by the metal-smiths were the hammer or ax (Isa 41:7), tongs (Isa. 6: 6), hatchet (Deut. 19:5), bellows (Jer. 6:29), fining-pot for , and a (melting) furnace for gold (Prov 17:3), whence the designation "furnace," for Egypt (Deut. 4:20) is derived. (Jacobs and Kraus 2004).

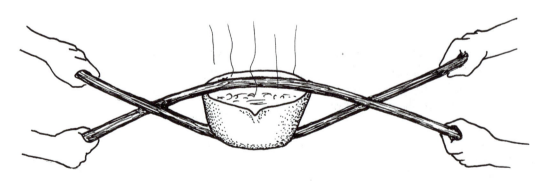

How the metal workers poured molten metals from hot crucible into molds (detail of Egyptian wall painting) as part of the process of making metal products. Smaller pans and molds would be used for jewelry, larger ones for bowls and cups.

Scripture mentions that ancient peoples knew how to solder (Isa. 41:7) to cast for images (2 Chron. 34:3f; Nahum 1:14) and to draw out gold to threadlike fineness for use in weaving into textiles and for embroidery (Exod. 28:6, 39:3). They were also skillful in beating, overlaying, and plating with gold (1 Kings 6:20ff.) (Madeleine S. Miller and J. Lane Miller 1961, 690). They had learned how to solder (Isa. 41:7) and how to cast (Job 11:15). They used "scoured" copper (1 Kings 7:45, 46) for the sanctuary, while for the Tabernacle in the wilderness they hammered the metal into shape. The excavations at the ancient Greek city of Mycenæ show that this process was known before casting, and was in use even in prehistoric times. The Hebrews knew also how to make gold and silver articles by this process (Joseph Jacobs and Samuel Krauss 2004).

The Israelites had probably learned some of these skills from traveling smiths who carried bellows and tools on their **donkeys**, living by their craftsmanship as well as their **music** and their wives' fortunetelling, like gypsies. They had also seen smiths at work in Egypt, where metal workers knew about smelting and casting. Tomb paintings show a charcoal fire glowing in a clay oven as two men work their foot bellows. Men with tongs grip a crucible containing molten metal. Another drawing shows the casting of large objects, using inlet funnels in the clay ground (Werner Keller 1982, 188).

The Israelites of the **Exodus** brought some precious metals with them to **Canaan**, mostly in the form of jewelry, but there is limited evidence that they were themselves skilled in the craft. The **Egyptians** had been shaping gold into beautiful ornaments for centuries, as had the other peoples of the Fertile Crescent. The Israelites were able to create only a few images: the golden calf and the figures for the **Tabernacle**. For these, they melted down their jewelry. The commandment prohibiting making graven images restricted them from developing their craftsmanship until a later time. When the Hebrews settled in Canaan, they had to rely wholly on the **Phoenicians**, even for such simple chores as the sharpening of **iron** implements.

In Saul's time, the **Philistines** were wary of any challenge to their monopoly position (1 Sam. 13:19, 20). "Not a blacksmith could be found in the whole land of Israel, because the Philistines had said, 'Otherwise the Hebrews will make swords or spears!' So all Israel went down to the Philistines to have their plowshares, mattocks, axes, and sickles sharpened. The price was two thirds of a shekel for sharpening plowshares and mattocks, and a third of a shekel for sharpening forks and axes and for repointing goads."

With the imported craftsmen who helped in the building of the **Temple** and the rest of his mighty works, Solomon created a local industry where native craftsmen could learn from foreigners. By the time Jerusalem fell to the Babylonians, smiths and locksmiths were significant members of the culture (2 Kings 24:10). This, of course, came to an end when "Nebuchadnezzar

Metal workers pictured in Egyptian wall painting (part of which is obscured), with mold, "refiner's fire," and finished product. Copper and bronze were refined in crucibles (Prov. 17:3) and then poured into stone or clay molds. The rough casting was then trimmed by hammering.

removed all the treasures from the temple of the Lord and from the royal palace, and took away all the gold articles that Solomon king of Israel had made for the temple of the Lord. He carried into exile all Jerusalem: all the craftsmen and artisans—a total of ten thousand."

Ezekiel's vision of God as the master craftsman portrays debased Israel as the worthless residue—the dross:

Son of man, the house of Israel is to me become dross: all they are brass, and tin, and iron, and lead, in the midst of the furnace; they are even the dross of silver. Therefore thus saith the Lord God; Because you are all become dross, behold, therefore I will gather you into the midst of Jerusalem. As they gather silver, and brass, and iron, and lead, and tin, into the midst of the furnace, to blow the fire upon it, to melt it; so will I gather you in mine anger and in my fury, and I will leave you there, and melt you. Yea, I will gather you, and blow upon you in the fire of my wrath, and you shall be melted in the midst thereof. As silver is melted in the midst of the furnace, so shall you be melted in the midst thereof; and ye shall know that I the Lord have poured out my fury upon you. (Ezek. 22:18–22)

Dross, the worthless residue, was a favorite image of Israel among the **prophets**, who saw God as the great refiner. Jeremiah speaks of refining and testing his people (Jer 9:7); Zechariah also speaks of refining them "like silver" (Zech. 13:9); and Malachi echoes this, saying that God will "refine them like gold and silver" (Mal. 3:3). The refiner's fire became one of the most powerful images of Scripture, vividly revealing the power of God and the purpose of suffering. *See also* Jewelry; Metal and Mines; Tabernacle; Temple.

Further Reading

Hirsch, Emil G. and Wilhelm Nowack, "Mines and Mining," http://www. jewishencyclopedia.com (accessed October 20, 2004). Jacobs, Joseph and Samuel Krauss "Metals," http://www.jewishencyclopedia.com (accessed October 18, 2004). Keller, Werner. *The Bible as History*. New York: Bantam Books, 1982. Miller, Madeleine S. and J. Lane Miller, "Smith," in *Harper's Bible Dictionary*. New York: Harper and Row, 1961.

Midian, Midianites

(Judg. 1:16, 4:11, 8:28; 1 Kings 11:18) Midian, the progenitor of the Midianites, was the son of Abraham and Keturah. The Midianites were a nomadic people who wandered into the Sinai and north into the eastern Jordan Valley and **Canaan**. They may have been attracted to the region by the famous copper mines. One group of Midianites were the Kenites, famous for their metal-working (Judg. 1:16, 4:11; Madeleine S. Miller 1961, 443). By the period of the **kings**, Midian appears to have occupied the land between **Edom** and Paran, on the way to **Egyp**t (1 Kings 11:18). It is also described as being in the vicinity of **Moab;** the elders of Midian joined with the elders of Moab in calling on Balaam to curse Israel (Num. 22:4, 7). The Midianites eventually seem to have lived in the Arabian Desert east of the Gulf of Aqaba, opposite the Sinai Peninsula.

They became rich in cattle and gold, dividing into tribes, each of which had its own city and fortresses. Unlike the other peoples of the region, these people enjoyed displays of treasure. Their kings wore golden earrings and other ornaments, and they ornamented their **camels** lavishly (Judg. 8:26). Some of the tribes continued the nomadic existence, lived in **tents** and were not part of the political life of the city-dwellers. They became **camel**-using merchants who traveled from Gilead to Egypt, a path that took them by the site where Joseph's brothers had him trapped (Gen. 37:25–27). Also called "Ishmaelites" (although the line of Ishmael was separate from theirs), they bought the boy and sold him in Egypt.

Later, when Moses escaped from Egypt after killing an Egyptian overseer, he fled to Midian and settled there, marrying a daughter of Jethro, a Midianite **shepherd**. Zipporah, his wife, was apparently brought up in the faith of Abraham, or at least in some of the customs. She, rather than Moses, insisted that their son be circumcised. After the **Exodus**, Jethro joined the Israelites for a time, offering Moses good advice, including the recommendation that he appoint **judges** to relieve himself of so much decision making (Exod. 18:1–14).

The friendship was apparently short-lived. Near the end of the 40 years of wandering, the Midianites and Moabites tried to exterminate the Israelites, leading Moses to dispatch an army of 12,000 men under Phinehas, the **priest**, to attack them, kill their five kings and set fire to all their cities and **fortresses**. The Israelites seized their cattle and goods, killed every Midianite male child and every woman, sparing only female children (Num. 31:2–18). From later stories, it becomes evident that this effort at extermination was a failure.

In the period of the judges, the Midianites had reappeared as a people and joined with the Amalekites to enter the territory claimed by Israel, driving them into mountain dens and caves (Judg. 6:1). In the time of Gideon, the allied army of Midianites and Amelekites crossed the Jordan and camped in the valley of Jezreel. Gideon, using only 300 men, surprised and routed them, driving them back across the Jordan in confusion (Judg. 7:1–24). By this point, only two princes, Oreb and Zeeb, were mentioned, suggesting that these were the tribes that were the surviving Midianites, while the other three tribes had joined with other Arab tribes (Isidore Singer and M. Seligsohn 2004). The story ends with this episode: Midian was "subdued before the children of Israel, so that they lifted up their heads no more" (Judg. 8:28). This is the final scriptural reference to the people. "Midian, however, continued to survive and play a role in the spice and gold trade from Arabia" (Wayne T. Pitard 1993, 519). *See also* Metal: Gold; Metalsmiths.

Further Reading

Miller, Madeleine S. and J. Lane Miller. "Midianites," in *Harper's Bible Dictionary*. New York: Harper and Row, 1961. Pitard, Wayne T. "Midian," in *The Oxford*

Companion to the Bible. New York: Oxford University Press, 1993. Singer, Isidore and M. Seligsohn, "Midian and Midianites," http://www. jewishencyclopedia.com (accessed June 20, 2004).

Moab, Moabites

(Gen. 19:30–37; Deut. 2:9; Ruth; Isa. 15, 16; Amos 2:1–3; Jer. 48)
Moab was the home of Ruth, the ancestor of both David and Jesus. It was a land adjacent to the Dead Sea, which was a close neighbor and occasional adversary to Israel. Sometimes it was even a part of Israel. In ancient times, it was apparently good farmland and a place where the Israelites would flee when they were suffering from droughts and famines.

Moab was located opposite Jericho, across from Bethlehem, and covered an area from north of the top of the Red Sea to the Arnon, 25 miles to the south. It was a well-watered tableland, a plateau about 4,300 feet above the Dead Sea. On the east was **Ammon** and the Arabian desert, with low, rolling hills separating the two related countries (the inhabitants being descended from half-brothers). "The limestone hills which form the almost treeless plateau are generally steep but fertile. In the spring they are covered with grass; and the table-land itself produces **grain**" (Joseph Jacobs and Louis H. Gray 2004). The rainfall is plentiful and the summers cooler than in western Palestine. Snow frequently falls in winter and spring. In the north there are a number of long, deep ravines, from which Moses climbed to Mount Nebo, where he died (Deut. 34:1–8). Ample rainfall and streams "enabled this lovely land to produce grain, fruit, and flocks of **sheep** on a scale large enough to support a considerable degree of city culture" (Madeleine S. Miller and J. Lane Miller 1961, 451).

As early as 3000 B.C., the Moabites had irrigation, but some catastrophe around 1900 B.C. caused the people to adopt a nomadic life. Gradually, hundreds of towns and walled fortresses emerged, forming a barrier to bedouins from the eastern desert steppes. Their strong-gated cities were sufficiently formidable that Moses and his fellow travelers "went around" the territory.

The name of the region appears to derive from the word meaning "seed of a father" or "to desire" (Joseph Jacobs and Louis H. Gray 2004). The Moabites' language and customs were much like those of the Hebrews, as is evidenced by the Moabite Stone, an enormous stone discovered in 1868, at Dhiban in Jordan by F. A. Klein. This stela describes the deeds of Mesha, a Moabite king of the mid-ninth century B.C. (2 Kings 3:4–5). The writing on it closely resembles early Hebrew inscriptions (Edward F. Campbell 1993, 522).

The people traditionally were considered descendants of Lot by an incestuous relationship with his daughter after the fall of Sodom and Gommorah

(Gen. 19:30–37). They were polytheists, but mainly worshipped **Chemosh**, a god who sometimes demanded human sacrifices, as in the case of Mesha who slaughtered his son and heir to this pagan deity (2 Kings 3:27). They were sometimes called the "people of Chemosh" (Num. 21:29, Jer. 48:46). They also worshipped **Baal**-peor (Num. 25:5) or Peor (Num. 31:16), whose cult was marked by its sensuality. Their worship of Ashtor-chemosh and her crude fertility gods and goddesses has been verified by the discovery of figurines from old Moabite farms. These practices caused the Hebrew prophets Isaiah, Jeremiah, Ezekiel, Amos, and Zephaniah to condemn them and cry down judgments on them.

Historically, the Moabites were adversaries to the Hebrews. The king of Moab would not allow Moses and the Israelites to cross his country, forcing them into a circuitous path to **Canaan** (Deut. 2:9). Numbers 22–23 records a sorry tale about King Balak of Moab, who was afraid that his own people could not match the physique or military skills of the "tough sons of the deserts." First, he strove to use **magic**, incantations, and **curses** to bring them under control, calling on Balaam for this purpose. When these measures failed, the Moabites undertook a more subtle strategy, assimilation. They allowed the Israelites to abide in their midst, "and the people began to commit whoredom with the daughters of Moab. And they called the people unto the sacrifice of their gods" (Num. 25:1–2). As Werner Keller noted, the daughters of the Moabites and the Midianites "enticed and seduced the men of Israel to take part in the rites of Baal, the fertility cult of Canaan. What Israel encountered, while still on the other side of the Jordan, was the voluptuous worship of the **Phoenician** gods." Phineas, the grand-nephew of Moses, killed all the wrongdoers, the Israelites, as well as the Moabites and the Midianites (Werner Keller 1982, 152–153).

After the conquest of Canaan, Moabite territory was given to the tribe of Reuben (Josh. 13:15–21), and for a time the Moabites appear to have submitted to Hebrew control. Then Eglon, King of Moab, joined with **Ammonites**, and Amelekites conquered the Hebrews and ruled over them for 18 years. At the end of this time, a Benjamite assassinated Eglon (Judg. 3:12–30). Later, Saul waged war against them (1 Sam. 14:47). Because of his kinship with Ruth, David sought and received help from Moab, but later he subdued them (2 Sam. 8:1–2; 11–12) and forced them to pay tribute.

The Moabite Stone, a famous discovery by archaeologists, asserts Mesha, king of Moab, liberated north Moab from control of the northern kingdom's Omri dynasty. This suggests that, sometime between Solomon and Omri, Moab had escaped subjugation. At the least there appears to have been a continuing struggle for independence over time, which may well have ended when the Moabites were taken over by Syria. They seem to have been vassals to **Assyria** around 732 B.C. and were clients of Nebuchadnezzar, (2 Kings 24:2), helping to put down Jehoiakim's revolt around 600 B.C.

This alliance with Assyria would help explain the antagonism of the **prophets:** Amos, Isaiah, and Jeremiah. The prophets speak of the "burden of Moab," referring to its prosperity and pride and calling the wrath of Jehovah down on the nation (Isa. 15, 16; Amos 2:1–3; Jer. 48). "These oracles judge Moab, lament over it, and convey to it divine promises" (Edward F. Campbell 1993, 522). After the Babylonian conquest, Moab finally disappeared as a nation, and it is Arabians instead of Moabites who are mentioned by the author of the book of the Maccabees (Joseph Jacobs and Louis H. Gray 2004).

Either because of their religion or their historic animosity to the Hebrews, they—like the Ammonites—were excluded from Hebrew congregations "unto the tenth generation" (Deut. 23:3–4). Nehemiah and Ezra, noting that this law had been ignored during the Exile, sought to "compel a return to the ancient custom of exclusion" (Jacobs and Gray 2004; Ezra 9:1–2; Neh. 13:23–25), probably as a part of their policy of ethnic purity.

Given this awkward relationship between the Moabites and the Israelites, it is interesting that Ruth, the Moabitess, is listed in Matthew's genealogy of Christ: "and Boaz begat Obed of Ruth" (Matt.1:5), probably a testimony to the universality of Christ's ministry. *See also* Ammon, Ammonites; Chemosh; Idols, Idolatry.

Further Reading

Campbell, Edward F. "Moab," in *The Oxford Companion to the Bible*. New York: Oxford University Press, 1993. Campbell, Edward F. "Moabite Stone," in *The Oxford Companion to the Bible*. New York: Oxford University Press, 1993. Jacobs, Joseph and Louis H. Gray, "Moab," http://wwwjewishencyclopedia. com (accessed June 16, 2004). Keller, Werner. *The Bible as History.* New York: Bantam Books, 1982. Miller, Madeleine S. and J. Lane Miller. "Moab," in *Harper's Bible Dictionary*. New York: Harper and Row, 1961.

Moloch

(Lev. 18:21, 20:2–5; 1 Kings 11:7; 2 Kings 21:6; Amos 5:26; Jer. 32:35) The name *molek* may derive from a Hebrew word for "kingdom, royalty" (William Albright 1969, 241). It was spelled "Molech" before being changed in the Septuagint to "Moloch." The actual god, who has been identified as the national god of the **Ammonites**, may be a more generic reference to the practice of child-sacrifice. A "royal sacrifice," in this interpretation would be "the noblest possible sacred act" or a "princely act," which may have been interpreted as the sacrifice of a child (William Albright 1969, 242).

After the interrupted sacrifice of Isaac by Abraham, such an offering was forbidden by Mosaic law (Lev. 18:21, 20:1–5), but was nevertheless eventually tolerated in Israel. Solomon, for example, built a **temple** for Moloch "on the hill over against Jerusalem" and is generally thought to have been the monarch who reintroduced this impious cult into Israel. After his time, traces of the cult reappeared in both Judah and Israel. The practice of "passing through the fire," or burning one's children seems to have become common in the Northern Kingdom (2 Kings 17:17, Ezek. 23:37) and even occurred in the Southern Kingdom (2 Kings 16:6). It was **King** Josiah who suppressed the worship of Moloch and defiled Tophet (2 Kings 23:13). The practice may have been revived under Joakim and continued after the **Babylonian** captivity, perhaps even reinforced by Babylonian worship customs (Francis E. Gigot 2005).

The place of sacrifice was "in the valley of the children of Hinnom," otherwise referred to as Topheth, a valley outside of Jerusalem. The children were killed and burned as a holocaust offering to God, in spite of the **prophets**' denunciation of this practice. The motive seems clear in Micah 6:7: "Shall I give my first-born for my transgression, the fruit of my body for the sin of my soul?" By following the hideous example of their Semitic kindred, the troubled **Hebrews** erected an **altar** or pyre in the Valley of Hinnom, while continuing their worship at the Temple as well (Isidore Singer and George A. Barton 2005). *See also* Sacrifice; Temple.

Further Reading

Albright, William Foxwell. *Yahweh and the Gods of Canaan*. Garden City, N.Y.: Doubleday & Company, Inc., 1969. Gigot, Francis E. "Moloch," http://www.newadvent.org (accessed January 12, 2005). Miller, Madeleine S. and J. Lane Miller. "Molech," in *Harper's Bible Dictionary*. New York: Harper and Row, 1961. Singer, Isidore and George A. Barton. "Moloch (Molech)," http://www. jewishencyclopedia.com (accessed January 12, 2005).

Money Changers

(Exod. 30:11–16; Mark 17:15–17) Mark tells us of Jesus's anger at the money changers and merchants in the **Temple**, who "sold and bought," overthrowing the "tables of the money changers and the seats of them that sold doves.... And he taught, saying unto them, Is it not written, My house shall be called of all nations the house of prayer? but ye have made it a den of thieves" (Mark 17:15–17).

Because of the variations of forms of money and the absence of anything like modern banks, money changing became a lucrative business. As described by one historian who had observed modern-day money changers and studied ancient ones: "These men change people's money from one type of currency to another, and also provide change within the same currency. The money changer sits beside the narrow street and behind a little glass-top table, under which his coins are on display" (Fred H. Wight 1953, 224).

Mosaic **law** (Exod. 30:11–16) required that every adult pay half a shekel annually to the sanctuary. Nehemiah mentions this requirement, which had been neglected in troubled times (Neh. 10:33). It continued into Jesus's day (John 2:14–22, Matt. 17:24–27). At the period of the Second Temple, the **tax** was paid at the time of the **Passover** pilgrimage.

Every male Israelite who was 20 years or older was expected to pay his half-shekel tribute using the exact Hebrew half-shekel. Because the tax was to be paid "on the first day of the twelfth month, Adar," that was the day the money-changers set up their tables in Jerusalem "for the purpose of exchanging foreign moneys for the coin in which the tax was payable.... On the twenty-fifth of Adar the changers set up their tables in the Temple itself; on the last-mentioned date also they began to take pledges from those persons who had not paid the tax, no pledges being exacted from the **priests**, although they were obliged to pay the tax, and committed a sin in refusing to do so; **women**, **slaves**, and minors were not required to pay the tax, though their money was accepted if they offered it, the tax was not accepted from pagans and Samaritans, even if they wished to pay it" (Wilhelm Bacher and Jacob Zallel Lauterbach 2004). These gold coins were used to purchase **animals** or doves for sacrifice in the Temple. The coins were later taken from the treasury, under tight security for fear of theft, and placed in three baskets, from which the money was subsequently taken for the purchase of **sacrifices**.

Wight notes that "these changers would reap a profit of from forty to forty-five thousand dollars" in modern terms for their work, charging twelve percent for each transaction (Fred Wight 1953, 225). The money changers would gather within the large open area of the Temple court, known as the "Court of Gentiles" or the porticoes around the Temple enclosure. It was their profiteering in God's house that infuriated Jesus (Mark 11:15–19, Michael D. Coogan 1993, 524). Both the half-shekel tax and the offering of the firstlings of the fruit ceased with the destruction of the Temple (Wilhelm Bacher and Jacob Lauterbach 2004).

In modern usage, "money changers in the Temple" refers to any commercial traffic in places which are considered sacred. *See also* Taxes, Tithes, Tributes; Temple.

Further Reading

Bacher, Wilhelm and Jacob Zallel Lauterbach, "Shekalim," http://www.jewishencyclopedia.com (accessed September 12, 2004). Coogan, Michael D. "Money Changers," in *The Oxford Companion to the Bible*. New York: Oxford University Press, 1993. Wight, Fred H. *Manners and Customs of Bible Lands*. Chicago: Moody Press, 1953.

Monsters

(Deut. 32:24; Job 12:7, 40:15; Pss. 49:12, 20; 50:10, 73:22; Jer. 12:4; Hab. 2:17) On the edges of medieval maps were sometimes warnings that, beyond a certain point, "there be monsters." This belief grew in part from the scriptural references to Leviathan, Behemoth, and dragons, as well as to discoveries and stories of travelers who returned from distant regions. Farmers digging in the fields or miners burrowing into the earth sometimes discovered enormous bones from prehistoric animals. Travelers returned from other countries with exaggerated descriptions of the marvels they had seen, making elephants and whales seem grotesque. In much of ancient folklore, monstrous creatures figure prominently, even in the various stories of the **creation** of the earth. Giant snakes, blends of animals, like the chimera or the satyr, were common among the countries encircling the Hebrews. For the most part, the Jews described in realistic detail the creatures they saw: the **sheep**, the **goats**, the lions, etc. But they too had memories and fears of mammoth beasts.

The Behemoth and Leviathan are usually mentioned together: one the land creature, the other the water. In Jewish tradition they were thought to have been created on the fifth day. Jewish tradition also suggested that God created only a single male and female of each and did not provide means for them to propagate for fear they would overrun the earth (Richard Schell 1992, 448). In most of literature, the Behemoth is male (and of the "dry land of the wilderness") and the Leviathan female (and of the "abysses of the sea"). These references come from the apocryphal book of 1 Enoch 60:7–10. Jewish literature, especially Talmudic, is full of explanations and elaborations of these mysterious creatures and their activities.

The name *leviathan* comes from a root for "bend" or "twist." Its literal meaning would be "wreathed" or "gathering itself into folds" (D. G. Stradling 1980, 896). One scholar in studying Leviathan in Job 3:8 and chapter 41, where so much of this description occurs, believes the writer is trying to describe a monstrous crocodile: "Canst thou fill his skin with barbed irons? or his head with fish spears? (41:26). As Cansdale notes, "An adult crocodile's skin is hard to penetrate with a bullet . . . , and the weapons used then would have been inadequate. . . . A wounded crocodile, lashing with its powerful tail and throwing its whole body about can make a tremendous disturbance" (George Cansdale 1970, 197). The Leviathan, "that crooked serpent" (Isa. 27:1), could well be a remembered crocodile, frightening and enormous, powerful and seemingly indestructible. Psalm 104:24–26 speaks of Leviathan frolicking at sea, suggesting a dolphin or a whale rather than a crocodile, but large crocodiles might be found at the edge of such water. They are river creatures, however, not salt-water and amphibious. They come ashore to bask in the sun and to lay eggs. Because the Leviathan so often appears in connection with references to foreign gods, it is thought to be tied to the **Babylonian** creation epic, where there was a mother goddess Tiamat, a "tortuous serpent" smitten by **Baal** (D.G. Stradling 1980, 896).

The Behemoth was the land creature of similar power. The references in Scripture (Deut. 32:24; Job 12:7, 40:15; Ps. 49:12, 20, 50:10, 73:22; Jer. 12:4; Hab. 2:17) tend to suggest a specific large animal, a "great beast" (T.C. Mitchell 1980,182). Some think that this was a remembered description of an elephant or a hippopotamus. The name is akin to that of cattle and may refer to a giant **ox**. Again, it is Job who mentions the creature, and Job may not have been a resident of **Canaan**. His own cloudy ancestry and his ties to **wisdom** literature suggest that he may have had experiences with fauna unfamiliar to the **Canaanite** residents. The Behemoth was thought to be the largest of the earth animals and remained hopelessly earthbound in his life. This imagery clearly opens the door for developing the creature into a metaphor for philosophies, states, religions, and people.

The dragon occurs primarily in **apocalyptic** literature and may be a vision of a large **snake** or lizard. The word appears to mean "whale" (Gen. 1:21; Job 7:12) or sea monster. Daniel had an encounter with a dragon in Bel and the Dragon, an **apocryphal** addition to the Book of Daniel. (He slays the monster by feeding him balls of hair mixed with fat and tar.)

Some believe that "the great dragon that lieth in the midst of his rivers" (Isa. 51:9 and Ezek. 29:3) is really a crocodile, although other anthropologists consider this a reference to the chaos dragon of Babylonian mythology (George Cansdale 1970, 197). The dragon of Revelation 12:3 is described colorfully: "a great red dragon, having seven heads and ten horns and seven crowns upon his heads." Like much of this grand apocalypse, the image is figurative, representing, many believe, the wild forces of chaos and destruction. Unlike the earlier dragons, it cannot be interpreted simply as a large snake or crocodile(Marjorie Reeves 1992, 210).

In Jewish messianic literature, the dragon, like the Behemoth and Leviathan, is to be released to torment the human race until finally slain by God and consumed in the messianic banquet. Revelation 13:1–18 described the two beasts that were to appear, one from the sea and one from the land, which will exercise great power over the dragon. The first had 7 heads and 10 horns. It was like a leopard, with the feet of a bear and the mouth of a lion. The second beast had two horns like a lamb, but he spoke like a dragon. This is the creature that forces the mark of the beast on everyone who hoped to live. Both of these seem to be creatures of vision, not of earthly experience. They are supernatural, and only God can slay them. He sends Michael and his **angels** to fight against the dragon, which they cast out, identifying him as "that old serpent, called the Devil and Satan" (Rev. 12:7–9).There are numerous references to the enormous feast that the believers will enjoy when the beasts are finally slain in a cosmic battle (Marjorie Reeves 1992, 211).

The Gnostics incorporated the Behemoth and Leviathan into their design of the seven circles or stations that the soul must pass for purgation and attainment of bliss. Their concept of the great banquet of the righteous was to be furnished with the abundant flesh of these monsters.

These creatures appear to be partially figments of the imagination, but based on animals that actually existed, although probably of less formidable size and form. The rich imagery of the entire book of Revelation makes literal interpretation difficult and unwise. The images live in their visionary truth, not in their references to actual snakes or elephants.

All three of these monsters are unusual in Scripture because of their strong ties to pagan thought and their vague meaning. Perhaps the Hebrews remembered the old Babylonian story of Marduk's victory over the dragon of the sea. Certainly, the Hebrew poets and **prophets** "were fond of using this old myth to symbolize the destruction of Israel's enemies" (Emil. G. Hirsch and Hermann Gunkel 2004).

In literature, not only did John Milton use both creatures in *Paradise Lost,* but so did Thomas Hobbes, who wrote *Leviathan* (1651), a famous political attack on the concept of the all-powerful king, who was like a massive, terrifying sea monster, "twisted" and "coiled." Shelley and Byron both used them, as did James Joyce and Robertson Davies. William Blake drew impressive pictures of both creatures. They have long fascinated poets. The most famous use for most modern Americans is to the great white whale, Moby Dick, which Melville referred to as the "Leviathan." *See also* Animals; Behemoth, Leviathan; Creation; Serpent.

Further Reading

Carsdale, George. *All the Animals of the Bible Lands.* Grand Rapids, Mich.: Zondervan Publishing House, 1970. Hirsch, Emil G. and Hermann Gunkel, "Dragon," http://www.jewishencyclopedia.com (accessed December 7, 2004). Mitchell, T. C. "Behemoth," in *The Illustrated Bible Dictionary.* Sydney, Australia: Tyndale House Publishers, 1980. Reeves, Marjorie, "Dragon of the Apocalypse," in *A Dictionary of Biblical Tradition in English Literature.* Grand Rapids, Mich.: William B. Eerdmans Publishing Company, 1992. Schell, Richard. "Behemoth," and "Leviathan," in *A Dictionary of the Biblical Tradition in English Literature.* Grand Rapids, Mich.: William B. Eerdmans Publishing Company, 1992. Stradling., D. G. "Leviathan," in *The Illustrated Bible Dictionary.* Sydney, Australia: Tyndale House Publishers, 1980.

Mourning

(Gen. 37:34; 2 Sam. 1:11–12; Job 1:20, John 11:44, 19:40) When a man or woman died in ancient Israel, the family set off a great cry that signaled the event to the whole village. The death itself was then announced with a cry or the blowing of the shofar. Others would come to the house and join in the **lamentation**, weeping with the family for days on end. Sometimes even hired mourners joined the keening.

The relatives of the deceased person followed a ritual that included tearing their garments and putting on sackcloth, a coarse material that they wore next to the skin below the waist and below the breast. They took off their shoes and headdress for the occasion, but covered their **beards** or veiled their faces, and wept prodigiously. People put their hands on their heads as a sign of sorrow (Roland deVaux 1961, 59; Gen. 37:34; 2 Sam. 1:11–12; Job 1:20). They sat on the ground or rolled in ashes to alter their appearance and mirror their misery. Some put earth on their heads or rolled their heads on the ground in the dust. They might tear out their hair and beards or shave their heads and beards (Jer. 7:29; Isa. 15:2). Sometimes they beat their breasts, or even gashed themselves, although this was forbidden by **law** (Deut. 12:1). They fasted and refrained from washing and using perfumes. Relatives and friends of the departed one felt free to demonstrate their grief openly and physically, rocking their bodies, wringing their hands, weeping and wailing, and singing an emotionally powerful expression from their hearts.

The dead were to be buried as quickly as possible, usually within 24 hours, even if they were criminals who had been hanged (Deut. 21:23). This stipulation probably derived from both the heat of the region and the law of **cleanliness** that forbade touching a corpse (Num. 19:11–14). The eyes of the dead were closed, The close relatives would embrace the body, and then the dead person would be prepared for burial. The body would be bathed and anointed with aromatic oils.

Because **cloth**, like flesh, decays over time and is not available for scholarly study, it is not clear how the bodies were clothed for death, but it seems to have been in their best clothes. Samuel, for example, still had his cloak around him when he came up from Sheol (1 Sam. 28:14). Only the **jewelry** that they wore as ornaments has survived—if it was not stolen. In other countries of the region, funeral masks of gold and rich apparel were placed on the corpses, but the Jews placed a napkin over the face and bound the whole body with linen wrappings. Soldiers had their swords under their heads and their shields under their bodies when they were laid to rest (Ezek. 32:27). The winding cloth was soaked in aromatic herbs: myrrh and bdellium, an aromatic gum resin resembling myrrh. The cloth was wound about the arms and legs and even around the head so that the jaw would not drop and then the body was placed on a bier for transport to the burial site. Both Lazarus (John 11:44) and Jesus (John 19:40) appear to have been prepared for burial in this mode.

They were sometimes buried in **graves**, without a coffin. Only Joseph, who had been influenced by his interactions with the **Egyptians**, was embalmed and buried in a coffin. Probably the oldest and simplest graves were dug into the ground and covered with piles of rock to keep wild **animals** from disturbing the corpse. Sometimes the dead were buried under trees, as in the case of Deborah, Rebekah's nurse (Gen. 35:19). More commonly, they were placed on shelves in **caves**, where they would be left to rot after which their bones would be dumped into a collective pit and "gathered with their fathers." Jacob and Joseph were unusual cases. Because they died in Egypt, they were embalmed and removed to **Canaan** later so that their bones could reside with their families. Israel never practiced embalming. In some ancient communities, infants were sometimes buried in jars (Madeleine S. Miller and J. Lane Miller 1961, 83).

For a corpse to remain unburied was considered a disgrace and perhaps even a sign of divine judgment (Philip J. King and Lawrence E. Stager 2001, 363). Improper burial was an insult, sometimes a deliberate one, as in the case of Jehoiakim, who was dragged off and thrown out beyond the **gates** of Jerusalem (Jer. 22:19, 36:30). When Jezebel died according to God's judgment, after being dashed to bits on the pavement, her carcass was eaten by **dogs**, except for her skull, her feet, and the palms of her hands (1 Kings 21:23; 2 Kings 9:30–37). This was considered an appropriate desecration of her body, even to the detail that even dogs would not eat certain parts of this infamous woman. Jeremiah used the threat of having neither burial nor lament as a recurrent **curse** on the people to whom he was preaching (Jer. 16:6, 7:33, 8:2, 9:21, 15:3). Even today, the desecration of a corpse is considered a crime in most cultures.

During the mourning, often a period of seven days, the mourners would **fast**. Afterwards, they would break the fast with a **meal** of **wine** and **bread**. In the case of Saul's burial, the whole nation fasted for seven days. Neighbors or friends would bring "mourning bread" and a "cup of consolation" to the house of the dead to break the fast. This was important because the uncleanness associated with death would have prevented the close relatives from preparing **food**.

According to the contemporary historian Josephus, the funeral of King Herod (4 B.C.) marked a gross exaggeration of these rituals: his body was displayed on a golden couch "studded with precious stones and [he] wore the royal purple and a golden crown.... His son Archelaus gave a sumptuous funerary banquet to the people.... King Herod himself had spent lavishly on the funeral of Antigonus (whom he murdered)—on the furnishing of a burial-vault, costly spices burnt as incense, the personal adornment ... of the corpse" (J. P. Kane, 1980, 213).

The death scene at the home of Lazarus in Bethany (John 11:38ff) provides insight into the New Testament ritual of preparing the dead for burial. At Nain, Jesus met with a procession of mourners on their way to the tomb. The family and the townspeople accompanied the body, which bearers carried on a bier. The burial of Christ himself, provides other indications of the preparation of the body and the use of a cave tomb with a rolling stone to cover the entrance (Mark 16:3). In the **Beatitudes**, Jesus makes especial note of those who mourn, "for they shall be comforted" (Matt. 5:4). This reflects a major purpose in the elaborate mourning tradition that had continued from ancient times. It is both a tribute to the dead and a comfort to the living. *See also* Afterlife; Caves; Dogs; Graves.

Further Reading

DeVaux, Roland. *Ancient Israel: Its Life and Institutions*. Grand Rapids, Mich.: William B. Eerdmans Publishing Company, 1961. Edersheim, Alfred. *The Life and Times of Jesus the Messiah*. Peabody, Mass.: Hendrickson Publishers, Inc., 2004. Kane, J. P. "Burial and Mourning," in *The Illustrated Bible Dictionary*. Sydney, Australia: Tyndale House Publishers, 1980. King, Philip J. and Lawrence E. Stager, *Life in Biblical Israel*. Louisville, Ky.: Westminster John Knox Press, 2001. Miller, Madeleine S. and J. Lane Miller. "Burial," in *Harper's Bible Dictionary*. New York: Harper and Row, 1961.

Music

(Gen. 4:21; 2 Sam. 19:36; Song of Solomon; the Book of Psalms) Singing and **dancing** were a regular part of life in ancient Israel. Whether for worship, celebration, homecoming, **work**, **festivals**, battles, **weddings**, or any number of other occasions, the people made music. Its importance is highlighted by the early and repeated references to musicians and to **songs**. We learn in Genesis (4:21) that Jubal, a descendant of Cain, "was the ancestor of all those who play the lyre and pipe." Abraham came from a land of sophisticated musicians and beautiful instruments, and he brought that musical tradition with him. The sojourn in **Egypt** further added to the knowledge of music among the Israelites. When Moses and Miriam crossed the Red Sea with their people, the women played on the tambourines and danced while singing a song of triumph over their Egyptian enemies.

Uses of Music in Scripture

In ancient Israel, music was used for a variety of purposes: As early as Jacob's escape from serfdom to Laban, we see that music was a part of domestic celebrations. Laban complains that, had he known the family was leaving, he would have planned a going-away party for them, "with mirth and songs, with tambourine and lyre" (Gen. 31:27). Weddings (as reflected in the Song of Solomon and Psalm 45) were times of song of the bride and bridegroom, or in the case of royal weddings, musical arrangements for the **king**. There would be singing and dancing at such events, including probably at the marriage at Cana. In one of his **parables**, Jesus mentions the joyous festivities at the return of the prodigal son, and we also know that the homecoming of Jephthah was greeted, tragically, by the dancing figure of his beloved daughter (Judg. 11:34).

Music was naturally used for **mourning**, when the people would join in lamenting national or personal tragedies. A song was also perfect for the celebration of harvest-time, as suggested by the song of the **vineyard** in Isaiah (5:1, 16:10–11). The Song of Solomon was probably a song of festivities in celebration of a wedding, as well as a memorial of the abduction of the Benjamite maidens (Judg. 21:20–21). Music also served in **warfare**, especially in victory celebrations. The famous songs of Miriam and Deborah (Exod. 15:20–21, Judg. 5:3) suggest this was a special role for women.

It was also used to induce prophetic ecstasy. A kind of divine madness was thought to come over the **prophets** when they were possessed by the spirit of Yahweh. "This ecstatic state was often accompanied by dancing, trances, and self-mutilation" (Philip J. King and Lawrence E. Stager 2001, 287). Samuel told Saul that he would meet a band of prophets coming to the shrine with harp, tambourine, flute, and lyre in front of them. "They will be in a prophetic frenzy along with them and be turned into a different person" (1 Sam.10:5–6). King notes that a terracotta cult stand from the tenth century B.C. has such figures of musicians playing instruments, including cymbals, double pipe, lyre, and tambourine. Elisha also used such musical ecstasy during the military campaign against the Moabites. When King Jehoram could not find water for his men and animals, he appealed to Elisha, who required musicians before the power of God "overtook him" and he uttered his prophesy (2 Kings 3:15–16).

Although there were no professional musicians among the Israelites until David's day, even the prophets used music in a variety of ways. David, an accomplished musician, inherited a tradition of **psalms** and dance. He and his son Solomon brought musicians to Jerusalem, where they collected, created, and preserved a rich heritage. David himself was the great creator of psalms. From the reign of David on, music formed a regular part of court life. Mention of the "voices of singing men and singing women" (2 Sam. 19:36) during the time of David, and at the coronation of Solomon, when the people went up after him "playing flutes and rejoicing"(1 Kings 1:34, 40), testify to this culture. It assumed a regular role at banquets as entertainment. From these early days of the monarchy also comes the rich heritage of the Psalms and the Song of Songs.

Its role was also firmly fixed in Hebrew liturgy. **Priests** came to see every detail of **Temple** music as symbolic of the universe (Eric Werner 1984, 1). The Temple singers are mentioned several times, apparently an impressive part of the pageant of worship. From the time of David, when music had first become an important part of worship, it was the practice to have thousands of Levites appointed for musical service (1 Chron. 9:33; 15:16,

19–24). The positions became hereditary in the tribe of Levi, perhaps following the pattern of **Egyptians**, who also divided their people into tribes with specific assigned duties for the members of the various tribes (Russel Squire 1962, 17–18).

In a more debased form, music was also a regular part of high society that was denounced by Amos, who complained that the Samaritans, during their revels at rich banquets, "sing idle songs to the sound of the harp, and ... improvise on musical instruments (Amos 6:5). Isaiah also referred to those "whose feasts consist of lyre and harp, tambourine and flute, and wine" (Isa, 5:12).

It was also a problem for the celebration of the Feast of the Tabernacles, which the Talmudic accounts suggest turned into a bacchic orgy. The two sexes intermingled and committed "light-headedness," leading the sages to require that the women be segregated and put in galleries to avoid "evil inclination." The only music specified by regulations was the priestly trumpet-blowing and the Levitical chant. Everything else was "improvised, noisy, and exuberant." The festival and its celebration fell into oblivion with the destruction of the Temple (Eric Werner 1984, 6–7).

When Sennacherib claimed tribute from Hezekiah in 701 B.C., among the treasures he sent to Nineveh were "male and female musicians." Later, among those deported to **Babylon** by Nebuchadnezzar, was the "director of the singers from Ashkelon" (Philip J. King and Lawrence E. Stage 2001, 286). In post-exilic worship, singers were awarded a priestly position and allowed to wear white priestly garments, which became ever more richly embellished. The congregation was also allowed to participate in the sing-ing, contributing certain responses, such as "Amen" or "Hallelujah;" or join in refrains, such as "Since His mercy endureth forever." In fact, Werner notes that, "Unique in the history of music is the firm belief in the purifying and sin-atoning power of the Temple's music, ascribed to both chant and instruments" (Eric Werner 1984, 8).

At the time of the dedication of the walls of Jerusalem, Nehemiah divided the levitical singers into two choruses that marched around the city in different directions and then stood opposite one another

Shofar, which was blown as a "trumpet" from the parapet before sacrifices began at the Temple in Jerusalem.

and sang alternate hymns of praise at the Temple (Neh. 12:31; Emil G. Hirsch and Wilhelm Nowack 2004).

In Hellenistic times, both the singers and the instrumentalists were strictly trained professions, studying for at least five years. The repertoire of the choir consisted of psalms, canticles, and other passages from Scripture. The singers in the Temple probably chanted the psalms in the manner of Greek choruses, which had strophe and antistrophe, verses that answered one another. The music would probably be neither tuneful nor appealing to modern ears. There was a set liturgy for the different days of the weeks, the different times of day, and the different festival days. Twelve adult choristers were the minimum for a chorus, to which could be added soprano and alto voices of their sons, who stood at their feet (and were called "their tormentors") (Eric Werner 1984, 14).

After the return from Exile, even though there was considerable tension between the Temple and the **synagogue**, the synagogues shared some of the musical culture of the Temple, but on a far smaller scale. One Levite noted that "the [temple] choristers used to go in a body to the synagogue from the orchestra by the altar, and so participated in both services." The synagogue worship, which did not include the sacrifice or the hereditary priesthood, was more informal, with psalms, prayers, and readings "which would be cantillated, that is recited in a heightened speech resembling simple song. Its basis was the chanting of the text on a single note, but with simple melodic alterations to indicate its grammatical structure." The rabbis and cantors led the musical sections of the service. This was important because of the nature of the Hebrew language, which has no punctuation. Thus, the leader divided the phrases and sentences, chanting them to show where the divisions occurred. This form of service, with a parallel role for music, appears to have become a natural part of the early Christian church services (Andrew Wilson-Dickson 1992, 22).

Musical Practices in Christianity

Early **Christians** shared with the synagogues a number of elements, among which were the "Liturgy of the Word," Scripture readings, teaching, prayers, fasting, and the singing of psalms and hymns. The interpretation of the word *hymns* has been a perennial subject of dispute. Paul said of the early Christians that they sang when filled with the Spirit: "Sing the words and tunes of the psalms and hymns when you are together, and go on singing and chanting to the Lord in your hearts" (Eph. 5:19). Of course, the whole concept of hymns, songs with rhyme and meter, did not exist at the time of Paul's epistles. It was centuries later when Augustine (354–430 A.D.) explained hymns: "A hymn is a song containing praise of God. If you praise God, but without song, you do not have a hymn. If you praise anything, which does not pertain to the glory of God, even if you sing it, you do not have a hymn. Hence, a hymn contains the three elements: *song* and *praise* of *God*" (Andrew Wilson-Dickson 1992, 25). Paul was probably speaking of spontaneous praise in song, such as that recorded in Revelation: "And I seemed to hear the voices of a huge crowd, like the sound of the ocean or the great roar of thunder, answering. 'Allelula! The reign of the Lord our God the Almighty has begun; let us be glad and joyful and give praise to God, because this is the time for the marriage of the Lamb'" (Rev. 19:6–7).

Because of abuses of music by pagan practitioners, many of the later Christian leaders rejected instrumental music in the Church. Like Paul, who referred to clanging cymbals (1 Cor. 13), these Church Fathers thought much of the music too noisy and distracting, too identified with debauchery and immorality to be appropriate for worship services. Obviously, this view was gradually relaxed in the Middle Ages, when liturgical music began to make its comeback, flourishing by the early Renaissance.

In Christian tradition, music continued to serve much the same purposes as in ancient Israel. It was a part of worship, celebration, mourning, etc. Debates that have arisen regarding the appropriate music for sacred occasions and the proper role of pagan music in the life of the believer have continued over the centuries.

Just as the early musicians came to understand the religious symbolism of their playing, so the musical symbolism expanded, especially with the **Essenes**. The Dead Sea Scrolls have revealed the popular image in intertestamental writings of **angels** surrounding the heavenly **throne**, singing and playing. This concept of the angelic concert parallels the described but not heard harmony of the spheres that appeared in Greek philosophy. **Apocalyptic** literature echoes the glory of the Temple, now understood as the Heavenly Temple, full of sacred music (Eric Werner 1984, 17). *See also* Angels; Dance; Musical Instruments; Psalms; Song.

Further Reading

Hirsch, Emil G. and Wilhelm Nowack, "Music and Musical Instruments," http://www.jewishencyclopedia.com (accessed October 11, 2004). King, Philip J. and Lawrence E. Stager, *Life in Biblical Israel*. Louisville, Ky.: Westminster John Knox Press, 2001. Seel, Thomas Allen. *A Theology of Music for Worship Derived from the Book of Revelation*. Metuchen, N.J.: The Scarecrow Press, Inc., 1995. Squire, Russel N. *Church Music: Musical and Hymnological Developments in Western Christianity*. Bloomington, Minn.: Bethany Press, 1952. Werner, Eric. *The Sacred Bridge: The Interdependence of Liturgy and Music in Synagogue and Church during the First Millennium*. New York: Ktav Publishing House, Inc., 1984. Wilson-Dickson, Andrew. *The Story of Christian Music: From Gregorian Chant to Black Gospel*. Minneapolis: Fortress Press, 1992.

Musical Instruments

(Ps. 150) Scripture is filled with references to **music** and musical instruments. These include:

The *halil* (1 Kings 1:40; Isa. 5:12), a pipe bored out of wood or bone, the name meaning "to bore." Some believe this to have been a fertility symbol, used at weddings and funerals, with a dionastic and orgaistic quality.

The *hazora* (Num. 10:5; 1 Cor. 14:8), a metal instrument which gave a sharp sound.

The *kinnor* (1 Chron. 15:16; 2 Chron. 5:12), a stringed instrument shaped like a harp with strings made of stretched sheepgut.

The *menanaim*, a percussion instrument made of metal plates, which looked something like a hand mirror, akin the Egyptian sistra.

The *meziltaim*, cymbals made of copper (1 Chron. 15:10).

The *nebel* (Ps. 71:22), a stringed instruments with up to ten strings.

The *qeren* (Ps. 98:6, 150:3), a wind instrument made of animal horn—also called a *shophar* or *shofar*.

The *tof* (Isa. 5:12), a percussion instrument with a membrane, a drum (Ralph Gower 1987, 305–309).

The *ugab*, or pipe, was not considered fit for use in the sanctuary, being related to pipe-playing prostitutes in Asia Minor and Rome. It was high-pitched, with a thin bodied, shill sound. The instruments were usually played in unison.

The bagpipe, which is mentioned in the book of Daniel, was used in Nebuchadnezzar's royal orchestra (Werner 1984, 2, 4).

Among the most famous listings of musical instruments appears in the **Psalms:**

Praise him with the blast of the horn;
praise him with harp and lyre;
praise him with tambourine and dance;
praise him with strings and pipe;
praise him with resounding cymbals;
praise him with clashing cymbals (Ps. 150:3–5)

The most prominent of the ancient instruments were percussion. There were bells made of gold on Aaron's high priestly robes, and there were cymbals made of copper or bronze, which were **metal** discs or cups fixed to the bridles of **horses** (1 Chron. 15:19). **Egyptians** and **Assyrians** also used cymbals. In fact, evidence of these small but effective musical instruments dates back to the end of the third millennium B.C. (Philip J. King and

Lawrence E. Stager 2001, 297). The musicians, who were often women, attached the shallow metal plates to their fingers with thin wires. Sometimes they held two cuplike metal plates so that one was stationary while the other was brought down sharply against it. One author speculates that the clashing of the "loud cymbals" was made by striking them together vertically. The "high-sounding cymbals" were struck horizontally (like hand-clapping), thereby giving off a clear ringing note (E.W. Heaton 1956, 198).

The timbrels and tabrets were a kind of tambourine that was held and struck with the hand, used as an accompaniment to singing and dancing (Exod. 15:20). The sistra was a small instrument that looked something like a hand mirror, with thick wires

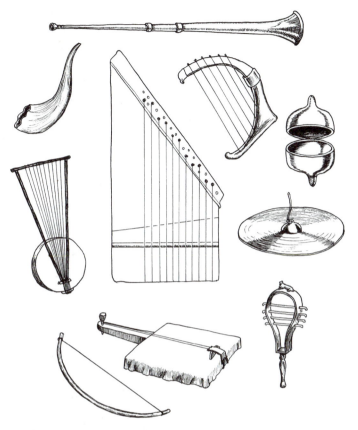

Center, zither; clockwise from top: trumpet, harp, "loud" cymbals, high-sounding cymbal, sistrum, viol and bow, ten-stringed instrument, ram's horn—instruments listed in Psalms and apparently used in worship services.

threaded across the frame through holes on each side. This allowed a kind of rattling sound. In addition, there may have actually been rattles, hollow clay pieces that contained pebbles (Heaton 1956, 199). Drums were usually small and shallow. Women would make them of two skins stretched over a wooden hoop frame. The musicians would beat out the rhythms with their bare hands, probably sounding like a tom-tom.

David was famous for his use of stringed instruments, specifically the lyre. The melodies he played and sang for **King** Saul were said to have had a therapeutic effect, calming the old king. Lyres (Gen. 4:21, 31:27), which were portable, usually had four to eight strings and were struck with a plectrum. Thick lyres, which had 10 to 13 strings and were plucked with the fingers, have not been found in Palestine. Also called "harps," these instruments were smaller and simpler than modern harps. They seem to have been what the **Greeks** and **Romans** called "cithara. "The harp had a wooden sounding box—sometimes cypress wood, later almug—that was

A kinnor, a harp like the one David played (below), contrasted with much more elaborate harps from an Egyptian wall painting.

asymmetrical in design. Lyres were frequently depicted in ancient **art**. The instruments were used by the **prophets** and by worshippers. Specifically mentioned in the poignant psalm of lament, "By the waters of Babylon we sat down and wept," the lyres were silent in this alien land. The Jews hung up their lyres, having nothing to sing about in exile (Ps. 137:2).

The favorite wind instruments were the flute, horn, trumpet, and ram's horn. The flute, also referred to as a "double-pipe," is often pictured in Greek art as the pagan god Pan's favorite instrument, a standard image of the **shepherd** figure. The wailing tone of the flute made it a good instrument for dirges or sad music (Jer. 48:36; Matt. 9:23).

The trumpet, on the other hand, or the horn, which might be made of beaten silver or bronze, had a limited range of notes (Num. 10:2–10). The term for *horn* occurs frequently in the Old Testament and may have been used both as a flask for carrying oil and as a kind of musical instrument. The earliest ones were made out of the horns of **animals**.

The shofar, which was often longer and shaped differently, was a ram's horn, turned up at one end. This is considered the national trumpet of the Israelites and is thought to be the only surviving instrument from ancient times (Russel Squire 1962, 22). It was blown at sacred occasions, for daily offerings of sacrifice, and at coronations or other festival occasions. It summoned the congregations, announced the breaking of camp, and signaled alarms in time of war. The **priests** used it exclusively on religious occasions, but it was also used for announcing majestic actions of the king (2 Kings 11:14). On the **Temple** Mount, one of the great discoveries was a stone indicating the place for the sounding of the trumpet. Some believe that this was the spot of Jesus's temptation by Satan. It was the ram's horn that was probably used in Joshua's capture of Jericho, with seven priests bearing seven rams' horns (Josh 6:4). Trumpets of beaten silver, which Moses was commanded by God to make, were used principally as sacred instruments (Num. 10:1–10). As Heaton notes, the ram's horn was not what we would now call a musical instrument: "It was used rather as we fire guns or ring church bells, not to play tunes but to give signals (like a hunting horn), and to announce national events, such as the outbreak of war, the coronation of a king, and the greater religious festivals. What it lacked in tone, it made up in volume" (Heaton 1956, 200). *See also* Dance; Music; Song.

Further Reading

Gower, Ralph. *The New Manners and Customs of Bible Times.* Chicago: Moody Press, 1987. Heaton, E. W. *Everyday Life in Old Testament Times.* New York: Charles Scribner's Sons, 1956. King, Philip J. and Lawrence E. Stager. *Life in Biblical Israel.* Louisville, Ky.: Westminster John Knox Press, 2001. Seel, Thomas Allen. *A Theology of Music for Worship Derived from the Book of Revelation.* Metuchen, N.J.: The Scarecrow Press, Inc., 1995. Squire, Russel N. *Church Music: Musical and Hymnological Developments in Western Christianity.* Bloomington, Minn.: Bethany Press, 1952.

N

Names for God

(Exod. 3:14, 20:7, 34:6, 7; Mark 14:36; Matt. 28:19; Rom. 8:15; Gal. 4:6) "The Name of the Lord is His Character and Conduct which constitutes the Eternal Glory of His Majestic Being" (Exod. 34:6, 7). The abuse of God's name was considered so serious that one of the commandments prohibits "taking the name of the Lord in vain" (Exod. 20:7). Blasphemy was punishable by death.

In the Old Testament, the three primary names of God are *Elohim, Jehovah,* or *Yahweh,* each of which emphasizes a different aspect of the nature of God. Genesis 1, which opens with, "In the beginning, God" uses the term *Elohim* 31 times. Here, we see him primarily as a creator and **judge.** This word is a plural of "majesty" and is used as a singular form when referring to God. The shortened form, *El,* appears frequently in names, especially names of holy places, such as *Beth-el,* meaning "the house of God" (J. A. Emerton, 1993, 548). It is the most commonly used appellative name for God in Scripture.

When Moses asked the name of the god of "Abraham, Isaac, and Jacob," God "said unto Moses, I AM THAT I AM: and he said, Thus shalt thou say unto the children of Israel, I AM hath sent me unto you" (Exod. 3:14). Scholars over the years have wrestled with this theophany (God's revelation to Moses) and tend to believe that it reveals "God as the Being who is absolutely self-existent, and who, in Himself, possesses essential life and permanent existence. To the Hebrew, *to be* does not just mean to exist, but to be active, to express oneself in active being" (*King James Study Bible,* 105). This is the *Yahweh* of the mighty acts, usually expressed in a tetragrammaton (four letters) YHWH to avoid using God's name in vain. It appears 6,823 times in the Old Testament (J. F. McLaughlin and Judah David Eisenstein 2004).

Adonai or Adoni, which means "master" or "lord," reveals God as the final authority in life. This is used in Isaiah, who ties it to God's redemptive work. It appears frequently in prophetic literature, but not in the Pentateuch, Joshua, or Judges.

Because **Baal** also means "lord," it may have been substituted instead of the traditional terms, as in 1 Chron. 12:6, where the name *Beealiah* means "Yah is Baal" (J. A. Emerton 1993, 549). *Adonai* also appears in the New Testament, and Jesus himself is often called "Lord" by his followers.

Another New Testament term common among the more loving of the prophets is *abba,* or "father." Jesus naturally uses this form frequently, emphasizing his relationship to his heavenly father, as he does in the famous lines of the **Lord's Prayer** (Mark 14:36; Rom. 8:15; Gal. 4:6). The more common formulation in the New Testament is Trinitarian: "in the name of the Father, and of the Son, and of the Holy Ghost" (Matt. 28:19).

The form that God's name takes in Hebrew scripture is often a compound: *El-olam* means "God-who-is-trustworthy" (Gen. 21:23); *El-roi* means "God sees me" (Gen. 16:13; *El-shaddai* means God who works the impossible (Gen. 17:1); *YHWH-sabaoth* means Lord of Hosts or "God who fights for me" (1 Sam. 17:45); *YHWH-shalom* means "Lord of Peace" (Judg. 6:24).

God was often described by his nature or activity: "the Holy One of Israel" is typical of Isaiah; "**king**" appears frequently in the Psalms (29:10, 47:2, 48:2, 5:2, etc.). He sometimes is referred to as a "shield" (Ps. 84:11), or as "fear" (Gen. 31:42, 53), or "the Mighty One" (Gen. 49:24). *See also* Baal, Baalim; Blasphemy; Creation; Law; Messiah.

Further Reading

Emerton, J. A. "Names of God in the Hebrew Bible," in *The Oxford Companion to the Bible*. New York: Oxford University Press, 1993. McLaughlin, J. F. and Judah David Eisenstein, "Names of God," http://www.jewishencyclopedia.com (accessed June 11, 2004).

Names: Hebrews'

Hebrew is the most ancient of all names given to the family of Abraham. Some scholars believe it derived from his ancestor Eber, whose name came to be used to designate a people. Others believe that it involved being "beyond" or "across" and designated the people who once dwelt in the land beyond the river Euphrates. Still others believe it meant those who dwelt "eastward" from the Jordan. Shem, whose name came to refer to the Semites, was called the "father of all the children of Eber," designating the Semitic peoples beyond the Jordan. It was in **Egypt** that the people, a distinctive group, were first referred to as *Hibiru* or *Hebrew,* suggesting that the term was once used by other nationalities in designating the tribe of Abraham. When used by adversaries or outsiders, the term often conveyed contempt, as in the **Philistines'** derision of the Hebrews as unworthy fighters who cowered in **caves** (1 Sam. 14:11).

By the time of the **Exodus,** they were also called *Israelites,* a term referring to their common ancestor, Israel or Jacob. Later, the term took on a more precise meaning: In the divided kingdom, after the death of Solomon, the Israelites were the people of the northern kingdom. The southern kingdom was known as *Judah.* It was Judah that survived the longest, and where Jerusalem was situated.

The citizens of Judah were known as *Jews,* a term that was gradually applied to all of the Hebrews who survived the Exile. After the period of division and chaos, first the northern kingdom and then the southern were taken captive, by **Assyria** first and then Babylonia and Persia. In the days of Cyrus the Persian, the clear distinctions between Jew and Israelite, as all the distinctions of the tribal loyalties, were lost on outsiders. The Persians called this group of people "Jews," "Hebrews," or "Israelites" without distinguishing subtle meanings.

In their diaspora (or scattering of the exiles), the Jews intermarried with other peoples and sometimes abandoned, but sometimes treasured, their faith and culture. They were forced by circumstances to learn other languages and to mingle with other peoples. A remnant returned to Jerusalem to rebuild their beloved **Temple,** living under one monarch after another, never again to be a free and distinctive people.

In the New Testament, the term *Hebrew* designates Jews, including Jewish **Christians** who continued to retain their ties to their Jewish heritage and their Aramaic or Hebrew language, as opposed to the *Hellenists,* who favored the Greeks (Acts 6:1). Paul was proud of his being a "Hebrew born of Hebrews" (Acts 22:2–3; Phil. 3:5; 2 Cor. 11:22). It was probably for this reason that the Christian writer who penned the letter to the "Hebrews" chose that term for his audience. Curiously, the **epistle** was written in Greek, the language of the famous Septuagint, the Greek translation of the Hebrew sacred writings. By the Christian era, Greek was the universal language, to be followed by Latin. *See also* Christian; History in the Bible; Israel.

Further Reading

Kline, M.G. "Hebrews," in *The Illustrated Bible Dictionary.* Sydney, Australia: Tyndale House Publishers, 1980. Knight, Douglas A. "Hebrews," in *The Oxford Companion to the Bible.* New York: Oxford University Press, 1993.

Names: Personal

(Gen. 2:19–20) Proverbs speaks of the value of a good name: "A good name is rather to be chosen than great riches" (Prov. 22:1). "Among primitive peoples, and throughout the ancient East, the name denotes the essence of a thing: to name it is to know it, and, consequently to have power over it" (Roland deVaux 1961, 43). This belief may be traced back to the **Garden of Eden,** when Adam was given authority over the **animals** and the task of naming them, a signal that they were in his power (Gen. 2:19–20).

In most of the Old Testament records, immediately after birth, the child was given his name, either by his mother or his father. (In some cases, an **angel** instructed the parents regarding the name of the child, Luke 1:13.) In New Testament times, the naming was delayed eight days until after the circumcision. The name denotes the character of the person, the circumstances of birth, the destiny, or the mood of the parents. Often in Scripture, immediately after the name is given, it is explained, especially when it is tied to events. A powerful example is the naming of Ichabod, or "Where is the glory?" after the **Ark of the Covenant** was captured by the **Philistines.** Eli's daughter-in-law, who gave birth to the child said, in explaining this strange name: "The glory is departed from Israel: the ark of God is taken" (1 Sam. 4:21–22).

Names might also be derived from the order of birth, as in the cases of Esau and Jacob, whose names probably mean "posthumous." Esau's name meant both "red" and "hairy mantle," a play on "Seir," where he settled. Jacob's name came from the Hebrew word for "heel," referring to his clasping of Esau's heel when he was born (*Harper-Collins Study Bible* 1989, 38–39). *Jephthah* implies "first-born," as does *Becher*; names such as *Manasseh, Nahum,* and *Nehemiah* probably refer to children who have come to take the place of others who have died in childhood" (Joseph Jacobs 2005). Personal peculiarities or physical appearance may give rise to a name, as *Laban* ("white," or "blond"); *Gideon* means "maimed;" *Harim* means "with pierced nose."

Mental qualities may determine a name, as in *Job* ("assailant") and *Barak* ("lightning"). Trade names, like *Smith, Carpenter,* or *Miller,* which are common in England and Germany, do not appear in Hebrew, largely because trades were not so specialized in ancient Israel.

Names taken from objects are found most frequently among females. The name *Rebekah* seems to be derived from a sheep-rope, *Peninnah* from coral, and *Keren-happuch* from a box of face-paint. Abstract names seem to be applied especially to women, as *Manoah* ("rest") and *Michal* ("power") (Jacobs 2005). Jewish names for baby girls often came from beautiful things in nature or qualities of character, for example, *Jemima* ("dove"), *Tabitha* or *Dorcas* ("gazelle"), *Rhoda* ("rose"), *Rachel* ("lamb"), *Salome* ("peace"), *Deborah* ("bee"), and *Esther* ("star"). One example of a woman's change of name is in the book of Ruth, when Naomi changes her own name to *Marah*. "Call me not, Pleasant, call me Bitter," she tells the women of Bethlehem (Ruth 1:20; Wight 1953, 111).

Although names may have been derived from the child's appearance or from animals or plants, much more common are "theophoric" names, which contain some divine name or title. Names such as *Baal* or *Yahweh* were common in shortened forms: "El" or "eh" were regularly a portion of the name. Such names were often used to express a religious idea, such as God's mercy or love, as for example, *Abijah*—"Whose father God is," *Ahiziah*—"Held by Jehovah," *Daniel*—"God is my Judge," or *Ezekiel*— "God will strengthen."

In fact, a distinctive characteristic of Bible naming practices is the frequent use of composite names. At times, they even form complete sentences: Isaiah's son Shear-jashub's name means "the remnant shall return." *Hephzibah* means "my pleasure is in her." Sometimes these composites begin with a preposition as their first element. *Bishlam* means "with peace" (Ezra 4: 7), and *Lemuel* means "belonging to God" Prov. 31: 4" (Jacobs 2005).

Toward the end of Old Testament times, a more common pattern was the use of a "patronymic"—the child was called after his grandfather, father, or uncle—as in our use of *son* (e.g., Patter*son* or Steven*son*) Considering the Jewish concern for the continuation of the family, this was a natural development. It was a common pattern in the Christian era (Luke 1:59)—with the given name first and the father's name indicated by *bar* or *ben*—as in *Jesus bar-Joseph* and *Peter bar-Jona. Ben* was also used, as in *Jaazaniah ben Shaphan* (Ezek. 8:11).

After the Exile, many of the Jews had foreign names—usually **Greek** or **Roman:** *John Mark,* for example. Some also had double names—as with *Thomas,* "which is called *Didymus*" (John 11:16). The first of these was Aramaic and the second Greek (Fred H. Wight 1953, 110).

When a change came into his life or he grew to manhood, a man might change his name, often with divine inspiration: Abram became *Abraham,* Jacob became *Israel,* Saul became *Paul* (Gen. 17:5, 32:29, 35:10). Jesus changed the name of Simon to *Peter* and called the colorful brothers "Sons of Thunder." Those in captivity might have their names changed for them: the pharaoh called Joseph *Saphenath-Paneah* (Gen. 41:45); the chief eunuch called Daniel, Ananias, Misael, and Azarias, *Baltassar, Shadrak, Meshak, and Abed Nego* (Dan. 1:6–7).

There are more than 2,800 names in Scripture. The full story of their meaning is a continuing study for scholars. Each of them has potential clues to the culture, history, life experience, parentage, or personality of the individual. *See also* History in the Bible.

Further Reading

DeVaux, Roland. *Ancient Israel: Its Life and Institutions.* Grand Rapids, Mich.: William B. Eerdmans Publishing Company, 1961. Jacobs, Joseph. "Names (Personal)" http://www.jewishencyclopedia.com (accessed January 14, 2005). Meeks, Wayne A., ed. *HarperCollins Study Bible.* New York: HarperCollins Publishers, Inc., 1989. Wight. Fred H. *Manners and Customs of Bible Lands.* Chicago: Moody Press, 1953 .

Nazarites

(**Num. 6:1–21**) *Nazarites* (the King James Version spelling, or "nazirites" elsewhere) were men or women who were set apart by vows to live an ascetic life, abstaining from **wine** or other grape products, refusing to cut their hair "lest a man-made tool profane this God-given growth," avoiding any contact with the dead, and refusing unclean foods (Madeleine S. Miller and J. Lane Miller 1961, 480). The rules for Nazarite life are found in Numbers 6:1–21, although it is believed that the custom of the ascetic life predated the Mosaic **law.** "Semites and other primitive peoples often left the hair uncut during some undertaking calling for divine help, and thereafter consecrated the hair" (J. D. Douglas 1980, 1063). Some Arab groups have continued this practice into modern times. The Nazarites' rules of behavior exceeded those of ordinary **priests** in their strictness, resembling more the high priest.

At the end of the period of the vow, the Nazarite was expected to offer burnt, cereal, peace, and sin offerings, as Aaron did at the time of his ordination. The Nazarite would also cut his hair at this time and offer it to the Lord. This hair was thought to parallel the high priest's diadem and was also spoken of as *nezer,* outward symbols of holiness (*The King James Study Bible,* footnote, 238). After the wave offering by the priest, the Nazarite was allowed to drink wine (Num. 6:20) and presumably return to his or her normal life.

The basic idea was that individuals who wished to consecrate themselves or their children "unto the Lord" undertook this regimen for a specific period of time—sometimes 30 days, sometimes for life. Samson, Samuel, and John the Baptist were probably lifelong Nazarites, dedicated by their mothers before their births. Some believe that the **Apostle** Paul was also a Nazarite.

In actuality, Samson broke his vows: he attended drinking parties and touched dead bodies. When Delilah cut his hair, his succumbing to her temptation and allowing her action broke his vow and removed the source of his strength—his close relationship with the Lord. Only as he regrew his hair did he regain that strength. Samuel seems to have chosen the priestly life instead of the Nazarite one in spite of his mother's solemn oath on his behalf. Joseph is also thought to have been a Nazarite (Gen. 49:26; Deut. 33:16), but this may be simply a metaphorical use of the term, meaning that he was separated from his brothers (Dennis T. Olson 1993, 552). The King James Version of the Bible does not use the term in connection with Joseph, only "separated" as a physical statement. The idea that David's son Absalom was a Nazarite is based primarily on his long hair, which eventually brought his death. His behavior hardly seems ascetic.

In John the Baptist's case, his father, Zechariah, seems to have made a vow for him when he was visited by the **angel,** who proclaimed: "For he shall be great in the sight of the Lord, and shall drink neither wine nor strong drink, and he shall be filled with the **Holy Ghost,** even from his mother's womb" (Luke 1:15). On the other hand, this may not indicate that John was a Nazarite, and there is no mention in Scripture of his having uncut hair, but he did live a saintly life, dedicated to the Lord.

Paul appears to have taken a limited vow, perhaps in gratitude for some **blessing.** He noted (Acts 18:18) that he shaved his head while he was in Corinth with Priscilla and Aquila, apparently as a sign that the duration of the vow was complete. He also demonstrated his respect for Nazarite vows by offering to finance the expenses connected with the **Temple** sacrifices of the four poor men who had completed their vows (Acts 21:20–30). In an effort to placate the Jews, who thought him a violator of the law, Paul even joined in the observations to show that he respected and observed the law himself, although he did not require such behavior of new **Christians.** The law was clear on strict rules for those who broke their vows by touching a dead relative or any other dead person: they were to shave their heads, bring two turtledoves or pigeons to the priest for sacrifice—one for a sin offering, the other for a burnt offering—and make atonement for their sins, making the offering of a lamb for the trespass (Num. 6:9–12).

Originally, this practice may have been a signal of the Hebrews' clear rejection of **Canaanite** practices. The hair was regarded as the seat of life among many primitive people and the abode of spirits and magical influences. The burning ensured that it was completely destroyed rather than used for pagan rituals. Later the vow seems to have been a promise to God in return for a blessing such as the **birth** of a son. In Paul's case, it would appear to have served as a symbol of gratitude for a special blessing, perhaps a miraculous escape from catastrophe.

The Nazarite dedication was symbolic of the holy calling of Israel (Jer. 7:29). The Nazarites did not live in communities, but were solitary lay-saints, proclaiming their love of God. They were men and women who dedicated both body and soul to holy service as individuals. Josephus's mention of them suggest that Nazarites were "a common feature of the contemporary scene" (Douglas 1980, 1064). *See also* Blessing; Curse; Oaths; Priest, High Priest.

Further Reading

Douglas, J. D. "Nazirite," in *The Illustrated Bible Dictionary.* Sydney, Australia: Tyndale House Publishers, 1980. Miller, Madeleine S. and J. Lane Miller. "Nazirites," in *Harper's Bible Dictionary.* New York: Harper and Row, 1961. Olson, Denis T. "Nazirite," in *The Oxford Companion to the Bible.* New York: Oxford University Press, 1993.

New Moon, Festival of the

(Num.10:10–15, 28) The Festival of the New Moon was a day of penitence for the sins of the previous month, marked by the appearance of the new moon. Some scholars believe that the festival's relevance to sin was tied to the jealousy that the moon was thought to have felt for the sun's superiority in size and splendor (Emil G. Hirsch 2005).

In Judeo-Christian thought, every day is a special day, a day the Lord has given. In Numbers 28, God commanded the children of Israel to show their gratitude to him with offerings, "in their due season." The due season began with daily offerings, morning and night, offerings by fire, one lamb in the morning, the other in the evening. This was then amplified to weekly celebrations of the **Sabbath.** The third set of offerings and celebrations were to mark the months—the Festival of the New Moon.

These "times of rejoicing" (Num. 10:10) were to be marked by the sound of the trumpets (probably a ram's horn) "over your burnt offerings and fellowship offerings, and they will be a memorial for you before your God." Two young bullocks, a ram, seven lambs "of the first year without a spot" (Num. 28:11) were to form the burnt offering; flour was to be mixed with oil for the grain offering, and wine served as the drink offering, and finally a **goat** as a "sin offering." This became an increasingly formal celebration, with the president of the **Sanhedrin** proclaiming, "The New Moon is consecrated," followed by a response from the whole Sanhedrin and the blowing of the shofar (Kauffmann Kohler 2005).

Historians note that the new moon celebrations would have been a useful way to mark the seasons for **shepherds** who moved their flocks to different pastures or to different climates as the seasons changed. For the Israelites, this probably evolved into harvest festivals as they moved to a more settled, agrarian culture. The scene in the book of Ruth—where Boaz and the other workers have spent their day harvesting the grain, ending with **food** and drink, finally lying on the ground to sleep, covered by their cloaks—suggests one form this celebration took. The **wine** harvest was also a significant time, with the community joining in the picking, stomping, and drinking the grape juice.

The gift of life—**bread** and drink—were solid reasons for gathering the community to praise God, the Creator and Sustainer of life. David, a shepherd and a man of faith, regularly noted the New Moon Festival, as did his friend Jonathan (1 Sam. 20:5, 18; 20:24). A lovely line in Psalm 81:3 proclaims, "Sound the ram's horn at the New Moon, and when the moon is full, on the day of our **Feast**" (New International Version translation; King James Version calls this a "trumpet").

Isaiah, however, notes that his soul "hates" the festivals and the New Moon festivals, which have become a "burden" to him and to his God (Isa. 1:14, 66:23). The Lord declares that he is "full of the burnt offerings of rams" and delights not "in the **blood** of bullocks, or of lambs, of he goats" because these are "vain oblations"—"the new moons and sabbaths" have become iniquity (Isa. 1:11–14). Rather than these vain offerings, God requires that they "cease to do evil." Hosea and Amos also complain about the evil ways of the people regardless of their display of piety. Hosea notes that they have illegitimate children (Hos. 5:7), and Amos laments that they cheat with inflated prices and dishonest scales for their wheat (Amos 8:5).

The festival lost some of its importance during the Exile, although women continued to celebrate it, altering it so as to make it a tribute to the "queen of **heaven**." They developed a theory, not supported by Scripture, that women were especially blessed because they (unlike the Hebrew men) refused to worship the Golden Calf (Kaufmann Kohler 2005).

During this time of Exile, needing a reminder of their old culture and their traditional faith, the remnant were encouraged to return once again to the time-honored festivals, including the New Moon Festival. Ezekiel rekindled enthusiasm for the feasts: "Thus saith the Lord God; The gate of the inner court that looketh toward the east shall be shut the six working days; but on the sabbath it shall be opened, and in the day of the new moon it shall be opened" (Ezek. 46:1). This prophecy is followed by the usual listing of burnt offerings required for solemn feasts. Ezra and Nehemiah both note that these festivals were regularly celebrated by the Israelites (Ezra 3:5; Neh. 10:33).

The celebration of New Moon festivals continued into New Testament times. Paul mentions them in his **epistle** to the Collosians (2:16), indicating that people should not judge us by what we eat or drink or "with regard to a religious festival, a New Moon celebration or a Sabbath day."

This ancient festival probably evolved into the **Day of Atonement** or Yom Kippur, the Jewish New Year celebration as **agriculture** diminished as a part of life, and the year began in the fall, not in the spring. *See also* Festivals; Sabbath; Sacrifice.

Further Reading

Hirsch, Emil G. "Festivals," http://www.jewishencyclopedia.com (accessed January 17, 2005). Kohler, Kaufmann. "New Moon," http://www. jewishencyclopedia.com (accessed January 17, 2005).

Oaths

(Exod. 22:6–12; Matt. 5:34–36) An oath is a promise to fulfill an obligation, usually attested to by some sacred object of deity. "I solemnly swear" is the beginning of our modern oaths, followed by promises to tell the truth, the whole truth, and nothing but the truth, or to uphold the Constitution and to fulfill the office to which the swearer is elected.

The usual form for the ceremony involves placing the right hand on the Bible and repeating the words slowly after the **judge** who administers them. This pattern derives from the Old Testament ritual of oaths, which were used in civil cases involving private property, where no other evidence was available (Exod. 22:6–10, Julius Rappoport 2005). The Code of the **Covenant** lists a number of cases where this procedure would apply: an object disappears and the thief cannot be identified, or a dispute has arisen over lost objects, stolen or wounded **animals.** The "judicial oath by the gods or the **king**" was practiced in **Babylonia, Assyria,** and in the Jewish colony of Elephantine, especially in issues of property rights. In cases where the accused man refused to take the oath, he was presumed guilty. He might be fearful that, if he perjured himself, "he would be stricken by the **curse** accompanying the oath" (Roland deVaux 1961, 157).

Oaths were also used in more general attestations of the truth of certain assertions or promises, and as a confirmation of one's intention to keep to the grounds of the agreement, as in the case of Abraham's covenant with God (Gen. 24:8) and with Moses (Deut. 29:12). Examples of solemn oaths are frequent in Scripture, often involving an affirming gesture, swearing by God, calling him to witness the agreement, placing a hand on the thigh of the individual, or appealing to some sacred object (Matt. 5:34–36; Madeleine S. Miller and J. Lane Miller 1961, 499). To confirm the seriousness of the words, the person might touch a sacred object, often the **Urim and Thummim** of the **priest.** Some considered such an oath a "**Trial** by Ordeal," based on the theory that God was the ultimate judge in such cases.

The formulas of the oath and the curse were similar: the person taking the oath would specify the consequences of lying (e.g., Is. 65:15; Jer. 29:22), saying: "God do thus to me and more also if " (1 Sam. 3:17). This was considered more effective if God was called as a witness (Ze'ev W. Falk 2001, 51–52).

In some cases, the court might have doubts about the truthfulness of the person, and would not accept an oath as adequate evidence of his innocence. Because God was the witness for him, he was obligated to cleanse himself by a sin offering if he had lied.

The **Essenes** avoided all forms of swearing, which they considered worse than perjury, noting: "he that can not be believed without an oath is already condemned" (Josephus B.J., ii, 8, 6, quoted by Julius Rappoport 2005). Jesus also insisted that his followers avoid oaths, "Again, ye have heard that it hath been said by them of old time, Thou shalt not forswear thyself, but shall perform unto the Lord thine oaths: But I say unto you, Swear not at all; neither by **heaven;** for it is God's **throne:** Nor by the earth; for it is his footstool: neither by Jerusalem; for it is the city of the great King. Neither shalt thou swear by thy head, because thou canst not make one hair white or black. But let your communication be, Yea, yea; Nay, nay: for whatsoever is more than these cometh of evil" (Matt. 5:33–37). *See also* Covenant; Law; Trials, Courts.

Further Reading

DeVaux, Roland. *Ancient Israel: Its Life and Institutions.* Grand Rapids, Mich.: William B. Eerdmans Publishing Company, 1961. Falk, Ze'ev W. *Hebrew Law in Biblical Times.* Provo, Utah: Brigham Young University Press, 2001. Miller, Madeleine S. and J. Lane Miller. "Oaths," in *Harper's Bible Dictionary.* New York: Harper and Row, 1961. Rappoport, Julius. "Oath," http://jewishencyclopedia.com (accessed January 17, 2005).

Offerings. *See Sacrifice*

Ointment. *See Perfume*

Olives, Olive Oil, Olive Trees

(Deut. 6:11; Judg. 9:9; Rom.11:17, 11:24) The berry-like fruit of the olive tree was one of the most useful and beloved of all agricultural products in ancient Israel. In the fable of the trees (Judg. 9:9), the other trees ask the olive tree to be their **king,** but the olive declines: "should I give up my oil, by which both gods and men are honored, to hold sway over the trees?" (Olive oil was used to anoint men, including **priests** and kings, and in the worship of God.)

Olive Trees

From early times, olive trees, which are thought to be native to Syria, grew abundantly in the rocky, hilly soil of **Israel.** Every family liked to have at least one of these productive trees in their **gardens.** Its blue-green leaves, with silver undersides, and dark, gnarled, twisted trunk make the trees picturesque and wonderful for shade. Olive groves lined the Phoenician Plain, causing the Promised Land to be proclaimed "a land of olive trees and honey"(2 Kings 18:32). Moses commanded the Israelites to be grateful to God for leading them to Palestine, "a land of **vineyards** and olive groves you did not plant" (Deut. 6:11). In later years, during the monarchy, the olive oil became the chief source of wealth in this "fat country" (Madeleine S. Miller and J. Lane Miller 1961, 504).

Planting and tending olive trees were not difficult tasks. The cultivated olive was grafted into the strong wild olive roots to produce a tree that would last for hundreds of years, the trunk twisting as it developed. Groves were often planted on terraced hillsides. The Garden of Gethsemane was such an olive orchard, and it still has trees from the stock of those among which Jesus prayed in the Mount of Olives (*Gethsemane* means "**olive press.**" *See* John 18:1). Trees required pruning, but little other care.

When the olive tree dies, the roots produce new shoots all around the site of the old tree, as the Psalmist notes, when describing a man's sons to be "like olive shoots around your table" (Ps. 128:3). The olive thus becomes the image of the blessed and healthy **family,** flourishing from generation to generation.

The fruit of the tree could be picked either green or ripe. Trees yielded some fruit within three of four years after the planting. In the fall, when the olives were ripe, the custom was to cover the ground with cloths and hit the limbs with sticks to make the olives fall (Isa. 24:13). (This damaged the branches, making the tree less likely to bear fruit more than once every two years.) As in the case of the other crops, the olive groves were to have a sabbatical. The **law** also allowed the "poor among your people" to get food from it, and the wild animals to eat what they wanted (Exod. 23:11). Some of the olives were left for the gleaners, even when the trees were beaten: "two or three olives on the topmost branches, four or five on the fruitful boughs" (Isa. 17:6).

The olive tree's natural enemies included the locust, blight, and mildew (Amos 4:9). As with other products, the human predator was often the most dangerous. When the olives were harvested and processed, marauders would swoop down to steal the jars of oil.

Olive Oil

The ripe olives were gathered in baskets and taken to the olive press, where they were ground in a handmill or crushed under a **stone** in a mortar (Num. 11:7). The oil was extracted in stages, with the "virgin" oil being the first and best. That which was pressed from the olives was considered the least desirable. This was stored in earthen jars, dispensed in smaller cruets, and used daily in the kitchens.

The first fruits of the harvest were owed to the Lord, to be apportioned like other sacrifices (Num. 18:12). Olive oil had many uses, in addition to its sacrificial role. It was used for light, for anointing, and for fragrant incense when mixed with other ingredients (Exod. 35:8). The 10 virgins of Jesus's **parable** (Matt. 25:1) probably used olive oil to light their **lamps**.

Olives and olive oil were staples at most meals. Olives were a handy snack, easy to carry in a bag into the field; olive oil was used by ancient peoples the way butter and animal fat are used for moderns. Olive oil was used to fry **foods**, to season them, and to give them moisture. A dish of oil was set in the mist of the meal, handy for dipping bread. The most popular use for oil was in the baking of **bread**, making the barley or wheat less tough.

As a balm for wounds, it helped to heal (as in the parable of the Good Samaritan) and was used in surgery. It served as a skin cream, as a regular lubricant after bathing. Mixed with other ingredients, it was essential in several ointments and hair tonics. Some believe that it may have been used for the making of soap even in biblical times, as it still is today.

As the most significant export for Israel, it provided exchange for spices and luxuries from other countries. Hosea notes that Ephraim "makes a treaty with **Assyria** and sends olive oil to **Egypt**" (Hos. 12:1). First Kings has a long list of kings and rulers who provided olive oil to surrounding peoples; Solomon considered it a great source of wealth (1 Kings 5:11; 2 Chron. 2:10). It was also used as a medium of exchange in negotiating agreements (1 Chron. 2:10). In Revelation, John listed the cargoes of the "merchants of the earth" who will weep when no man will buy their merchandise: "cargoes of cinnamon and spice, of incense, myrrh and frankincense, of **wine** and olive oil, of fine flour and wheat; cattle and **sheep**; **horses** and carriages; and bodies and souls of men" (Rev. 18:13).

Olive Wood

The roots of the olive tree provided fine fuel. And the wood was used for carving various decorative designs, including the **cherubim** at the doors of the **Temple.** Olive wood is a deep amber color; it is very dense and fine-grained, and can be polished to a rich sheen. Solomon had the inner and outer doors of the Temple and the posts of the sanctuary all made of olive wood (1 Kings 6:23, 31, 33). Furthermore, the twigs of the olive tree might be woven into a wreath or **crown** and used to celebrate victories in the Greco-Roman games that Paul witnessed (Madeleine S. Miller and J. Lane Miller 1961, 505). Olive branches also were used in constructing the booths for the Feast of **Tabernacles** (Neh. 8:15).

Symbolism

The symbolism of abundance and joy in the olive carries all through Scripture: The Psalmist speaks of a man "like an olive tree flourishing in the house of God" (Ps. 52:8). Jeremiah warns that although "The Lord called you a thriving olive tree with fruit beautiful in form," he will come "with the roar of a might storm . . .set it on fire, and its branches will be broken" (Jer. 11:16). Isaiah uses the beating of the tree to console people that a remnant will survive, like the gleanings on the topmost branches of the olive trees (Isa. 17:6).

Paul used the grafting process as an image of gentile Christians—wild olive shoots—growing out of the "roots" of Judaism: "you, though a wild olive shoot, have been grafted in among others and now share in the nourishing sap from the olive root." He noted that Jews—the natural branches—could also grow in this faith: "After all, if you were cut out of an olive tree that is wild by nature, and contrary to nature were grafted into a cultivated olive tree, how much more readily will these, the natural branches, be grafted into their own olive tree!" (Rom. 11:17–24).

The most famous olive-branch symbol derives from Noah's dove, which brought back an olive leaf as a signal that the flood had receded (Gen. 8:11). From this came the olive branch as the image of peace. Because of the connection with the dove, with peace, and with anointing, it has also become the symbol of the **Holy Spirit** (1 John 2:27). *See also* Agriculture; Anointing; Food; Lamp; Olive Press; Perfume.

Further Reading
King, Philip J. and Lawrence E. Stager. *Life in Biblical Israel.* Louisville, Ky.: Westminster John Knox Press, 2001. Miller, Madeleine S. and J. Lane Miller. "Olive," in *Harper's Bible Dictionary.* New York: Harper and Row, 1961.

Olive Press

The ripe black olives or the green ones were knocked off the trees by sticks, then gathered in reed or wicker baskets, and carried to the olive mill. This mill was a circular **stone** base eight feet or so in diameter, in which was fitted a millstone, which revolved around a central pivot. The millstone, which was placed on its edge, was fastened to a beam through the central hold and turned by two people who pushed the beam as they walked around the basin. The oil that flowed from this grinding would run down a trough into a large tub. Before such mills were constructed, the farmers probably pulped the olives much the same way they did the ripe grapes, by treading on them with their bare feet.

This first product of the grinding was the virgin olive oil, the most highly prized of the oil products. The pulp was then packed into baskets and taken to the oil presses. The baskets were placed on a stone tablet (the "sea"),

stacked two or three on top of one another. A wooden beam was wedged into a hole in the face of a rock or in a wooden frame (the "maidens") just slightly above the level of the top of the baskets. On one end of the pole were tied heavy stones, pulling the beam against the baskets with an even pressure. The oil would drip down under this pressure and collect in basins at the base that had been hewn out of the rock (E.W. Heaton 1956, 107–108).

It was important that this oil be purified by allowing it to settle in vats, sometimes treated with hot water. It was then stored in large jars and skins for use. Only the best of the purified oil was to be used in **sacrifice.** *See also* Agriculture; Food; Olives, Olive Oil, Olive Trees; Perfume.

Olive mill grinding the ripe olives and producing "virgin" oil, and olive press with bags of smashed olives pressed down by weights that release the oil to the jar at the bottom.

Further Reading

Jacobs, Joseph and Lewis N. Demleitz. "Sale," http://www.jewish-encyclopedia.com (accessed June 1, 2005). Heaton, E. W. *Everyday Life in Old Testament Times*. New York: Charles Scribner's Sons, 1956.

Ox, Oxen

Oxen were first tamed in Neolithic times, somewhat later than **goats** and **sheep.** "Bringing under control such massive and powerful beasts—the bull standing about 6 ft. at the shoulder—would be hard enough today, with all modern aids, yet these men did it before the age of **metals.**...We must assume that it happened after man had worked out a more or less settled form of **agriculture,** for these huge cattle would need to be both enclosed and fed" (George Cansdale 1970, 57). They need regular water and good pasture. In fact, it was probably because of the great number of cattle owned by both Abram and Lot that they were obliged to divide up the countryside near the southern end of the Dead Sea.

In the beginning, it was probably their meat that led men to bring oxen under control. Later, the milk from the cows proved a further benefit. This was placed in goatskin receptacles where it quickly curdled. When shaken, it soon became butter or curds (Prov. 30:33; Deut. 32:14). The dung of cattle was also useful, both as fertilizer and as fuel. Droppings from cud-chewing animals is full of fiber. When dried, it burns easily, with good heat, making it useful in baking.

The great strength of the oxen led owners to use them for draft purposes, first with sleds and later, with the invention of the wheel, pulling wagons. A clay model of a wagon, found in Mesopotamia, is dated ca. 2500 B.C. Cansdale notes that the spoked wheel was invented about the time of Hammurabi (ca. 1750 B.C.) The first biblical mention of a cart, probably drawn by horses or oxen, is in Genesis 45:19, when the Pharaoh "sent wagons to fetch the aged Jacob" (George Cansdale 1970, 57–59). Generally, a pair of oxen would be used to draw carts, as in the transport of the **Ark of the Covenant** (1 Sam. 6; 2 Sam. 5).

In Scripture, the terms for oxen may be *cattle, bullock*, or *calf*. There are three principal types of ox: the longifrons (long-headed), the primigenius (the main type of Aurochs or wild ox), and the Zebu (with the typical hump on the neck). Cattle were already part of Abram's caravan when he left his home country. At this time, there were still wild oxen around the countryside, and apparently they were considered dangerous.

Ancient peoples admired the enormous strength of these animals. The people of Ephraim, the "thousands of Manesseh" who are described in Deuteronomy 33, are said to be majestic "like a firstborn bull; his horns are the horns of a wild ox. With them he will gore the nations, even those at the ends of the earth." (An ox could fatally gore a man or animal.) Isaiah prophesies the disaster of having the wild oxen fall on the people, "the bull calves and the great bulls. Their land will be drenched with **blood,** and the dust will be soaked with fat" (Isa. 34:7).

Yet Isaiah also notes that the oxen can be docile. Once domesticated, and usually castrated, the ox was a hard worker, apparently willing to labor for hours carrying heavy burdens. He was patient beyond measure. Isaiah notes that the ox knows his master (Isa. 1:3), and his dumb obedience became proverbial, as Solomon tells us that a young man following a wicked woman is "like an ox going to slaughter" (Prov. 7:22).

Although they preferred working with **donkeys,** the Israelites found there were some loads these small beasts could not haul and some rocky land they could not plow. When they saw the usage among the **Egyptians** the Hebrews may have begun to employ oxen, using **yokes** to harness their oxen together for maximum power. From the Egyptians they may have also discovered the value of the **goad** to keep the animals moving. The **law** of

Oxen yoked together. The strongest animals farmers had for pulling heavy loads, and also used as sacrificial animals in large numbers.

Moses clearly indicates that the agricultural uses of the oxen and the concerns for their care were well understood. Their value was obvious, to the point that coveting ones neighbor's ox was explicitly forbidden by the Ten Commandments. The unequal strength of the great ox and the small donkey is also noted in the commandment to avoid yoking an ox with an ass (Deut. 22:10). Because the ox was a clean animal, chewing the cud and being endowed with hoofs and horns, it had some of the same uses as sheep and goats: hides, milk, and flesh.

Because oxen were dangerous, the damage one might do to a neighbor or a neighbor's property was covered by the **law**, demanding blood money for a "goring ox" (Exod. 21:28–32). On the other hand, because they were valuable, the theft of oxen or cruelty in dealing with them also deserved punishment. People should not dig pits that an ox or a donkey might fall into (Exod. 21:33), nor should they steal and sell them, or slaughter another person's animal (Exod. 21:1). One of the first biblical references to oxen is in regard to evil men who have murdered other men and hamstrung their oxen (Gen. 49:6), rendering them lame and useless.

Like the other animals, they were included in the **Sabbath** rest (Exod. 23:12). One interesting consideration is the law against muzzling an ox when he is treading out the **grain** (Deut. 25:4). Oxen usually were used in the heavy labor of threshing the grain, and an occasional nibble of the grain at their feet was considered proper reward. Jesus mentioned the ox in his reference to necessary labor on the Sabbath: "Doesn't each of you on the Sabbath untie his ox or donkey from the stall and lead it out to give it water?" (Luke 13:15) and "If one of you has a son or an ox that falls into a well on the Sabbath day, will you not immediately pull him out?" (Luke 14:5).

They also had religious significance, probably because they were the most valuable of the sacrificial animals. Leviticus (4:10, 9:4, 9:18) is specific about the ritual for the sacrifice of the ox as a peace offering: First the animal (without flaw, according to Deut. 17:1) was led to the **altar,** where his throat was slit and the blood collected in a vessel. This blood was then sprinkled "against the altar, on all sides"; then the animal was skinned (the skin being valuable for various uses); then the fat portions of the ox and the ram, the kidneys, and the covering of the liver, as well as the head were removed and burned by fire—"an aroma pleasing to the Lord" (Num. 18:17). This was the sin offering. Finally the **priest** washed the "inwards and legs" and burned them on the altar. Then the priest came down to the people and blessed them.

On occasion, the people might share with the priests in the eating of the roasted flesh, but usually this was **food** reserved for the priesthood. Solomon sacrificed 22,000 oxen in the dedication of the **Temple,** burning only token parts of the fat, so that the meat could serve for a huge public **feast** of thanksgiving, going on for days. This must have been a great treat, as the usual family rarely had beef at home.

Usually a single animal or a pair, or even a dozen might be sacrificed, often in conjunction with other sacrificial beasts such as the sheep and the goats. Sometimes a hundred or more oxen were sacrificed at a time. Archaeologists have verified that this was also a pattern of other cultures. It is mentioned repeatedly in Homer's epics and it is reported that the funeral of Prince Hepzefa, an Egyptian government official, had such a lavish slaughter to honor the dead ruler. Skulls of 100 oxen have been found around the tomb (Brian Fagan 1996).

Wild oxen were respected and worshipped in ancient Babylon. Some cultures believe that an ox tail hung between the eyes may protect one against the "evil eye." The earliest money—copper ingots—were called "ox-hide ingots" because their value was equal to that of an ox hide. Ulysses's adventure with the oxen of the sun was revived in James Joyce's famous novel, *Ulysses.* This giant animal has been a source of wonder and service for millennia. It is also figured as the basis of the simple man's wealth.

Images of oxen early became part of culture: And we know from Scripture that in Solomon's Temple, despite the prohibition of graven images, the great laver, or "molten sea," in the Temple was held up by oxen, lions, and **cherubim** (1 Kings 7:22). As one of the images that also appears among

461

the "creatures" in Ezekiel's famous vision, the image is repeated in Revelation: "The first living creature was like a lion, the second was like an ox, the third had a face like a man, the fourth was like a flying eagle" (Rev. 4:7). Based on this image, which **Church** Fathers took to symbolize the four **Gospels,** the ox persisted in Church **art** as the symbol for the Gospel of Luke. This identification was chosen because of Luke's emphasis on the sacrificial atonement of Christ and his divine priesthood. Thus his image in art was the winged ox (George Ferguson 1966, 22). *See also* Agriculture; Animals; Food.

Further Reading

Cansdale, George. *All the Animals of the Bible Lands.* Grand Rapids, Mich.: Zondervan Publishing House, 1970. Fagan, Brian. *Eyewitness to Discovery.* Oxford: Oxford University Press, 1996. Ferguson, George. *Signs and Symbols in Christian Art.* New York: Oxford University Press, 1966.

Palaces

(2 Sam. 5:11–12, 7:1–2; 1 Kings 7:2–8; Jer. 22:6–13) The term *palace* was applied to any structures that housed people in authority, no matter how modest the structure or the authority. They were centers of power and intrigue. In earlier Hebrew history, the palace was the dwelling place of the **king**. Later it became the center for the high **priest** or the governor.

Abraham came from Mesopotamia, a region full of grand building programs. Sumer (and later Babylon) had lavish constructions for their rulers long before Abram set out for the Promised Land. He and Sarai saw palaces in **Egypt**, as did his great-grandson Joseph, who was given "charge" of the pharaoh's palace (Gen. 41:40). Moses grew up in the palace household, but for the most part the early Israelites had little contact with such grandeur. They were affluent herdsmen, who lived most of their migratory existence in **tents**.

Leaders from nearby **Moab**, such as Balak and Ehud, appear to have built regal dwellings that the Scripture calls "palaces" (Num. 22:18; Judg. 3:20). "Castles" (which may have been storehouses for communities with officers in charge) were common among various peoples. Jehosophat, for example, had them, and Moses commanded Israel to burn the "castles" of the **Midianites** (Num. 31:10). Later, the **Roman** Castle of Antonia was clearly a fortress, built to house and protect the Roman forces in Jerusalem.

In Israel, from the beginning of the monarchy, the need for a fortified camp proved essential for the **warrior** kings to protect their soldiers and to store their supplies. Saul probably had his "palace" (nothing more than the **house** of the king, with a "**throne**" of sorts) on an acropolis, a high rocky area that could be easily defended. When he went home to Gibeah (1 Sam.10:26), "he went to a crude rustic stone stronghold." Dr. W.F. Albright has excavated what appears to be Saul's fortress castle at Gibeah (Tell el-Ful) north of Jerusalem, probably erected between ca.1020 and 1000 B.C. with "casemated walls and separately bonded corner towers." It measured 170 × 1554 feet, had two stories and a strong stone stairway (1 Sam 15:34; Madeleine S. Miller and J. Lane Miller 1961, 39)

From the beginning of the monarchy, the appetite for regal splendor grew to match the assertion of authority. David built his house—or palace—on the acropolis in Jerusalem, bringing carpenters and builders from Tyre, a region that had talented artisans (2 Sam. 5:11–12, 7:1–2). Compared with his previous life in tents and **caves**, this must have seemed lavish. Chronicles notes that Hiram, king of Tyre, sent him cedar logs, stonemasons, and carpenters (1 Chron. 14:1). He was concerned, when he settled into his palace, that the **Ark of the Covenant** was still under a tent while he had a palace (1 Chron. 17:1; 2 Sam 7:2), but he was strictly forbidden to build the permanent **Temple** in Jerusalem. This awaited the reign of Solomon. David's headquarters in Jerusalem were large enough to assemble all "the property and livestock belonging to the king and his sons, together with the palace officials, the mighty men and all the brave warriors"(1 Chron. 28:1). It also was large enough to house his wives and his 10 concubines who were kept under guard (2 Sam. 20:3).

As the monarchy flourished, David's son Solomon also imported foreign architects and began constructing lavish palaces at the same time that he undertook the building of the Temple. The description of his palace is quite detailed. Solomon

> built the House of the Forest of Lebanon one hundred cubits long, fifty wide, and thirty high; it was supported by four rows of cedar columns, with cedar capitals upon the columns. It had a ceiling of cedar above the beams resting on the columns; these beams numbered forty-five, fifteen to a row. There were three window frames at either end, with windows in strict alignment. The posts of all the doorways were rectangular, and the doorways faced each other, three at either end. He made the Hall of Pillars, fifty cubits long and thirty cubits wide. There was a portico in front with pillars, and a canopy in front of them. He made the Hall of the Throne where he was to pronounce judgment, the Hall of Justice, covered with cedar from floor to ceiling beams. His own house where he would reside, in the other court back of the hall, was of the same construction. Solomon also made a House for Pharaoh's Daughter, whom he had married. (1 Kings 7:2–8)

This elaborate description reveals a separation between private quarters and public ones. In addition to the "House for Pharaoh's Daughter," there was also a harem for his hundreds of wives and concubines. During the 13 years it took to build all this, he also undertook the building of the Temple.

Using forced labor he conscripted, King Solomon also arranged the building of "the supporting terraces, the wall of Jerusalem, and Hazor, Megiddo and Gezer" (1 Kings 9:15). We know that these constructions involved other palaces and quarters in Megiddo for his horsemen and his **horses** and **chariots**, as well as storehouses. He had all of his palaces decorated with pillars and capitals carved to look like palm trees, and he had the walls of his house covered with engravings of cherubim, palm trees, and rosettes. Bits of this carving have been discovered at Hazor, Dan, Megiddo, Samaria, and Jerusalem. His 300 hammered-gold shields and his gold goblets (nothing of silver, which was considered an inferior metal) drew the envy of other monarchs and eventually invited looting (1 Chron. 9:16; 1 Kings 14:26).

From Solomon's time forward, palaces grew ever more ornate, with elaborate gates and doorways). The courtyards grew more elegant, with **gardens** enclosed for the use of the family. This grandiose lifestyle, requiring **slave** labor and heavy taxes, set the tone for later monarchs. By the time of the northern kingdom's Omri dynasty, in the early ninth century B.C., royal quarters had been constructed on the summit of a hill in Samaria (1 Kings 16:24). There King Ahab enclosed the acropolis with a casement wall in Phoenician style of stone. The royal living quarters had masonry-trellised windows, like Jezebel's (2 Kings 9:30.) The remains of the palace reveal rooms grouped around a central courtyard, the palace inlaid with carved **ivory**. "Archaeologists have recovered more than five hundred ivory fragments dating to the eighth century, including two hundred decorated pieces, from the palace debris" (Philip J. King and Lawrence E. Stager 2001, 204) The **prophet** Amos saw their "beds of ivory" as evidence of the decadence of the Northern Kingdom (Amos 6:4, 3:15).

Another archaeological dig at Ramat Rahel, on a hill midway between Jerusalem and Bethlehem, may have uncovered where Jehoiakim, king of Judah (609–598), built his palace "by unrighteousness, and his upper stories by injustice; who makes his neighbors work for nothing and does not give them their wages; who says, 'I will build myself a spacious house with large upper stories,' and who cuts out windows for it, paneling it with cedar and painting it with vermilion" (Jer. 22:13–14).

The period of the Jews' deportation and bondage introduced them to royalty of other lands, altering their taste and making their royal architecture even more imperial in scope. With foreign governors who brought alien styles, the palaces displayed eclectic details. From **Assyria** came the idea of the open court, a large courtyard surrounded by rooms on all sides (Philip J. King and Lawrence E. Stager 2001, 208). From the Persians, they brought home memories of impressive throne rooms and well-furnished harems. The Book of Esther describes details of the Persian palace at Susa: the harem in which she was prepared for her role as queen, the beautiful courtyard that separated the women's quarters from the palace, and the banquet room and throne room of the king. The Old Testament has numerous references to palaces in Mesopotamia (Isa. 39:7; 2 Kings 20:18), especially the palace of the king of **Babylon**, to which Israelites dreaded being taken as eunuchs, perfumers, and servants (Dan.1:4). Such splendor of foreign monarchs' palaces impressed the Hebrews. They brought home bits of this elegant life to furnish their own homes: Assyrian artifacts have been discovered all over Israel, in Hazor, Megiddo, and elsewhere. Sargon, who rebuilt Samaria and settled Assyrians in the cites, had a palace that occupied 25 acres, with walls from 9 to 16 feet thick. Large stone winged bulls stood at the entrance with inscribed bricks to identify the palace. "In the palace courtyard were three temples, a towering ziggurat, luxurious harems, and spacious domestic quarters" (Robert T. Boyd 1969, 203).

When these empires were replaced by the Greeks and Romans, with their governors and kings, they brought their own styles and their impressive engineering feats. The Jewish palaces by Jesus's day had double gates, massive pillars, great courtyards, lovely gardens, impressive anterooms, and even bathrooms. Yet the king who reigned was not of their choosing. Grandeur came at a great price.

The prophets came to see the palaces as evidence of Israel's corruption and foreigners' decadence. Much of Jeremiah's prophecy refers to the destruction of the disobedient, whose great buildings and towns will be "like a desert" (Jer. 22:6). "Woe to him who builds his palace by unrighteousness, his upper rooms by injustice, making his countrymen work for nothing, not paying them for their labor" (Jer. 22:13). If Judah should prove obedient to God, her palaces will be restored, along with her city (Jer. 30:18). Jeremiah lived to see the Babylonians set fire to the royal palace and to the houses of the people and break down the walls of Jerusalem (Jer. 39:8). This catastrophe was to be repeated at the time of the Jewish rebellion against Rome in 70 A.D. By then, palaces had become symbols of foreign tyranny.

The author of Lamentations noted that the Lord "has swallowed up all" Israel's "palaces and destroyed her strongholds" (Lam. 2:5). Isaiah portrayed a time when "Hyenas will howl in her strongholds, jackals in her luxurious palaces"(Isa. 13:22). Amos turned the earthly palace into an immortal image in his famous declaration: "he who builds his lofty palace in the heavens and sets it foundation on the earth, who calls for the waters of the sea and pours them out over the face of the land—the Lord is his name" (Amos 9:6).

Numerous palaces around the countryside formed the background for Jesus's ministry. In Jerusalem stood Herod's spectacular palace, not to mention the palace of the high priest, and the palace of the governor. The

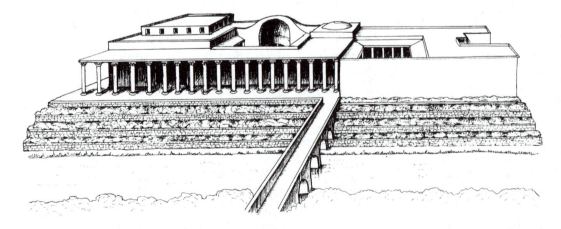

Herod's palace at Jericho with terraced gardens and classical columns.

Fortress of Antonia was also there. Other of Herod's grand fortress-palaces were at various places in the land, including the famous one at Masada. It was after a feast and dancing entertainment in one of Herod's palaces that another Herod arranged to have John the Baptist beheaded.

Jesus's ministry was primarily among simpler folk with simpler dwellings, but even they understood when he explained that in his father's house were "many mansions." His own life ended with exposure, torture, trial, and imprisonment in a series of palaces: Caiaphas's, Herod's, and Pilate's. So the early **Disciples** and **apostles** found that their contact with palace life was usually one of trial or imprisonment (Acts 23:35). It was in palace dungeons that Paul and others were kept "in chains for Christ" (Phil. 1:13). *See also* Houses; Kings; War, Warfare: General.

Further Reading

Boyd, Robert T. *Tells, Tombs and Treasure: A Pictorial Guide to Biblical Archaeology*. New York: Bonanza Books, 1969. King, Philip J. and Lawrence E. Stager. *Life in Biblical Israel*. Louisville, Ky.: Westminster John Knox Press, 2001. Miller, Madeleine S. and J. Lane Miller. "Palaces," in *Harper's Bible Dictionary*. New York: Harper and Row, 1961. Wright, George Ernest. *Biblical Archaeology*. Philadelphia: The Westminster Press, 1957.

Parable

(2 Sam. 12:1–4; Isa. 5:1–6; Mark 4:1–33) The word *parable* literally means "putting things side by side" (R.V.G. Tasker and I.H. Marshall 1980, 1153). It derives from the concept of saying things a different way, usually by telling an illustrative story. As used in Scripture, a parable is a short allegory, often religious or moral, which is followed by an explanation of its meaning. The Old Testament has five such narratives:

1. The story of the poor man who had raised a single lamb, which a wealthy neighbor took from him to set before a guest (2 Sam. 7:1–4), illustrative of the sin that David had committed with Bathsheba, Uriah's wife
2. The story of the wise woman of Tekoah, who induced David to make peace with his son Absalom (2 Sam. 14:6–8)
3. The story of the **prophet's disciple**, showing Ahab the wrong course that he had adopted toward Ben-hadad (1 Kings 20:39–40)
4. The tale of the **vineyard** that does not thrive despite the care bestowed on it (Isa. 5:1–6), illustrating Israel's degeneracy
5. The allegory of the farmer who does not plow continually but prepares the field and sows his seed, arranging all his work in due

order (Isa. 28:24–28); it is intended to show the methodical activity of God.

All of these parables were based on people and situations familiar to the audience at the time. Even the event described in 2 Sam. 14:6–8 "was probably no rare occurrence, in view of the custom which then prevailed of avenging bloodshed" (Wilhelm Bacher and Jacob Zallel Lauterbach 2005).

Jesus frequently used this literary form as a pedagogical device. The **Gospels** record 41 parables, some of which overlap, are variations, or are repeated in other gospels (Buckner B. Trawick 1968, 12). Jesus preferred to illustrate his principles concretely with homespun analogies drawn from everyday life in Palestine: a lost coin, a farmer sowing seed, a blighted fig tree, a **shepherd** looking for his **sheep**, or a good Samaritan helping out a Jewish victim of a robbery. They include such stories as the **house** built on the rock (Matt. 7:24–27; Luke 6:47–49), sewing new patches on old garments or putting new **wine** in old wineskins (Mark 2:21; Matt 9:16; Luke 5:36), the two debtors (Luke 7:36–50), and the mustard seed (Mark 4:30–32; Matt.13:31–32; Luke 13:18–19).

Each of the Gospels except John's seems to record numerous stories of sons, husbandmen, wedding feasts, wise and unwise servants, virgins, and builders. Luke is usually credited with being the best of the evangelists in recording these stories. If we consider the figurative statements in John regarding the Good Shepherd and the Vine and the Branches (10:7–16, 15:1–8), even he demonstrates that this was a favorite device used by Jesus to clarify his ideas and preserve them in the memories of his listeners. Some of his parables may blend with allegories or other image formations.

In most cases, Jesus would ask the disciples if they understood. If there was some doubt, he would explain himself in plain words. Sometimes, the failure to understand is attributed to hardness of heart. The parables were apparently used to target that section of his audience that had "ears to hear" while leaving the others confused. As Mark recorded the purpose of the parables, Jesus told his disciples that they had been given the "secret of the kingdom of God, but for those outside, everything comes in parables" so that "they may indeed look, but not perceive, and may indeed listen, but not understand; so that they may not turn again and be forgiven" (Mark 4:10–13). This enigmatic statement is followed by a series of parables: the **lamp** under a bushel basket, the growing seed, the mustard seed. Then Mark concludes the scene noting: "With many such parables he spoke the word to them, as they were able to hear it; he did not speak to them except in parables, but he explained everything in private to his disciples" (Mark 4:33). Sometimes, his gesture becomes an image of his idea, as in the cursing of the fig tree that fails to bear fruit. Jesus even spoke of his own life in figurative terms, comparing his body to the stones of the **Temple** and his death and **resurrection** to the destruction and rebuilding of it.

Preachers and evangelists over the centuries have found that this is indeed an impressive rhetorical device, ideal for teaching. It touches the experience of the listener, forces him or her to reach for meaning in order to interpret it, and generally makes the point more memorable. The believers are encouraged in their faith, and the unbelievers are tempted to seek a deeper understanding. The vivid images hold the listeners' attention, making the message more memorable. *See also* Gospel, Gospels.

Further Reading

Bacher, Wilhelm and Jacob Zallel Lauterbach. "Parable." http://jewishencyclopedia.com (accessed January 18, 2005). Tasker. R.V.G. and I.H. Marshall "Parable," in *The Illustrated Bible Dictionary*. Sydney, Australia: Tyndale House Publishers, 1980. Trawick, Buckner B. *The Bible as Literature*. New York: Harper and Row, Publishers, 1968.

Passover, or the Feast of Unleavened Bread

(Exod. 12:7–17, 34:18; Lev. 23:5; 2 Kings 23:21–23; Matt. 26:17; Mark 14:1, 12; Luke 22:1; John 18:28, 1; Cor. 5:7) Passover, or *Pesach,* also known as *Hag Ha Aviv,* the Holiday of Spring, is the joyous **feast** that celebrates God's protection of his children. When God passed over the **houses** of all the families in **Egypt**, killing the firstborn sons, he preserved the sons of his people, who put lambs' **blood** on the doorposts. The term *Passover* is sometimes used for the feast that opens the seven-day Feast of Unleavened **Bread** and sometimes only for the ceremonial meal held on the first day, also called the *Seder* after biblical times. The Hebrew name, *Pesah* means "to protect or have compassion." The unleavened bread is a memorial to the haste with which the Hebrews fled from Egypt, not taking time to allow their bread to rise. The whole period of the festival commemorates God's grace in releasing his people from bondage, a time of liberation.

Moses told the Hebrews in the wilderness that God had instructed him to "celebrate the Feast of Unleavened Bread, because it was on this very day that I brought your divisions out of Egypt. Celebrate this day as a lasting ordinance for years to come" (Exod.12:17). The day was set as the 14th day of the first month, Nisan until the 21st day of the month "at even" (Lev. 23:5), "for in that month you came out of Egypt" (Exod. 34:18). The directions for the entire feast are quite specific: first, the household must be scoured and rid of any fragment of leavening. (Moses had told the fleeing Israelites to eat "with your cloak tucked into your belt, your sandals on your feet and your staff in your hand" (Exod. 12:11)—signs of their haste. The first celebration occurred on the anniversary of the events of the Exodus, when the Hebrews were in the Sinai Desert.

Because God had instructed the Israelites to slaughter a lamb and paint the doorways of their houses with that blood, the Passover, or pascal was lamb served as a natural part of the celebration. The selection and offering of the sacrificial **animals** were important parts of the ceremony. At noon on the 14th of Nisan, Jews were to bring their animals to the **altar**. The worshipers slaughtered their animals, the **priests** caught the blood, and then tossed it against the altar. While this was happening, the Levites sang psalms (Psalms 113–118). The worshipers carried their animals home and roasted them in portable clay stoves set up in their courtyards, in a manner that avoided breaking any of the animal's bones. Every person was to eat at least a small portion of the lamb, along with symbolic herbs dipped in vinegar or red wine, accompanied by the matzah (or unleavened bread). The **Pharisees** established the first Seder (the specific order of service), which included wine-drinking and reclining on sofas so that the participants could eat their food in a leisurely manner and discuss the events of the Exodus.

The traditional ceremony of the eating involved questions and answers by fathers and sons, and psalms of praise were sung after the drinking of the cups of **wine**. At the end of the meal, the people were encouraged to go out "from sorrow to gladness, and from mourning to festival day, and from darkness to great light, and from servitude to redemption" (quoted from Pesah. 10.5 by John H. Hayes 1993, 573).

No foreigner was to celebrate the Passover unless he was **circumcised** and had all of the males in his household circumcised (Exod. 12:43). After all, this was a feast commemorating God's special blessing on his chosen people. The people themselves were to be ceremonially **clean**, that is, not having touched an unclean woman or a dead body (Num. 9:6). He might be excused from the feast if he were on a journey, but he was encouraged to remember this day rather than "bear the consequences of his sin" (Num. 9:13).

Apparently, during the time of the **Judges**, the people neglected their duties and let this celebration fall by the way. **King** Josiah, in his renewal of the **Covenant** (619 B.C.), gave the order to "celebrate the Passover to the Lord your God" (2 Kings 23:21–23). Giving special prominence to this festival, he insisted that it be observed in Jerusalem, making it a grand national event. Many who traveled to the **Temple** in Jerusalem were not ceremonially clean, requiring that the Levites slaughter the Passover lambs for them (2 Chron. 30:17–18, 35:6–8). In a lavish display of generosity, Josiah's officials helped with the total of 30,000 sheep and goats and 3,000 cattle; they also contributed additional money and animals to the people, the priests, and the Levites.

This massive slaughter was followed with the sprinkling of blood, the skinning of the animals, the roasting of the animals over the fire, and boiling of "the holy offerings in pots, caldrons and pans" (2 Chron. 35:11–13). When all was accomplished, the people sat down together and ate, observing the Feast of Unleavened Bread for seven days (2 Chron. 35:17).

The requirement that Passover be celebrated in Jerusalem resulted in another break in the tradition that was forced on the Jews during their period of captivity (586 B.C.). Even in Exile, however, they kept the Passover, leaving out only the pascal offering, which required the ceremony to be performed at the Temple in Jerusalem. After the return from Exile (516 B.C.), Ezra noted that the people celebrated the feast again "with joy" when the King of **Assyria** allowed them to rebuild the Temple and assisted them in their work (Ezra 6:22). The celebration must have continued to be observed in the following years, until the destruction of the Temple in 70 A.D. by the **Romans**.

By Jesus's time, this celebration had become an established tradition of Jewish life. In the final weeks of his life, Jesus and his disciples traveled to Jerusalem for this great event, joining the overflow crowds that jammed the streets, the city, and the Temple. Matthew, Mark, and Luke all mention that the **disciples** planned with Jesus where they should celebrate the event, probably because of the elaborate preparations that were necessary in their own rituals of cleansing and the sacrifice of the lamb. (See Matt. 26:17, Mark 14:1, 12, Luke 22:1. Curiously, John 18:28 notes that this was the time of "preparation" for the feast.)

Because of this clear evidence in three of the **Gospels**, most **Christians** believe that the **Last Supper** was the Jewish Passover. Paul seems to have thought so, using the symbolism of the "old yeast" and the "Passover lamb" as signs of Christ's immaculate life and sacrificial death (1 Cor. 5:7). This symbolism carried over in Christian worship as the sacrament of communion.

In modern Judaism, the Passover Seder is one of the most commonly observed of all the festivals. The celebrants use a book known as the *Haggadah,* literally "telling." Over time, this tradition has been expanded to include contemporary readings, medieval song, and references to the Holocaust (Jonathan Klawans 2002). Throughout history, the Passover symbols have remained constant: the story of the Exodus and the Passover lamb, the unleavened bread to signify the haste of the Israelites when they left Egypt, and the bitter herbs to recall the bitter life in Egypt. Even the song of Moses, recorded in Exodus, remains a portion of the service. *See also* Exodus; Feasting.

Further Reading

Hayes, John H. "Passover," in *Oxford Companion to the Bible*. New York: Oxford University Press, 1993. Klawans, Jonathan. "Was Jesus' Last Supper a Seder," in *Bible Review* October 2001. http://www.bib-arch/bswb.com (accessed

June 15, 2002). Kramer, Amy J. "Passover," http://www.everythingjewish. com (accessed June 3, 2005).

Pentecost or the Day of the First Fruits

(Exod. 23:16, 34:22; Lev. 23:15–21; Num. 28:20) Pentecost was originally a Jewish **feast** deriving its name from the fact it occurred 50 (or *pentekostos* in Greek) days after the **Sabbath** following **Passover**, also known as the Feast of the Weeks or the Day of the First Fruits. Ordained by God through Moses (Exod. 23:16, 34:22; Num. 28:20), it was also a joyous festival celebrated at the sanctuary by every male, and marking the end of the wheat harvest and the beginning of the fruit harvest. As one of the Sabbatical system of feasts, the standard obligations applied: ceasing from labor, gathering in a holy convocation, burnt **offerings**, wave offerings, and peace offerings (Lev. 23:15–21). For the "wave offering," the worshippers would bake two loaves of **bread** from the first fruits of the **grain**, and the **priest** would wave them prior to the feast. One unusual note was the admonition that the harvesters should leave gleanings for the poor and the sojourners (Lev. 23:22). This echoes the experience of Ruth who gleaned in the fields of Boaz.

At certain times in later years, some of the celebrants would climb to the roof of the **synagogue** and throw apples down to the crowd below, who picked them up saying, "As these apples are gathered up, so may we be gathered together from our dispersion among the heathen" (David L. Jeffrey 1992, 597). Later traditions connected this celebration to God's covenant with Noah, and the giving of the **law** to Moses at Mt. Sinai. Over time, it gathered more traditions for commemoration.

It is not surprising, therefore, that the followers of Christ would have gathered together to celebrate this festival after the death and **crucifixion** of their Lord during Passover. Scripture indicates that Jews and converts to Judaism came together from all over the Roman Empire for this celebration: Parthians, Medes, Elamites, residents of Mesopotamia, Judea, and Cappadocia, Pontus, and Asia, Phrygia and Pamphylia, Egypt and parts of Libya near Cyrene, Romans, Cretans, and Arabs (Acts 2:8).

As Luke reports the events of that day in the book of Acts, his narrative of the early **Church**: "Suddenly a sound like the blowing of a violent wind came from **heaven** and filled the whole **house** where they were sitting. They saw what seemed to be tongues of fire that separated and came to rest on each of them. All of them were filled with the **Holy Spirit** and began to speak in other tongues as the Spirit enabled them....When they heard this sound, a crowd came together in bewilderment, because each one heard them speaking in his own language" (Acts 2:2–7). The members of the crowd were amazed and perplexed. Finally, assuming the celebrants were drunk, they began taunting them. At this point, Peter preached a sermon that converted three thousand listeners.

For **Christians**, these events of Pentecost signaled the outpouring of the Holy Spirit, the empowerment of the new Church, and the beginning of the outreach to the whole world. The day was therefore set aside as a special event in the Christian calendar. Whit Sunday, which falls 50 days after Easter, is the Christian Pentecost, symbolized by the cloven tongues of fire that descended on the early Christians (Madeleine S. Miller and J. Lane Miller 1961, 537). The celebration of "first fruits" took on new meaning with the first conversions, becoming the harvest of souls for Christ with this miraculous outpouring of the Spirit on Jew and Gentile alike.

For some the gift of tongues experienced at Pentecost is the mark of the true Christian: *glossolalia,* or speaking in tongues, marks a number of charismatic and Pentecostal denominations. Others consider it the gift of communication to people of all cultures. Symbolically, it is the antithesis of the Tower of **Babel**, when humankind was cursed with the multiplication of languages. In the power of the Holy Spirit, humans were united in love and in understanding. John Wesley believed that "the whole world should in due time praise God in various tongues" (David L. Jeffrey 1992 600). *See also* Babel, Tower of; Bread; Feasting; Holy Spirit, Holy Ghost.

Further Reading

Jeffrey, David Lyle. "Pentecost," in *A Dictionary of the Biblical Tradition in English Literature*. Grand Rapids, Mich.: William B. Eerdmans Publishing Company, 1992. Miller, Madeleine S. and J. Lyle Miller. "Pentecost," in *Harper's Bible Dictionary*. New York: Harper and Row, 1961.

Perfume

(Exod. 30:22–33; 1 Chron. 9:30; 1 Sam. 8:13; Ruth 3:3; Esther 2:12; John 12:2, 19:39) In the ancient world, both men and women wore perfumed oils if they could afford the luxury. From early times in **Egypt** and Mesopotamia, perfumers were a standard part of the **king**'s household, classed along with the cooks and bakers (1 Sam. 8:13). Archaeologists have discovered that the great palace at Mari, on the Euphrates, had its own perfumery as early as the eighteenth century B.C. (K. A. Kitchen 1980, 320). The king and his court required ointments for their rituals, for bathing, and for banquets.

The English word *perfume* comes from the Latin meaning "through smoke." One of the oldest uses of perfume was for the burning of incense and aromatic herbs in religious services. The Chinese, Hindus, Carthaginians, Arabs, Persians, **Greeks**, and **Romans**, as well as the **Israelites** and

Egyptians, used perfumes as a regular part of their culture, particularly in caring for the dead. One story relates how an odor, perhaps of fragrant kyphi or myrrh, issued forth from the tomb of Tutankhamen when it was opened thousands of years after it was first sealed. Glass perfume bottles were found in Egypt that are thought to date to around 1000 B.C. (Mary Bellis 2002).

Perfumes were used regularly for the burial of honored persons and were burned at their **funerals**. The symbolism of frankincense and myrrh as gifts for the Christ child suggest both royalty and death. The great expense of fragrant ointments is suggested in John 12:3, when Mary uses a pound of "ointment of spikenard, very costly" to anoint Jesus's feet, and elicited an angry rebuke by Judas Iscariot, "Why was not this ointment sold for three hundred pence, and given to the poor?" When Jesus died, Nicodemus anointed him, bringing " a mixture of myrrh and aloes, about a hundred pound weight" (John 19:39).

The Priestly code of Israel, a part of the Mosaic **law**, required rituals of **anointing** and of preparing and using **incense** (Exod. 30:22–33). Here the references are to myrrh and cinnamon, sweet calamus, cassia, and **olive oil**. The "apothecary" was to make a holy oil of these materials. Also mentioned are "sweet spices, stacte, and onycha, and galbanum; these sweet spices with pure frankincense" from which was to be manufactured a perfume. David and Saul both commissioned **priests** to make "ointment and spices" for the **tabernacle** (1 Chron. 9:30).

The myrrh, mentioned here and also listed among the gifts brought to the Christ child by the Wisemen, came from a fragrant gum resin of a tree that grew in Arabia and Somaliland. The actual identity of cinnamon is in doubt, but it may refer to an aromatic bark of wood like that from Ceylon. The "sweet calamus," which is also referred to as an aromatic cane, was the "sweet cane from a far country" mentioned by Jeremiah (6:20). Scholars have not determined the identity of cassia.

The personal, bodily use of perfumed oil was common after a **bath**, for lubrication of the skin. "Practically everyone used scented oils to mask offensive odors and to protect the skin from the dry heat and bright sun" (Philip J. King and Lawrence E. Stager 2001, 280). Naomi recommended this as a beauty treatment for Ruth, her daughter-in-law: "Bathe and oil yourself and put on your best attire" (Ruth 3:3). The lavish application of a combination of oils with appealing odors became a ritual of beautification. In harems, for example, new recruits such as Esther were treated to several months of bathing and rubbing with aromatic oils until they were deemed adequate for presentation to the monarch and, if he so desired, to spend one night with him. "Now when every maid's turn was come to go in to king Ahasuerus, after that she had been twelve months, according to the manner of the women, (for so were the days of their purification accomplished, to wit, six months with oil of myrrh, and six months with sweet odors, and other things for the purifying of the women)" (Esther 2:12).

These fragrances were used on **clothes**, as well as on the body, sprinkled on couches for banquets or poured on the head. David records the **blessings** of sweet-smelling garments, which "smell of myrrh, and aloes, and cassia" (Ps. 45:8). The Queen of Sheba brought such spices to King Solomon (1 Kings 10:2, 10), perhaps introducing him to additional exotic blends from far distant African and Arabian lands. With the monarchy, the references to perfumes and spices increase, especially in the Song of Solomon. They were among the treasures that the foolish King Hezekiah showed to envoys from Babylon (2 Kings 20:13). Because they had to be imported and were consequently expensive, they were the gifts appropriate for kings. For this, they were bottled in tiny jugs or boxes, many of which have survived.

The Craft of the Perfumer

The perfumer was a kind of combination of cook and chemist. He would extract the perfume of flowers or herbs and fix them by one of three processes:

1. *Enfleurage,* the steeping of flowers in fat and continually changing them
2. *Maceration,* the dipping of flowers or other fragrant items in hot fats or oils at 65 degrees Celsius
3. *Expressing,* the squeezing out of the scent-bearing juices by compressing the flowers or other objects in a bag

"Oil of myrrh and other gum-resins were obtained by heating the substance concerned in a greasy-type 'fixative' oil/fat (plus water to avoid scent-evaporation); the perfume-essence of the myrrh or other 'resin' was thereby transferred to the greasy oil/fat which could then be strained off as a liquid perfume" (K. A. Kitchen 1980, 321).

Egyptian tomb paintings of the fifteenth century B.C. demonstrate the manufacture of incense, using this method. In fact, the Egyptian word for "perfumer" was "cooker of ointment." The Hebrew word for the process was "to mix" or "to compound," indicating that the "perfumer's techniques in blending ointments resemble a chef's preparations for a banquet" (Philip J. King and Lawrence E. Stager 2001, 281). *See also* Anointing; Bath, Bathing; Hospitality; Olives, Olive Oil, Olive Trees.

Further Reading

Bellis, Mary. "History of Perfume," http://www.inventors.about.com (accessed January 2, 2002). King, Philip J. and Lawrence E. Stager. *Life in Biblical*

Israel. Louisville, Ky.: Westminster John Knox Press, 2001. Kitchen, K. A. "Cosmetics and Perfumery," in *The Illustrated Bible Dictionary*. Sydney, Australia: Tyndale House Publishers, 1980.

Pharisees

(Matt. 23:15, 23, 25, 27, 29; Mark 2:16, 7:5; Luke 5:21; John 12:42)
The three prominent religious parties of the two centuries around the birth of Jesus appear to have risen in response to the acts of desecration during the time of Antiochus Epiphanes (168 B.C.). The Jewish historian Josephus tells of this tyrant's efforts to turn the **Temple** into a place of heathen worship, erecting statues of pagan gods and sacrificing swine on the **altar**. These violations of **law** and custom, which gave rise to the wars of the Maccabees, also seem to have stirred some true believers to separate themselves from the community of worshippers, taking the name of *Pharisees*.

They were first mentioned in the time of John Hycanus, the warrior-priest, and appear to have been successors to the *Hasidim* (or "Pious ones"). The other two contemporary sects that Josephus mentions were "the aristocratic **Sadducees** and the ascetic **Essenes**" (Madeleine S. Miller 1961, 546 and Josephus's *The Wars of the Jews,* I:1; 2 Macc. 6:7). The Pharisees had a great deal of influence and popular support under John Hyrcanus (134–76 B.C.) for a while and later under Alexandra Salome, his successor (76–67 B.C.). Out of favor during Herod's time, they petitioned **Rome** for direct rule and opposed the revolt of the Jews against Rome (66–70 A.D.) (H. L. Ellison 1980, 1209).

The Pharisees were noted for their scrupulous adherence to every jot and tittle of the law, including the traditions of the elders. They were known as the successors of the early **scribes**, the men of the Great **Synagogue**, especially Ezra and the Hasidaeans. They were the chief advocates of the synagogue, a place of teaching, as opposed to the exclusive emphasis on the Temple, a place of **sacrifice**. The Pharisees insisted on the unity and holiness of God, the election of **Israel**, and the absolute authority of the Torah (the first five books of the Bible), but largely stressed ethical rather than theological issues. They argued with the Sadducees regarding a number of the rites in the Temple, insisting that the **priests** were only deputies of the people. They brought a sense of festivity and cheerfulness to the celebration of the **Sabbath** and holy days, emphasizing domestic joy. They showed themselves to be more lenient in their regulations regarding women by relaxing some of the laws of levitical purity and **divorce**, encouraging peace in the home based on affection rather than arbitrary regulation. As a result, they "stood in high favor with Jewish women" (Kaufmann Kohler 2004).

Among the points of theology they did profess were beliefs in the coming of the **Kingdom of God**, the hope for a **Messiah**, predestination of all things by God, the importance of acting out the faith one professes, the **resurrection** of the body, and divine **judgment**. They also believed in **angels** and **demons**.

In most of these and other views, the Pharisees stood in opposition to the aristocratic priesthood of the Sadducees, which relied on the Torah, not on the Mishnah and the Talmud (the writings of the **rabbis** and the scribes that interpreted the law of Moses in great detail). They believed that the spiritual life of the people should be centered on the synagogue, replacing the aristocracy of the priesthood with an aristocracy of learning. One of their more flamboyant statements was that "a bastard who is a student of the Law" is "higher in rank than an ignorant high priest" (Kaufmann Kohler 2004).

In an effort to keep the people safely away from sinful acts, they added numerous restrictions to the biblical law, especially in connection with the company they kept, their eating and drinking, their marriages to heathens, and Sabbath observance. This multiplication of the details of the law, with precise regulation of the people, led to an excess of legalism that offended Jesus and his followers.

The air of piety that they assumed led to challenges that were particularly offensive to them. Nothing could have been more loathsome to a genuine Pharisee than to be charged with **hypocrisy**. Yet, this was the very charge that Jesus made against them: "Woe to you, teachers of the law and Pharisees, you hypocrites!" he says five times (Matt 23:15, 23, 25, 27, 29), calling them "whitewashed tombs, which look clean on the outside but on the inside are full of dead men's bones and everything unclean." He accused them of missing the important matters of the law, "justice, mercy, and faithfulness," while they observed legalistic niceties.

In their religious punctiliousness, they exaggerated some earlier laws, especially in their dress, emphasizing these rules to the point that they became distinctive. One was the phylactery, a little metal box or band of parchment, which Jews were required to fasten to the forehead or hand by straps. It contained passages of Scripture, reminding the bearer of the **Passover** and the redemption of the firstborn at the time of the **Exodus** (Exod. 13:9, 16). The blue fringes on the edges of the mantle, again commanded by the law of Moses (Num. 15:37, 38; Deut. 22:12), became ridiculously long on Pharisees' clothing. Their extraordinarily broad phylacteries and long fringes (Matt. 23:5) made these appendages seem to be objects of pride rather than reminders of God's grace (Fred Wight 1953, 101).

Jesus was questioned or "tested" by Pharisees on several occasions. He chided his accusers, who were less interested in his views of Sabbath observance and relations between religion and state than in trapping him into making blasphemous statements. On some occasions, he turned the tables on them and questioned them right back (Luke 14:3). Sometimes he attacked them directly for their ostentatious display of piety and their hunger for political and religious power.

The Pharisees disapproved of Jesus's loose interpretation of the law that uncovered the true meaning of the commandments, preferring instead their own many tidy rules. They were shocked that Jesus ate with sinners and **tax collectors** (Mark 2:16), that he ignored the "tradition of the elders" (Mark 7:5). They were the ones who noted that he spoke "**blasphemy**" when he asserted that he forgave sins, a power belonging to God alone (Luke 5:21). They joined with others in the **Sanhedrin** to bring Jesus to trial, muzzling his defenders. John notes that "many even among the leaders believed in him," but because of the Pharisees, they would not confess their faith for fear they would be put out of the synagogue (John 12:42).

Nicodemus, who provided the tomb in which Jesus was buried, was a Pharisee as was Paul, before his conversion experience on the road to Damascus. In fact, it was the Pharisees, the "teachers of the law," who argued for Paul, "a Pharisee, the son of a Pharisee" saying, "We find nothing wrong with this man. . . . What if a spirit or an angel has spoken to him?" (Acts 23:6, 9).

In the later years, the Pharisees gradually triumphed over the Sadducees, who disappeared with the destruction of the Temple (70 A.D.), leaving the regulation of Jewish affairs in the hands of this group, who as Kohler notes "shaped the character of Judaism and the life and thought of the Jew for all the future." Although this series of events gave the Jewish religion a legalistic tendency and made "separatism" its chief characteristic, "yet only thus were the pure monotheistic faith, the ethical ideal, and the intellectual and spiritual character of the Jew preserved in the midst of the downfall of the old world and the deluge of barbarism which swept over the medieval world" (Kaufmann Kohler 2004). *See also* Sadducees; Scribes; Synagogue; Tabernacle.

Further Reading

Ellison, H. L. "Pharisees," in *The Illustrated Bible Dictionary*. Sydney, Australia: Tyndale House Publishers, 1980. Kohler, Kaufmann. "Pharisees," http://www.jewishencyclopedia.com (accessed June 3, 2004). Miller, Madeleine S. and J. Lane Miller. "Pharisees," in *Harper's Bible Dictionary*. New York: Harper and Row, 1961. Wight, Fred Hartley. *Manners and Customs of Bible Lands*. Chicago: Moody Press, 1953.

Philistines

(**Deut. 2:23; Josh. 13:2, 3; 1 Kings 15:27, 16:15–17; 2 Chron. 26:6–7, 28:18; Amos 9:7**) The perennial adversaries of the Hebrews during the period of the **Judges** and the early days of the monarchy were the Philistines. Philistia was the coastal strip of land next to **Israel**, from Gaza to Joppa along the Mediterranean Sea (Josh. 13:2, 3). In addition to their port cities, the region included a wide, fertile plain that stretched to the Judean hills and was productive agricultural territory.

The Philistines were thought to have come from Caphtor (Amos 9:7; Deut. 2:23), the location of which has long been disputed, but the "prevailing opinion among scholars is that the Philistines were roving pirates from some northern coast on the Mediterranean Sea. Finding a fertile plain south of Joppa, they landed and forced a foothold. Their settlement was made by such a gradual process that they adopted both the language and the religion of the conquered peoples" (Emil G. Hirsch and Ira Maurice Price 2005). We know that they were not Semites but Aryans or Indo-Europeans, uncircumcised, skilled in sea craft, with a fully developed culture that remained a mystery to the Israelites. They appear to be one of the Sea Peoples who "ravaged the eastern Mediterranean world subsequent to the collapse of Mycenean civilization" at the end of the Bronze Age. The **Egyptians** repulsed them in a great sea battle with Ramses III (ca. 1190 B.C.), driving them to settle on the southwestern coast of Canaan (Carl S. Ehrlich 1993, 591).

Their arts and crafts show strong relationships with **Greece** and Crete. Wherever archaeologists have dug in Philistine cities, they have discovered large quantities of **pottery** that is distinctive from the Israelite or **Canaanite**, which was crude and largely unadorned. The Philistine ceramics, by contrast, is made of fine, well-baked clay, in classic shapes, with spirals, and birds (George Ernest Wright 1957, 91).

Their **metal** arts amazed the Hebrews, who were dazzled at the Philistine hero Goliath's armor and shield. Their war dress was especially striking. A high headdress with plumes resembled a horse's mane and made their large stature even more impressive. As they were already larger than the usual Hebrew, this and their **chariots** and **horses** made them seem like giants to the simple nomads. The contemporary drawings show them bare-chested and bare-footed wearing kilts with tassels (Pat Alexander 1978, 17). Wright notes that, although copper, which was easy to smelt and work, had been the dominant metal for tools and **weapons** since 4000 B.C., the Philistines learned to mix a little tin with the copper to make it harder, as bronze. Then iron came into use sometime after 1200 B.C., and was seen as a **magic** product, treasured like a precious metal. It is complicated to smelt and the secrets of the process were jealously guarded by the Hittites, and later by the Philistines (George Ernest Wright 1957, 92).

Except during the period of the Judges, the Philistines did not threaten Israel's territory, but they did remain a constant menace, both politically and socially (Madeleine S. Miller and J. Lane Miller 1961, 551). Their constant raids, especially at harvest time, forced the Israelites to organize as a monarchy to resist them. The Philistines were able to prevail against Saul (1 Sam. 31), but David defeated them decisively. From that time on, their expansion was halted and their battles with the Israelites were limited to border skirmishes (1 Kings 15:27, 16:15–17; 2 Chron. 26:6–7, 28:18).

By the tenth century, Philistia came under Egyptian hegemony and then, in the eighth century, under **Assyrian** rule. They revolted from time to time against their overlords, but remained part of the Assyrian empire, prospering during the seventh century, until the fall of Assyria (612 B.C.) Then, caught between the powers of Egypt and **Babylonia**, they were conquered and their land was ravaged by Nebuchadnezzar in 604 B.C. (Carl S. Ehrich 1993, 591). Like the Israelites, they fell before the marauding armies of Alexander the Great, finally being absorbed by other peoples and passing from history (Madeleine S. Miller and J. Lane Miller 1961, 553).

Their monopoly on iron (knowing where to find it, how to shape and use it) gave them a strategic superiority. They had iron-rimmed chariots and iron weapons, including iron swords. In the meantime, they not only blocked Israel from learning the secrets of the forge, but even held the monopoly on sharpening of tools and weapons. David's victories over them (1 Sam. 13:19–22) put an end to this situation.

The five Philistine cities (Gaza, Gath, Ashkelon, Ashdod, and Ekron) never united into a kingdom. Their rulers were called the "lords of the Philistines" (Josh. 13:3; Judg. 3:3; 1 Sam. 7:7). They governed with councils of co-equals, voting on actions and then acting as one, as in the case of Samson's fateful feast and imprisonment (1 Sam. 6:18, 27–29). Some believe the role of "lord" was hereditary. Archaeological digs in some of these cities in recent years have proven fruitful, allowing a picture of this extremely rich and highly developed civilization to emerge, in contrast to the traditional understanding of the term *philistine*. (The nineteenth-century British essayist Matthew Arnold had pictured middle-class money-grubbers as *philistines* in *Culture and Anarchy*.) It was the word *Philistine* that gave the name *Palestine* to the region (George Ernest Wright 1956, 45). The modern term refers to Arab people now living in the region, not to this ancient, extinct race.

Archaeologists have discovered evidence of iron forges, as well as other industrial activity, some dating as far back as ca.1300 B.C. They have also found pottery and potsherds scattered among the Israelite cities, indicating a significant level of interaction. That Samson visited them and was attracted to their women and that David hid out among them demonstrate that close relationships were not uncommon.

As the Millers sum up this competition: "It was inevitable that the ambitious Philistines and Israelites, both having a sense of destiny, and both arriving in Canaan at about the same time, should clash in their struggle for political and economic control" (Madeleine S. Miller and J. Lane Miller 1961, 552). It is no surprise that the Philistines eventually joined cause with the Canaanites, adopting their language and gods. They did have some differences, worshipping the god **Dagon** (Judg. 13–16), whose temple Samson, "eyeless in Gaza," brought down, along with all those worshipping therein. They also had a fish goddess, as well as Marna, Derketo, Baalzebal or Baal-zebub, of which Baal-zebub, also called "lord of the flies" was the most famous. *See also* Metals: Iron; Pots and Pottery.

Further Reading

Alexander, Pat, ed. "Nations Within the Promised Land," in *Eerdmans' Family Encyclopedia of the Bible*. Grand Rapids, Mich.: William B. Eerdmans Publishing Company, 1978. Ehrlich, Carl S. "Philistines," in *The Oxford Companion to the Bible*. New York: Oxford University Press, 1993. Hirsch, Emil G. and Ira Maurice Price. "Philistines," http://www.jewishencyclopedia.com (accessed January 20, 2005). Miller, Madeleine S. and J. Lane Miller. *Harper's Bible Dictionary*. New York: Harper and Row, 1961. Wright, George Ernest. *Biblical Archaeology*. Philadelphia: The Westminster Press, 1957. Wright, George Ernest, *The Westminster Historical Atlas to the Bible*. Philadelphia: The Westminster Press, 1956.

Physicians

Because illness was considered a divinely ordained **punishment**, physicians were rare in the Old Testament. Most problems were taken to the Lord in **prayer** or handled by offering **sacrifices**. All true healing was thought to come from God, the Great Physician. The gift of healing, which some of the **prophets** (Elijah and Elisha) demonstrated, was considered an attribute of the prophets, curing the sick through miracles. This gift was also shared by Jesus and his **disciples**. Most of medical treatment was undoubtedly informal and administered in the home, being mentioned in Scripture primarily as an occasion for miraculous intervention.

Childbirth was not considered an illness and was usually handled by midwives rather than physicians. Housewives were probably expected to deal with childhood disorders and most of the common problems such as fevers, indigestion, and accidents, which could be treated with herbs or simple poultices.

On a few occasions, physicians were mentioned. For example, Joseph employed house physicians (Gen. 50:2), possibly because **Egypt** had a fully developed system of medicine by this time. And Isaiah refers to a surgeon or "wound-dresser"(Isa. 3:7), suggesting that this was a profession by his time.

From the evidence archaeologists have discovered among the peoples of **Babylonia** and Egypt, we must assume that the Hebrews had seen doctors at work, but thought them not worth mentioning in their sacred scripture. The medical profession, represented primarily by foreign doctors, were held in low esteem. In fact Job asserts that they were "of no value" (Job 13:4), and King Asa was criticized for seeking physicians instead of looking for God's will.

The pious Hebrew would seek out a prophet or a **priest** and pray to the Lord. Moses prayed for those who had been bitten by snakes (Num. 21:7); David prayed in his time of sickness as he had earlier prayed for his sick son (Ps. 6). When these individuals were healed, they also gave God thanks for this healing (2 Kings 20; Ps. 107:17–21). When the patient died, the bereaved accepted this as God's will. It was the custom to give thanksgiving or "well-being" offerings (Lev. 7:11–36) after an illness was cured.

Elijah was noted as a healer who dealt with many painful disorders, and even brought a dead child back to life. That David consulted a prophet when his child was dying suggests that the holy man was thought to serve as a healer as well as a counselor. Jesus himself was considered a miraculous healer, able to cure many who were diseased (Mark 1:32–34). His disciples also had the gift of healing well into the Apostolic Age.

Gradually, this reliance on the priests and prophets changed. Conquest by great powers and mingling with other cultures led to more respect for the profession of medicine. The apocryphal book of Ecclesiasticus (or Sirach) suggests that we "honor physicians for their services, for the Lord created them." Their "gift of healing comes from the most high, and they are rewarded by the **king**" (Ecclus. 38:1–2). This extended description in Ecclesiasticus, "or the wisdom of Jesus son of Sirach" (a widely read handbook by a teacher in Jerusalem 200–180 B.C.) indicates that physicians were active in the households of the wealthy and powerful, distributing medicines and that they were skillful in healing and relieving pain. Nonetheless, the writer recommends that "when you are ill, do not delay but pray to the Lord, and he will heal you," adding, "Offer a sweet-smelling sacrifice, and a memorial portion of choice flour, and pour oil on your offering, as much as you can afford." At this point the patient is to "give the physician his place," and there may come a time when "recovery lies in the hands of physician" (Ecclus. 38: 9–13).

This advice suggests that many considered sin to be the root cause of illness, but others considered a less judgmental approach. Fundamentally, Original Sin introduced all of the evils into human life, including diseases and other disorders. The Priestly code was used to keep chronically ill people, who were ceremonially unclean, away from the **Temple**. (This practice also limited the spread of infectious diseases.)

By New Testament times, the blind and the lame appeared to receive little help from the priests. Jesus and his disciples spent much of their time ministering to this excluded group. This focus has led some to believe that early Christianity was considered, in part, a critique of the "priestly healthcare system" (Hector Ignacio Avalo 1993, 509). Jesus also argued against the yoking of sin with illness, indicating that a man's blindness was not necessarily a result of his or his parents' sinful behavior. Yet, in the case of the paralytic (Mark 2), he did include the statement, "Your sins are forgiven" when performing the cure.

Most physicians in ancient Israel were probably foreigners rather than Jews (Fred H. Wight 1953, 139). After all, in the surrounding countries, particularly in Mesopotamia and Egypt, the practice of medicine was more advanced, although often tied to a local goddess or god. Even as late as New Testament times, those who practiced medicine were seen as pagan, useless and even detrimental. The woman with the issue of **blood**, for example, "had suffered many things of many physicians" (Mark 5:26). **Rabbis** sometimes "posed as physicians, and very queer remedies indeed were prescribed by them" (Fred H. Wight 1953, 140). For example, to **cure** the bleeding, she was to dig seven pits, put vine branches (not yet f our years old) in them, and then carry a cup of wine in her hand, coming up to each pit, sitting down beside it, and repeating the words, "Be free from thy sickness" (Fred H. Wight 1953, 140). This smacks of magic rather than medicine.

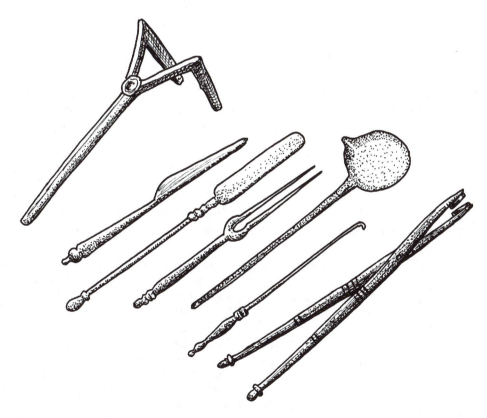

Surgery was practiced among Egyptians and other cultures in the ancient world, using tools like these that have been discovered by archaeologists: speculum, scalpels (2), retractor for removing arrowheads, spoon for warming salves, hook for excising tissue, and retractor.

Luke, the "beloved physician," used a large number of specific medical terms in his writing of his **Gospel** and in the Book of Acts. He is the one who quotes the famous "Physician, heal thyself" (Luke 4:23). The reference to "thrown him down" in Luke 4:35 is the term used for epileptic convulsions. "Idle tale" (Luke 24:11) is a medical term used to describe the babblings of an insane or feverish patient (D. H. Trapnell 1980, 616). Some believe that Luke's kind manner endeared him to Mary, encouraging her to share with him many of the stories of Jesus's birth and early childhood not recorded by the other Gospel writers. This suggests that the Jews, having lived with the Greeks and Romans, finally saw the role of the physician as respectable. *See also* Birth; Cures, Medicine; Disease.

Further Reading

Avalon, Hector Ignacio. "Medicine," in *The Oxford Companion to the Bible.* New York: Oxford University Press, 1993. Trapnell, D. H. "Health, Disease and Healing," in *The Illustrated Bible Dictionary.* Sydney, Australia: Tyndale House Publishers, 1980. Wight, Fred Hartley. *Manners and Customs of Bible Lands.* Chicago: Moody Press, 1953.

Plagues

(**Exod. 7–12**) When Moses confronted the pharaoh, telling him that God demanded that he let his people go, the monarch refused. Each time he refused, Moses warned him that a plague would follow and each time it did. Each time, the pharaoh repented, begging Moses to pray for relief, in return for which he would let the Israelites leave. Then, each time the pharaoh found the situation returning to normal, he "hardened his heart" and reversed his orders. This ritual, with variations, was repeated 10 times, resulting in 10 plagues, the last being the most fearful and the most successful. Several were connected with some aspect of Egyptian worship of a pantheon of gods:

1. The plague of **blood** in the Nile. Ha'pi was the Nile god of inundation. The Nile, with its periodic floods, was the source of fertility for Egyptian agriculture. The turning of the river into blood, perhaps through the death of fish, would have made the water unpalatable and bred the following plagues.
2. The plague of frogs. Hequit, a goddess of fruitfulness had the frog as her symbol. She was thought to assist women in childbirth. Excessive inundation, which makes the Nile red, brings down microcosms known as *flagellates,* creating conditions that cause a terrible stench and pollute the river shore where the frogs live, perhaps resulting in internal anthrax.
3. The plague of lice. This may actually refer to mosquitoes, which would have bred at a great rate with the high Nile.

4. The plague of flies. Like the lice, these insects, probably worshipped by the Egyptians, would also result from the high waters of the Nile.
5. Plague on the cattle. The Egyptians worshipped many animal gods, including the bull-gods Apis and Mnevis, and the cow-god Hathor, as well as the ram-god Khnum. The frogs probably carried their anthrax infection into the fields, causing peril to the Egyptian cattle, which would not be in their stalls, as were the Israelites' cattle.
6. The plague of boils. This attack on the humans probably came from the flies.
7. The plague of hail. This plague struck the crops, as did the following plague.
8. The plague of **locusts**. The previous plagues would make this the ideal situation for the attack of locusts.
9. The plague of darkness. This would have blotted out the light of the sun, which the Egyptians worshipped as the sun god Re.
10. The death of first-born sons of the **Egyptians**. The Lord passed over the homes of the Israelites, preserving their children, while destroying the Egyptian boys, commemorated in tradition as the **Passover** (K. A. Kitchen 1980, 1234–1237).

These 10 plagues are justified in Scripture by God's decision to show his power to the oppressors of his chosen people so that they should turn and worship him. He is in control of the waters of the Nile, insect and animal life, crops, and humans themselves, demonstrating by means of the plagues a far more comprehensive power than that of any of the multitude of Egyptian gods. (We know of the Egyptian worship of insects and animals, as well as human images and blends of human and animals, by their tomb paintings. The scarab, a beetle image, for example, has been discovered in numerous sites.)

The plagues have been explained by a number of critics as "natural scourges" in the region that God used and ordered in such a way as to effect his providential purposes. Observers note that they correspond to the annual events in Egypt: The Nile, after reaching its height in August, "often becomes dull red in color, due to large numbers of tiny organisms. Under certain conditions the water might easily become foul and undrinkable." This sometimes leads to plagues of frogs in September, which would be more frequent if it were not for the ibis, a **bird** that feeds on vermin. "The decomposition of dead frogs easily explains the third and fourth plagues, those of lice and flies; and such conditions would certainly bring pestilence to cattle and men (fifth and sixth plagues)." As for the hail storms, though they are rare, they do sometimes occur. Locusts have caused damage of plague proportions in the Near East on many occasions and continue to do so to this day. "The thick darkness (ninth plague) can be explain as a terrible sand and dust storm, brought in by the *Khamsin,* the hot desert wind which is one of the most disagreeable features of the Egyptian spring. The *Khamsin* blows for two to four days at a time, while the 'thick darkness' is said to have lasted for three days" (George E. Wright 1957, 54).

Many of these plagues continue in Egypt into modern times. Werner Keller notes that, "Deposits from the Abyssinian lakes often colour the flood waters a dark reddish-brown, especially in the Upper Nile" so that it might look like blood. "Under the heading of 'lice' would come undoubtedly the dog-fly. These often attack whole areas in swarms, affect eyes, nose and ears, and can be very painful." Keller also notes, "Cattle pest is known all over the world. The 'boils' which attack human beings as well as animals may be the so-called 'Nile-heat' or 'Nile-itch'. This is an irritating and stinging rash which often develops into spreading ulcers." The hail storms give the sun a "dull yellowish appearance and turn daylight into darkness" (Werner Keller 1982, 116–117).

Other than these famous plagues, the Israelites most certainly had experiences with the plagues that struck the ancient world. In fact, some of them continue into the present. For example, the sickness that decimated the invading armies of Sennacherib may well have been a plague spread by rats. Because the writers of Scripture usually saw plagues as a punishment sent by God, they did not identify outbreaks of disease by their symptoms so that modern doctors can diagnose them. Instead, they presented them as evidence of God's providence, his miraculous intervention in the lives of his people. *See also* Animals; Disease; Egypt, Egyptians; Insects; Locusts.

Further Reading

Keller, Werner. *The Bible as History.* New York: Bantam Books, 1982. Kitchen, K. A. "Plagues of Egypt," in *The Illustrated Bible Dictionary,* 3 volumes. Sydney, Australia: Tyndale House Publishers, 1980. Wright, G. Ernest, *Biblical Archaeology.* Philadelphia: The Westminster Press, 1957.

Plants

What is a "mustard seed?" And how big does it grow? Why were "tares" such a problem? What kind of "reeds" did Moses's mother use to make a basket for her son? What is a "juniper"? What kind of vine shaded Jonah—and then suddenly wilted? These and many other questions about plants spring from the reading of Scripture, and scholars have provided little more than guesses.

Time, nomenclature, and changes in vegetation patterns in the Holy Land have clouded the details of most biblical botanical references. **Trees** and crops, such as the **grains, olives,** and grapes, were so valuable that their specific seed time and harvest dominated the calendar. But wild plants, flowers, and weeds had no such claim to the attention of the ancient scribes. Living in a period before botany was a science, they used general terms that often covered a number of types of vegetation. Translators have clouded the picture even more with their guesses and efforts to equate ancient plants with familiar modern ones. Many of the plants mentioned in Scripture may, in fact, have disappeared from Palestine. Some have been replaced by new varieties unknown to the ancients.

The greatest list of plants in the Bible is in the Song of Solomon, which has 74 references to plants, most of them a mystery to the moderns. In the poet's zeal to describe his bride, he says, "A garden enclosed is my sister, my spouse" (Song of Sol. 4:12). After this lovely image, he goes on to describe her plants as "an orchard of pomegranates, with pleasant fruits; camphire, with spikenard," and from there completes a listing of spices, trees, and flowers. He compares her belly to a heap of wheat "set about with lilies" and ends by calling her a vineyard full of fruit. This brief marriage song has a host of lavish (and sometimes unlikely) images.

The following listing, drawn from various portions of Scripture, partially describes the scholarly identification of plants (other than those covered in individual sections of this study).

Broom, Shrub

(1 Kings 19:4–5; Ps. 120:4; Job 30:4; Jer. 17:6) Broom, which is also referred to in the King James Version of the Bible as *juniper,* was a common shrub in Palestine. It grew two to four feet high and had small white flowers in the spring. Elijah sat under a broom bush, a reference that T. S. Eliot used in his poetry. It was thought to have been used for making charcoal and for incendiary arrows.

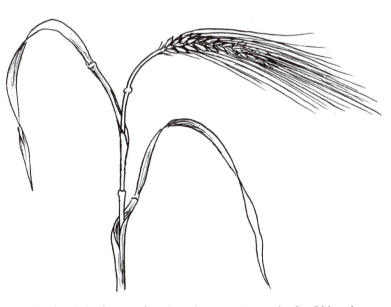

Barley (*Hordeum vulgare*), an important crop in the Old and New Testaments, noted as early as Ruth.

489

Some believe that the reference to broom in Job may be to an edible parasitic plant that grows on the roots of broom.

In Jeremiah, the translation is shrub in the King James Version, apparently referring to the Phoenician juniper or even the tamarisk.

Castor-Oil, Vine of Sodom

(Deut. 32:32; Jonah 4:6; Isa. 1:8) This rapidly growing shrub may have been the one that provided shade to Jonah. It is also called the gourd-vine and is used by Zora Neale Hurston in her novel *Jonah's Gourd Vine*, a story of African American life in rural Florida. This plant was known to wither rapidly, as did Jonah's shade-provider, but it is not a vine. It is instead a small tree. Some believe that Jonah's shade came from the bottle-gourd, which was used to provide shelter for the "watchers over cucumbers," mentioned in Isa. 1:8. It also withers quickly.

In the Song of Moses, the reference to a wild gourd or colocynth may be purely figurative, "describing the bitterness of Israel's enemies" (F. N. Hepper 1980, 1243). The plant conceals a powdery substance under an attractive rind. The New English Bible describes them this way:

> Their vines are vines of Sodom,
> grown on the terraces of Gomorrah;
> Their grapes are poisonous,
> the clusters bitter to the taste.
> Their wine is the venom of **serpents**,
> the cruel poison of asps (Deut. 32:32).

The additional reference to *asps* suggests that this is an Egyptian gourd, perhaps symbolizing the judgment brought on God's people because of their infidelity to their Rock.

Crocus

(Isa. 35:1) This "bulb" or "corm" may have referred to a rose, an asphodel, or a polyanthus narcissus. Crocus may actually be the name used for the "rose of Sharon." It does not seem to be the crocus that moderns know, a lovely bloom (usually white, yellow, or lavender) that appears early in the springtime.

Hyssop

(Exod. 12:22; Lev. 14:4, 6; 14:49–52; Num. 19:2–6; Heb. 9:19; Ps. 51:7) The general name *hyssop* may actually refer to several different plants in Scripture. In the Old Testament, a Syrian marjoram, a fragrant perennial herb, with gray leaves and wiry stems, was used for purifying lepers and those stricken with the plague. It was also used in the Passover rites for the sprinkling of blood of sacrificed animals on lintels and doorposts (Exod. 12:22). It was additionally part of the "red heifer sacrifice" (Num. 19:2–67). This plant grows in dry, rocky places and produces tiny white flowers. Some believe it may have been the reedlike 5-foot tall sorghum (Madeleine S. Miller 1961, 275).

The reference in 1 Kings 4:33 seems to be to the caper, a prickly woody flower that was often seen in the walls of old buildings. It also had white flowers, but they were large.

The New Testament references involve the Crucifixion. John 19:29 mentions that hyssop was lifted up to Christ on a javelin (perhaps a reed or stick). Hepper believes that this may have been "the reed-like cereal durra (*Sorghum vulgare*)" (F. N. Hepper 1980, 1238).

Lily

(Hos. 14:5; 1 Kings 7:19, 22, 26; 2 Chron. 4:5; Matt. 6:28; Luke 12:27) The term *lily* may have referred to a number of flowers that come from a bulb and have a distinctive flower. Candidates include the hyacinth, scarlet tulip, red poppy anemone, white madonna lily, yellow flag, water lily, white daisy, crown marguerite, and lotus. When the rains finally come to the dry land in Palestine, many wild flowers blossom briefly. Jesus's reference to the "lilies of the field" with all their beauty may easily refer to any of these.

The Old Testament has more specific mentions of "lily-work" on the columns and the "molten sea" of King Solomon's **Temple** (1 Kings 7:19, 22, 26). These probably reveal his debt to foreign architecture. In Egyptian art, the water lily or lotus often formed a prominent portion of design. It was widely used in ancient Near Eastern art and probably influenced the Ionic column style in Greece. In Egypt, the lotus was abundant in the Nile fields, making it a natural symbol of the United

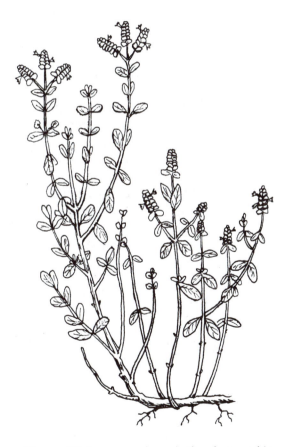

Hyssop (*Origanum syriacum*), the plant used in worship services and also famously at the Crucifixion.

491

Lotus, a water plant common in Egypt, used extensively as a design in Egyptian art.

Kingdom. Later, it was used on the coinage of the Maccabees, and a form of the lily—the *fleur-de-lis*—became the emblem chosen by King Clovis for the French royalty.

Because the lily of the valley is one of the first flowers of the year, announcing the return of spring, it became a symbol for the Advent of Christ. The whiteness of its flowers and the sweetness of its scent made it a perfect symbol of the Virgin Mary and the Immaculate Conception, often with references to the Song of Solomon 2:1: "I am the rose of Sharon, and the lily of the valleys" (George Ferguson 1966, 34).

Mallow

(Job 30:4) The term *mallow* means "saltiness," perhaps because of its taste or its native habitat. Hepper notes that this "shrubby orache" comes from the salty places by the Dead Sea or Mediterranean, and may be used like spinach. It is a weed commonly found in wastelands.

Mandrake

(Gen. 30:14) John Donne referred to the mythic powers of this herb, saying to his beloved, "Get with child a mandrake root." The mandrake plant is a perennial, a member of the nightshade family. A rosette with large leaves and mauve flowers, it produces round yellow fruits in the spring. Rachel and Leah (and King Solomon) thought it would help their love life, as it was noted for its aphrodisiac properties, as well as its emetic, purgative, and narcotic qualities. The tap roots are forked in such a way as to resemble a man's torso, perhaps the reason for Donne's little joke.

Mildew

(Deut. 28:22; Amos 4:9; Hag. 2:17; 1 Kings 8:37; 2 Chron. 6:28) Moist weather can attack crops, inviting the growth of this common species of fungus, whose name means "paleness," or "greenness." The Israelites thought of it as God's punishment. The opposite condition was the blasting hot wind that scorched the crops. Modern farmers face much the same conditions. King Solomon prayed for deliverance from mildew.

Mustard

(Matt. 13:31, 17:20; Mark 4:31; Luke 13:19, 17:6) A frequently quoted saying of

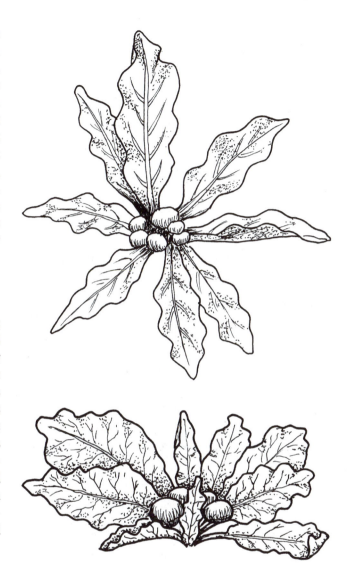

Mandrake (*Mandragora officinarum*) was considered an aphrodisiac; its roots were thought to be shaped like a human body.

Jesus was, "If ye have faith as a grain of mustard seed, ye shall say unto this mountain, Remove hence to yonder place, and it shall remove; and nothing shall be impossible unto you." He spoke of the Kingdom of Heaven as a mustard seed that grew from a tiny seed to an enormous tree. No one is quite sure what plant is the object of his references, but speculations have settled on black mustard, the seeds of which were cultivated for their oil, as well as for cooking. It can grow as high as five meters, so that birds can perch on it. "Mustard grows wild along the Plain of Gennesaret, where Jesus taught the multitudes" (Madeleine S. Miller 1961, 470).

Myrtle

(Lev. 23:40; Deut. 16:16; Isa. 41:19, 55:13; Zac. 1:8–11; Neh. 8:15) The myrtle is a fragrant evergreen shrub that grows two to three meters high, and has edible berries and white flowers, which are used as perfumes. In Scripture, myrtle symbolized divine generosity: Isaiah saw it replacing the brier in the wilderness. The shelters at the Feast of Booths or the Feast of Tabernacles were constructed of myrtle. In fact the name *Hadassah*, or *Esther,* derived from the Hebrew word for *myrtle.*

The plant became a symbol of love in the Greco-Roman world, where it was sacred to Venus. Because of the vision of Zechariah 1:8: "I saw by night, and behold a man riding upon a red horse, and he stood among the myrtle trees that were in the bottom; and behind him there were **horses**, red, speckled, and white," the Christians believed that the myrtle was an allusion to the Gentiles who were converted by Christ, the rider of the red horse (George Ferguson 1966, 34).

Christ thorn (*Paliurus spina-christi*) named for the crown of thorns that may have been the one was thrust upon Christ's head before the Crucifixion (John 19:2).

Nettles, Thistles, Thorns

(Gen. 3:18; Num. 33:55; Joshua 23:13; Ezek. 2:6; Isa. 34:13; Hosea 9:6; Prov. 24:31; Job 30:7) Shakespeare uses the term *nettle* to refer to a prickly plant. The word itself seems to derive from "to be sharp" or "to sting." It may refer to wild brushwood, wild vetches, or thistles. Botanists speculate that these terms are used for any number of thorns, briers, bramble, and other weeds that are thorny and without fruit or beauty. They may have been acacia, boxthorn, or spiny burnet, among other types.

They occur frequently in Scripture, most significantly in the crown of thorns placed on Jesus's head at the Crucifixion in mockery of his "kingdom" (Matt. 27:29; Mark 15:17; John 19:5). In the Old Testament, thorns in the wilderness were often used as makeshift fences to protect the **sheep** from wild animals. They made excellent hedges and were also good fuel for fires because they were dry and quick-burning.

In much of Scripture, thorny shrubs are used as images of divine judgment and fruitlessness. In much of later iconography, the thistle or the thorn is the symbol of earthly sorrow (based on the pronouncement against Adam in Gen. 3:17–18). Because of the crown of thorns worn by Christ, later saints, such as St. Catherine of Siena, are also pictured with such a crown to signify their identification with Christ's suffering.

Milk thistle flower (*Silybum marianum*), a common weed that was thought to have medicinal powers.

Pods

(Luke 15:16) When the Prodigal Son found himself eating pods along with the swine, he knew he had hit bottom and swore to return to his father. The **parable** Jesus told refers to the seedpods of the carob tree, which was common in the Mediterranean region. It is also called the "locust bean." Some think this may have been the food John the Baptist ate, but others believe he ate the insects instead (F. N. Hepper 1980, 1239).

Reeds and Rush

(Gen. 41:2, 18; Exod. 2:3, 5; Isa. 19:6, 42:3; 1 Kings 14:15; Ezek. 40:3–8, 41:8, 42:16–19; Matt. 11:7–8, 12:20; Luke 7:24; Rev. 11:1, 21:15–16) This general word for water-growing plants describes a number of species found in swamps and by riverbank. The cattail or reed-mace was common around the Nile; the Red Sea was called "the sea of Reeds." It appears in Scripture as a measuring rod (in Ezekiel and Revelation) and as a symbol of weakness, such as a "bruised reed." A form of reed was also cut and shaped to serve as a primitive flute among **shepherds**.

Rush was a term used to other water-loving plants with more fiber, such as sedges and papyrus. They were useful for weaving into rope or as fuel. The papyrus was especially important in the development of **writing materials**. It could be dried, sliced into strips, and pasted together so as to form scrolls.

Boxthorn (*Lycium europaeum*), another common thorny plant that was used for hedges and fuel.

Wheat and tares, or bearded darnel grass, contrasted. They grew up together and looked much alike, but the differences between the plants showed most clearly when they were mature. Tares, which were poisonous, had yellow grain at maturity and were pulled out of the crop one-by-one by women and children.

Rose

(Song of Sol. 2:1, 4:13; Isa. 35:1) Although roses are grown in Syria today in vast numbers, cultivated for perfume and flavoring extract, the rose was probably not the flower cited in Scripture. Most scholars agree that there were very few true roses in Palestine in biblical times, largely wild roses, with a few cultivated varieties that may have been introduced from Persia. Roses now bloom "along garden pools or in broken jars on peasant roofs," but the biblical rose of Sharon was probably a form of narcissus. (The plant now known by this name is native to China.) Miller notes that the flower cited in Isaiah 35:1, "the desert shall blossom as the rose," was "the true rose of the genus *Rosa*" (Madeleine S. Miller 1961, 629).

The rose image appears on ancient coins, like those of Rhodes, and on crosses and other forms of art. Ferguson notes that, "Traditionally, among the ancient Romans, the rose was the symbol of victory, pride, and triumphant love. It was the flower of Venus, goddess of love." Among Christians, the red rose became a symbol of martyrdom, "while the white rose is a symbol of purity. . . . St. Ambrose relates how the rose came to have thorns: Before it became one of the flowers of the earth, the rose grew in Paradise without thorns. Only after the fall of man did the rose take on its thorns to remind man of the sins he had committed and his fall from grace; whereas its fragrance and beauty continued to remind him of the splendor of Paradise" (George Ferguson 1966, 37). It also became the image for the Virgin Mary, who was referred to as "a rose without thorns," largely because of the tradition that she was without original sin. Thus the garlands of roses in Renaissance art are allusions to Mary, and wreaths of roses that adorn angels, saints, or human souls just entered into heavenly bliss indicate heavenly joy. Eventually, it also became the sign of papal benediction.

In medieval cathedrals, the great rose window, traditionally on the east side of the building, is a beautiful tribute in stained glass to the Virgin. In the *Divine Comedy*, Dante approached the presence of God in the *Paradiso*, discovering that the saints were like so many bees flitting in and out of the petals of a great heavenly rose, which was in the presence of God himself.

Weeds, Tumbleweed, Tares

(2 Kings 4:39; Job 31:38–40; Matt. 13:25) In the midst of the grain that the Israelites had planted, they often discovered tares, a weed that bore a resemblance to the grain in its early development. Hepper identifies it as darnel grass: "In the leafy stage this grass resembles wheat, but if the biblical counsel be followed and both are allowed to grow together till harvest (Mt. 13:30) the small ear is clearly distinguished, and usually to women and children falls the tedious manual task of separation. If the wheat grain is contaminated with the bitter darnel grains subsequent poisoning causes illness and vomiting" (F. N. Hepper 1980, 1243). This was sometimes used as a means to revenge a wrong: deliberately planting tares among the grain. This makes clear Jesus's parable about the tares in the midst of the good grain and the need to root it out before it chokes out the good food.

Job's reference to weeds (31:38–40) is thought to be a prickly weed such as the oyster thistle and rest-harrow. Another reference is to "wild gourds" in 2 Kings 4:39, thought to be colocynth, a vine that produces small melons that are dangerous to eat. They grow in sandy spots near the Dead Sea.

Tumbleweed is a form of weed that rolls in the wind, distributing the seeds in open, dry countryside. We see this in the desert regions in the western part of America, where grasses can form rolling balls blown to and fro.

Wormwood (*Artemisia herba-alba*) was famous for its bitter taste.

Wormwood

(Deut. 29:18; Prov. 5:4; Lam. 3:15, 19; Amos 5:7, 6:12; Jer. 9:15, 23:15) *Wormwood,* sometimes translated as "hemlock," is the classic symbol of bitterness. Both Moses and Jeremiah used it to point out the perils of idolatry, and Jeremiah spoke of it as the punishment awaiting the disobedient people of God. It is the ideal image for **lamentations**, as the plants all have a strong bitter taste, a physical manifestation of spiritual sorrow. *See also* Agriculture; Food; Olives, Olive Oil, Olive Trees; Trees; Vineyards.

Further Reading

Ferguson, George. *Signs and Symbols in Christian Art.* New York: Oxford University Press, 1966. Hepper, F. N. "Plants," in *The Illustrated Bible Dictionary.* Sydney, Australia: Tyndale House Publishers, 1980. Hirsch, Emil G. and Immanuel Low. "Plants," http://www.jewishencyclopedia.com (accessed

August 10, 2005). Miller, Madeleine S. and J. Lane Miller *Harper's Bible Dictionary.* New York: Harper and Row, 1961.

Plow

(Isa. 2:4; Mic. 4:3) "They will beat their swords into plowshares and their spears into pruning hooks," according to the **prophet**s Isaiah and Micah (Isa. 2:4; Mic. 4:3). Apparently this was a common practice in ancient Israel, the transforming of instruments of war into instruments of **agriculture** and, when forced, turning the plowshares back into spears (Joel 3:10). This handful of tools were the only **metal** objects in most households. The **Philistines** held a monopoly over their manufacture, forcing the Israelites to make every possible use out of these valuable bits of iron.

The primitive plow in Palestine was often little more than a forked tree bough to which a plowshare, a piece of sharp metal, was attached by a peg or a nail. It was usually bound to a second piece of wood that could be tied onto the **yoke** of the **oxen** or **donkeys**. The plowshares and **goads**, which the farmers bought in town markets, were shaped like arrows or spears and had to be sharpened regularly.

These plows did not turn the soil over; they merely scratched it. This plowing process might be either before or after the seed was scattered, but usually followed the broadcasting of the seed. Isaiah does mention "harrowing" the ground and Hosea refers to breaking the ground after it is plowed

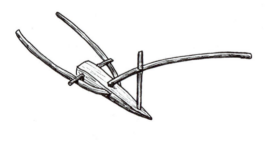

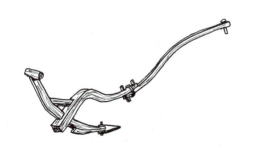

A two-handed plow used in Mesopotamia ca. 2000 B.C., a one-handed plow.

(Isa. 28:24; Hos.10:11), suggesting that the double process was usually seen as essential. Although the plow was light enough for the plowman to carry it on his shoulder, the digging into the hard soil required steady effort, often involving teams of yoked animals and plowmen following one after another.

It was important to focus on maintaining the momentum, goading the **animals** forward, watching for rocks, and keeping the furrow straight. Jesus admonished his followers that they should remember the lessons of the good worker, "No one who puts his hand to the plow and looks back is fit for service in the kingdom of God" (Luke 9:62). Amos also used the careful ordering of the process of plowing for his prophesy of chaos: "The days are coming . . . when the reaper will be overtaken by the plowman and the planter by one treading grapes" (Amos 9:13). The writer of **Proverbs** also reminds us of the proper order of things: "A sluggard does not plow in season; so at harvest time he looks but finds nothing" (Prov. 20:4).

Although the work of plowing the fields was often done by hired workers or sons of foreigners, not members of the family, every Israelite apparently knew how important it was to use the right animals, the right tools, and the right attitude to accomplish this essential work. *See also* Agriculture; Animals; Donkey, Ass; Grain; Metal: Iron; Philistines.

Pots and Pottery

Pots were everywhere in ancient Israel's life. From Neolithic times, some primitive forms of baked clay were available for use as dishes for eating and serving, pots for cooking, and urns for storage. The ancient folk also used the baked clay for small figures of gods and children's toys. The discovery that clay, when baked at an intense heat, could hold water and withstand continued handling must have been a major step forward in human civilization. The invention of the **potter's wheel** in the fourth millennium B.C. added to the attractiveness and utility of pots. They became more symmetrical and varied in their design, with thinner and higher walls, making them lighter and more elegant.

Ancient tells (flat-topped hills containing ruins of cities) usually contain large quantities of broken pottery, which helps archaeologists to differentiate cultures, to identify interaction of various peoples, and to speculate on habits of the folk who lived in these locations. The types and colors of the clay used, and the sequence of forms and of decoration can help date sites, establish trade routes, and reveal cultural boundaries (A. R. Millard 1982, 1249–50).

Before they had ceramic pots, the nomadic Hebrews used skins for water and wine, baskets made of reeds for holding dry produce, and **metal** vessels for cooking. Because pottery was fragile, it was not a convenient implement to carry on their frequent treks from site to site; the little they had was bought from other people. It was only when they settled that they developed the skill of pottery-making (Madeleine S. Miller and J. Lane Miller 1961, 569).

The earliest pots resembled baskets. They were coarse, heavy, formed by hand, and had rims and handles. Some were cups and some big, barrel-like vessels. These early designs were frequently imitations of wineskins in shape and were probably used for storage, carrying liquids, drinking, and serving food, as well as cooking it. Pottery might have painted or incised decorations and some burnishing so that they looked like **leather**.

The early Bronze Age produced globular jars with crisscross lines of reddish paint, some gray-burnished vessels that looked like stone, some single-handled pitchers, and red- and black-burnished dishes. The middle Bronze Age produced jars with short, narrow necks and broad flat bases, spouted pots, and

Samples of pottery in ancient Palestine: a pitcher with a handle for pouring liquids, a bowl that might be used for mixing wine with water, smaller serving bowls for bread, meat, or fruit; and a large urn that might be used for storing water. The graceful design and curvilinear pattern on the pitcher would mark it as more common among the Philistines than the Israelites, who used plain pottery.

very fine pottery, now made on the potter's wheel. **Lamps**, juglets, and jars and pitchers with small round or pointed bases were more common, as were metal or **stone** vessels. These would have been the pots made and taken from **Egypt**, where they were used for religious purposes, explaining the Israelites' preference for bronze ware in the **Tabernacle**.

The later stages of Israel's pottery reveal the influence of other cultures, especially the Myceneans, with their red and black geometric designs. The **Philistines** used large two-handled bowls and jugs of cream ware. The Israelite pottery tended to be much more primitive in design and decoration, allowing scholars to spot where there was interaction between the cultures and where only Israelites were settled.

During the period of the monarchy, when the Hebrews traveled more widely and imported more goods, the pottery improved conspicuously. During this period, very thin pottery was often decorated with bands of red slip, and large storage jars were often stamped on the handles with a royal seal (A. R. Millard 1980, 1252). More Persian and Hellenistic pottery is seen during this period including the amphora, with the black-and red-figured wares; narrow, elongated flasks; floral designs; and beautiful glazes.

More expensive pots, especially those designed for the Tabernacle and **Temple**, were made of bronze. The priests roasted the holy offerings, in "cauldrons and pans and served them quickly to all the people" (2 Chron. 35:13). These bronze utensils included "pots to remove the ashes, and . . . shovels, sprinkling bowls, meat forks and firepans" (Exod. 27:3). Metal was so precious and so rare among the early Israelites that these were clearly exceptional vessels, of great value. Ezekiel spoke of putting the empty pot on the coals "till it becomes hot and its copper glows so its impurities may be melted and its deposit burned away" (Ezek. 24:11). These were among the Temple objects that Hiram made for King Solomon (1 Kings 7:45; 2 Chron. 4:11). Jeremiah also mentions in his description of the looting of the Temple taking away pots, sprinkling bowls, dishes, and all of the bronze articles (Jer. 52:18). The repeated references suggest their great value and the pride with which the Israelites viewed them.

Items that figured most prominently in Hebrew life and imagery were the large cooking pot, water jar, large storage jars for **grain** and smaller ones for oil or ointments, washbasin (which was used in **foot-washing**), flasks , and cups. Archaeologists have also found that **lamps** were made of clay, as were children's toys and cheap **jewelry;** businessmen used jars for safe-keeping of contracts; miniature jugs were used for perfume, ointment, and oils.

For common folk, the cooking pot in which their dinner was boiled was made of baked clay. They bought it from the **potter**, and if it was soiled or marred, it could be smashed and replaced. Jeremiah spoke of the "despised, broken pot, an object no one wants" as being like God's despised people, to be hurled out, cast into a land they do not know" (Jer. 22:28). The law notes that a pot in which meat has been cooked was considered unclean and must be broken (Lev. 6:28). On the other hand, if it was made of metal, it may be scoured and rinsed with water.

Even the shards of the broken vessel then found use—as handy scoops for carrying live coals, as scrapers (Job 2:8), or surfaces for writing. These potsherds have survived over the centuries, providing archaeologists with a continuing record of the people who lived in the Promised Land. *See also* Metal: Iron; Olives, Olive Oil, Olive Trees; Potters and Pottery-Making; Potter's Wheel; Washing of Feet.

A water-pot, on display at the Archaeological Museum in Jerusalem, has a round base and therefore is on a stand that allows the server to tilt the pot to pour its contents into a pitcher.

Further Reading

Millard, A. R. "Potter, Pottery," in *The Illustrated Bible Dictionary*. Sydney, Australia: Tyndale House Publishers, 1980. Miller, Madeleine S. and J. Lane Miller. "Pottery," in *Harper's Bible Dictionary*. New York: Harper and Row, 1961.

Potters and Pottery-Making

(1 Chron. 4:23; Isa. 41:25, 64:8; Jer.18:4; Rom. 9:21) Even before recorded history, potters all over the world shaped their wares much as they do today. Using special clay, these potters (usually men) found they could form receptacles of use in the household. When the clay hardened in the sun, it held its shape. Later, they found that they could bake it so that it could be used to hold liquids, and even glaze it to make it more attractive. Because clay was free and the process was simple, they used pottery for everything from **lamps** to storage vessels.

No complete potter's studio from biblical times has been excavated in **Israel**, although a Palestinian ceramic workshop has been found at Lachish that dates back to 1500 B.C. "It contains a stone seat near a limestone pivot on which a simple potter's wheel once turned. Near it were potsherds [scraps of broken pottery] worn smooth from having been used to shape revolving masses of wet clay, pebbles probably used to burnish vessels, and a sharp piece of stone for incising designs on the pots" (Madeleine S. Miller and J. Lane Miller 1961, 569).

The skill of pottery-making often was passed down from father to son within families, and the children were probably apprenticed in the shop. This family industry was probably located near good clay pits and convenient to villages, although some potters were in the **king**'s hire and probably carried their pots to the royal residence. Some believe that there were ceramic quarters in Jerusalem. Jeremiah speaks of visiting a potter, as does the Chronicler mention the neighborhood: "These were the potters . . . there they dwelt with the king for his work" (1 Chron. 4:23).

Potters found their clay in various locations around the countryside—clay pits, some of which are still prized today. The quality of the clay was important to the production of their work. It had varying chemical composition: sand, gravel, sometimes foreign animal, or vegetable matter. It had to be properly weathered (a process of spreading it out on the hillside to dry) and then cleaned. It was washed and purified in a series of vats on descending levels, with the finest of the clay strained through a cloth. The colors varied, from white to gray, red, or yellow. Next, water was added to the product, and the men would "tread it" (Isa. 41:25) until it was malleable. The next stage was to cover it and store it, taking out smaller lumps for use. These would be worked further, usually on a clean, flat surface by throwing and kneading them until all the air bubbles were gone and they were pliable while still able to hold a shape. Sometimes other elements, such as straw or broken bits of pottery, were added to give the clay greater strength.

The actual shaping of the bowl was determined partially by custom, usage, and the equipment available to the potter. If he had only his hands to work with, he would press the lump onto a flat surface and make an opening at the top, gradually working this larger with his hands and building up the sides. When he had reached the proper size and shape, he would finish off the edges, using water to smooth the clay, and let it dry before he cut it off the surface on which he had formed the vessel.

One early technique was to roll the clay into long coils, which the potter would place on top of a round surface, building a larger, higher bowl or pot, pressing the coil flat with his wet fingers. Using water, he would gradually smooth the coils into a shape that hid the transitions from base to sides and from coil to coil. The top coil would often be shaped into a lip for the vessel, making the pot easier to lift. These primitive vessels might be decorated by a red slip coating, a surface of a different colored clay, made liquid by mixing it with water. These red-slipped ware were often burnished—rubbed with a hard tool before baking (Avraham Faust 2004, 53).

A Philistine vessel from Beth-shemesh, with an elaborate decoration, a spout, and a lid that is far more sophisticated than most Israelite ware.

Another technique was to use another bowl that had the desired shape, turned upside down. He would press wet clay on this mold to form a shape that he could leave to dry before he removed it. For small items, such as drinking cups, liquid clay could be poured into a mold and allowed to dry slightly, and then the excess poured out, leaving a thin layer of clay and forming a more delicate vessel.

If the potter had a wheel, either one managed by hand or one turned by foot, he had to center the lump of clay, turning the wheel and the clay until it was firmly fixed in the middle of the wheel so that it would not wobble when he worked it. He would then build it up to the shape he desired, turning and working it with his hands or using various instruments he would hold against the rising sides of the clay. By keeping his hands wet and responding to the strength and shape of the clay, he might bring the pot to a great size and relatively thin walls. An experienced potter might use a large lump of clay, forming a hollow cone, from which he might cut off a series of smaller vessels, one after another, from the top of the half-shaped vessel, planning to finish each at a later point.

When the pot had arrived at the desired shape, and the potter had fixed the handles or lips and perhaps added a simple design using a piece of string or a comb to give it some markings, he would cut it from the wheel, using a string held tautly between his hands. He would then let the newly formed pot rest and dry in the sun until it began to harden to a leather-like constituency. When it was partially toughened, he might burnish it to give it a gloss or paint it with slip (liquid clay), or incise designs on it. Some potters painted the outside with a liquid clay of a different color, allowed it to dry, and then cut designs to reveal the underlying surface.

The final task was baking the pot in a kiln, a tall oven, sometimes a pit that had shelves in it and could be brought to an intense temperature. An extended period of baking and an equally long, slow cooling followed. The pots were

Egyptian pottery kiln, apparently made of brick, with numerous clay vessels being submitted to intense heat to produce pottery.

then removed from the kiln. The more primitive ones were ready for use; the more sophisticated ones were glazed and rebaked. Glazes that turned to a glasslike finish under heat were a late development in pottery-making, at least for the Hebrews. The **Egyptians** had discovered glazes quite early, using mixes of soda, lead, silver, copper, or tin, and developing splendid colors—green, turquoise, purple, and blue (Madeleine S. Miller and J. Lane Miller 1961, 571). For the most part, however, the Palestinian potters did not glaze, preferring burnishing or rubbing to finish the product.

Among the products of the potter were clay rattles and toys, small figurines, candlesticks, jewelry, buttons, and spindle whorls, all of which were discovered in archaeological digs at Jericho (Madeleine S. Miller and J. Lane Miller 1961, 571). Ceramic tiles were used for decorative purposes, especially by the **Greeks** and **Romans**. Development of this skill was considerably more advanced among the people at Corinth, for example, than among the Jews. Paul may have worked near such a shop with Priscilla and Aquila when he shared their tent-making tasks.

The work of potters was so intimately understood by the Israelites that the **prophets** were able to use the image of the potter and his clay as God forming man. "Yet, O Lord, you are our Father. We are the clay, you are the potter; we are all the work of your hand" (Isa. 64:8). Man, formed out of the dirt, shaped by the hand of God, conforms beautifully with the image of creation in Genesis 2:7. Thus, the will of the potter determines the shape of the pot, the manipulation of the clay. "But the pot he was shaping from the clay was marred in his hands; so the potter formed it into another pot, shaping it as seemed best to him" (Jer. 18:4). Paul also uses the image of God as the potter: "Does not the potter have the right to make out of the same lump of clay some pottery for noble purposes and some for common use?" (Rom. 9:21)

The potter, who also made burial urns, became the image of death as well. The "Potter's Field" was a term used for graveyards where tombs for wealthy people were constructed by potters, although in Jerusalem, where Judas was buried, the field also appears to have been used primarily for the poor and the strangers (Matt. 27:7). *See also* Pots and Pottery; Potter's Wheel.

Further Reading

Faust, Avraham. "Pottery Talks," in *Biblical Archaeology Review*, March/April 2004, 53. Millard, A. R. "Potter, Pottery," in *The Illustrated Bible Dictionary*. Sydney, Australia: Tyndale House Publishers, 1980. Miller, Madeleine S. and J. Lane Miller. "Pottery," in *Harper's Bible Dictionary*. New York: Harper and Row, 1961.

Potter's Wheel

Potter's wheel driven by foot power, allowing the potter to use both hands to shape the vessel.

The potter's wheel was often a pair of **stones**, one of which fit on top of the other and rotated. The most convenient form involved a foot rest that moved the top so that both hands could be used for shaping of the clay on the flat surface. The simpler and older wheel, which was designed to turn counter-clockwise by the potter's hand, might also be turned by an apprentice, leaving both hands of the potter to work the clay.

Real freedom of movement came with the double-wheeled **pottery** wheel, allowing the **potter** to use both hands and not requiring the help of a turner. This became the standard for pottery making. A good description of the process appears in the apocryphal Book of Ecclesiasticus 38:29–30: "So it is the potter sitting at his work, and turning the wheel with his feet, he is always deeply concerned over his products, and he produces them in quantity. He molds the clay with his arm and makes it pliable with his feet; he sets his heart to finish the glazing, and he takes care in firing the kiln" (*Harper Collins Study Bible* 1989, 1592). Even today, the potter works with two wooden discs with an axle or spindle, which runs from the bottom of the top wheel through the center of another, somewhat larger, wheel below. When the potter moves the lower disc with his or her foot, the upper disc spins around, allowing the potter to control the speed of the action with his or her foot.

As the wheel spins, the potter centers and shapes the lump of clay, always keeping the hands moving gently along the inside and outside of the clay vessel, sprinkling the clay with water while proceeding (Fred H. Wight, *Manners and Customs of Bible Lands,* 205). The potter uses a small piece of wood with one hand to smooth the outside of the vessel when he or she is ready to finish the vessel and continues spinning the wheel even as he or she incises decorations with a shard or piece of flint.

After the vessel was shaped and cut from the wheel, it was sun-dried until it had a leather-like texture. Then it was returned to the wheel for further reinforcement, decoration, and shaping. For much of this, a cutting tool was used—sometimes a piece of broken pottery, sometimes a bit of metal or stone. *See also* Pots and Pottery; Potters and Pottery-Making.

Further Reading

Meeks, Wayne A., ed. *HarperCollins Study Bible.* New York: HarperCollins Publishers, Inc., 1989. Wight, Fred Hartley. *Manners and Customs of Bible Lands.* Chicago: Moody Press, 1953.

Prayer

(1 Sam 1:10, 2:1–10; 2 Kings 19:15–19; Neh. 1:4–11; Matt. 6:9–13, 15:36, 26:39; Luke 11:2–4; Acts 27:37) Deliberate efforts of humans to communicate with God are virtually universal. These prayers may take many forms from simple communion (as when Adam and God walked and talked together in the **Garden of Eden**) to "wrestling" with God (as Jacob did in his dream-filled night). David wrote many of the **Psalms** as prayers of thanksgiving to God and praise of his glory and creativity; others are pleas for forgiveness or help. Solomon prayed for wisdom (1 Kings 3:4–15); numerous others used prayer for thanksgiving, vows, petitions, **blessing**s, etc. Some 85 prayers have been identified in the Old Testament alone—and many others in the New Testament (E.L.S. Thompson 1980, 1257).

Most of the early prayers were voluntary and spontaneous, even silent. "The building of the **Temple** naturally invited public prayer. Indeed, the prayer ascribed to Solomon at its dedication (1 Kings 8:12–53) includes every form of prayer—adoration, thanksgiving, petition, and confession" (Cyrus Adler and M. H. Harris 2005). The first "ritual" prayer of the Jews occurs in Deuteronomy (26:5–10, 13–15), connected with the bringing of first fruits and tithes. Aaron used prayer in connection with the atonement-sacrifice, when the **priest** laid his hands on the head of the **goat** and confessed over it "all the iniquities of the children of Israel" (Lev. 16:21). Adler notes that much of the Bible incorporates bits of liturgy in the form of prayers.

The older prayers were probably chanted (Exod. 15); the Psalms were sung. The more common prayer was an individual prayer, either silent or vocal. The Old Testament did not limit prayer to any particular time or place, although the formal prayers were usually uttered in the Temple. By the time of the **prophets**, regular times were set apart for prayers. Daniel prayed three times a day; later, Maimonides indicated that at least one prayer a day was obligatory (Cyrus Adler and M.H. Harris 2005). In fact, after the destruction of the First Temple, prayers came to replace **sacrifice**.

In the New Testament, the spontaneous, private prayer was encouraged. Jesus spoke often of the need for prayer and its efficacy, indicating that God does hear prayer and respond to it. He himself prayed fervently in the Garden of Gethsemane, "O my Father, if it be possible, let this cup pass from me; nevertheless not as I will, but as thou wilt" (Matt. 26:39). Jesus frequently admonished his disciples to pray, even providing them the model with the **Lord's Prayer**, although he did not indicate that this was an exclusive prayer for their use.

An Israelite man dressed in shawl for prayer, preparing for the reading of Torah, the scroll in his hands.

Paul exhorted the **Christian**s to "pray without ceasing" (1 Thess. 5:17; Eph. 6:18). The gathering of the early Christians for communal prayer was a typical part of the worship experience. As the **Church** became more formal and used more liturgy, the *pater noster* ("Our Father") was typically recited by the people; and prayers were said, chanted, and sung by the clergy. The ritualized use of set prayers came under attack in the Protestant Reformation. The followers of Wycliffe, among others, objected to using a set form except for the Lord's Prayer.

Some have determined that certain postures are more appropriate than others: standing with hands extended (like Christ on the cross), or with hands raised toward **Heaven**, bowing heads or lifting the eyes toward heaven; prostration, kneeling, even beating the breast or tearing the hair (John J. Wynne 2005). More important is the attitude of the heart: reverent, sincere, humble, and faithful (1 Pet. 1:17–23). As the Psalmist explained, the best sacrifices are a "broken spirit: a broken and a contrite heart" (Ps. 51:17)

Although the Old Testament has no requirement for intermediaries, the Cabalists prayed to **angels**, expecting that they would carry the supplication to God and were more likely to be heeded than a mere mortal. In the Christian tradition, Christ may intercede for the suppliant, thereby encouraging Christians to pray "in the name of Christ." The **Roman** Catholic tradition added to this the intercession of the saints and held to the idea that even souls in purgatory pray to God for those on earth and for themselves (John J. Wynne 2005).

This whole range of prayer continues into modern times, with songs, chants, poetry, and prose being used. The approaches, adoration, confession, supplication, thanksgiving, and intercession remain much the same. The tendency toward imprecatory prayer (cursing one's enemies) has diminished, perhaps because of the admonition to love our enemies. But the need to speak to God, especially in times of great joy or sorrow, remains constant in the human heart. *See also* Lord's Prayer; Sacrifice.

Further Reading

Adler, Cyrus and M. H. Harris. "Prayer," http://jewishencyclopedia.com (accessed January 23, 2005). Lewis, Edwin. "Prayer," in *Harper's Bible Dictionary*. New York: Oxford University Press, 1961. Schuller, Eileen. "Prayer(s)," in *The Oxford Companion to the Bible*. New York: Oxford University Press, 1993. Thompson, J.G.H.S. "Prayer," in *The Illustrated Bible Dictionary*. Sydney, Australia: Tyndale House Publishers, 1980. Wynne, John J. "Prayer," http://newadvent.org (accessed January 23, 2005).

Priest, High Priest

(Exod. 28:1–30, 29, 39; Lev. 21; Heb. 7:21, 9; Rev. 1:6) The term *priest* derives from *presbyter* or "elder" (A. Boudinhon 2005). Priests are the ministers of divine worship, the professional men of God, who lead the **prayers**, regulate the worship practices, and perform the **sacrifices**. Among the **Hebrews**, these descendants of Moses's brother, Aaron, were born to their tasks, not called by God like the **prophets**. They were of the tribe of Levi and the household of Aaron. After the Israelites escaped from **Egypt**, which had a strong priesthood, Moses was told to anoint his brother as a priest.

The Levites

Until this time, the Hebrew patriarchs had spoken directly to God, needing no professional mediators. Abraham and his children had performed their own sacrificial offerings and offered their own prayers. But in **Exodus**, after receiving the directions for constructing the **Tabernacle**, Moses was instructed regarding the priests: "And take thou unto thee Aaron thy brother, and his sons with him, from among the children of Israel, that he may minister unto me in the priest's office" (Exod. 28:1).

The Levites, members of the tribe of Levi, were dedicated to the care of the Tabernacle, and later the **Temple**. They performed the manual labor in such sacred places. In addition, they were established as substitutes for the other families' first-born, considered "the tribe of the first-born." They had no land of their own, living off the tithe that the people paid for their upkeep in return for the Levites' performing religious obligations. The sons of Kohath were in charge of carrying the religious furnishings. The sons of Gershon cared for the coverings, screens, and hangings. And the sons of Merari carried and erected the frame of the tabernacle and its court (Num. 3–4).

The Levites, who were set aside by Moses as a permanent priesthood, especially the children of Aaron's son Eleazar, were expected to care for the **Ark**, the Tabernacle, and the sacred lots (**Urim and Thummim**) and teach the people the ways of God. Their tasks were also to minister in the house of the Lord with reverence, to judge, mediate, and sacrifice for the people. Each of these tasks is clearly outlined in the Holiness Code, with special detail to the sacrifices. In the earliest days, there was little distinction between Levites and priests. The main concerns of both were to be the interpreters of the **law** and the protectors, "doorkeepers," of the sanctuary and its sacred contents. Until the time of the Exile, the terms *Levite* and *priest* were synonymous (Moses Buttenwieser 2005).

The Priestly Code, starting in Leviticus 21, outlines the duties and responsibilities of the priests in detail. They were to remain holy, refraining from shaving their heads or cutting their **beards**. They were to refrain from bad **marriage**s (to whores or divorced women). They were encouraged to marry Israelite maidens who had never been held captive, to guarantee their purity. (This seems to assume that captives were probably raped.) And they were to avoid dead bodies, even the dead within their own families. A "blemished" man was not eligible to sacrifice—a person who is blind, lame, with a flat nose, or hunchbacked. Only the unblemished seed of Aaron was to come "nigh to offer the offerings of the Lord made by fire" (Lev. 21:21).

The code stipulates the members of the priest's family who may eat the **food** that has been made holy by offerings (Lev. 22) and the **curses** that will follow if the rules are violated. The nature of the offerings are also stipulated—nothing "bruised, or crushed, or broken, or cut" (Lev. 22:24) and nothing that comes from a stranger's hand, for fear it is corrupt. The food is to be eaten the same day as the sacrifice.

The feasts and the sacrifices are carefully outlined in both Exodus and Leviticus, along with the manner in which the priest must make his offerings. The household of Aaron was dedicated to learning the procedures and following them precisely. When Joshua was confronted with the task of dividing the lands among the **tribes**, he excluded the Levites from ownership, stipulating instead that they had their portion in the Lord and that they were to be dispersed among the other tribes to serve as God's ministers. This seems to have uneven success in the days of the **Judges**, with Levites often wandering unemployed and untutored across the countryside. Sometimes wealthy landowners had their own private priests and supported them; sometimes they maintained sanctuaries, such as the one at Dan.

The High Priest

Apparently, where the different worship centers were active in various parts of **Canaan**, many of the priests were fully employed and honored, but with the unified monarchy, the center of the worship, and the authority moved to Jerusalem, where Zadok was considered the founding head (Bruce M. Metzger and Michael D. Coogan 1993, 610). Until Solomon appointed Zadok, even laymen were known to function as priests on occasion. David sometimes functioned as a priest himself, in his role bringing the Ark to Jerusalem. For the most part, he honored the priests and prophets in his household, respecting their advice. Solomon was anointed by a priest (1 Kings 4:2, 4). With Josiah's abolition of all sanctuaries except Jerusalem, three centuries later, the "sons of Zadok" were firmly in power.

With this shift of worship to Jerusalem, the role of the chief priests and the high priest became more significant: The "chief" priests were those who ministered at the Temple. And the "high" priest was chosen by the **king** to preside over the others, in judgment and in authority. He was the only anointed priest, in the tradition of Aaron, and the only priest allowed to enter into the Holy of Holies on the **Day of Atonement**. It was particularly important that he be at least 20 years old, of legitimate birth, and married to a virgin. He was specifically forbidden to touch the dead, to trim his beard, or to rend his garments. His sins were regarded as the sins of the people (Lev. 4:3, 22). He presided over the **Sanhedrin**, the council of chief priests, which had the right to confirm the appointment of the high priest. He was considered the holiest man in Israel, the spiritual head over the congregation.

The powerful "high priest"(otherwise known as "the priest" or "the anointed priest") thus took on special authority. Although this man was supposed to be the eldest representative of Eleazar's family, there was no age limit. As a result, very young men (as young as 17 or 24) became high priests with the approval of the Sanhedrin. After the Exile, there was no longer an **anointing**, just a simple investiture ceremony.

Although he was consecrated in the same manner as other priests and shared their routine duties, the high priest alone wore the special vestments enumerated in Exodus 28. He represented the chosen people before God, sprinkling the **blood** of the sacrificial **goat** on the Mercy Seat. (Josephus, the famous Jewish historian, described their dress and activities in some detail in *Antiquities* III. 7.)

The elements of the priests' **clothing** were carefully enumerated in the Priestly Code. They were intended for "glory and beauty" and included linen undergarments, the jeweled breastplate, an ephod, a robe, an embroidered coat, a miter, and a girdle (or belt). These were to be made of gold and fine linen, with accents of blue, purple and scarlet (Exod. 28). The Code specifies the engraving, the kinds of stones to be used as decoration, and the chains of pure gold. In a pocket in his "breastplate of judgment," the priest was to have the Urim and Thummim, allowing him to bear the judgment of God, as they were upon his heart (Exod. 28:30). Further details of the priestly vestments appear in Exodus 39, with explanations of the beaten gold and the twined linen and the bells at the hem of the robe. (There was even a rope that allowed other priests to pull him out of the Holy of Holies if he should faint or die in that sacred space that they were forbidden to enter.) The needlework and the engravings, the blue lace on the miter, all suggest a lavish display of color and splendor, rich with symbolic meaning.

The high priests became counselors to wealthy households and to kings, powerful at some times, powerless at others. Some of the Maccabees were both rulers and priests. Mattathias was the high priest and one of his sons became both high priest and general of the army (Madeleine S. Miller and J. Lane Miller 1961, 578). By the time of Jesus, Herod was the real authority who appointed the high priests, often designating members of wealthy families not known for their purity or faith so much as their friendship with him and willingness to follow his commands.

Under Herod, in the time of the Roman occupation, some six high priests were appointed, noted for their corruption and wealth. By this time, the high priest at Jerusalem not only received offerings of tithes but demanded them (Madeleine S Miller and J. Lane Miller 1961, 579). The family of Annas, which included his son-in-law, Caiphas, was noted for their lavish lifestyle and political power. They formed the aristocratic priestly party of the **Sadducees** and turned over their old teaching office to the **scribes**. These were the leaders who sat in judgment over Jesus, when he was accused of **blasphemy** (Mark 14:53ff). Later, Ananias was the high priest who brought the same charges against Paul.

Priest wearing the clothing of the high priest, including the turban, the ephod with the inscriptions of the Twelve Tribes on precious stones, the apron, and the bells shaped like pomegranates on the hem of his garment.

In view of the increasing deterioration of the standards of the office of high priest, the author of Hebrews notes that, with the New **Covenant**, Christ has become the high priest of the order of Melchizedek (Heb 7:21), a better mediator because he sits on the right hand of God, he has power and authority. He is sinless and eternal. In Revelation (1:6; 5:10), all Christian believers are seen as their own kings and priests, no longer in need of earthly representatives of God. (This is the image that Dante uses at the top of Mt. Purgatory, when the pilgrim is empowered with full spiritual and political power, ready for his ascent into God's presence.)

With the destruction of the Temple in 70 A.D., the role of the high priest, along with the task of sacrifice, disappeared. Modern Jewish congregations have **rabbis**, but not priests. Without a Temple or a Holy of Holies or a place for sacrifice, there is no occasion for a high priest. The tradition of priests continues in the Roman Catholic, Eastern Orthodox, Episcopal, and some other churches, but has disappeared from most Protestant denominations. *See also* Ark of the Covenant; Law; Sacrifice; Tabernacle; Temple; Tribes of Israel.

Further Reading

Boudinhon, A. "Priest," http://www.newadvent.org (accessed January 24, 2005). Buttenwieser, Moses and the Executive Committee of the Editorial Board. "Priest," http://www.jewishencyclopedia.com (accessed September 20, 2005). Hirsch, Emil G. "High Priest," http://www.jewishencyclopedia.com (accessed January 24, 2005). Hubbard, D. A. "Priests and Levites," in *The Illustrated Bible Encyclopedia*. Sydney, Australia: Tyndale House Publishers, 1980. Metzger, Bruce M. and Michael D. Coogan. "Priests and High Priest," in *The Oxford Companion to the Bible*. New York: Oxford University Press, 1993. Miller, Madeleine S. and J. Lane Miller. "Priests," in *Harper's Bible Dictionary*. New York: Oxford University Press, 1961. Tierney, John J. "The High Priest," http://www.newadvent.org (accessed January 24, 2005).

Promised Land. *See Israel*

Prophet

A prophet is a divinely inspired preacher who speaks for God. He or she might predict the future, but that was not the typical message the prophets delivered. There were women prophets, including Miriam, the sister of Moses; Huldah, who lived in the time of Josiah; and Anna, who foretold the birth of Christ; but most of the prophets were men.

Examples appear throughout Scripture, beginning with Abraham and ending with John, in his powerful Revelation of the times to come. The earlier prophets did not write their messages, nor did some of the later ones, such as John the Baptist.

Prophets

Prophet	King/s or Country	Approx. Dates
Moses	Pharaoh of Egypt	c. 1290 BC
Samuel (also judge & priest)	Saul & David	c. 1105–1020 BC
Nathan	David	c. 1000 BC
Ahijah	Jereboam	c. 922–901 BC
Elijah	Ahab . etc.	c. 869–850 BC
Elisha	Joram, etc.	c. 840
Joel	Judah, etc.	c. ? 830–820 BC
Jonah	Nineveh	c. 786–746 BC

Hosea	Israel	755–715 BC
Isaiah	Judah, Exiles in Babylon	739–690 BC
Micah	Judah, Jotham, Ahaz, etc.	735–700 BC
Nahum	Judah, Josiah	c. 650–620 BC
Zephaniah	Judah, Josiah	626 BC
Jeremiah	Judah, Manesseh etc.	627–575 BC
Habakkuk	Jerusalem, pre-Exile	605–600 BC
Daniel	Babylonians & Persians	605–536 BC
Ezekiel	Exiles in Babylon	593–560 BC
Haggai	Jerusalem, post-Exile	520–505 BC
Zechariah	Judah, Darius	520–519 BC
Malachi	Jerusalem	460 BC
Obadiah	Edom	450–350 BC
Joel	Judah, Jerusalem	c. 350 BC
John the Baptist	Herod	c. AD 30

Based on listings in Eugene H. Merrill 1972, 268; Madeleine S. Miller and J. Lane Miller 1961, 584. Other listings vary by as much as 50 years for some prophets.

The role of the prophet was to speak the truth that he or she received from God to a ruler or to a people. Prophets and their prophesies are deeply imbedded in Scripture, serving from earliest times to the concluding words of Revelation as intermediaries between God and humans. From Moses to John, the prophets were the preachers, the advisors, and sometimes the leaders who comforted, warned, lamented, blessed, and instructed God's chosen people in times of confusion, sorrow, imprisonment, and doubt. They spoke to specific situations faced by specific communities, often fore-telling the future for either the Jews or their enemies.

The prophets usually had a clear call from God, who instructed them to deliver specific messages to God's chosen people. In the days of the patri-archs and earlier, God occasionally spoke directly to men, as in the cases of Adam, Cain, Noah, and Abraham. The "seed of Abraham" were blessed by their special relationship with God, allowing them unusual mystical powers: Jacob saw a ladder coming down from heaven and later wrestled all night with God; Joseph could interpret **dreams**. But it was Moses who clearly interpreted God's word for the Hebrews. He talked with God "face to face," leaving a legacy of history and **law** unmatched by any other Hebrew prophet. These early prophets had broad powers: Moses brought the people out of **Egypt;** Samuel instructed the people on the choice of their first **kings.**

Later, during the days of the **Judges,** certain men who gathered in "schools of prophecy," are called by some commentators "ecstatic proph-ets." Their messages have not been recorded, although we know that David met a group of them along the road. The far more impressive Samuel was not only a prophet, but also a **priest**. He was a transitional figure between the age of the judges and that of the kings. He sternly warned the Hebrews against selecting an earthly king to rule them, thereby replacing the rule of God. When they insisted, he anointed first Saul and later David, thereafter playing the role of the kings' conscience. This became the model for prophets in the days of the united monarchy. Theirs were the voices that balanced those of the **warrior**-kings. In this vein, the prophet Nathan, facing King David in his adultery with Bathsheba, spoke truth to power, using a **parable** to accomplish his task (2 Sam. 12: 1–15).

Later, in the divided kingdom that followed Solomon's death, specific prophets spoke to Israel or Judah, sometimes just to the people of Jerusalem. During their times of exile in **Babylonia** and among the Persians, different prophets also spoke out to both Jews and gentiles, giving advice to the people, pointing the future to Nebuchadnezzar, interpreting the dreams of Balthazar.

In the final days of the Old Testament, much of the prophesy became increasingly apocalyptic, pointing to the "**Day of the Lord**" and the concept of a **Messiah** and a Heavenly Jerusalem. It was these prophesies that John the Baptist and Jesus echoed, pointing to the fulfillment of prophesy in the birth, life, death, and resurrection of Christ. At the time of the Transfiguration, when Jesus asked Peter who men said that he was, Peter told him that many thought him to be Elijah, the prophet who never died. After **Pentecost**, Peter and the other **Disciples** looked back at the pattern of Jewish prophesy to explain their own faith. Paul, on his missionary journeys, often echoed the messages of the prophets, especially when addressing fellow Jews.

When John recorded his revelation in the final book of the New Testament, he used the tone of Daniel and other Old Testament apocalyptic prophesy, once again touching on the Heavenly Jerusalem, the **Temple**, and the hopes for the Day of the Lord.

We have only a scattering of the prophesies of the earliest prophets. We know little of Nathan beyond his parable, which he used to upbraid the sinful David, or Ahijah, beyond his prophesy of the division of the kingdom (1 Kings 11:29ff). Some of the later "literary" or "writing prophets," such as Isaiah, are recorded in far greater detail. Jeremiah allowed Baruch to serve as his amanuensis, preserving his prophesies for posterity. Jonah's life rather than his actual message delivered to the people of Nineveh is the only surviving record of his prophetic career.

We also know of false prophets, such as Baalam, who could sometimes hear God's voice, but also listened to alien deities. The priests that Jezebel brought with her into Israel were seen as "prophets" of Ashtar and Baal, not reliable in their messages. One of the tasks of the Temple priests was to weed out these false prophets. Later, Jesus also warned the people against false prophets.

Scripture divides these spokesmen for God into the major and minor prophets, largely determined by the authority and size of their writings. Although the minor prophets are placed in the Bible in approximate chronological order, the major prophets are not. Establishing the "canon" of the prophets probably began during the era of Nehemiah (Madeleine S. Miller and J. Lane Miller 1961, 584)

Although women could be prophets, just as they could be judges, this was a rare occurrence. More often, prophets were solitary men such as Elijah or John the Baptist. Holy, ascetic, steeped in Scripture, and sensitive to the problems of the people as well as the voice of God, called to live lonely lives, they sometimes met tragic deaths. Some of God's prophets were married, some achieved special status at the court, but most found that their profession excluded them from normal human activities and ambitions.

Artistic interpretations of the prophets dominate much of medieval **art**. The cathedrals are full of carvings of their elongated bodies and anguished faces; the stained glass windows portray events in their sacrificial lives. The idea of the prophet continues into the present: many ministers consider their sermons divinely inspired words provided by the Holy Spirit to be delivered to their congregations. The rich tradition of prophetic utterance is very much alive in our day. *See also* Apocalypse; Day of Judgment, Day of the Lord; History in the Bible; Judges; Kings.

Further Reading

Hamilton, Edith. *Spokesmen for God: The Great Teachers of the Old Testament.* New York: W.W. Norton and Company, Inc., 1936. Merrill, Eugene H. *An Historical Survey of the Old Testament.* Nutley, N.J.: The Craig Press, 1972. Miller, Madeleine S. and J. Lane Miller. *Harper's Bible Dictionary.* New York: Harper and Row, 1961. Tischler, Nancy M. *Men and Women of the Bible.* Westport, Conn.: Greenwood Press, 2002.

Proverbs

In the Old Testament, the term *masal* or "to be like" is used to denote a pithy saying that condenses the wisdom of experience. In the New Testament, *parabole* or *paroimia,* or "dark sayings," is used the same way, much like **parables**. A proverb is an ancient saying often without a definite source. Although considered a part of folk wisdom, it was sometimes attributed to a famous person. In the case of Scripture, the Book of Proverbs mentions both Solomon and Lemuel (31:1–9). Proverbs are quoted throughout Scripture, especially in Ecclesiastes and the Book of Job. In the New Testament, proverbs are liberally sprinkled through the **Gospels** and **Epistles**. Numerous books of the **Apocrypha**, such as Ecclesiasticus, are also full of folk sayings.

Proverbs usually have a didactic role, serving as a memorable means of teaching an ancient truth. They provide advice regarding wisdom and foolishness, reverence, education, marriage, lust, money, thrift, religion, and many of the other elements of human existence. It is from proverbs we learn that "Fear of the Lord is the beginning of wisdom," and that "a dog returns to its vomit." We discover the habits of the ant and are encouraged to emulate his industry. And we are taught to honor our fathers, and not to provoke our children. We learn about a "good woman" and a "harlot" and the temptations of young men and old.

Some proverbs are enigmatic, forcing the listener to puzzle over the idea. The Beatitudes are of this nature, bringing together curious contradictions such as, "Blessed are they that mourn, for they shall be comforted." Some summarize the experience of a people, such as the Jewish saying, "Man strives and God laughs." Paul frequently used proverbs to sum up his ideas, often drawing on ancient Jewish wisdom.

These proverbs, which appear throughout Scripture, are the most quoted portions of the Bible, lending themselves to specific circumstances, providing help and advice for young and old alike. *See also* Beatitudes; Education.

Further Reading

Cox, Dermott. "Proverbs, The Book of," in *The Oxford Companion to the Bible*. New York: Oxford University Press, 1993. Hubbard, D. A. "Proverb," in *The Illustrated Bible Dictionary*. Sydney, Australia: Tyndale House Publishers, 1980. Jacobs, Joseph, M. Grunwald, Marcus Jastrow, and Louis Lewin. "Proverbs," http://www.jewishencyclopedia.com (accessed January 25, 2005).

Psalms

The title *Psalms* derives from the Greek *psalmoi,* "sacred songs chanted with accompaniment." This term derives from the classical Greek word *psalmos,* meaning the "twanging of strings." In one manuscript of the Septuagint, the book is entitled *Psalterion,* from which we take our term *Psalter,* meaning songs sung or chanted in accompaniment with a stringed instrument (Bruckner B. Trawick 1970, 241). Today we use the term *Psalms* to designate the book in the Bible and *Psalter* to indicate a collection of Psalms set to music for singing.

The Psalms were the **songs** of ancient Israel; the Psalter was their hymnal. "Let us come into his house with singing" "Sing unto the Lord a new song." Songs were clearly a major means of expressing God's glory and testifying to man's awe at his majesty and power. In their psalms, the Jews sang of the wonders of nature, the history of their people, the rich rewards in the **law** of Moses, their anger at their enemies, their advice to young and old. These inspired songs prophesied the wonders to come, proclaimed the glorious kingdom of their monarch, and expressed their deep sorrow and shame. They are wide ranging and full of details of everyday life, of politics, history, geography, and faith.

The major songs were hymns of praise, which glorify God, celebrating his loving-kindness, his creation of nature, his gift of the law, and his concern for his chosen people. These tend to be psalms of gratitude, which constitute about one-third of the Psalter. The enthronement psalms, royal psalms, and songs of thanksgiving are part of this category (Philip J. King and Lawrence E. Stager 2001, 286). The pilgrim songs, which were sung by participants in processions to the three pilgrim **festivals**, were probably sung by the Levites standing on the 15 steps between the Court of the Women and courts of the Israelites (Emil G. Hirsch 2005).

There were also didactic psalms, which were quieter, providing advice on conduct and speech. The imprecatory psalms, which have the same character, tend toward stronger language, with details about consequences of evil-doing and denunciation of wrong-doers, often enemies. They frequently seek God's judgment on Israel's (and God's) enemies.

Finally, there are the elegies or laments, which express grief at the spread of iniquity, the sufferings of the people, and the abandonment of Israel. Such moving laments as "By the waters of **Babylon**, we sat down, yea, we wept, when we remembered Zion"(Ps. 137) are of this grouping. They usually end with supplication for the restoration of **Israel** to grace or the repentance of sinners. Pure **lamentations** end with the expression of sorrow, with or without confessions of sin and hope for forgiveness. They tend to be inspired by a consciousness of guilt (Emil G. Hirsch 2005).

The Psalter contains more notations regarding musical arrangements and performance, both vocal and instrumental, than any other book in the Bible. Psalm 68, for example, describes the processions into the sanctuary: the singers in front, the musicians last, between them girls playing tambourines. Psalm 81 adds: "Blow the ram's horn at the new moon, at the full moon, on our festal day"(81:3–4). Psalm 98 names all the instruments. Twelve adult Levites were the minimum membership of a chorus; boys and perhaps women seem to have been added to their numbers after the Exile. The singers also played instruments to accompany themselves.

The Form of the Psalms

The basic form of the psalms is parallelism, a device that allows great variety in length and substance. It is also open to translation in a way that a heavily metrical and rhymed verse-form is not. The psalms are noted for the richness of metaphor, the great extended images that carry through entire poems. Balanced contrasts, listings culminating in powerful statements, and repetition with variations are the techniques of the writers. Some are acrostics or alphabetical in their arrangement. Some are designed as couplets (2-line groupings) or triplets (3-line groupings).

The Psalter consists of five books, with each section recognizable because it is closed with a doxology. The divisions are Book I: 1–41; Book II: 42–72; Book III: 73–89; Book IV: 90–106; Book V: 107–150. These divisions have different titles for God and may have been used by different centers of worship at different periods in history. One scholar classified the Psalms by these main types: Hymns of Praise, Personal Thanksgivings, Communal Laments and Personal Laments, Entrance Liturgies, Blessings and Cursings, Wisdom Psalms, Royal Psalms, and mixed types (F. D. Kidner 1980, 1295–1297).

The History of the Psalms

Although tradition has named David the author of 73 of the psalms, modern scholars believe that as many as 10 authors might well have contributed to this collection (F. D. Kidner 1980, 1294). The Book of Psalms constituted the hymn book of Israel during the time of the Second Temple. The major portion of the Book of Psalms was probably already established by the time of Jesus's ministry. Jesus knew the psalms by heart and quoted from them frequently. **Christians** make particular reference to the Messianic Psalms, such as Psalm 2.

Much of **Church music** is built on the foundation of the psalms, even for those denominations that do not adhere to the exclusive use of psalmody. Medieval chants, Reformation hymns, and modern religious songs often take their inspiration from one of the Psalms. Martin Luther drew on Psalm 46 for his great hymn *Ein' Feste Burg* or "A Mighty Fortress Is Our God." "Old Hundred," also known as the *Jubilate* (Latin for "Rejoice") is still used at many Thanksgiving services. And Psalm 150, "Praise ye the Lord," is considered the great Doxology, a great favorite through the ages. The most famous and most widely used of the psalms, especially at funerals is the twenty-third: "The Lord is my shepherd; I shall not want." *See also* Music; Musical Instruments; Song; Temple.

Further Reading

Hirsch, Emil G. "Psalms," http://www.jewishencyclopedia.com (accessed January 24, 2005). Kidner, F. D. "Psalms, " in *The Illustrated Bible Dictionary*. Sydney, Australia: Tyndale House Publishers, 1980. King, Philip J. and Lawrence E. Stager. *Life in Biblical Israel*. Louisville, Ky.: Westminster John Knox Press, 2001. Trawick, Buckner G. *The Bible as Literature: The Old Testament and the Apocrypha*. New York: Harper and Row, 1970.

𝔓unishments

In many primitive societies, especially in the Mideast, offenses have traditionally been considered to involve clans, or extended families not just individuals. They were therefore judged and punished within the clan or between clans, usually applying either *lex talionis,* the **law** of retaliation, or vengeance. In Hebrew law, this rule of "an eye for an eye, a tooth for a tooth, a life for a life" was restricted, allowing blood-revenge only in some cases that were seen as a danger to the general society and only falling on the accused individual. In the older, more brutal systems, whole clans might be destroyed because of a violation. The Hebrew code restricted the retribution to the individual, although divine justice might be visited "upon the children even unto the third and fourth generation" (Exod. 20:5; Lev. 26:39; Deut. 5:9; Lam. 5:7).

Evidence of the earlier code can be seen in the description of Cain's descendent Lemech (Gen. 4:24), reckoning that he would visit his revenge on the evildoer at a rate of seven times the original violation. In another violent act of vengeance, some of Jacob's son were infuriated at the seduction or rape of their sister Dinah; they demanded that the evildoer marry her, and that all the men of the town be circumcised. While the citizens of Shechem were recovering from this surgery, the brothers killed every man in the whole town, all for the transgressions of one man.

Most of the punishments that are outlined in the law of Moses are prescribed in Exodus and Deuteronomy. Here we find some orderly listings (such as the Ten Commandments) and some rules that seem a jumble of complicated and detailed regulations that intermingle livestock, rape, sacrilege, and lying. The major offenses that merited extreme punishment were crimes against other men: murder and assault, theft, and damage to property—usually **animals**. Sexual offenses fell within the property regulations, assuming that wives and children were the man's property. Some crimes against God, such as **blasphemy**, false swearing, or ritual offenses, were also punished in public ways. Actual punishment would be determined in part by the motivation of the malefactor. Intentional crimes were considered more serious than crimes of the moment: accidental killings, carelessness, or justifiable homicide (Exod. 2113–14; Num. 15:27–31, 35:11; Deut. 17:12). Others resulted from ignorance of the law and mistakes of fact, which might be more easily forgiven.

The punishments were proportional to the crimes, but usually much harsher than in modern times, in part because there were no prisons available and because violations were considered a blow to the entire community:

Death Penalty

The most serious crimes was the shedding of blood, especially premeditated murder, which was to be punished by death, probably stoning (Exod. 21:12; Lev. 24:17; Num. 35:16–21). For especially egregious cases, the body was dishonored by impaling or burning after being stoned. **Crucifixion** was a later practice.

Other serious crimes were offences against God or the family as the sources of life, deserving the most serious punishment. They included:

1. Rebellion or other grave sins against parents, such as striking or cursing them (Exod. 21:15–17; Deut. 22:23–27), carrying the death penalty.
2. Sexual sins, which were considered offences against the family, the community, and God, including:
   - Adultery of men and women (Lev. 20:10; Deut. 22:23–27), punishable by stoning to death;
   - Incest with various members of the family, including the wife's family (Lev. 20:11–12), punishable by burning to death;
   - Sodomy, a man lying with another man "as with a woman" (Lev. 20:13), punishable by death;
   - Bestiality, humans involved with animals in sexual and other "unnatural" relations (Exod. 22:19; Lev 20:15–16), punishable by death for both the humans and the animals involved.
3. Grave sins against God, including:
   - Idolatry, sacrificing a child to Molech or leading others to serve other gods (Lev. 20:1–5; Deut. 13:2–19, 17:1–7), could result in the death penalty for the individual or for entire cities, which might be "destroyed utterly" with fire for their perfidy (as when Joshua declared "harem" against Jericho);
   - Blasphemy (Lev. 24:15–16) (the charge brought against christ);
   - Profanation of the Sabbath, including working on the Sabbath (Exod. 31:14–15) could result in the death penalty;
   - Sorcery or witchcraft, dealing with the spirits of the dead (Lev. 20:27), was punished by stoning to death;
   - Prostitution of the priest's daughter, who profaned her father when she "played the whore" (Lev. 21:9), was punished by death by burning;
   - Abduction of a man in order to make him a slave (Exod. 21:16; Deut. 24:7), merited the death penalty.

Lesser Penalties

Less heinous sins might be punished by flogging, that is beating with a rod (up to 40 stripes) (Deut. 25:3). These included:

- Slander of wife, accusing her falsely of not being a virgin at the time of the marriage (Deut. 22:18), which might be punished by either flogging or paying of 100 shekels to the wife's father. (This explains wives' saving the bloodied bedsheets from the wedding night as proof of virginity.)

- Disobedience of son, not rising to the level of violence or cursing, might be punished by flogging instead of stoning (Deut. 21:18).

The mutilation of body as symbolic retaliation was rarely the punishment for a crime, but was prescribed for the peculiar example of a woman interfering with a fight between her husband and another man, grabbing the other man's genitals. She was to have her hand amputated as punishment (Deut. 25: 11–12).

For a crime or sin, other than intentional homicide, a fine (often in excess of the amount of damage actually caused) was to paid to the person harmed or perhaps to the **priests** as an act of contrition (2 Kings 12:17). Fines were not to be paid to the state and were not considered appropriate for serious offences. These fines were considered appropriate punishment for minor offences such as:

- Violations of animals, women, crops, and so on (Deut. 22:19). A man who raped a virgin might be expected both to pay a fine and to marry the woman.
- Enslavement for a debt when there was failure to make restitution (Deut. 15:2; Lev. 25:39).

Ordeals were also employed as tests, rather than punishments, requiring the suspected person to take an oath or drink the "cup of bitterness." (The **Assyrian** practice of drowning—or ordeal by water—was not practiced by Israelites.) Exile was rarely used, whereby one was "cut off from people."

Imprisonment was not a punishment until after the Exile, probably considered a foreign punishment. In the New Testament, Peter and Paul were imprisoned by Roman authorities, as were other **apostles**. (See Roland deVaux 1961, 158–160.)

In the period of the Exile, other patterns of justice are seen, apparently foreign ones. According to the Book of Daniel, Shadrach, Meshach, and Abednego were thrown into a fiery furnace. Daniel was thrown into the lions' den without any judgment other than the **king's**. In the Book of Esther, the king's word was sufficient to determine the life or death of whole groups of people, with no call for trial by jury. Of course, in time of war, violations of persons and property were a matter of course.

Under **Roman** law, various other punishments were added. One form of capital punishment practiced by both Greeks and Romans was tying of millstones around the necks of the condemned and tossing them into the sea. Jesus made reference to this when he noted that, if anyone offended the children who had come to him, "It were better for him that a millstone were hanged about his neck and that he were drowned in the depth of the sea" (Matt. 18:6).

Jesus himself was scourged and then crucified, neither of which forms of punishment was a part of Hebrew law (although Josephus mentions that the

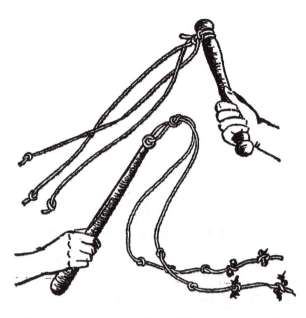

Scourges were commonly used for punishment, the stripes limited by law so that the person being punished would not die, but the bits of glass or metal in the knots often tore the skin off the body.

Seleucids also crucified criminals and troublemakers). Paul was imprisoned and beaten without a trial, also forbidden under the law, especially for Roman citizens. The tension between Hebrew courts and the Roman ones became increasingly apparent as Paul was accused by Jews of various violations of the religious law, but was judged in Roman courts, which required special treatment for Roman citizens. As a Jew, he might have been tried and punished locally, but as a citizen, he had the right to appeal to the Emperor. The **Sanhedrin** was limited to trials for religious matters; the Roman courts dealt with matters of state such as stirring up rebellion.

In addition to these punishments, atonement might be achieved through **sacrifices**, especially in cases involving the breach of sacred law. Because the purpose of the law was to return the offender to harmony with his or her community (or rid the community of the offender), this ritual was significant for the act of reconciliation. Regular worship, with offerings on the **Sabbath**, on festival days, and on special days of obligation, also served to cleanse the individual or family of violations of the law. In addition, sinners who were in breach of the law, although not necessarily facing a trial, might be reconciled with God and their fellow beings through the scapegoat, on whom they placed their sins before sending him off into the wilderness. The **Day of Atonement** was the special festival for such reconciliation.

In his interruption of the stoning of the woman taken in adultery, Jesus called for a greater leniency in treatment of malefactors, recommending that "He who is without sin" should cast the first stone (John 8:7). Likewise, he rejected the old law of "an eye for an eye," suggesting instead that we love and forgive the one who has transgressed. In affirmation of this New **Covenant**, he himself forgave his tormentors, asking that God "Forgive them, for they know not what they do" (Luke 23:34). His refusal to judge or condemn others was a personal choice rather than a rejection of governments, judicial proceedings, and authority. He accepted his own trial and punishment as "rendering unto Caesar that which is Caesar's," a sign of the need for judicial systems, even when they prove unjust. His forgiving tone has led many Christians to a modified view of judgment, preferring mercy rather than justice. Even though Christ came as the merciful redeemer of humankind, he not only allowed the world to condemn him, but announced that a time would come when all of humankind would face God's great **Judgment Day**. *See also* Atonement, Day of; Crucifixion, Cross; Day of Judgment, Day of the Lord; Judges; Law; Redeemer, Redeemer-of-Blood; Trials, Courts.

Further Reading

Boyd, Robert T. *Tells, Tombs and Treasure: A Pictorial Guide to Biblical Archaeology.* New York: Bonanza Books, 1969. DeVaux, Roland. *Ancient Israel: Its Life and Institutions.* Grand Rapids, Mich.: William B. Eerdmans Publishing Company, 1961. Falk, Ze'ev W. *Hebrew Law in Biblical Times.* Provo, Utah: Brigham Young University Press, 1966.

Purim

Purim, a celebration of Esther's heroic efforts to save the Jewish people from death, is a festival that falls on the thirteenth to the fifteenth days of the month of Adar. The admonition to reserve this day is in Esther 9:28: "These days should be remembered and observed in every generation of every family, and in every province and in every city. And these days of Purim should never cease to be celebrated by the Jews, nor should the memory of them die out among their descendants." These days of fasting and **lamentation** commemorated Mordecai's ingenious plan to trick King Ahasuerus to punish the sinister Haman, his vizier, rather than the innocent Jews. The day before Purim was a **fast** day, with all the appropriate restrictions, making the feast day that followed all the more joyous.

The name of the day is thought to derive from the word *pur,* which Esther 3:7; 9:24, 26 indicates means "lot." This is not a Hebrew word, but probably the **Assyrian** word *puru,* "which means a pebble, or small stone, which would be used for casting lots" (J. S. Wright 1980, 1306). It is not considered a religious celebration; some even think of it as pagan in origin. The Jewish community does use this eternal story of Jews threatened in a strange land to remind one another that they must be always vigilant to resist complacency.

The celebration involves the reading of the book of Esther in the **synagogue**, with participation from the congregation, which "boos" and shouts whenever Haman's name is mentioned. In thanksgiving for their salvation from destruction, the community share their food with others. This is a time for making up *Mishloach Manots,* or food packages for friends and family. The favorite pastries connected with the day are small three-cornered cakes filled with poppy seeds or fruit jam, called *Hamantashen.*

Purim is a time of merriment, gift-giving, and more drinking than is usual in festivals. In the carnival atmosphere of the celebration, the children sometimes put on grotesque masks and perform plays, masquerades, or parodies. The older boys may construct an effigy of Haman, which they burn in a bonfire or enjoy the *graggers,* or noisemakers. The foods and festivities date from the Middle Ages, and the deeper meaning of the day is cherished by families as a time of family parties and a reminder of God's hand preserving his chosen people. *See also* Feasting; Lamentations.

Further Reading

Kohler, Kaufmann and Henry Malter. "Purim," http://www.jewishencyclopedia.com (accessed January 25, 2005). Kramer, Amy J. "Purim, Festival of Lots," http://www.jewishencyclopedia.com (accessed June 5, 2005). Wright, J. S. "Purim," in *The Illustrated Bible Dictionary.* Sydney, Australia: Tyndale House Publishers, 1980.

R

Rabbi

The idea of using rabbis for the teachers of the Jewish law had developed in the first century B.C. It was and still is a title for those "who are distinguished for learning, who are the authoritative teachers of the Law, and who are appointed spiritual heads of the community" (Isidore Singer et al. 2004). The term was first used to describe Rabban Gamaliel the elder, along with others who were patriarchs or presidents of the **Sanhedrin.** It came to mean those (not necessarily Levites) who taught the Scriptures and the oral and traditional laws to members of the community.

When Judas betrayed Jesus in the **Garden** of Gethsemane, he kissed him, saying, "Greetings, Rabbi!" (Matt 26:49; Mark 14:45) The term *rabbi,* which Scripture says means "teacher" (John 1:38), was used by Matthew, Mark, and John to refer to Jesus. It is not a term that occurs in the Old Testament. It was also used for John the Baptist by his disciples (John 3:26). When the blind man greeted Jesus as "Master" and "Lord" (Mark 10:51), and when Mary confronted her lord at the open tomb (John 20:16), both used the term *rabboni,* which implied even more respect.

In Jesus's day, *rabbi* and *rabboni* were comparatively new titles given to learned teachers regardless of their antecedents. (Previously, scholars as well as **priests** were from the line of Levi.) The respect afforded the rabbi was comparable to that given parents or those "elder in years." Unlike priests, the rabbi had no power beyond the ability to expound the **law** and give solid information. He "is no priest, no **apostle;** he has no hierarchical power" (Isidore Singer et al. 2004). As "great rabbis," they nonetheless, had attributed to them miraculous cures and help. It was thought by some of the simple folk that "by a look or word" they could kill or restore to life. "At their bidding the eyes of a rival fall out, and are again inserted" according to stories popular in the first century B.C. (Alfred Edersheim 2004, 74).

The rabbi was supposed to set an example, leading the community "in the fear of God and in a life of purity and sanctity." He was "expected to embody the Torah in his own life, conduct himself with dignity, manifest graciousness to all, supply means of charity to the needy, guide his people to the righteous life, preach to men and women in the **synagogue** on the **Sabbath,**" discuss the intricacies of the Law on other occasions with the more learned, "and study the Torah systematically" (Madeleine S. Miller and J. Lane Miller 1961, 598).

His appearance should command respect: "The rabbi should appear as clean and pure as an **angel.** . . . The Rabbis generally dressed in long, flowing white robes, and sometimes wore gold-trimmed official cloaks" (Isidore Singer et al. 2004). This was clearly not the case for Jesus, who had a commanding presence, but dressed simply in peasant clothing.

It was not a paid position until the Middle Ages, but disciples often helped to cover the rabbi's living expenses. Rabbis often worked at least one-third of the time at some other occupation to support themselves and their families. These were often humble tradesmen: wood-choppers, laundrymen, winetasters, brewers, and **carpenters.** They might also be merchants and farmers. Rabbis were exempt from **taxes** and from labor on public works. They were usually married, and their wives had precisely circumscribed lives. The rabbi's wife did not mix in society beyond her own family circle or even do her own marketing.

As rabbis believed in living the holy life through observance of the Torah, they assumed many activities in the community, helping in disasters, judging small claims among the poor, and teaching the young. They shared the traditions and views of the **Pharisees,** "embracing an all-knowing, all-wise, just, merciful, and loving God who supervised the lives of individuals and decreed the fates, even while giving room for free will to choose beyond good and evil." Their religion "exalted the holy faith, the holy man, and the pursuit of a holy way of life...It was only by pursuing the holy on a daily basis that salvation could be achieved and the **Messiah** would come" (Philip Stern 1993, 641).

"Rabbinism" was not a system of theology, but rather a collection of ideas, conjectures, and fancies regarding God, angels, **demons,** humankind, and the future. A major criticism was that it demanded "outward obedience and righteousness, and pointed to sonship as its goal." By contrast, the Gospel of Jesus Christ started "with the free gift of forgiveness through faith and sonship, and pointed to obedience and righteousness" as fruits of this faith (Alfred Edersheim 2004, 74). Jesus, therefore, rarely addressed himself to the rabbis, but rather cited the Pentateuch, the first five books of the Bible, in his debates with the authorities. *See also* Education; Pharisees; Scribes.

Further Reading

Edersheim, Alfred. *The Life and Times of Jesus the Messiah.* Peabody, Mass.: Hendrickson Publishers, Inc., 2004. Miller, Madeleine S. and J. Lane Miller. "Rabbi, Rabboni," in *Harper's Bible Dictionary.* New York: Harper and Row, Publishers, 1961. Singer, Isidore, Isaac Broydé, Joseph Jacobs, Judah David Eisenstein, Kaufmann Kohler, and Max Landsberg. "Rabbi," www. jewishencyclopedia.com (accessed November 20, 2004). Stern, Philip. "Rabbi," in *The Oxford Companion to the Bible.* New York: Oxford University Press, 1993.

Redeemer, Redeemer-of-Blood

(**Lev. 25:25–49; Ruth 3:9, 12–13; Eph.1:7**) When the immediate family was unable to deal with a violation of the **law,** either to extract vengeance for the honor of the family or to fulfill an obligation, a kinsman might serve in their stead. For example, a kinsman was obliged to carry on the line of Ruth's dead **husband,** but was reluctant to assume the obligation. He and Boaz agreed that Boaz would instead accept the responsibility for taking Ruth as his wife, thereby continuing the family's name and inheritance (Ruth 3:9, 12–13). This was a fulfillment of the leverite law.

A redeemer might also "redeem a relative sold into slavery for defaulting on a debt" (Lev. 25:48–49) as in the case of Jeremiah's purchase of the "ancestral state of Anathoth, which was not to be alienated since property was to remain in the family" (Lev. 25:25–33; Jer. 32:8). When Jeremiah's cousin was forced to sell his field, "Jeremiah was obliged to buy it back" (Philip J. King and Lawrence E. Stager, 2001, 39).

The most perilous role for the kinsman-redeemer was blood vengeance. If a gross offense had been committed against a family, the redeemer-in-blood was obliged to seek revenge. Such a crime was forgiven if he killed the slayer outside a city of asylum (Num. 35:27). This private justice, or "redemption" of blood, was a concept preserved till late into the monarchical period (2 Sam. 3:27, 30). However, this right was limited by the institution of the cities of asylum (Num. 35; Deut. 19) and by the creation of a distinction between unintentional and premeditated killing (Deut. 19; Exod. 21:13) (Ze'ev W. Falk 2001, 56). As a result, there arose a need for judicial decision. Judgment was given either by the community or by the elders after hearing both the accused and the avenger. The intervention of a **judge** was also necessary for the infliction of *talion* (or *Lex talionis,* the principle of exacting compensation in return for the wrong done, also known as "an eye for an eye"). This limited the plaintiff's right to revenge himself on the assailant to the decision of the judge. A wrong committed against a member of the same clan was adjudicated by the common chief (Ze'ev W. Falk 2001, 57).

In much of law, the concept of the redeemer is used in connection with slavery, ransom allowing the release of the person held in bondage. The term is used in a hopeful manner by Job, who exclaims, "I know that my redeemer liveth!" and is used in a fuller sense in the New Testament, where Jesus is referred to as the Redeemer of humankind because of his sacrificial death. If the penalty for sin is death, then Christ's death in place of his people, which offers the promise of life and salvation, is redemption, payment by his death on behalf of humankind to free them from the slavery to sin (John 8:34; Rom. 7:14). Here the concept appears to be that one person pays the price for another to satisfy justice. Paul refers to this as "redemption through his blood" (Eph. 1:7).

Thus, in a court of law, a relative or friend might pay the fine or assume the penalty for another. In theology, this comes to mean far more, including the deliverance from death or damnation, the just penalty for sin, being "bought at a price" (1 Cor. 6:20). *See also* Cities of Refuge; Law; Punishments.

Further Reading

Falk, Ze'ev W. *Hebrew Law in Biblical Times.* Provo, Utah: Brigham Young University Press, 2001. King, Philip J. and Lawrence E. Stager. *Life in Biblical Israel.* Louisville, Ky.: Westminster John Knox Press, 2001. Schechter, Solomon and S. Mendelsohn. "Homicide," http://www.jewishenclyclopedia. com (accessed June 10, 2005).

Resurrection

(Job 14:13–15, 19:25–27; Isa. 26:19; Jer. 31:29; Ezek. 18; Dan. 12:1–4; Matt. 26:28; Rom 5:18–19; John 11:24) Resurrection is the rising again from the dead in the flesh, an ancient belief that was a significant part of Christ's experience and teaching. It became a core belief of most Christian churches, affirmed in the Apostles' and Nicene Creeds: "I believe in … the resurrection of the dead."

The concept of the immortality of the soul has been common to many civilizations, developed in particular detail by the **Greeks,** most notably Plato. But the idea of the resurrection of the body was less common, shared primarily by the **Egyptians** and the Persians. The Jewish scriptures, both canonical and apocryphal, refer to the resurrection of the dead on numerous occasions. The Book of Job expresses this hope beautifully: "I know that my **Redeemer** liveth, and in the last day I shall rise out of the earth. And I shall be clothed again with my skin, and in my flesh I shall see God" (Job 19:25–27). The Book of Daniel indicates something of the same belief: "Many of those that sleep in the dust, shall awake: some unto life everlasting, and others unto reproach, to see it always" (Dan. 12:2). This passage relates the Resurrection Day to the Last Judgment, an idea that carries over into much of **apocalyptic** literature. Ezekiel's vision of the dry bones that will "rise again" is thought to refer to both the individual rebirth and to Israel's revival (Ezek. 37, 36:19–21).

Christ, in the tradition of the **Essenes** and the **Pharisees,** taught this idea expressly, confronting the **Sadducees** who appeared to doubt the power of God and the meaning of the Scripture (Matt. 22:29; Luke 20:37). Some weeks before his **crucifixion,** Christ began preparing his **disciples** for his death and resurrection. He told his followers that he would be put to death and, after three days, would rise again from the dead. In Mark's **Gospel** it is clear that these followers did not understand him or preferred not to consider the possibility of his death (Mark 8–9).

In other gospels, Jesus used the words, "I am the life and the Resurrection." At the time, he was discussing with Martha life after death. Martha, the sister of Lazarus, noted that she knew her brother "shall rise again, in the resurrection at the last day" (John 11:24). On three occasions, Christ brought people back from the dead: Lazarus, the daughter of Jarius, and the son of the widow of Nain.

The experience of Easter morning further reinforced the reality of this idea: the women who carried spices to the sepulchre before dawn found the heavy stone rolled away and the body of their Lord was gone (Matt. 28:1–3; Mark 16:1–3; Luke 24:1; John 20:1). Having been told of the resurrection, Peter and John ran to the tomb. There they found the linen **cloth** in which the body had been wrapped (John 20:3–10). Mary Magdalene returned to the sepulchre, saw two **angels,** and then Jesus himself (John 20:11–16; Mark 16:9). Jesus appeared to the disciples on the road to Emmaus, walking beside them (Mark 16:12–13; Luke 24:13–35). Christ also appeared to Peter and finally to all the **apostles** (Mark 16:14; Luke 24:36–43; John 20:19–25). On these occasions, Jesus broke **bread** and ate with his followers. He walked with them, talked with them, and cooked **fish** for them beside the sea. He even invited "doubting Thomas" to put his hands on his wounds. The body was clearly physical and recognizable, although different enough that even his best friends were slow to recognize him. This, of course, might also have been a result of their certainty of his death and failure to anticipate that he would reappear in their midst.

For the early **Church,** the events of Jesus's resurrection testified to his conquest of Death, justifying their faith. For Paul in particular, certainty that Christ was the **Messiah** came largely from the fact that he had defeated Death. "If Christ has not been raised, then our preaching is in vain, and your faith is in vain. . . . If Christ has not been raised, your faith is futile and you are still in your sins" (1 Cor. 15:14, 17). Peter also spoke of the resurrection of Christ as the basis for his faith that "we have been born anew to a living hope" (1 Pet. 1:3).

The centrality of this doctrine of the **Christian** Church led to a number of attacks. Some insisted it never happened, that Jesus did not really die, but only swooned. Some thought it was all a plot invented by the disciples. Many modern critics continue this litany of rejection, insisting that it is a fantastic and unnecessary belief. But even today, most Christians continue to recite their faith in the "resurrection of the body and the life everlasting." And even the Jews continue to express it in their morning benediction: "O God, the soul which Thou hast set within me is pure. . . . As long as it is within me I will give homage to Thee, O divine Master, Lord of all spirits, who givest back the soul to dead bodies" (George A. Barton and Kaufmann Kohler 2005). *See also* Afterlife; Mourning.

Further Reading

Barton, George A. and Kaufmann Kohler. "Resurrection," http://www.jewishencyclopedia.com (accessed January 28, 2005). Fuller, Reginald H. "Resurrection of Christ," in *The Oxford Companion to the Bible.* New York: Oxford University Press, 1993. Mass, A. J. "General Resurrection," http://www.newadvent.org (accessed January 28, 2005). Mass, A. J. "Resurrection of Jesus Christ," http:www.newadvent.org (accessed January 28, 2005). Segal, Alan F. *Life After Death: A History of the Afterlife in Western Literature.* New York: Doubleday, 2004.

Rod. *See* Shepherds

Rome, Romans

The events of the New Testament all occurred in the time when the Roman Empire was the dominant power in the world. Jesus was born in Bethlehem, rather than his family's hometown of Nazareth, because the Roman emperor Augustus Caesar ordered that a census be taken at that time and that citizens enlist in their ancestral home regions. Jesus was nearly killed as an infant when the Roman-appointed **King** Herod learned that a new king, the **Messiah,** was born and might supplant him. Jesus lived in a country full of Roman troops, including centurions who sometimes sought his help for their own families. He traveled on roads built by Roman engineers. He passed Roman cities, such as Tiberius and Caesarea, named after Roman emperors and full of Roman citizens, constructed according to the Greco-Roman designs so popular at the time. These cities were full of testimonies to Roman culture with their amphitheatres, temples, baths, and courts. When asked about his proper relationship with Rome, Jesus used a Roman coin to make his point about the allegiance owed to God and the allegiance owed to government. Jesus was eventually tried by the Roman Procurator, Pontius Pilate. He died on the cross, a Roman form of punishment, with Roman soldiers at his feet, casting lots for his robe

In the early years of the **Church,** one of its key leaders, Paul, was a Roman citizen who was proud of his citizenship. He was eventually imprisoned in a Roman city, Caesarea Maritima, and tried by Roman **judges** according to Roman **law,** which allowed him to claim the right to appeal to the emperor and travel to Rome. He previously had written to the **Christians** in Rome (the famous **epistle** to the Romans). In Rome, he is thought to have been held in prison for some time before he was finally executed by Roman officials.

Rome itself became the new center for the early Church after the destruction of Jerusalem in 70 A.D. by Roman legions. Peter, like Paul, was taken there and was also executed in Rome. The catacombs of Rome became famous as meeting places of the Christians, who grew in number even as they were persecuted by a series of emperors, as John had prophesied in the book of Revelation. The infamous Coliseum was the scene of hideous atrocities, many involving Christian martyrs, who refused to bow the knee to the emperor as a god.

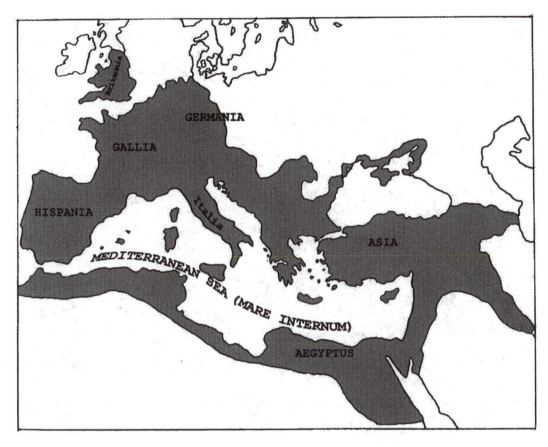

Map showing the extensive reach of the Roman Empire, from Britain across Asia and into Africa.

The spread of the faith among the gentiles was finally encouraged by the Roman Emperor Constantine, who became a Christian and proclaimed Christianity the official faith of the Empire, for the first time stamping a cross on his coinage in 314 A.D. (Kenneth Scott Latourette 1953, 91). The early ecclesiastical historian Eusebius, a contemporary of Constantine (ca. 260–340 A.D.), has told much of this story in detail from the vantage point of the time.

Years before Christ was born, the Romans had overthrown Hannibal of Carthage and took over the land previously controlled by the Seleucids, expanding their sovereignty beyond Greece into Asia Minor. The Roman general Pompey marched through the kingdom of the Seleucids, launched a three-month siege of Jerusalem, and made Judah a Roman province in 63 B.C. The famous historian Flavius Josephus, an eyewitness to the Roman conquest of Palestine, has left a vivid account in *The Wars of the Jews*. In a vivid chapter of his history, Josephus describes the destruction of Jerusalem and of the Temple under Titus. They starved the citizens during a long siege, rammed in the walls of the city, looted all the treasures of the great citadel, burned the palaces and the places of worship, sent many of the citizens into slavery, and took a host of captives back to Rome for a triumphant victory parade. The city was eventually rebuilt as a Roman city, with its amphitheatre, baths, etc., but it was no longer David's holy city. The country never again was truly independent.

Many attribute the rapid rise of Christianity to the Roman Empire, with its good roads, safe travel, easy communication, and peaceful administration of a vast realm. "Under Augustus and his successors, the empire stretched from the north-west corner of Europe to **Egypt** and from Mauratania to the Black Sea. It brought fifty million or more inhabitants under relatively stable rule, an ideal setting for the growth of a new religion" (Richard P. Saller 1993, 657).

Some historians note that the Roman Empire was the ideal seedbed for the new religion, where many faiths were contending for the hearts and minds of the people: "Better than its rivals, Christianity gave to the Greco-Roman world what so many were craving from a religion"—for those seeking immortality, the promise of eternal life; for those craving high moral values, an ideal vision of the sacrificial life of servanthood; for those seeking fellowship, a community of worshippers who loved one another; for those distrustful of reason, a deep faith rooted in an ancient set of beliefs; for those seeking intellectual satisfaction, a challenging set of ideas and a developing theology (Kenneth Scott Latourette 1953, 107). *See also* Law; War, Warfare: General.

Further Reading

Josephus, Flavius. *The Works of Josephus*. Peabody, Mass.: Hendrickson Publishers, Inc., 2001. Latourette, Kenneth Scott. *A History of Christianity*. New York: Harper and Row, 1953. Saller, Richard P. "Roman Empire," in *The Oxford Companion to the Bible*. New York: Oxford University Press, 1993. Wright, G. Ernest. *Biblical Archaeology*. Philadelphia: The Westminster Press, 1957. Keller, Werner. *The Bible as History*. New York: Bantam Books, 1982.

S

Sabbath

(**Gen. 2:2–3; Exod. 20:8; Num. 28:9–10; Ps. 92; Matt. 12:1–14; Mark 2:23–28; Luke 6 1–11**) The majestic account of God's work of **creation** in Genesis concluded with these words: "And on the seventh day God ended his work which he had made; and he rested on the seventh day from all his work which he had made. And God blessed the seventh day, and sanctified it: because that in it he had rested from all his work which God created and made" (Gen. 2:2–3). Even as late as Moses, this was the only day of the week that had a name, the *Sabbath,* probably meaning "to cease" or "bring to an end." It was also the only day designated by a commandment as a perpetual ordinance: "Remember the Sabbath day to keep it holy" (Exod. 20:8). Neither man nor beast was to work on this day of rest. God even provided his people with a double portion of manna on the day before, thereby freeing them from the need to labor on his holy day.

The details of this special day are spelled out in some of the **law** applicable to every living creature in the household: the children, the servants, even the aliens and the **animals** (Exod. 20:10). The **sacrifices** for the Sabbath involve burnt offerings, drink offerings, and grain offerings (Num. 28:9–10). The **punishment** for failing the observance was also clear: it was death. "Whoever does any work on the Sabbath day must be put to death"(Exod. 31:15). Scripture also details the **blessings**. In Psalm 92, designated a song for the Sabbath day, the Psalmist proclaims that "It is a good thing to give thanks unto the Lord, and to sing praises unto thy name, O most High," and Isaiah proclaims the blessings that come to the man who "keeps the Sabbath without desecrating it" (Isa. 56:2).

Within the Jewish home, Sabbath observance meant that the family attended worship services and refrained from all activity that might be classified as work: lighting fires, preparing **food**, buying and selling products, or walking farther than needed to go to the **synagogue**. The observance began with the blast of the ram's horn, after which the mother lit the Candle of Joy. The members of the family put on their best **clothing** and enjoyed the best **meal** of the week, which began with the father's special blessing over the **bread** and **wine**, thus making every Hebrew home a kind of sanctuary in which God was worshipped (Madeleine S. Miller and J. Lane Miller 1961, 632).

Apparently, over time the Hebrews grew careless in their observation of the day, leading a number of the **prophets** to rail against them. Jeremiah, for example, prophesied that if the people refused to obey God and "keep the Sabbath day holy by not carrying any load as you come through the **gates** of Jerusalem on the Sabbath day, then I will kindle an unquenchable fire in the gates of Jerusalem that will consume her **fortresses**" (Jer.17:27). Hosea,

Ezekiel, and Isaiah also denounced the "sabbaths" and new moons—the perversions of **festivals** and violation of their **covenant** (Hos. 2:11; Is 1:13; Ezek. 46:3).

During the **Babylonian** exile, the celebration of the Sabbath became a binding force to hold the people together in a common culture and faith. When the **Israelites** returned to rebuild Jerusalem under the Persians, Nehemiah led them to a fresh orthodoxy regarding the Sabbath. He admonished them to refuse to buy from foreign merchants who brought **fish**, grain, and other merchandise into the city to sell on the Sabbath (Neh. 10:31; 13:16). He ordered that the doors be shut "when evening shadows fell on the gates of Jerusalem before the Sabbath" so that no one could enter, and they should not be opened until the Sabbath was over (Neh. 13:19). This was a span of 24 hours, sundown on Friday until sundown on Saturday.

In the period between the Testaments, Jewish **priests** and scholars in the synagogues studied and elaborated the minutiae of Sabbath observance, developing a host of rules and regulations, already elaborated over the years in oral tradition, for the orthodox to observe (E. J. Young and F. F. Bruce 1980, 1355).

It was to this expansion of regulations that Jesus objected. He observed Sabbath worship, going regularly to the synagogue or **Temple** (as did his **disciples**). But when he healed on the Sabbath or fed his disciples with bits of grain gathered in the field, he was violating the rules of the Mishnah (the works of the **scribes** that expand on the words of Scripture) (Matt. 12:1–14; Mark 2:23–28; Luke 6 1–11). He responded to the Pharisees' charges by explaining that the Sabbath was made for man, not man for the Sabbath. He also claimed to be "Lord of the Sabbath" (Mark 12:8). His practice of healing on the Sabbath became a special bone of contention. The **Pharisees** quizzed him about this and spied on him to catch him in the act of violating the Sabbath (Mark 3:2–4).

After the death and **resurrection** of Jesus, his followers continued to observe the Sabbath. Paul, however, did not insist that converts follow this part of the law of Moses. At the Council of Jerusalem, the **apostles** determined that they need not impose a Sabbath observance on **Christian churches**. Nonetheless, because so many of the converts were Jews, they continued their observance even after this declaration, celebrating Saturday as the Sabbath. They continued this practice until late in the first century when they gradually chose to observe the first day—Sunday or the Lord's Day—as their day of rest and worship in commemoration of the Resurrection.

In later history, Sabbath observance has been disputed periodically. The Roman Catholic Church debated the need for **fasting** on the Sabbath; Luther and other reformers were inclined to reject any emphasis on the Sabbath, but Calvin (in the *Institutes:* 2.8.28) emphasized the Bible's clear proclamation of this as a day "to hear the Law, and perform religious rites" and to rest. Rather than *Sunday* or *Sabbath*, some Reformers refer to the day as the "Lord's Day." Later times have seen arguments about Sabbath observance in America and England (the so-called Blue Laws), which enforce the closing of stores even for nonbelievers. Another debate has involved the Seventh Day Adventists' insistence on return to the original meaning of the Sabbath as Saturday (Paul Garnet and David L. Jeffrey 1992, 673).

All of this history points to the human observance of the Sabbath Day, but there were other details in the law as well. Just as animals were to rest on the seventh day, so on the "sabbatical year"—that is, the seventh year, the land was to rest, to lie fallow. That was also the year that **slaves** were to be set free and debts forgiven. The Jubilee Year, the 50-year Sabbath, marked the culmination of the sabbatical years. The trumpet was to be sounded, property was to return to its original owners, debts were remitted, and those enslaved for debt were to be freed (D. Freeman 1980, 1356). This tradition may have led some to describe the age to come as a "perpetual Sabbath" (Heb. 4:9) for the people of God. *See also* Festivals; Law; Meals; Punishments; Synagogue.

Further Reading

Freeman, D. "Sabbath," in *The Illustrated Bible Dictionary*. Sydney, Australia: Tyndale House Publishers, 1980. Garnet, Paul and David L. Jeffrey. "Sabbath," in *A Dictionary of the Biblical Tradition in English Literature*. Grand Rapids, Mich.: William B. Eerdmans Publishing Company, 1992. Miller, Madeleine S. and J. Jane Miller. "Sabbath," in *Harper's Bible Dictionary*. New York: Harper and Row, 1961.

Sacrifice

(Gen. 4:3–4, 8:20; Lev. 1–7; Heb. 9:19–28) Cain and Abel brought to God their offerings of their flock and grain (Gen. 4:3–4), the first recorded sacrifice in Scripture. In both cases, God observed both the offering brought and the spirit in which it was brought. Abel's offering was the "firstlings" of his flock, but Cain brought some of the fruit of the ground, not the choicest and not involving the sacrifice of **blood** or life. Noah built an **altar** and gave to the Lord a burnt offering of every clean beast and fowl (Gen. 8:20). His offering sent forth a "sweet savor" that pleased the Lord. When Abraham went to the Promised Land, he built altars along the way (Gen. 12:6–8), and when God instructed him to place his son on the altar as a sacrifice, both father and son revealed that they were accustomed to blood sacrifice (Gen. 22:7). The replacement provided by

God himself, the wild ram, marks the first recorded substitutionary sacrifice. Later in the **law** of Moses, the scapegoat became such a substitute for the offending party.

Other patriarchs built and used altars regularly, marking places where special events occurred. It is only when the children of **Israel** escaped from **Egypt** and received the law and the **Covenant** that the specific terms of sacrifice were outlined for them, with special days and reasons; special sacrifices; and special functionaries, the **priests**, to perform the ceremonies. Much of this is contained in the Holiness Code, in Leviticus 1–7 especially.

The best known of the regular offerings occurred at the **Passover**, the **Day of Atonement**, and the **Festival of First Fruits**. Each of the daily rituals that the priests were commanded to follow also called for the sacrifice of lambs, as did the **Sabbaths**. The **Festival of New Moons** required bullocks, rams, and **goats** as well. The Festival of **Tabernacles** also required the full range of offerings, with the sacrifices spread out over eight days. The Lord commanded some of these festivals in Exodus 23:15, insisting that "none shall appear before me empty handed." Some also involved a communion **meal**, where the family and the priests joined to enjoy food and fellowship after the cleansing had occurred. In some cases, only the priests and their families were allowed to eat the sacrificial offering.

With the advent of the monarchy, Solomon provided the place and pattern for regular sacrifices involving royal participation, which sometimes replaced participation of the entire community. Although the sacrifices were supposed to be limited to the altar at the **Temple** in Jerusalem, some of the old **sanctuaries** were probably used as well. Scripture follows the activities of the **kings** and the ceremonies at the Temple, but local worship probably continued as well. As Solomon opened other worship centers out of respect for the faiths of his various wives and concubines, sacrifices must have also proliferated outside of Jerusalem.

For centuries, the great holocausts were performed at the altar at the Temple, involving hundreds of **animals**. The ritual became increasingly elaborate. Psalm 51 summarizes the message of many of the **prophets** regarding the outward show of most sacrifice: "For thou desirest not sacrifice, else would I give it: thou delightest not in burnt offering. The sacrifices of God are a broken spirit; a broken and a contrite heart, O God, thou wilt not despise" (Ps. 51:16–17).

The destruction of the First Temple and the period of the Exile interrupted the sacrificial rituals, forcing the faithful into the more limited mode of worship in the **synagogues**, where prayers and study rather than bloodletting and feasting were the norm. With the restoration of the remnant of Judah and the building of the Second Temple, however, the Jews did revive their old tribal practices. These continued until the Romans destroyed Herod's Temple in 70 A.D.

Jesus was circumcised at the Temple, and his mother offered the usual poor-person's sacrifice for the birth of a firstborn son—two pigeons. He and his family seem to have made the pilgrimage to Jerusalem for some of the regular festivals, including the **Passover**. His outrage at the excessive charges for the **clean animals** and the manner in which **money changers** were abusing God's law suggest that he was concerned with the behavior of the priests and officials, not with the sacrifice itself.

His own **crucifixion** became the culmination of the sacrifice for Christians, who believed that this sacrifice was once and for all. The Book of Hebrews explains this theology fully, starting with Mosaic law:

> For when Moses had spoken every precept to all the people according to the law, he took the blood of calves and of goats, with water, and scarlet wool, and hyssop, and sprinkled both the book and all the people, Saying, This is the blood of the Testament which God hath enjoined unto you. Moreover he sprinkled with blood both the tabernacle, and all the vessels of the ministry. And almost all things are by the law purged with blood; and without shedding of blood is no remission. It was therefore necessary that the patterns of things in the heavens should be purified with these; but the heavenly things themselves with better sacrifices than these. For Christ is not entered into the holy places made with hands, which are the figures of the true; but into heaven itself, now to appear in the presence of God for us ... but now once in the end of the world hath he appeared to put away sin by the sacrifice of himself. ... So Christ was once offered to bear the sins of many. (Hebrews 9: 19–28)

Sacrifice, Offerings

The laws for sacrifice appear all through Exodus 20–24, 34; Leviticus 17, 19; Numbers 15 and in various other places. They specify the materials, the occasions, and the rituals required for appropriate sacrifice. Among the standard materials were the **clean animals** and **birds**: the bullock, **goat**, **sheep**, dove, or pigeon. The basic principle was that these animals were valuable property lawfully acquired. The ram that Abraham offered was the rare exception of a wild animal that God found acceptable for sacrifice. The sacrificial offerings were also to be the best of the animals, unblemished and male (except in the case of birds, where sex was not a consideration).

In addition to the animals, cereal offering was regularly included, although it was not so highly regarded as "blood" sacrifice. The first fruits or the best of the harvest were considered suitable, often baked into loaves of **bread** and eaten. The loaves of showbread (or *shewbread*) were placed on the golden table in the Holy Place.

Libations of oil, **wine**, and water were also used, although only the wine-offerings were named among the first legal offerings (Num. 28:7). Honey and leaven were prohibited. **Incense** was also used as an accompaniment to cereal offering, especially frankincense.

The Ritual of Sacrifices

1. *Holocausts or burnt offerings:* Leviticus 1–5 outlined the major altar sacrifices, particularly the complete burning of the sacrificial animal, called a "holocaust." These voluntary acts of worship were intended to atone for unintentional sin in general, or to express devotion, commitment, and complete surrender to God. The ritual included five acts, used in the holocaust:

   a. The worshipper, presenting himself in a state of ritual purity, brought his offering of a clean, unblemished male beast to the place of sacrifice, usually the **tabernacle** forecourt, the local sanctuary, a rough **stone** or earth altar, or the great brazen altar at the **Temple**.
   b. He laid hands—or perhaps one hand—on the victim, either confessing his sin at this time or certifying that this victim came from him.
   c. At some distance from the altar, he slaughtered the animal, cutting its throat, or he gave it to the priest or Levites for slaughter (in the case of national offerings).
   d. The **blood** was collected in a basin by the **priest**, who dashed it against two corners of the altar so as to splatter all four sides. In the case of birds, where the blood was insufficient for this practice, the priest wrung its neck and drained the blood out on the side of the altar. The remainder of the blood was then poured out at the base of the altar. In certain ceremonies, it was sprinkled or flung over various other items or rubbed on still others. "The life of all flesh is its blood" (Lev. 7:26–27, 17:14; Gen. 9:4; Deut. 12:23) and therefore all blood belongs to God.
   e. The carcass, which was skinned and quartered, was placed on the altar by the priests, to be burned by a fire that was never allowed to die out. The rest of the body, including the head, intestines, and hooves or feet, were then washed and placed on the altar to be burned. Different kinds of burning were prescribed for different forms of offering. The holocaust was a complete burning, in which nothing survived but ashes. The skin usually was given to the priests, although it too might be burned (R. T. Beckwith 1980, 1360–1361).

When **grain** offering was included, an offering of fine flour was kneaded with **olive oil**, incense, and salt. The flour was burned in the holocaust and a libation of wine was poured out at the foot of the altar, like the blood of the victim (Roland deVaux 1961, 416).

2. *Communion sacrifices or fellowship offerings.* The communion sacrifices were voluntary acts of worship, expressing thanksgiving to God to bring about union with him. The three types were the sacrifice of praise, the voluntary sacrifice offered out of devotion, and the votive sacrifice, in which the participant has bound himself by a vow (Lev. 7:16–17, 22:18–23). Birds were not allowed for this sacrifice, but female animals with minor blemishes were sometimes tolerated.

The same process for the laying on of hands, sprinkling of blood, and so on was used, with the fat that was mentioned for the burning was considered, like blood, to be life-giving. Specifically, the fat from the kidneys, liver, and intestines was put on the fire, explaining the phrase "a feast of fat things." Offerings of unleavened cakes and leavened bread were part of this sacrifice. For communion sacrifices, the portions of the sacrifice that were not wholly burnt up were then eaten as a sacrificial **meal**. The priest was assigned the breast and the right leg of the animal, and the remainder belonged to the person offering the sacrifice. He and his family would join with any guests in a communion **feast;** all of those participating were expected to be in a state of ritual purity (Roland deVaux 1961, 417–418).

3. *Expiatory sacrifices.* There were two types of mandatory offering to atone for unintentional sin. The confession, forgiveness, and cleansing were different from the voluntary forms of sacrifice listed earlier. They were used to reestablish the **covenant** with God that had been broken by the sins of man: the sacrifice for sin and the sacrifice of reparation.

The sacrifice for sin (Lev. 4:1–5, 13:6:17–23) was used to obliterate sin, even the sins of the high priest. The rank of the sinner determined the animal used for sacrifice, with a bull offered for the high priest, a he-goat for a prince, and a she-goat or sheep for the private individual. Two parts of the ritual distinguished it from others: blood was more important, with the ritual involving collecting, sprinkling, rubbing, and pouring blood in an elaborate ceremony. This blood was intended to make expiation: "Without the shedding of blood, there is no forgiveness at all" (Heb. 9:22). In addition, the fat was burnt on the altar but the person offering the sacrifice received no part of the victim, which was reserved for the priests. In the case of the high priest's sin, even the priests were not allowed to eat any part of the victim: all the remains were carried out and placed on the ash heap (Roland de Vaux 1961, 419). This ceremony was especially important as a part of the Day of Atonement.

The sacrifice of reparation dealt with a specific offense, usually against a specific individual. In addition to the sacrifice, the guilty man had to offer a ram for reparation and restore to the priests or the person he had wronged the monetary equivalent of the damage he had caused.

Alfred Edersheim describes vividly the morning sacrifice at the Temple that Jesus would have experienced:

As the massive Temple-gates slowly swung on their hinges, a three-fold blast from the silver trumpets of the Priests seemed to waken the City, as with the Voice of God, to the life of another day.... It had not come too soon. The Levites on ministry, and those of the laity, whose 'course' it was to act as representatives of Israel ... hastened to their duties. For already the blush of dawn, for which the Priest on the highest pinnacle of the Temple had watched, to give the signal for beginning the services of the day, had shot its brightness far away to Hebron and beyond. Within the Courts below all had long been busy. At some time previously ... the superintending Priest had summoned to their sacred functions those who had 'washed,' according to the ordinance. There must have been each day about fifty priests on duty. Such of them as were ready now divided into two parties, to make inspection of the Temple courts by torchlights. Presently they met, and trooped to the well-known Hall of Hewn Polished Stones.... It was scarcely daybreak, when a second time they met for the 'lot,' which designated those who were to take part in the sacrifice itself, and who were to trim the golden candlestick, and make ready the altar of incense within the Holy Place. And now morn had broken, and nothing remained before the admission of worshippers but to bring out the lamb, once again to make sure of its fitness for sacrifice, to water it from a golden bowl, and then to lay it in mystic fashion—as tradition described the binding of Isaac—on the north side of the altar, with its face to the west.

All, priests and laity, were present as the Priest, standing on the east side of the altar, from a golden bowl sprinkled with sacrificial blood two sides of the altar, below the red line which marked the difference between ordinary sacrifices and those that were to be wholly consumed. While the sacrifice was prepared for the altar, the priests, whose lot it was, had made ready all within the Holy Place, where the most solemn part of the day's service was to take place—that of offering the incense, which symbolised Israel's accepted prayers. (Alfred Edersheim 2004, 94–95)

In all cases, the sacrifices were powerful expressions of worship, acknowledging that God is the creator and sustainer of the universe, that he deserves our praise and obedience. The purpose was to bring a valuable gift to him and to seek to reestablish fellowship with him. *See also* Altar; Feasting; Festivals; Law; Tabernacle; Temple.

Further Reading

Beckwith, R. T. "Sacrifice," in *The Illustrated Bible Dictionary.* Sydney, Australia: Tyndale House Publishers, 1980. DeVaux, Roland. *Ancient Israel: Its Life and Institutions.* Grand Rapids, Mich.: William B. Eerdmans Publishing Company, 1961. Edersheim, Alfred. *The Life and Times of Jesus the Messiah.* Peabody, Mass.: Hendrickson Publishers, Inc., 2004.

Sadducees

(Mark 12:18; Luke 20:27; Acts 23:8) The Sadducees were a group of **priests** who became the "**Temple** party" in the days after the return from Exile, a powerful and aristocratic group during the first century B.C. until the destruction of the Temple in 70 A.D., when the Romans put down the rebellion of the Jews. They were mentioned several times by Jesus in the **Gospels**. Most frequently, they are paired with the **Pharisees** as the establishment parties in Jewish life, but with strong differences. Several times, the Scripture notes that they "say there is no **resurrection**" (Mark 12:18; Luke 20:27; Acts 23:8), while the Pharisees did believe in the resurrection.

The Sadducees were educated and wealthy men who traced their traditions back to Zadok, high priest in Solomon's reign (1 Kings 1:39; 1 Chron. 12:28; Madeleine S. Miller and J. Lane Miller 1961, 634). Some believe that they emerged as a semi-political party because of the crisis brought about by the usurpation of the high priesthood by Jonathan in 152 B.C. (This was the moment when the **Essenes** were thought to have broken away to move into the desert (John Riches 1993, 667). Under **Roman** rule, the Sadducees compromised with authorities, thereby becoming very influential. Among their ranks were nobles, high priests, and members of the **Sanhedrin**. They dominated the rule of the Temple and its ritual until they were pushed aside by the Pharisees, who disagreed with many of their ideas and were more numerous and more political.

The Sadducees were more literal than the Pharisees in their interpretation of the **law** of Moses, insisting on adherence to the written documents, not the interpretations and traditions of the **scribes** and **rabbis**, also known as the "elders." They rejected not only the doctrine of the resurrection, which the Pharisees held, but even the immortality of the soul. Although they were the chief ecclesiastical rulers, they were not believers in Divine Providence. According to Josephus, they "took the people's destiny into their own hands, fighting or negotiating with the heathen nations" as they thought best (Kaufmann Kohler 2004). They believed that Jews could influence their own destiny; "if they obeyed the Law and repented and made due restitution when they sinned, then all would be well" (John Riches 1993, 667). They also denied the Pharisaic belief in **angels** and **demons**, and they rejected the Essenes' practice of incantation and conjuration for the cure of **diseases**.

As literalists, they insisted on the law of retaliation—"Eye for eye, tooth for tooth" (Exod. 21:24). They argued over which of the Temple ceremonies was appropriate in the celebration of certain **festivals**, especially the proper distribution of offerings, the use of **incense**, water libation, the Sukkot feast, etc. In a few instances, they were less strict than the Pharisees, who were much more numerous, and gradually stood much higher in the people's esteem. Over time, the Sadducees modified many of their ideas to coincide with those of the Pharisees.

With the destruction of the Temple in Jerusalem, including its altar, its holy precincts, and its many services, the Sadducees no longer had an object for which to live. They disappeared from history, although their views lived on. We know of them chiefly from Josephus and the New Testament, both unsympathetic sources. They argued with Jesus, imprisoned Peter and John, and arraigned Paul. Jesus warned his disciples, "Be on your guard against the yeast of the Pharisees and Sadducees" (Matt. 16:6). *See also* Pharisees; Temple.

Further Reading

Josephus, Flavius. *The Works of Josephus.* Peabody, Mass.: Hendrickson Publishers, Inc., 2001. Kohler, Kaufmann. "Sadducees," www.jewishencyclopedia.com (accessed December 20, 2004). Miller, Madeleine S. and J. Lane Miller. "Sadducees," in *Harper's Bible Dictionary.* New York: Harper and Row, 1961. Riches, John. "Sadducees," in *The Oxford Companion to the Bible.* New York: Oxford University Press, 1993.

Salt

(2 Lev. 2:13; Num. 18:19; 2 Chron. 13:5; Kings 2:19–23; Matt. 5:13; Mark 9:50) The most famous scene related to salt occurred in Genesis 19:26, when Lot's reluctant wife turned back to view the cities doomed for destruction and was transformed into a pillar of salt. Travelers to the Dead Sea often mention the remarkable salt formation to the west of the southern shore of this region, where they see a range of hills "150 feet high and

10 miles from north to south. Their slopes sparkle and glitter in the sunshine like diamonds" (Werner Keller 1982, 80). This range is pure rock salt: "Many blocks of salt have been worn away by the rain and have crashed downhill. They have odd shapes and some of them stand on end, looking like statues." It is easy to identify them with this ancient story of the end of Sodom and Gamorah and the death of Lot's wife.

This formation was the source for Israel's salt supply, of sufficient quality and quantity to allow them to make salt one of their major exports. "The Dead or 'Salt' Sea (Gen. xiv. 3, Josh. iii. 16) holds in solution not less than 24.57 kg. of salt in 100 kg. of water, and after every flood, upon the evaporation of the water, a coarse-grained salt is left behind in the pools and ditches. Saltpits, in which salt was thus obtained, are mentioned in Zeph. ii. 9 and in I Macc. ii. 35" (Emil Hirsch et al. 2005). One of the outrages in the regime of Antiochus Epiphanes was the **taxation** of salt to pay tribute to Rome.

In Scripture, salt was used for a variety of purposes:

1. *For seasoning food*. Every culture requires salt for good health and tasty cuisine. Both humans and **animals** require it. The Hebrews were particularly blessed by their large natural supply. It was so important to them that the Talmud used salt to symbolize the Torah (the five books of Moses), assuming that humans could not survive without it.

   Because the salt from the Dead Sea region was of fossil variety with impurities and because of chemical changes, the outer layer often lacked flavor. This was thrown away because it was worthless for its main purpose, just as Jesus notes in his famous quotation (Matt. 5:13). He has spoken of his followers as the "salt of the earth," who must maintain their "saltiness" to be of value.

2. *For preserving food*. Salt has long been known as one of the best and handiest of preservatives for foods, especially fish and meats. Because of this usage, it became the image of perpetuity, as in the "covenant of salt" that existed between God and Israel (Num. 18:19; 2 Chron. 13:5).

3. *In offerings*. Because of its symbolism as a preservative, salt was used in the levitical cereal-offerings (Lev. 2:13). "Every oblation of thy meal-offering shalt thou season with salt." This regulation also referred to the burnt offering of animals (Ezek 43:24). Salt was used also in the showbread and the **incense**. It is clear that Temple services required great quantities of salt (Ezra 6:9, 7:22).

4. *In agreements*. Harrison notes that it was often used by Oriental peoples in ratifying agreements, as a symbol of fidelity and constancy (R. K. Harrison 1980, 1370). It was also customary for people to assume, when they ate salted food together, that they had made

a pact of friendship. "Eating the salt of a man" means that a person derives his sustenance from him or takes pay from him (Ezra 4:14). Therefore, *salarium* or "salt money," represents "salary."

5. *For healing.* Newborn babies were rubbed all over with salt before they were swaddled (Ezek. 16:4). Elisha used salt on the brackish waters of the spring at Jericho to "sweeten" (or "heal") it (2 Kings 2:19–22). Folk medicine used salt for a number of purposes, even developing a series of superstitions regarding the condiment. Among those that have survived is the idea it is "bad luck" to spill salt. Some of it must be thrown over the left shoulder to avoid this outcome.

6. *In warfare.* Because excess salt in the ground renders it sterile, it became a custom to salt the ground of defeated cities. Abimelech sowed salt on Shechem as a "token of perpetual desolation" (R. K. Harrison 1980, 1370) as did other conquerors who wanted to make certain that their enemies would never rise again. *See also* Food; Sacrifice.

Further Reading

Bruce, F. F. "Salt, City of," in *The Illustrated Bible Dictionary,* 3 volumes. Sydney, Australia: Tyndale House Publishers, 1980. Harrison, R. K. "Salt," in *The Illustrated Bible Dictionary,* 3 volumes. Sydney, Australia: Tyndale House Publishers, 1980. Hirsch, Emil G., Immanuel Benzinger, Cyrus Adler, and M. Seligsohn. "Salt," http://www.jewishencyclopedia.com (accessed July 11, 2005). Keller, Werner. *The Bible as History.* New York: Bantam Books, 1982. Miller, Madeleine S. and J. Lane Miller. "Salt," in *Harper's Bible Dictionary.* New York: Harper and Row, 1961.

Sanctuary

"High places" or sanctuaries appear through much of the Old Testament as places of worship. These appear to be sacred spaces, often tied by tradition to experiences of the patriarchs when God revealed himself to his chosen ones. Sometimes, as at Carmel, the location had a long tradition of local people's worshipping other gods. Although called "high," these places were not always on mountains or hills, but were sometimes in cities or even valleys. They might even be under large trees. They were distinguished by having a raised area to signify that the space was set aside for worship.

The term *bamah* or *high place* usually referred to a space with an **altar**, which marked some historical event, such as a conquest. The altar traditionally was of uncut stone. Often these shrines marked the location of a **burial** and were used by the **Canaanites** for ancestral worship. The **Moabites** tended to believe that the god dwelt at the spot, especially on mountain tops. These ancient Canaanite sanctuaries may have marked nature worship and most certainly were cultic.

In addition to the altar, they often had a *massebah* and an *asherah*. The *massebah* was a stone standing upright, a commemorative stele (such as the stone set up by Joshua at Shechem (Josh. 24:26–27). Sometimes, God instructed the worshipper to set a stone on a special spot as a memorial of a theophany, in the case of Jacob's vision of the ladder to **Heaven**. Jacob had set up such a stone after his vision at Bethel, using the stone that had previously served as a pillow (Gen. 28:18, 31:13). This *massebah* was not a sculptured idol, but often symbolized a male deity such as **Baal** (2 Kings 3:2). The *ashrah*, a name for both the goddess and her cultic symbol, was made of wood cut into shape by a man, and could be burned (Judg. 3:7; 2 Kings 23:14, 23:6, 15; Deut. 12:3). It could even be a living tree or a post or stake (Roland deVaux, 1961, 285–286).

When the Israelites entered Canaan and settled the land under Joshua and the **judges**, they were too scattered to continue the centralized reverence for the **Tabernacle** that had been their sanctuary during the sojourn in the wilderness. The **Ark of the Covenant** was moved from one location to another, as the people found local sanctuaries to satisfy their need for regular worship. Rough sanctuaries (sacred space marked off by rings of rocks) were apparently established at a variety of places:

Shechem, where Abraham first stopped in Canaan, at the tree of Moreh—also called the Oak of the Teacher (Gen. 12:6–7);

Bethel, where Abraham erected his second altar in Canaan and where Jacob had set up his stone and anointed it with oil (Gen. 12:8, 28:10–22);

Mambre, where Abraham erected an altar under the Oak of Mambre (Gen. 13:18) and welcomed his three mysterious guests;

Beersheba, where Isaac saw God one night at the **Well** of the Oath, confirming Abraham's promise to his seed (Gen. 21:22–31, 26:33).

Once the Israelites settled into Canaan, the patriarchal centers of worship were rarely mentioned, but other sanctuaries emerged:

Gilgal, probably in the area near Jericho (Josh. 4:20), where the Ark came to rest after the crossing of the Jordan (Josh. 4:19, 7:6) and where the people circumcised themselves and celebrated the first **Passover** in Canaan. It was at Gilgal that the manna ceased to fall (Josh. 5:10–12), marking the end of the desert wanderings. Here Samuel came to judge Israel. It was also an important place in Saul's life: He was proclaimed **king** at Gilgal, and later was rejected as king in that same place.

Shiloh became the central sanctuary during the tribal confederation, serving as a meeting place for the **tribes**. The Tabernacle was set up there, and lots were cast for the territory of the seven tribes. Tradition holds that the Ark was kept there, in the first "temple" of Yahweh Sabbaoth (1 Sam. 1:3).

Mispah in Benjamin, where the Israelites took a solemn **oath** (Judg. 20:1), was mentioned in stories of Samuel and Saul. It was here that Saul was chosen king, and sacred lots were drawn (1 Sam. 10:17–24).

Gibeon, called "the greatest high place," was associated with a grotesque act of vengeance, in which the victims were dismembered (2 Sam. 21:1–14).

Ophra, where the **Angel** of the Lord appeared under a tree, charging Gideon to save Israel from the **Midianite** oppressors. In a dream, Gideon was instructed to destroy the altar of Baal and cut the asherah into pieces and burn it (Judg. 6:25–32).

Dan, the history of which seems to be associated with the migration of the tribe of Dan (Judg. 17–18) and a scandalous story that resulted in a false sanctuary served by a false priest.

Jerusalem, where David finally brought the Ark, and his son Solomon built the Temple. This hill was mentioned in the story of Abraham meeting with Melchisedek, king and priest of Salem, or Jerusalem. (For a more complete description, see deVaux 1961, 302–312.)

Six major sanctuaries emerged over time:

1. The Tabernacle in the wilderness shortly after the **Exodus**
2. The Tabernacle at Shiloh, built by Joshua after the conquest of Palestine (Josh 18:1)
3. The Tabernacle at Nob, the city of priests, which stood till the reign of Saul
4. The Tabernacle at Gibeon (2 Chron 1:3), which stood 50 years until Solomon completed the Temple
5. The first Temple, destroyed in 422 B.C.
6. The Second Temple, built in 352 B.C. and destroyed in 68 or 70 A.D. (Judah David Eisenstein 2005)

Each of these sanctuaries was considered legitimate at some time, but they often were profaned by the worship of heathen gods. Solomon was notorious for his encouragement of worship in high places, apparently under the influence of his foreign wives. The worship of Baal and his consorts along with the heathenish practices caused Amos, Ezekiel, and Hosea to denounce them. Especially in the Northern Kingdom, where phallic **idols** were introduced, Josiah killed the priests and burned their bones on the altar (1 Kings 13:32). Under Rehoboam and Asa, the high places flourished, as they did after the Exile.

The sacredness of space surrounding the Temple or the Ark proved very powerful in Hebrew thought. Gentiles might not enter the inner courts of the Temple, and lay persons (such as Jesus) might not enter the Holy Place. No one but the high priest might enter the Holy of Holies. The Temple itself was built with each increasingly sacred area higher than the previous one, echoing the notion that "high places" had some mystical value.

The concept of holy space, or sanctuary, has continued over time. Certain places are revered because of events such as visions or miracles that are associated with them. Thus, pilgrims will flock to a site, hoping that the spot where one person was miraculously healed might prove the place for their own healing. The pilgrimages to Canterbury Cathedral or to Lourdes are a part of this tradition. *See also* Altar; Asherah, Ashtoreth, Ashtaroth; Baal, Baalim; Tabernacle; Temple.

Further Reading

DeVaux, Roland. *Ancient Israel: Its Life and Institutions*. Grand Rapids, Mich.: William B. Eerdmans Publishing Company, 1961. Eisenstein, Judah David. "Sanctuary," http://www.jewishencyclopedia.com (accessed June 14, 2005).

Sanhedrin

(Matt. 26:59; Mark 14:55, 15:1; Luke 22:66; John 11:47; Acts 4:5–21, 5:17–41, 6:12, 22:30, 23:15, 24:20) The term *Sanhedrin* was first used by Josephus to designate the Jewish supreme court under the **Romans**. It is Greek for "sitting together." Not an original concept, the court was a successor to a series of councils that had met to confer and judge from the time of Moses. The 70 elders who governed **Israel** at Moses's request (Num.11:4–31) were followed after the Exile by the Great **Synagogue**, or the "Great Assembly," convened by Ezra and Nehemiah (Neh. 8–10) to deliberate on important questions and issue regulations (Wilhelm Bacher, Jacob Zallel Lauterbach 2005). Although there is no record of the composition of this assembly or the number of its members, it probably consisted of "leading men in Church and State, the chief priests, elders, and 'judges'—the latter two classes including 'the **Scribes**'" (Ezra 10:14; Neh. 5:7; Alfred Edersheim 2004, 66).

The Sanhedrin was limited to 70 elders (some believe 71), selected originally from **priests** belonging to prominent families, with the high priest presiding. Gradually, the **Pharisees** gained some authority in the council, especially during the time of Herod. These laymen were devoted to the law and interpreted it logically and meticulously. Also, pairs of leaders, teachers, and scribes presided over the body and debated to present rival points of view. Records note that they were chosen for their scholarship, modesty, and popularity. They were expected to be strong and courageous. They had to have previously filled three offices of increasing dignity, such as magistrate or **judge**. They also "must be tall, of imposing appearance, and of advanced age; and they must be learned and must understand foreign languages as well as some of the arts of the necromancer" (Wilhelm Bacher and Jacob Zallel Lauterbach 2005).

The assembly was first called *Sanhedrin* when the Roman governor of Syria, Gabinius (57 B.C.) abolished the constitution of Palestine and divided it into five provinces, with a sanhedrin at the head of each. The assembly at Jerusalem came to be known as the "Great Sanhedrin." This is the council that appears prominently in the New Testament, particularly in the trial and execution of Jesus (Matt. 26:59; Mark 14:55, 15:1; Luke 22:66; John 11:47).

There may have been two such bodies, one for secular concerns that met outside of the **Temple**, and one for religious judgments that met adjacent to the **altar**. The religious group dealt with questions relating to the Temple, the priesthood, the **sacrifices**, and such religious issues. The other functioned as a kind of supreme court in political cases, having the highest political authority, being empowered to deal with criminal cases and to impose the sentence of capital punishment—but only if the Roman procurator was present. It had authority only in Judea, a limitation explaining why the Sanhedrin could not lay hands on Jesus when he was working in Galilee. The charge brought against him, **blasphemy**, was typical "of its arraignments, for it was the court of highest appeal in matters based on the Mosaic **Law**" (Madeleine S. Miller and J. Lane Miller 1961, 644).

The Great Sanhedrin met on the southern side of the inner court of the Temple, the site of the "court of laymen," which was called "the hall of hewn stone." Impressive with its great colonnade and majestic situation, it was accessible to any Jew who wished to bring before it complicated details of Jewish law. "The learned council sat in a semi-circle with the accused in front of them; attended by court clerks; and observed by three rows of **disciples** who might be candidates for the body. The prisoner was appareled in mourning garments" (Madeleine S. Miller and J. Lane Miller 1961, 644).

After the execution of Jesus, the Sanhedrin persecuted his followers, questioning Peter, John, and other **apostles**, commanding them to refrain from preaching in the name of Jesus, and threatening and beating them. The Sanhedrin questioned Stephen and sentenced him to be stoned, and Paul later faced them (Acts 4:5–21, 5:17–41, 6:12, 22:30, 23:15, 24:20).

Although the Sanhedrin was disbanded with the destruction of the Temple and the downfall of the Jewish state (70 A.D.), it was succeeded by a series of academies under the presidency of the patriarchs of the family of Hillel. During the rabbinic period (ca. 200 A.D.), the *Sanhedrin* became a technical term for the rabbinic court, which determined many of the rulings that formed the Mishnah, the first codification of rabbinic law and debate (J. Andrew Overman 1993, 678). *See also* Court Officials; Judges; Law; Pharisees; Sadducees.

Further Reading

Bacher, Wilhelm and Jacob Zallel Lauterbach "Sanhedrin," http://www.jewishencyclopedia.com (accessed January 29, 2005); Edersheim, Alfred. *The Life and Times of Jesus the Messiah* Peabody, Mass.: Hendrickson Publishers, Inc., 2004. Josephus, Flavius. *The Works of Josephus.* Peabody, Mass: Hendrickson Publishers, Inc., 2001. Miller, Madeleine S. and J. Lane Miller. "Sanhedrin," in *Harper's Bible Dictionary.* New York: Harper and Row, 1961. Overman, J. Andrew. "Sanhedrin," in *The Oxford Companion to the Bible.* New York: Oxford University Press, 1993.

Scepter

(Gen 49:10; Num. 24:17; Judg. 5:14; Ps. 23:4; Esther 4:11) The scepter is a staff that a ruler holds to signify his authority. It may be long, topped by a symbolic insignia, or short, like a mace. In ancient Greece, the leader of the clan often had such a staff in his hand and gave it to others when he allowed them to speak (as in Homer's epics). In many of the ancient kingdoms, the ruler would extend the scepter to someone to allow that person to approach his throne. Men of rank often carried a rod as a symbol of their authority.

"Thy rod and thy staff they comfort me," sang the Psalmist. This **Shepherd**'s Psalm (Ps. 23:4) suggests the origins of the **king's** scepter in Israel. The shepherd used his rod for protection from wild **animals**, for separating sheep from the **goats**, for inspecting them, and for guiding them, and for **punishment**. "Passing under the rod" was the shepherd's way of counting his sheep (Lev. 27:32; Ezek. 20:37). He also carried a staff, with a crook on the end, to pull the sheep toward him and save them from trouble. Soldiers, like shepherds, carried clubs as primitive and effective weapons (1 Sam. 14:27; 2 Sam. 23:21).

The rod or staff was also a support for travelers (Gen 32:10; Mark 6:8) or for old men or cripples (Zech. 8:4). In Babylon, every man carried a staff, as did most men in Israel, probably as a heritage from their nomadic days, when the heavy piece of wood was a steadying influence on hills and in rocky terrain.

As an instrument of punishment (1 Cor. 4:21), it is best known from the Proverb, "Spare the rod and spoil the child" (Prov. 13:24), suggesting that reasonable control and guidance of youngsters will save them from more serious problems later in life. In this case, the term may be a reference to the shepherd's concern for careful watching rather than violent punishment.

Hebrew pedagogy, however, did recommend beatings to keep order in the classroom (Joseph Jacobs and Louis Grossman 2005).

When finally the Israelites chose to have a king, it was natural to see him as a shepherd of his people. In archaeological sites around Egypt, the **Egyptian** rulers are pictured holding two crossed symbols, one a staff and the other a flail. (Aaron's rod appears to have been a direct reference to this imagery.) For the Israelite monarch, the scepter symbolized the power of God's authority, confirming his divine appointment (Judg. 5:14).

Over time, the scepter itself became a metaphor for the monarchy. Thus, the promise that "the scepter will not depart from Judah" (Gen. 49:10) became a promise of the lineage of the kings. David also used it—along with the **throne** metaphor—to stand for the God's regent on earth: "Your throne, O God, will last for ever and ever; a scepter of justice will be the scepter of your kingdom" (Ps. 45:6). In a call for God's judgment of the heathen, the Psalmist prays that God "break them with a rod [or scepter] of **iron**" and dash them to pieces like a **potter**'s vessel (Ps. 2:9).

As a contrary image of opposing authority, it became the "scepter of the wicked" (Ps. 125:3; Isa. 14:5). In Isaiah's prophecy, the scepter is a symbol for God's power: "with his scepter he will strike them down" (Isa. 30:31). In Jeremiah's prophesy, it stands for the loss of power: "How broken is the mighty scepter, how broken the glorious staff" (Jer. 48:17). Ezekiel shifts the imagery to underscore the tree (or heritage) from which the scepter is made, noting the great branches of the tree that were "fit for a ruler's scepter" and the destruction of that tree and its branches by fire (Ezek. 19:11–14), a prophecy of Judah's fall.

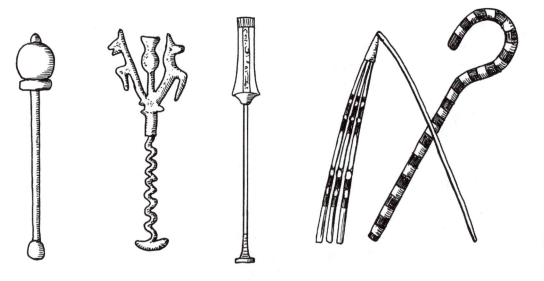

Scepters used among ancient kings: a royal mace, Ishtar's scepter, Pharoah's scepter in the era of King Tut, Egyptian flail and crook (often pictured in Pharoah's hands).

The scepters of conquering peoples are indicated in much the same way. The Book of Esther, which includes more details of the regal imagery than most books of the Old Testament, describes the gold scepter in the king's hand, which he held out to her when he wished her to rise and speak. When she rose and touched the tip of the gold scepter, she begged for the life of her mentor and kinsman (Esther 5:2; 8:4). In this case, the king's authority is suggested by the autocratic gesture, which did not occur in Israel's court. Amos spoke of "holding the scepter" when pointing to various rulers (Amos 1:5, 1:8).

Thus, when the writer of Hebrews said: "Your throne, O God, will last for ever and ever, and righteousness will be the scepter of your kingdom" (Heb. 1:8), the Jewish Christians he was addressing would have understood the meaning of the imagery. So also, the Christians must have understood John's Revelation, prophesying (like the Psalmist) that "He will rule them with an iron scepter, he will dash them to pieces like **pottery**" (Rev. 2:27, 19:15; echoing Psalm 2).

Staff (left) and rod, the tools of the shepherd, guiding and defending his sheep became symbols of authority, as scepters and maces for the kings who were tasked with guiding and defending their people.

The rod of Aaron, one of the earliest references to a rod in Scripture, was a **magic** one, which could turn into a **serpent** or flower with almond blossoms. In confrontation with the power and majesty of the Pharaoh and his court magicians, Aaron's rod proved superior. The rod was evidence of Aaron's divine election; it became a favorite symbol in literature and art for other miracles such as the birth of Jesus (a blossom from the root of Jesse) and the salvific power of the Crucifixion. The **angel** Gabriel, when portrayed at the Annunciation in medieval paintings, carries a scepter or wand, indicating that he is a herald of God (George Ferguson 1966, 73).

The simple wooden rod, known to every Jew, thus became a tool for shepherds, pilgrims, soldiers, schoolmasters, poets, painters, and kings. *See also* Kings; Magic; Shepherds.

Further Reading

Allen, L. C. "Rod," in *The Illustrated Bible Dictionary,* 3 volumes. Sydney, Australia: Tyndale House Publishers, 1980. Ferguson, George. *Signs and Symbols in Christian Art.* New York: Oxford University Press, 1966. Hirsch, Emil G. and

Immanuel Benzinger. "Staff," http://www.jewishencyclopedia.com (accessed June 5, 2005). Jacobs, Joseph and Louis Grossman. "Pedagogics," http://www.jewishencyclopedia.com (accessed June 5, 2005). Jeffrey, David Lyle. "Aaron," in *A Dictionary of the Biblical Tradition in English Literature*. Grand Rapids, Mich.: William B. Eerdmans Publishing Company, 1992.

Scribes

Because most people in ancient times were illiterate, the scribe (usually a copyist or "penman") was an honored and essential member of the community. He could make the marks on clay or stone or papyrus or vellum to document the **laws**, accounts, and messages of the powerful and wealthy.

The earliest indication of scribes appears to be in Sumer, the original home of the Hebrew people. Abraham probably brought an understanding of their usefulness with him on his travels. Very early, these men had learned to make marks on clay *bullae* that would certify the contents of shipments of merchandise. As a trader himself, Abraham would have found these skills invaluable.

During the centuries that the **Israelites** lived among the **Egyptian**s, they adopted many of their customs, including the regular use of scribes. In

Scribe at work with reed pen, ink, and scrolls.

Egypt, the royal secretaries were more than simple copyists; they also were officials in the royal palace, functioning as "ministers of finance or secretaries of state." They even served as advisors to the **king** (George Wesley Buchanan 1993, 684; Roland deVaux 1961, 131). The Hebrew scribe performed a role that mimicked the royal scribes of the Egyptian court in a much more modest manner.

In Hebrew culture during the monarchy, the scribes were scholars who dedicated their lives to the study of the sacred law. They preserved the law, administered it as **judges** in the **Sanhedrin**, and served as teachers of the law, or lawyers. Some scholars believe that scribes may have banded together into families and guilds (1 Chron. 2:55). They were significant enough that their names were recorded in Scripture and in other ancient Hebrew records (Roland deVaux 1961, 131).

In the Old Testament, the first scribe mentioned was Shemaiah, son of Nathaniel, "a Levite" who recorded the names of the people and documented the census (1 Chron. 24:6). Later in Chronicles (1 Chron. 27:32), David's uncle Jonathan was a scribe, as well as a counselor and a man of insight. This suggests that he was a learned man who advised the king. It was Shaphan, the secretary to King Josiah, who brought the recently discovered book of the law to the king and read it to him, consulted Huldah the prophetess for him, and thereby initiated the religious reformation (2 Kings 22–23).

The most impressive of the Old Testament scribes was Ezra, who seems to have been the preserver of the law of Moses, as well as a **priest** and a Levite. (Apparently, the roles of priest and scribe frequently overlapped.) Among the duties of the priest enumerated in Deuteronomy 33:10 was that he was to "instruct the people." Ezra read the book of the law to the people and instructed them in its meaning (Neh. 8:1, 8:4, 8:9). Later, when the wall of Jerusalem was being dedicated, Ezra led the procession that included singing accompanied by cymbals, psalteries, and harps (Neh.12:27, 36). Another scribe served with Jeremiah, recording his words. Baruch the scribe appears to have been a close associate of the **prophet**, writing the words that he dictated and restoring the scrolls that the king Jehoiakim had burned in the fire (Jer. 36:26, 32).

These famous scribes were more influential than earlier ones and more respected. Their intimate knowledge of the sacred books of Judaism made them natural teachers. Scribes were also the originators of the **synagogue** service—an extension of their teaching role. From the time of the Exile, the task of teaching was separated from the regular duties of the priesthood. The Levites became the preachers and catechists. Teaching was separated from worship, restricted to the synagogues, where the scribes and teachers of the law were the authorities. "This class was open to all, priests and Levites and layfolk alike, and eventually it displaced the priestly caste in the work of teaching" (Roland deVaux, 1961, 355).

After the dispersion of the Jews, the scribes became the representatives of the people and the recognized authorities, solemnly ordained by the laying on of hands. As Edersheim notes, the scribe was "the Divine aristocrat, among the vulgar herd of rude and profane 'country-people'—who 'know not the Law' and are 'cursed.' More than that, his order constitute[d] the ultimate authority on all questions of faith and practice." He was the teacher of the law, along with the chief priests and elders, a judge in ecclesiastical tribunals. Although often in the company of Pharisees, he was not necessarily a member of that group. "Each Scribe outweighed all the common people, who must accordingly pay him every honour" (Alfred Edersheim 2004, 65).

By the time of Jesus's ministry, as the priesthood itself had become increasingly corrupt, the scribes had emerged as the professional students of the law and its defenders. They tried to apply the law of Moses to everyday life. They gathered pupils about them, insisting that their students learn their lessons verbatim, without variation. They were the teachers who lectured in the **Temple** (C. L. Feinberg 1980, 1404) and probably the "doctors" that the young Jesus stayed behind to debate there (Luke 2:46).

In his own defense at his **trial** before the high priest, Jesus indicated that he, like the scribes, had taught openly in the Temple (John 18:20). He apparently infuriated the others, however, because he taught as "one having authority" (Matt. 7:29). It was frequently these legalists against whom Jesus preached. They, with the **Pharisees**, had reduced the faith to cold formalism, with an ever-expanding set of rules and regulations.

Later, the scribes persecuted Peter and John and facilitated Stephen's death (Acts 4:5, 6:12). Over time they had moved from being mere students of the law and transcribers of the documents to becoming central players in religious politics.

Recent discoveries of the Dead Sea Scrolls testify to the care with which scribes copied biblical texts. Scholars have discovered few differences in their documents from medieval texts, most of which are not the result of scribal errors but rather of variant texts. As one commentator notes, "At the ends of some books, the scribe gave the total number of words in the book and told which word was the exact middle, so that later scribes could count both ways to be sure they had not omitted a single letter." (George W. Buchanan 1993, 685). Moderns owe much of the authenticity of Scripture to the care and dedication of these industrious men. *See also* Education; Law; Pharisees; Rabbi; Sadducees; Writing Materials.

Further Reading

Buchanan, George Wesley. "Scribes," in *The Oxford Companion to the Bible*. New York: Oxford University Press, 1993. DeVaux, Roland. *Ancient Israel: Its Life and Institutions*. Grand Rapids, Mich.: William B. Eerdmans Publishing

Company, 1961. Edersheim, Alfred. *The Life and Times of Jesus the Messiah*. Peabody, Mass.: Hendrickson Publishers, Inc., 2004. Feinberg, C. L. "Scribes, in *The Illustrated Bible Dictionary*. Sydney, Australia: Tyndale House Publishers, 1980.

Seals

(Gen. 38:18, 25; Exod. 28:11, 21; 39:6, 14; 28:11–23;1 Kings 21:8; Dan. 12:1; 2 Cor. 1:22; Eph. 4:30; Rev. 5:1, 9:4, 22:10) The word *seal* is used to describe both the device for making an impression on clay or wax

This seal cylinder would be rolled on hot wax or wet clay to form a rectangular impression, sometimes very artistic and stylish.

and for the impression itself. Seals, also known as *bullae*, have been discovered all over the ancient world. These small bits of clay or wax were to ancient peoples what signatures are to moderns: They authenticated the document and were used to seal documents or purchases. If the package or letter had a string holding it together, the bit of clay (or later wax) was put on the opening and pressed against a marker that would leave the official impression. A broken seal revealed that someone had tampered with the letter or the measurement in the bag.

Because the bags and papyri that the clay protected have long since disintegrated, the seals themselves alone have survived to testify to the activities and products they authenticated. Clay grows even harder when burned or dried over the centuries, making the bullae among the best indicators of trade and people of the various eras.

Cylinder seals, popular in Babylonia and Assyria, often had pictures on them that told of the major achievements of the seal owner. With the invention of **writing** in the fourth millennium B.C., cylinder and stamp seals became popular. In **Egypt**, scarab seals were often used, making both the surface and the object itself interesting. The seal was so important as a mark of authenticity that it often was pierced so that a cord could be run through it and it could be worn around the neck (D. J. Wiseman, A. R. Millard 1980, 1408). They were used by a large segment of the population, even by comparatively poor people, who could purchase roughly engraved seals.

Seals might be made of local terracotta, bitumen, limestone, frit, or wood. In Palestine, engraved stones were usually semi-precious: carnelian, chalcedony, agate, jasper, rock crystal, and hematite. Egyptian ones were often glazed. The more valuable ones were made by skilled seal-cutters who used "copper gravers, a cutting wheel, and sometimes a small bow-drill, and perhaps a 'pen of iron, with a point of diamond'" (Wiseman and Millard, 1408). Later, these carefully designed stones were mounted on bands to make signet rings. They remain in use even today, usually for special documents, which are sealed with sealing wax. Notarized government documents, for example, usually require a seal that testifies to their authenticity. (In modern legal

Seal of Hezekiah that says: "Belonging to Hezekiah, son of Ahaz." This could be the impression made by a signet ring.

Seal from the time of Hezekiah that says: "Ma'sheyahu, the Judge."

procedures, the official seal of the state or other entity of government is used on birth certificates, death certificates, and sworn affidavits. It is usually impressed on the paper.)

The writing and images on seals reveal names, contents, agreements, or relationships and have proven invaluable to historians. Cylinder seals in particular, which portrayed a variety of figures, might include rows of men, lions, winged human-headed lions or sphinxes (**cherubim**), griffins, or winged snakes. Egyptian motifs included the lotus flower and the ankh-symbol of life, scenes of **worship**, **animal** deities, etc. Apparently the figures carved on these did not offend the Hebrews who chose not to see them as a violation of God's prohibition of graven images. The inscriptions on them might include owners' names and sometimes the fathers' names as well.

The Hebrew Use of Seals

The Hebrews may have learned about the design and usages of seals in Sumer. They clearly used them before their time in Egypt. A seal and its cord were used as a bit of evidence in the case of Tamar against Judah, who demanded his signet as a pledge and later used it to prove that he had fathered her child (Gen. 38:18, 25). The Egyptians, in fact, probably borrowed the commercial use of seals from the Sumerians, who appear to be the first to use them (Leonard Wooley 1965, 47). When the Israelites returned from Egypt and were instructed on the design for the high priest's garments, they engraved the names of the sons of Jacob/**Israel** on two stones "the way a gem cutter engraves a seal" and they were also instructed to "make a plate of pure gold and ingrave on it as on a seal: Holy to the Lord." This same passage indicates they used onyx stones in gold filigree settings, 12 stones, one for each of the sons of Israel, and each with its own imagery (Exod. 28:11, 21; 39:6, 14). They also used engraved stones as insets in the high **priest**'s breast ornament (Exod. 28:11–23).

Later, we see the wicked queen Jezebel using the **king**'s signet ring to issue a decree allowing Ahab to appropriate Naboth's **vineyard** (1 Kings 21:8). Foreigners also impressed the Israelites with their use of seals: The Book of Esther notes that no document was official without the king's signet ring's seal to affix his name and assurance (Esther 8:8).

Seals have been found in various excavations in the Holy Land, including Megiddo and Lachish. In addition, archaeologists have found as many as 1,000 jar-handles with seal impressions. A hoard of 50 clay seal impressions for documents from the time of Hezekiah, king of Judah in the late eighth century B.C., is among the latest discoveries. On the front of these is the raised imprint of the seal, and on the back is usually the mark of the rope that tied the document being sealed or the textile that held an agricultural product (Hershel Shanks 2003, 25). Thousands of these relics, some of them quite artistic, have been discovered all over North Africa and in the Near and Middle East. Their greatest value is in the identification of names from their periods. They also testify to the widespread ability to read, at least to decipher pictograms and cuneiform on a primitive level.

Meaning of the Seal in Scripture

The use of the seal as the image of ownership and fidelity in **marriage** is very effective in the Song of Solomon: "Place me like a seal over your heart, like a seal on your arm; for love is as strong as death, its jealousy unyielding as the grave" (Song of Sol. 8:6). Paul echoes and expands this usage as a theological image in Corinthians, where he speaks of Christ's "seal of ownership on us" (2 Cor. 1:22), and in Ephesians, where he speaks of being marked "in him with a seal" (Eph. 1:13). Christians used the term "sealed with the promise of the **Holy Spirit**" (Eph. 4:30) as a mark that they have been baptized of the spirit and anointed by God, who had put his seal upon them, in promise of redemption at the Last Judgment (Eph. 1:13, 4:30; 2 Cor 1:22, etc.). Generally, in the New Testament, the term *seal* means "ownership, authentication and security" (S. S. Smalley 1980, 1411).

Early in Scripture, the image of "sealing" or placing the "seal" on a person was commonly used and clearly understandable. It ranged from the use of the priests' placing their seals (Neh. 9:38) to John's revelation of the Lamb, sitting on his throne, "a scroll with writing on both sides and sealed with seven seals" (Rev 5:1), each of which was broken as the scroll was opened. The concept of the unbroken seal was understood to mean the unrevealed prophecy. Daniel, for example, is instructed to "seal the words of the scroll until the time of the end" (Dan.12:4). This foreshadows the image of the seven scrolls in Revelation, which have their seals broken and their contents revealed. At first John noted that the seven thunders spoke and "I was about to write; but I heard a voice from **heaven** say, 'Seal up what the seven thunders have said and do not write it down'" (Rev. 9:4). This is followed by the admonition, "Do not seal up the words of the **prophecy** of this book, because the time is near" (Rev. 22:10). *See also* Jewelry; Stone; Writing Materials.

Further Reading

Boyd, Robert T. *Tells, Tombs and Treasure: A Pictorial Guide to Biblical Archaeology.* New York: Bonanza Books, 1969. Shanks, Hershel. "Festschrift for Monssaieff," in *Biblical Archaeology Review* (November/December 2003,

25). Smalley, S. S. "Seals: New Testament," in *The Illustrated Bible Dictionary*. Sydney, Australia: Tyndale House Publishers, 1980. Wiseman, D. J. and A. R. Millard. "Seals," in *The Illustrated Bible Dictionary*. Sydney, Australia: Tyndale House Publishers, 1980. Woolley, C. Leonard. *The Sumerians*. New York: W. W. Norton & Company, 1965.

Sermon on the Mount

(Matt. 5–7; Luke 6:17) The Sermon on the Mount is sometimes spoken of as the "Sermon on the Plain" because Luke spoke of its being delivered on a "level place' (Luke 56:1), but Matthew specifically mentioned a mountain (Matt. 5:1). Matthew's account of the sermon that Jesus preached to his **disciples** and a large group of listeners constitutes some of his most significant statements about the Christian life. It includes the **Beatitudes**, his discussion of the fresh interpretations of the **law** under the New **Covenant**, and the **Lord's Prayer**.

Many of the ideas may, in fact, have been repeated under different circumstances, as they are so central to Christ's message. The ideas are presented more as a teaching than a preaching, with questions from the Disciples and responses from Jesus. The Beatitudes and the following ideas on the true disciple being salt and light seem to be addressed to his closest followers. The Lord's Prayer is provided in response to a request: "Lord, teach us to pray."

The whole extended sermon is poetic in nature, full of strong images, memorable and striking. The examination of law of Moses, with the fuller consideration of why people commit adultery, kill one another, or swear falsely exposes the real nature of sin, which is rooted in man's fallen nature. In each case, Jesus sees the beginning of the sin in anger or lust or covetousness that leads the person into wrong actions. The practical instructions on giving alms, praying, and fasting suggest his concern with daily life, as well as the life in the **Kingdom of God**.

It is an excellent summing up of "essential Christianity." *See also* Beatitudes; Law; Lord's Prayer.

Serpent

(Gen. 3:1–4; Exod. 4:2–5, 7:8–12; Num. 2:1, 21:8; John 3:14; Acts 28:3; Rev. 12:90; 20:2) Only two animals in all of Scripture speak—Balaam's ass and the serpent in the **Garden of Eden** (Num. 22:30; Gen. 3:1–14). One speaks for God, the other for Satan. When we first see the serpent in the Garden, he is described as "more crafty than any of the animals the Lord God has made." The teasing questions he poses to the woman, his clever undercutting of God's clear command, and his blunt lie

("You will not die") made him the world's first villain. Eve blamed him for her **fall**, but it is clear that God blamed her and Adam as well, and punished them each according to their actions. He told the serpent, "Because you have done this, Cursed are you and above all the livestock and all the wild **animals!** You will crawl on your belly and you will eat dust all the days of your life." He also indicated that the serpent would be in enmity with man forever.

The venomous serpent has indeed proven to be man's enemy, lurking by the side of the road, coiling and slithering to attack humans silently and often fatally. As scholars have noted, the region around Palestine has an enormous variety of serpents, including all the main families except rattlesnakes, and ranging from less than a foot in length to more than six feet. Most are harmless, but six species are potentially lethal. Their cold-blooded system forces them to depend on the local extreme climate of the region: basking in the sun or moving out of it, hibernating underground, or searching for food in early morning or evening to avoid the extremes of noonday and night temperatures. They are carnivorous, eating worms, **insects**, fish, frogs, lizards, **birds**, eggs, mammals, and even other snakes.

Although snakes appear frequently in Scripture, the individual species, including the harmless ones, are not generally noted. George Cansdale has tried to identify some of the species in various parts of Scripture, noting

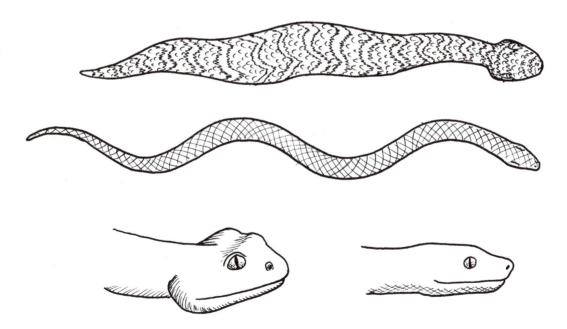

Viper and snake, both of which appear in Scripture. Note the differences in heads, body shape, and markings.

that the **Egyptian** cobra may have been the one used in the snake-charming scenes in Egypt. The asp was the Egyptian snake used by Cleopatra to commit suicide; Isaiah 11:8 mentions the "hole of the asp," although cobras are more often found in holes in the ground. The "adder" (Ps. 58:4, 5) is probably an asp. In the desert, the sand vipers and false cerastes were probably present, inspiring the "fiery serpent" of Numbers 21, the "serpent in the wilderness" of John 3:14. The snake that bit Paul (Acts 28:3) was probably the common viper, which is still found on Sicily and other islands, although not on Malta (George Cansdale 1970, 204–10).

Snake Symbolism

Throughout most of the Bible, the serpent is identified with the Devil, "or Satan, who leads the whole world astray" (Rev. 12:9). Thus, when a man or nation is compared to a snake, his wicked ways are clear. For example, Jeremiah laments that "Nebuchadnezzar king of **Babylon** has devoured us, he has thrown us into confusion, he has made us an empty jar. Like a serpent he has swallowed us and filled his stomach with our delicacies and then spewed us out" (Jer. 51:34).

When the Hebrews lived in Egypt, they encountered the snake charmers there, and Moses worked his own God-ordained snake sorcery to confound theirs. When Moses and Aaron confronted the Pharaoh, demanding the freedom of their people, Aaron cast down his rod, which became a serpent that subsequently swallowed up the rods of the Egyptian magicians (Exod. 4:2–5, 7:8–12). Egyptian art testifies to the significance of snakes in this culture and worship, appearing in headdresses, on statues, and on urns and **pottery**.

While the children of Israel were still in the wilderness, they were tormented by venomous snakes, and many of them died of their bites. After they begged Moses for relief, God ordered him to "Make a snake and put it up on a pole; anyone who is bitten can look at it and live" (Num. 21:8–9). This healing power became a symbol in medicine, the Caduceus, probably a combination of Greek and Hebrew imagery. In the Greek mythology, Asclepius, the ancient Greek physician deified as the god of medicine, is pictured holding a staff with his sacred serpent coiled around it, symbolizing renewal of youth as the serpent casts off its skin. (This has been confused with the staff of Hermes in much iconography, using the divine messenger with his wings to speed his way and his staff, with two snakes coiled around it. Actually the snakes here are an error in understanding the heraldic white ribbons.)

This "caduceus" survives as a symbol for medicine in general and specifically for natural healing, but it also suggests occult powers connected with alchemy; Moses merely held up the snake as a sign of God's healing power. Later, when the Israelites began worshipping this image rather than God himself, Hezekiah, the **king** of Judah, had the bronze figure (the *Nehush-tan*) destroyed (2 Kings18:4). John recalled this prophetic salvation from the serpent in the words of Jesus: "Just as Moses lifted up the snake in the desert, so the Son of Man must be lifted up, that everyone who believes in him may have eternal life" (John 3:14).

The "divine serpent" has been an element of worship since "the very beginnings of time, on every continent of this earth where humanity has worshipped divinity.... From Africa's steaming jungle to the icy wastes of northern Europe; from the fertile crescent to the deserted outback of Australia" (Robert T. Mason 2004). Jung, the famous psychoanalyst, considered the snake a chthonic and spiritual being, symbolizing the unconscious memories of ancient ancestors. "The mysterious dynamism of the snake, its extraordinary vitality and its seeming immortality through the periodic rejuvenation of shedding the old and appearing new each year must have instilled a sense of awe and invoked a powerful response in" our earliest ancestors (Robert Mason 2004). Some ancient vases show gigantic snakes coiling over the whole universe, apparently a symbol of energy and immortality.

It was also considered a sign of wisdom. Jesus warned his **disciples** that they must be as "wise as serpents" (Matt. 10:16). In Greek culture, the Delphic Oracle was thought to derive her wise sayings from a snake, probably a python. The form of knowledge the snake has is seen as "subtle" or "crafty"—not the kind of wisdom that comes from the fear of God and knowledge of his Word.

The snake was also a symbol of eternity in many cultures: *The Gilgamesh Epic* of ancient Sumeria contains the story of the hero descending to the bottom of a lake to find and bring back the plant of eternal life. When he retrieved it and lay resting after his exertion, a snake came along and ate the plant, thus giving the snake rather than the man the gift of eternal life. Some believe that the way the snake can form a circle of its body may have led to this identification of the snake with eternity.

Its shape also made it a natural phallic symbol. In the Egyptian creation story, we find "the serpent and the primordial egg" that produce the "Bird of Light" (Robert Mason 2004). Some students of myth relate this to the "plumed serpent" image in Mexican folk lore that D. H. Lawrence wrote about in his novels, essays, and poetry. In addition, the Phoenicians had a serpent god called the Basilisk, which may have been a serpentine form. It killed with its gaze, routed all snakes with its hiss, and moved its body forward in coils. Variations of this semi-human kind of snake appear in numerous cultures. The Romantic poets were particularly interested in the Lamia, a snake-woman, who lures and infects man. Coleridge used the figure in his narrative poem "Christabel," and Keats wrote a poem entitled "Lamia."

Another sinister use of the snake may be implied by a repeated term in Scripture—"the leviathan." Some believe it may have been a form of snake. Some suspect it was the crocodile. "Thou brakest the heads of leviathan in pieces," said the Psalmist (Ps. 74:14). Isaiah also described how the Lord breaks "the heads of leviathan in pieces" (Isa. 27:1). Both of these spoke of multiple heads, but in another Psalm (104:25, 26), the leviathan was described as playing in "this great and wide sea," suggesting a dolphin rather than a river creature. Most certainly the Israelites knew the crocodile from their stay in **Egypt**, where these reptiles were hunted, feared, and revered. "In Ancient Egypt the crocodile was venerated as a symbol of sunrise, for which it became a hieroglyph. At Thebes a young crocodile used to be reared in the temple and decorated with **jewels** of all kinds; at Ombi it was worshipped and its mummies have been found in the catacombs there and elsewhere" (George Cansdale 1970, 196). Cansdale notes that evidence suggests that reports of varying trustworthiness indicate the presence of crocodiles in **Canaan** as well. The creatures would have been considered unclean and frightening. Primitive weapons were virtually useless against them.

Some even speculate that the crocodile may have served as the model for the great serpent figure of the dragon—the Satanic image in Revelation. As John said, "The great dragon was hurled down—that ancient serpent called the devil, or Satan, who leads the whole world astray. He was hurled to the earth, and his **angels** with him." Somewhat later, John pictured this final epic battle between God and the rebellious angels to be fought in the Last Days: "He seized the dragon, that ancient serpent . . . and bound him for a thousand years" (Rev. 12:90, 20:2). It is amazing that the snake—or the dragon—is a major figure in one of the first scenes in Scripture, and in one of the last. *See also* Animals; Fall of Man; Monsters.

Further Reading

Cansdale, George. *All the Animals of the Bible Lands*. Grand Rapids, Mich.: Zondervan Publishing House, 1970. Kitchen, K. A. "Snakes," in *Illustrated Bible Dictionary*. Sydney, Australia: Tyndale House Publishers, 1980. Mason, Robert T. "The Divine Serpent in Myth and Legend," http://www.geocities.com/Athens/Delphi/5789/serpent.htm (accessed June 20, 2004)

𝔖𝔥𝔢𝔢𝔭

(Gen. 30:32–35, 31:19; 2 Sam. 13:23; Ps. 23; John 1:29, 10:14; Rev. 5:6) Constant companions of humans, sheep were the primary source of meat for **food** and **sacrifice**. They were also the source of **work**, **clothing**, fuel, and economic prosperity for the Old Testament families. Hundreds of references to them are scattered all through Scripture, from the sacrifice of Abel to the Feast of the Lamb. Their habits have provided a rich source of imagery for writers, who have detailed their combination of helplessness and guilelessness: they are afraid of gushing streams and prefer still waters, they flock together, yet individual sheep will often stray from the flock; they are without natural protection against predators, such as snakes and wild beasts, but wander off where they may be attacked; they love to seek the grasses on mountainous terrain, but get their feet lodged between rocks and can only bleat their dismay; they have no sense of direction; they tumble down rocky hillsides, and they need protection from thieves and lions in the night. They tend to be gregarious creatures, eager to be led, responsive to guidance, docile and affectionate. They respond to the **shepherd**'s rod or the sheep **dog**'s nudge or bark, and they know their master's voice.

Evidence points to the domestication of sheep very early: an Asiatic variety appeared on a Sumerian vase dated approximately 3000 B.C. (Madeleine S. Miller and J. Lane Miller 1961, 671). They formed the bulk of Abraham's wealth when he traveled from Ur to **Canaan**. Usually the head of a clan was the owner of the sheep, and the rest of the family became the shepherds and minders of the products yielded by the animals. The early sheep were probably brown, like their wild ancestors. The references to Jacob's efforts at selective breeding (Gen. 30:32) suggest that he may have tended sheep of various colors (George Cansdale 1970, 50).

Scholars note that three types of sheep, both rams (male) and ewes (female), appear in Scripture:

1. The short-tailed and horned sheep
2. The curling horned, broad-tailed sheep, also known as "fat tailed," which was much cherished for the food fats in this tail (Exod. 29:32), for its deep wool, often colored black and white (Gen. 30:33, 35). These were perhaps originally from Kurdistan.
3. The long-legged, short fleeced sheep, which were originally from Asia, but bred in **Egypt** (Madeleine S. Miller and J. Lane Miller 1961, 671–672)

The fat-tailed sheep was a favorite of the ancient Israelites.

All three types of sheep were a good source of food, not only the flesh itself, but also the milk produced by the ewes. The "fatted" lamb was kept in a pen and protected, overfed, and saved for **feasts**, such as the one given by the father on the return of a prodigal son.

Ram's horn or shofar, used as a trumpet.

The unblemished lamb, white and without spots, was the ideal sacrifice for the many feast days. The rules for sacrificial offerings, that the animals be "without spot," may mean "without blemish" or imperfections. It was a ram, a male sheep, that appeared from the thicket to provide a substitute for the sacrifice of Isaac (Gen. 22:8, 13). It was the blood of a lamb that was wiped across the doorways, when the Israelites faced the final **plague** in their sojourn in Egypt, that marked their special relationship with God. The sacrificial lamb is a key image in Hebrew **festivals** and holy days—the **blood** shed and the flesh eaten by the **priests** and the other worshippers. Roasted or boiled, the meat was considered a delicacy. The lamb was the ceremonial center of the feast of **Passover**, the **Last Supper**, that Jesus and his **disciples** observed.

Lambs were also apparently considered good pets for children. Such **animals** often lived in the house with the Israelites. When Nathan sought to show King David the cruelty of his adulterous affair with Uriah's wife, Bathsheba, he used the story of a thoughtless rich man's taking of the pet lamb for a feast.

The wool of sheep was also valuable, as were their hides. Some shepherds wore cloaks or overgarments that were sheepskins, with wool still intact, a warm wrap against night chills in the mountains. Sheep-shearing season usually occurred in the springtime, after lambing season. The first scriptural reference to shearing of sheep is part of Jacob's story: Laban was busy with sheep-shearing when Jacob and his wives stole away, taking their flocks with them (Gen. 31:19). It was another sheep-shearing that led to trouble in David's reign (2 Sam. 13:23).

After the shearing, the wool was then carded, dyed, spun, and woven into fabric for various uses. Wool, which is characterized as "white" in several Scripture passages, may have been bleached to that level of purity in the process of making it into **cloth**. Or perhaps, through selective breeding, the shepherds had finally produced white sheep to replace the early brown ones.

The close relationship between sheep and their owners led to the thorough understanding of the animals' habits, weaknesses, and problems. It also accounts for the imagery in so much of Scripture, as in Psalm 23 and John 10. Most often, sheep symbolize God's people, needing the help of a good shepherd to keep out of trouble and find safe shelter for the coming night. As one author expressed it: "The sheep is consistently a picture of man—lost, helpless, easily led astray, essentially sociable, and unable to fend for himself or find his way back.... The New Testament unfolds the great paradox of John 1:29, 'Behold the Lamb of God which taketh away the sins of the world', and John 10:14 'I am the Good Shepherd' with its climax in Rev. 5:6, 'In the midst of the throne ... stood a Lamb as it had been slain'" (George Cansdale 1970, 55–6). *See also* Animals; Cloth; Cloth: Goat's Hair and Wool; Clothing; Sheepfold; Shepherds.

Further Reading

Cansdale, George. *All the Animals of the Bible Lands*. Grand Rapids, Mich.: Zondervan Publishing House, 1970. Miller, Madeleine S. and J. Lane Miller. "Sheep," in *Harper's Bible Dictionary*. New York: Harper and Row, 1961.

Sheepfold

(John 10:7) Night is a hazardous time for sheep: they stray if not kept enclosed, and they are subject to numerous **animal** predators that stalk them in the night, not to mention human thieves who are hungry for a good meal or a valuable asset. Therefore, the good **shepherd** would plan carefully where he should settle his flock for the night.

The animals were usually kept close to the family that owned them. If their number was small, they might even come into the **house** at night, staying in the separate portion set aside for livestock, safe from robbers and other animals. In some cases, the owner had sufficient sheep to construct a sheepfold, a shelter that was built to protect the sheep from the cold winds. "This fold is a low building with arches in front of it, and a wall forming an outdoor enclosure, joining the building" (Fred H. Wight 1953, 154). The walls were wider at the bottom than at the top, usually four to six feet high, made of stone with thorn bushes on the top for further protection.

A watchman usually guarded the **gate** to the enclosure. In very simple enclosures, he might even lie across the opening, serving as a human gate. This makes Jesus's statement, "I am the door of the sheep" (John 10:7) quite literal.

When away from home, the shepherd might chose a sheepcote that used a **cave** as its enclosure and source of protection. Caves are common in the countryside of Palestine and might be protected with a stone wall enclosure that had a small entrance way, which was easy to watch. If no caves were available, the shepherd might instead settle for a makeshift enclosure in the open field, made of brambles and thorns piled up in a kind of fence.

The shepherds who "watched their flocks by night" in Luke's memorable narrative are thought to have been at the "tower of the flock," the *Migdal Eder*, a watchtower near the road to Jerusalem that was used to oversee the sheep designated for Temple **sacrifice**. These sheep were kept isolated and protected all year round so as to remain unblemished for the **Passover** services. *See also* Caves; Sheep; Shepherds.

Further Reading

Edersheim, Alfred. *The Life and Times of Jesus the Messiah*. Peabody, Mass.: Hendrickson Publishers, Inc., 2004. Wight, Fred Hartley. *Manners and Customs of Bible Lands*. Chicago: Moody Press, 1953.

Sheol. See Hell

Shepherds

(Ps. 23, John 10:14) Abraham led his flocks through the wilderness; Jacob tended **sheep** to win his brides; Joseph found his brothers in the wilderness tending their sheep just before they beat him and threw him into a **cistern;** Moses ran to Midian and spent years in shepherding in preparation for the **Exodus;** David was tending his sheep when Samuel found him and anointed him **king;** shepherds were watching over their flocks by night when Christ was born. Many of the great events of Scripture involve the shepherd.

The good shepherd was exceptionally close to his sheep. He led them from pasture to pasture, keeping them in line with his slingshot and rod; he found the best and safest grazing areas for them—green grass sheltered from the sun. He herded them into **sheepfolds** or sheepcotes at night; he played **music** for them on his homemade flute to calm them; he rescued them from rocky places with his staff, protected them from predators with his heavy rod; he carried the new lambs in his cloak or on his shoulders and dedicated one out of every ten to the Lord.

The task of shepherding the family's sheep and **goats** usually fell to the youngest son (like young David), who learned from his elder brothers how to use his rod and his staff. The rod was a stick with a knob at one end, which could be used to hit wild **animals** or to hold over the sheep to count and mark them. (It became the **scepter** in later years, a symbol of the king's power and authority.) The staff often had a crook at one end as a tool for pulling sheep gently back into line or out of trouble.

Most shepherds also learned to use the sling (two strings of leather with a receptacle for stones), which they carried in their scrip (a leather bag made of dried skin). They could frighten wandering sheep, hit animals lurking along the way, or warn off a robber with this fast and silent weapon. David advertised its power to the whole region with his use of a sling to kill the giant **Philistine**, Goliath.

The shepherd usually dressed in a tunic, covered by a cloak. His girdle or belt held his scrip (his small bag or wallet for money) and could also be used to turn his cloak into a pouch for carrying newborn lambs. He often carried a flute: a reed instrument that makes a tune in minor strains. Considering David's talent in music and his beautiful **psalms**, it is interesting that the Arab word equivalent to the Hebrew word for *psalm* is *mazmoor*, or "played on a pipe or flute" *See also* Kings; Music; Musical Instruments; Sheep; Sheepfold.

Further Reading

Wight, Fred Hartley. *Manners and Customs of Bible Lands.* Chicago: Moody Press, 1953.

Ships. *See* Boats and Ships

Slavery, Laws of

(Exod. 21:1–11, Lev. 25:39–55, Deut. 15:12–18) The Law of Moses deals with slaves in some detail These regulations grant them far more lenient treatment than in most of the Near East while still considering them chattel, to be bought and sold. The Israelites' treatment of slaves, as a consequence of their close personal relations within the home and in the fields, tended to be personal and benign by contrast with other cultures. Slaves were also seen as God's creatures, deserving protection and respect—to a certain degree. Because many of the Hebrews found themselves temporarily forced to become slaves because of conquest or debt, they were more likely to view slaves as unfortunates rather than as inferiors.

During the years of foreign conquest by many powers, including **Egyptian**, **Babylonian**, **Assyrian**, and so on, the people of Israel developed a deep personal understanding of the nature of slavery. The Assyrians forced the Hebrew slaves from their land, yet included them in their society. The Persians were inclined to allow them to return to their homeland and their old activities, while remaining as servants of the king. The **Greeks** considered that, in the natural order of things, slaves were inferior to citizens. Greek citizens were thought to be, strictly speaking, *human,* but the slaves were *chattel.* Among the **Romans**, a slave was considered a person without rights like any other form of personal property. (E.A. Judge 1980, 1462–1464).

The different laws of Jews refer to slaves according to various categories and behaviors: whether they were male or female, whether they were Israelites or foreigners, and whether they were obedient or disobedient.

Foreign Slaves

Foreign peoples who had been taken in battle were bought and sold freely, not subject to the restrictions that limited the terms of Israelite slaves. They were most often slaves for life, at one time known as "Slaves of Solomon." These were state slaves laboring in the remote regions and mines, performing work no free men could be hired to perform. Some even became crews for Hiram's ships, working alongside the slaves from Tyre (1 Kings 9:27; 2 Chron. 8:18, 9:10). Some (known as "dedicated") became servants of the Levites in the **Temple**. Seen as hewers of wood and carriers of water (Josh. 9:27), this cultic guild of religious functionaries returned from Babylonian exile together with the Hebrews (1 Chron. 9:2; Neh. 7:57, 10:29, 11:3; Ezra 2:55, 7:7; Ezek. 44:7–9; Ze'ev W. Falk 2001, 115).

Israelite Slaves—Male

Hebrews became slaves most frequently to fellow countrymen because of poverty. Unable to pay their debts, they would sell their children or themselves into slavery. The term of indenture or service for such people was limited to six years unless the slaves chose of their own accord to continue in service. The slave was to be provided with sufficient assets to begin life on his own, but for various reasons, he might prefer the security of life under a master. In this case, he pledged to remain in the service for life, and his earlobe was pierced with an awl to mark his status. Even such slaves, however, were to be freed in the Jubilee year (the 50th year, when all debts were forgiven and all land returned to its owner).

Israelite Slaves—Female

Female slaves were a special category: they attended to the personal needs of the mistress of the household or nursed the children. Their master was expected to arrange their **marriages** at his own discretion (Exod. 21:4). He might, for example, take a slave woman as his concubine or as a wife for himself or his son. If he grew dissatisfied with her and chose to divorce her, he was not allowed to sell her as a slave, but was obliged to return her to her family. If she became his daughter-in-law, he was expected to treat her as a member of the family (Roland deVaux 1961, 86). As in many other cultures, slave women were often used for sexual satisfaction and for breeding, with little concern about their personal tastes and preferences.

Slave women were usually daughters of debtors, as it was forbidden for a man to sell his wife into slavery. They might also be "house-born slaves"—children of slaves, who consequently belonged to the master. They might be married to another of his servants if he so chose, and their children would belong to him. A Hebrew daughter, when sold by her father, often was bought with the understanding that she would become her master's concubine or a member of his family, not a prostitute (Exod. 21:7–11).

Women captured in war were usually considered part of the booty due the victor. In early times, women were often enslaved for life. In later periods, Deuteronomic law suggests that women, like men, were to be freed in the seventh year, the standard period of indenture. Like a man, she might refuse her freedom and retain her status if she chose (Deut. 15:12, 17).

Protections

Although they were clearly of a lower social status, slaves were often treated as members of the family, circumcised, expected to follow the laws of the **Sabbath**, and share the festivals with the rest of the group. A trusted male slave might be appointed the heir of the master. If the master had only daughters, the slave might marry one of them and become an adopted son.

Slaves might be beaten and punished, but they were protected from excessive violence, with fines imposed on those who hurt them (although lesser penalties than those levied for damage to freemen). Fines were usually calculated by the price of the slave. If a master killed his slave, he might be put to death himself as guilty of manslaughter.

Runaway Slaves

When a slave was desperate with his circumstances, he might choose to flee his master's cruelty or simply seek freedom. Apparently this became something of a problem in David's day, when workers were impounded for the tasks of the new monarch (1 Sam. 25:10; 1 Kings 2:39). Anyone discovering a fugitive slave was expected to return him or her (1 Sam. 30:15; 1 Kings 2:39). Centuries later, when Paul found that Onesimus was a runaway slave, he encouraged him to return to his master, Philemon. There seems to be a change with later history, especially relating to the Israelites. When these slaves fled to other countries seeking refuge, the Israelite law forbade their return. They were to be welcomed and treated well in the town they had chosen, a regulation that is unique in ancient laws. This rule apparently applied only when the slave was an Israelite escaping from a foreign master, not when his master was also an Israelite (Roland deVaux 1961, 87).

Manumission

A master could free his slave at any time he so chose. On certain occasions, he was obliged to allow his slave to go free, for example, to compensate for bodily injury (Exod. 21:26–27). Also, if a man took a slave for his wife, she became a free woman (Deut. 21:10–14). If a slave could pay his purchase price, he could buy his freedom, although usually the debt needed to be worked off through labor.

Each type of slave had his or her own legal status and protections. Those who had voluntarily sold themselves into slavery to pay off debts had a time limit set to their service. If they continued as servants to the master, they were guaranteed a seventh year sabbatical and a 50th year release for the Year of the Jubilee (Exod. 21-:2–6; Lev. 25:10, 38:41). If their enslavement was a result of a crime, they had no benefits of release, but they were guaranteed decent treatment (Exod. 22:21, 23:9). Those who were sold into slavery could be redeemed at any time by a relative or friend and must be freed in the Jubilee Year (Lev. 25:42–43).

If a man took his wife with him into slavery, he was free to take her with him when he was released. But if his master provided him with a wife, and he had children by her, both the wife and children belonged to the master and remained at the master's house. Some might find the separation from family so wrenching that they preferred to remain in slavery, and provision in the law allowed for this (Exod. 21:6; Deut. 15:16), with the understanding that the whole family would be freed at Jubilee.

Many of these laws were adopted by other countries in later years, assuming that these were scriptural advice to slaveholders. In the American South, for instance, the same laws regarding the children of slaves caused great hardship for slaves seeking freedom. The Fugitive Slave Act also was based on the scriptural pattern, causing considerable consternation among abolitionists and others. The basic differences between biblical slavery and the American system was the permanent nature of the American slaves and the fact that their slave condition was determined by their race. White indentured servants brought to America were released after their contractual time, but eighteenth-century laws established perpetual bondage for African Americans, a custom contrary to Scripture. *See also* Slavery, Slaves.

Further Reading

DeVaux, Roland. *Ancient Israel: Its Life and Institutions.* Grand Rapids, Mich.: William B. Eerdmans Publishing Company, 1961. Falk, Ze'ev W. *Hebrew Law in Biblical Times.* Provo, Utah: Brigham Young University Press, 2001. Judge, E. A. "Slave," in *The Illustrated Bible Dictionary.* Sydney, Australia. Tyndale House Publishers, 1980.

Slavery, Slaves

(**Exod. 21:5; Deut.15:17; Rom. 8:15–17; Gal. 4:5–7, 23–31; Philemon**) The English term *slavery* derives from the bondage of the Slavic peoples, but the scriptural usage has a much wider range of meanings than either the enforced labor of the Slavs or of the African slaves, which is our usual conception. In Scripture, the term often referred to prisoners of war or those sold for debt, who could be Israelites or anyone else. It could mean anything from domestic service to enforced labor (Willard M. Swartley 1993, 701).

From earliest times to the present, slavery has been a persistent reality of human society. Abraham's family undoubtedly knew slave holders in Haran, and he probably had slaves in his caravan as he left for the Promised Land. He apparently had sufficient "servants" and to tend to his host of **animals** along the way to man his army when he needed to fight. When Sarah and Abraham were visiting **Egypt**, Sarah was given an Egyptian princess as a "maidservant." At Sarah's suggestion, Hagar subsequently became the mother for Abraham's first son, Ishmael, and thereby progenetrix of the Arab peoples.

Abraham's grandson Jacob, fleeing from his homeland, had no money to pay the bride price for his beloved Rachel. He indentured himself to Laban, his wily relative, in return for wives and livestock, agreeing to work seven years for each wife. Each of these wives had slaves, who served as additional "wives" for Jacob, contributing to the large family that eventually returned to Canaan. Continuing the legacy of slavery, Jacob's son Joseph was kidnapped and sold into slavery by his brothers, and the tribe's descendants became the slaves of the Egyptian pharaoh, helping in the building of Ramses's grand monuments. Later, the Hebrews knew slavery under Babylonians, Assyrians, Persians, Greeks, and Romans. Even their own kings enslaved them.

All through the Old Testament, slavery played a significant role. The actual words used for slavery varied: sometimes *maidservant* or *manservant*, sometimes just *servant*, and sometimes *slave*. These nouns and their related verb, *to serve*, were occasionally used metaphorically rather than as actual descriptors of social roles. In fact, as a matter of courtesy, a host might refer to himself as "your most humble servant," not meaning that he was a literal slave to his guest. The custom of self-abasement took on more significance in religious speech: David, for example, was called a "servant of the Lord" (Ps. 18:1), and the Israelites were admonished to "serve Jehovah" (Deut.11:12). Other times the words referred to actual servitude, as in the enslavement to the Egyptians or to the **kings** of **Israel**. The **prophets**, for example, criticized King Ahaz for taking captives from Judah (2 Chron. 28:8–15), and Isaiah called on Israel to let the captives go free (Isa. 58:6).

There were three types of servile status in ancient Israel:

1. An Israelite might become a servant to a fellow Israelite voluntarily because of debt or poverty. The usual term of indenture was six years. Nehemiah, however, complained that pervasive poverty was forcing more and more Israelites into perpetual bondage, frequently causing them to sell their sons or daughters to pay their debts (Neh. 5:1–13). Hebrew **law** explicitly forbade the selling of wives into slavery.
2. He or she might have been born a slave or have been purchased. Children of slave parents were called "house-born" slaves, and might or might not become free people later, depending on the status of their parents.
3. An Israelite might be the victim of forcible enslavement by foreigner conquerors, or of foreigners by Israelites who sold them into slavery (William M. Swartley, 1993, 700). In some cases, the captives probably thought themselves saved by slavery, because the law of **warfare** often required the condemnation of whole cities:

the men were put to death and the women and children reckoned as booty (Roland deVaux 1961, 81).

There were slaves of every type: poor children who were sold into slavery by their father, upper-class maidens seized in battle or given as tribute to serve as concubines to the conqueror, laborers working on the king's palatial construction sites, and debtors seeking security with a wealthy landowner. The owner-slave relationship was also varied: A slave owner might love his slave and adopt him as a son, as Abraham was tempted to do with Eliezer. He might even choose to marry a slave woman or make her his concubine. On the other hand, he might have a host of foreign slaves who served as field hands or as laborers in mines—faceless, nameless figures who toiled for his profit. Paintings of slave laborers usually show them with overseers who carried whips.

Some believe that slaves were marked in some manner. Scripture notes that a slave who chose the security of perpetual enslavement rather than manumission at the end of his six years was to have his ears pierced (Exod. 21:6; Deut. 15:17). They may also have been tattooed or branded, like cattle. This may explain the concept in Isaiah of having the name of Yahweh written on the hands of the faithful (Isa. 44:5) to show that they belonged to God. It may also explain the mark of the Beast in Revelation (13:16–17), which echoed the tattoo marks of Hellenistic cults (Roland deVaux 1961, 84).

Slaves tied together in a "human train" by the neck, from a wall mural 1186 B.C.

The law of Moses deals in some detail with the rights and rules regarding slavery, suggesting that it was a firmly established part of Hebrew culture even at the time of the **Exodus**. The incursions into **Canaan**, first under Joshua, and later under the **Judges** and the Kings, undoubtedly resulted in many captives who were put to work in the fields of the new settlers. Certain kinds of labor considered too menial for free men to perform were handed over to servants or slaves: washing of feet, making of bricks, carrying of heavy loads at construction sites and in mines.

In most Hebrew households, the maidservant or manservant was considered a member of the family. The menservants were circumcised and became members of the local congregation of worshippers. Servants of the **priests** were allowed to share in the sacrificial meat. When women slaves were taken as concubines or wives by their masters, the children of these relationships became part of the family, as with the sons of Jacob.

The monarchy conscripted large numbers of Israelites, as well as Canaanite, **Midianite**, and **Moabite** captives. They were reduced to the status of slaves and put to work on the many public and royal buildings of David and Solomon.

In later years, the various conquerors transported the captive Hebrews off to **Babylon** or Suza or other exotic places, where they frequently served as slaves for foreign peoples. Later, Herod enslaved Jews to work on his massive building programs. The **Romans** used many of the Jews, along with other laborers in the building of roads, aqueducts, baths, amphitheatres, and temples. When the Romans put down the Jewish Rebellion in 70 A.D. and burned Jerusalem, they took thousands of Jews to Corinth to construct the great canal there. They took others with them to Rome to parade them through the streets as a testimony to their victory over these rebels.

All through the New Testament, slaves appeared as a regular part of the social fabric. Although they were not mentioned in the households of Jesus and his **disciples**, slaves were present in some of the upper-class homes where Jesus visited (Luke 7:1–10, 12:37–46; Matt. 26:51, 24:45–51, 25:14–30). In these instances and in the homes Paul and his friends stayed, affection and a sense of mutual respect and responsibility appear to have prevailed, leading New Testament writers to speak of the "household of God (Eph. 2:19) in a positive manner.

Some of the households mentioned, like that of Lydia, may well have had paid servants rather than slaves for the labor. In fact, slaves themselves were allowed to have possessions, including their own slaves, and to carry on their own businesses. The household slave was considered a domestic, joining in the family worship, resting on the **Sabbath**, celebrating at religious **feasts**, and even marrying into his master's family or becoming an adopted son and heir. (Abraham's servant Eliezer was such a trusted family member, considered a likely heir to Abraham should the old man remain childless) (Gen. 15:3).

Paul himself is thought to have come from a family that had once been enslaved and were "freemen" by his day. He attended the Synagogue of the Freemen or "Libertines" in Jerusalem and had Roman citizenship—both indicators of a possible family history of slavery. He showed great concern with the "yoke of slavery" and was clearly thrilled with his freedom in Christ, perhaps his legacy of servitude giving his words additional power and poignancy. (C. L. Fineberg 1980, 1503). When Paul sent the runaway slave Onisemus back to his owner, Philemon, he acknowledged the authority of the system of slavery but implored mutual respect within it. Both master and slave were **Christians** and therefore brothers "both in the flesh and in the Lord" (Philem.16:17).

Under the **Greeks** and Romans, house slaves were sometimes educated men, serving as tutors to the children of the household. Some believe that many were authors as well. The fortune-telling slave girl, who annoyed Paul and his group, was being exploited by an owner who used her for their own gain. They were furious when Paul exorcised the spirit and left her "worthless." Consequently, they dragged Paul and his companions to the "marketplace to face authorities" (Acts 16:16–19).

The pervasiveness of slavery and its temporary nature made it less of a matter of shame for the family than a simple indication of status. It was used in Scripture to describe the worshipper's relationship to God and the true believer's relationship to his fellow Christians. Christ took the role of the slave in washing his disciples' feet, and spoke of making himself a servant to others. His death on the cross was the punishment Romans usually reserved for slaves (Philem. 2:7).

Paul spoke of mutual service and of becoming a slave to Christ (Rom. 1:1; Philem. 1:1). He used the tradition of the heir-slave in his statement to the Galatians, "So you are no longer a slave, but a son; and since you are a son, God has made you also an heir" (Gal. 4:7). He compared Abraham's two sons, "one by the slave woman and the other by the free woman," using the law to explain that it is the free woman's child who is the legal heir, and that we are adopted by God to be heirs to eternal life (Gal. 4:23–31). And it was Paul who proclaimed that, in Christ Jesus, "there is neither Jew nor Greek, slave nor free, male nor female" (Gal. 3:28). The concept of manumission (freedom from slavery) and adoption by the owner as a son and heir became powerful images of the work of Christ and his followers (Rom. 8:15–17; Gal. 4:5–7). *See also* Slavery, Laws of.

Further Reading

DeVaux, Roland. *Ancient Israel: Its Life and Institutions.* Grand Rapids, Mich.: William B. Eerdmans Publishing Company, 1961. Fineberg, C. L. "Synagogues," in *The Illustrated Bible Dictionary.* Sydney, Australia: Tyndale

House Publishers, 1980. Swartley, Willard M. "Slavery," in *The Oxford Companion to the Bible*. New York: Oxford University Press, 1993.

Song

From early times, both men and women sang. They sang with delight when they were victorious in battle, when they worked or worshipped or wedded or feasted. They played instruments and danced as they sang, putting their whole body and spirit into exuberant expressions. They also sang their lamentations and their prayers. The Hebrew custom was to express their moods with great vigor, sharing pain and delight, triumph or sorrow. For instance, when David returned from the slaughter of the Philistines, "the women came out of all the cities of Israel, singing and dancing, to meet king Saul, with timbrels, with joy, and with instruments of music. And the women sang one to another in their play, and said, Saul hath slain his thousands, And David his ten thousands" (1 Sam. 18:6f).

This bit of Scripture would appear to suggest a fairly developed form of music—antiphonal song, with one group responding to the other. A number of the **Psalms** are also constructed so that this kind of answering song is implied, with the lines divided for responses. Over the years, traditional tunes developed, and the singers freely improvised variations. These eventually became the stock musical phrases that were used for liturgical music as well, especially for the Psalms.

There were songs for all occasions. Like the songs sung for David, there were numerous war songs, as in Deborah's victory song and Miriam's (Exod. 15:20; Judg. 5). There were musical laments, as David's poignant cry for the death of Saul and Jonathan (2 Sam. 1). Men sang at their work when gathering grapes or drinking the vintage.

Weddings had songs, as the Song of Solomon attests. Psalm 45 is the anthem composed for a royal marriage. Some believe that the words of Song of Songs (2:15) are actually lyrics for a popular song:

Catch for us the foxes,
The tiny, little foxes;
For they ruin all our **vineyards**,
When our vineyards are in bloom.

Certainly most of Solomon's Song of Songs must have derived not just from individual creativity, but from popular numbers sung at weddings. Ezekiel complained that people listened to singers of love ballads more closely than they listened to his admonitions (Ezek. 33:32).

The other famous words, "Let us eat and drink, for tomorrow we shall die" may also be lyrics for a drinking song, perhaps sung at the harvest of grapes (E.W. Heaton 1956 , 202–204). There were probably a number of songs connected with different crops that the community joined to harvest or process.

Public **prayer**, which regularly accompanied **sacrifice** in ancient Hebrew rituals, apparently turned to song quite early. Amos (5:23) tells us that hymns were sung, and instruments were played when the **priests** were offering sacrifices. Because it is rhythmic and choral, public prayer naturally lends itself to musical renditions. "Liturgical singing made its appearance once the cult and the priesthood were organized in a public sanctuary, and Solomon's **Temple** had a group of singers attached to it from its earliest days. After the Exile, the members of this Temple choir became more important and more highly esteemed.... The hymn book, or the prayer book, of the second Temple was the Psalter" (Roland deVaux 1961, 457).

Some scholars believe that Scripture was often recited with musical accompaniment (Neh. 8:8). A "sort of musical declamation for the passages uttered aloud in the **synagogue**," as well as lessons, prayers, and praises "have always been thus musically declaimed; and this declamation, developing in many lands under the influence of varying tonal surroundings through long centuries, has gradually become extended into the vocal melody, solo or choral, in which the whole of the traditional services are now presented" (Cyrus Adler and Francis L. Cohen 2004).

The Temple had singers, who ceased in their work only when the Temple itself was first destroyed. When the Temple was restored after the Exile, the singers were provided with priestly garments and high status. Nehemiah describes the remarkable scene of the dedication of the wall, when he divided the singers into two groups. They marched around the walls in separate directions, returning to the Temple itself, where they sang alternating hymns of praise to God (Neh. 12:31). This use of strophe, antistrophe echoes the pattern of the Greek chorus and anticipates much early Christian music. Some believe that, after the Exile, there may have been mixed voices in the choir, both male and female (Ezra 2:65).

In post-exilic times, with the development of the synagogues, the music was transferred to the more informal sphere, where it underwent a gradual development. The melody and the form of the music, which may have been like Greek music, were probably determined by the syntactical structure of the sentence instead of by the metrical form of the musical phrase. Some believe there were no regular strophes, allowing great freedom in melody. The melodies would have been earnest and simple, with the singers making every word intelligible.

We do not know quite what the style of singing would have been in Jesus's day, but we do know that after the **Last Supper**, the **disciples** joined in singing (or chanting) a hymn before they went out to the Mount of Olives. This would probably have been a Psalm, because the **Passover** meal was traditionally closed with the singing of Psalms 115 and 118. The early **Church** continued the practice of singing a hymn at their gatherings.

John echoes this tradition by picturing the "new song" sung in **Heaven** (Rev. 5:9, 10), and the singing of the angelic hosts, especially the "Song of the Lamb."

Numerous of the poetic passages in the New Testament are interpreted as songs: the angelic appearance to the Bethlehem **shepherds** (Luke 2:14), the song of Zacharias after the birth of John the Baptist (Luke 1:67–79), the song of Mary in anticipation of the birth of Christ (Luke 1:46–55), Paul's hymn of redemption (Eph. 1:3–14), the hymn of the early Church (1 Tim 3:16), and the songs of Moses and of the Lamb (Rev. 15:3–4; Fred H. Wight 1953, 237).

The style of singing, nasal, shrill, and alternately full of intricate graces and sudden pressures on emphatic notes, would not "altogether commend itself to Western ears as graceful or harmonious" (Cyrus Adler and Francis L. Cohen 2004). The most elaborate of these songs were probably the Psalms, which were a regular part of the Temple ritual.

The scale forms of this singing were probably like the plain song of the Catholics, Byzantine, and Armenian churches. The songs also drew from a wide variety of other musical traditions. Eventually, a style of florid melodious intonation came into fashion, requiring the exercise of vocal agility that restricted the singing to specialists.

Some scholars speculate that the music would have been without harmony, a tradition that is incomprehensible to the Arabs, who consider it "a wild and unpleasant noise, in which no sensible person can take pleasure." Apparently this means that musicians play on different instruments and sing at the same time, all using the same melody or singing or playing one and the same note throughout. Thus, the singers and the instruments, including the blaring trumpets, would make "one sound" (2 Chron. 5:13, 15:25). *See also* Music; Musical Instruments; Psalms.

Further Reading

Adler, Cyrus and Francis L. Cohen. "Music, Synagogal," http: www. jewishencyclopoedia. com (accessed July 7, 2004). DeVaux, Roland. *Ancient Israel: Its Life and Institutions*. Grand Rapids, Mich.: William B. Eerdmans Publishing Company, 1961. Heaton, E. W. *Everyday Life in Old Testament Times*. New York: Charles Scribner's Sons, 1956. Wight, Fred H. *Manners and Customs of Bible Lands*. Chicago: Moody Press, 1953.

Sports

(Rom. 15:30; 1 Cor. 9:25–27; Heb. 12:1; 2 Tim. 4:7) From ancient times, although Jews were a strong and healthy people, they were not concerned with sports or the cultivation of muscular bodies. They were hardworking outdoors people. They could walk or run for miles. Their heroes were strong wrestlers: Samson even wrestled a lion, and Jacob wrestled an **angel**. They were fierce fighters when they needed to be, yet they did not cultivate gladiators who fought for the joy of battle. They could endure **slavery**, even the arduous labor in the brickyards and yet grow as a people. With physical work to be done in the fields or in the town, these people needed all their strength and courage for real life, not for games that only imitate life.

By contrast, the **Greeks** were famous for their games, especially for the Olympic games, which were held every four years at Olympia in honor of their god Zeus. Admirers of bodily strength and agility, they focused their attention on physical cultivation and brought that taste to their empire. The Greeks and their Hellenistic successors ruled over the Hebrews from the time of Alexander the Great until the invasion of the Romans, another people who shared this zeal for sports.

Menelaus, the brother of the high priest Jason (170 B.C.), hoping to ingratiate himself to the king Antiochus Epiphanes, was the first to build a gymnasium in Jerusalem. It was close to the **Temple** and modeled on the Greek plan, with space for "wrestling, boxing, ball-playing, throwing, slinging, archery, jumping, riding, swimming, diving," and other events under the supervision of a "gymnasiarch" (Frank H. Vizetelly and Cyrus Adler 2004). At first, the conservative Jews were shocked at the naked men cavorting in public, but eventually, athletics became popular, even among the **priests**. Young Jewish men were enticed to join the activities, even foregoing or seeking to reverse **circumcision** so that they could look more Hellenistic.

Evidence of this period is still available for archaeological study in the Holy Land. Any visitor to modern Israel is struck by the remarkable remains of the Greek and Roman cities with temples and marketplaces, gymnasia, and baths. Under the Romans, gladiators performed amazing feats of strength and heroism in the great amphitheatres. The Roman genius for plumbing was put to use in the series of baths, graduating the temperature of the waters from hot to cold, with steam rooms, much like modern athletic clubs. The Romans had adopted the Greek admiration for athletes and for competition. Working out in the nude, these well-oiled men were thoroughly un-Jewish.

The Hasmonean (or Maccabean) rebellion rid the land of Hellenism, including the love of the athlete, for the time being. But Herod the Great reintroduced athletics into Jewish life. He "appointed solemn games to be celebrated every fifth year in honor of Caesar, and built a theatre at Jerusalem, and also a very great amphitheater in the plain" (Vizetelly and Adler 2004, quoting Josephus).

Most of the Jews continued to consider sports a corrupting influence, but a few rabbis considered the games a good way for young Hebrew men to develop physically and become acculturated to their Roman rulers. Weightlifting, archery, javelin-throwing, and other gladiatorial skills gradually became much admired even by the conquered peoples.

Saul, later Paul the evangelist, was a Roman citizen with thorough grounding in the Greek culture. In his **epistles** to individuals and churches, Paul used more athletic imagery than any other writer of Scripture. He drew lessons from many aspects of the Olympic games: he noted that the contestants were under rigid rules, including dietary regulations. From this Paul drew the analogy of "self-control in all things" if one planned to strive at the games (1 Cor. 9:25). When he considered the great but temporary prize for the winner, which was proclaimed by the herald, the palm branch awarded by the **judges,** and the crowning with a sacred olive wreath, he was led to note the *incorruptible* nature of the Christian rewards: "Ye shall receive a **crown** of glory that fadeth not away" (1 Pet. 5:4). He portrayed himself as a man running a race for "the prize of the high calling of God in Christ Jesus" (Phil. 3:14). At the end, he noted that he had run his race (2 Tim. 4:7).

The author of Hebrews, who may not have been Paul, also used the race and the grandstands in his imagery of the great "cloud of witnesses" and the running of the race "with endurance" (Heb. 12:1). He spoke of the team spirit—"striving together," or acting as athletes as a team (Fred H. Wight 1953, 296). Such is the nature of those who have the "same mind" and work together for the good of the whole group. They become "spiritual athletes" in so doing (Fred H. Wight 1953, 297). Paul also referred to boxing and wrestling, echoing Jacob's wrestling with the angel as he spoke of "striving" against evil (Rom 15:30). Like a good boxer, he did not flail around, "as one that beateth the air: but I keep under my body, and bring it into subjection" (1 Cor. 9:26–27).

The gladiatorial shows, usually performed by professional athletes, became more and more degenerate over time as the crowds demanded more action and more **blood**. Huge crowds would gather in the amphitheatres all over the empire to watch battles between slaves and criminals against one another or in combat with lions, bears, elephants, and tigers. **Christians,** because they refused to acknowledge Caesar as a god, were frequently the victims in these increasingly vicious games. Paul referred metaphorically to "fighting with the beasts" at Ephesus (Acts 19). The custom was to allow the gladiators to have armor and equipment for battle against the **animals** in the morning, but to be stripped of **clothing** and weapons by noon, when the animals were turned loose on them. Fred Wight believes this is Paul's meaning when he describes the sufferings of the **apostles** this way: "For I think that God hath set forth us the apostles last, as it were appointed to death: for we are made a spectacle unto the world, and to angels, and to men" (1 Cor. 4:9; Fred R. Wight 1953, 298).

Further Reading

Vizetelly, Frank H. and Cyrus Adler. "Athletes, Athletics, and Field-Sports," http://www.jewishencyclopedia.com (accessed June 12, 2004). Wight, Fred H. *Manners and Customs of Bible Lands.* Chicago: Moody Press, 1953.

Staff. *See* Scepter

Stars. *See* Cosmology

Stone

(Gen. 28:18, 38:20, 31:52; Exod. 24:4; Deut. 12:31, 6:22; Josh. 24:26; 1 Sam. 7:12; 1 Kings 7:15) Large stones have long held a fascination for people, many of whom have been inclined to worship them. For Canaanites, Phoenicians, and most of the Arab peoples, stones often came to be seen as the habitat of a god. Impressive and oddly shaped stones also became landmarks or boundary stones.

Stones were commonly used as **altars** by the ancient Hebrews. Jacob, who once used a stone as a pillow, set up numerous stone altars to commemorate various experiences in his life. He set up one at Bethel, where he wrestled with an angel, and at Gilead and Shechem. He set one to mark Rachel's grave. When Moses built his altar at the foot of Mt. Sinai, he set 12 stones around the mountain, one for each of the 12 tribes. Joshua used a stone for an altar in the sanctuary at Shechem, following Jacob's tradition. And Samuel set up a sacred stone, known as a *mazzebah*.

Most of these were not "hewn" stone, not shaped by the iron tools of human hands. The stone was just as it had been the first day of **Creation**. These altar stones were usually wide and flat, with space for a sacrifice. They had **blood** splashed on them and **oil** poured on them in an anointment ceremony. On them the sacrifices were burned. The exception to the rule of natural stone was Solomon's use of carved pillars, which were typical parts of Phoenician temples.

Later kings and prophets grew concerned that people might worship the stones rather than the God to whom they were sacrificing their goats and bulls. As a result of the association with Astarte and worship in "high places," they were rejected by Hebrew law and destroyed by kings (Deut 12:31, 16:22; 2 Kings 3:2, 10:26).

Like the stones used among many other primitive peoples, the ancient markers did take on a sacred quality for the Jews. The Greeks believed that humans derived from stones, others believed that stones could produce rain, but the Jews were less superstitious. They acknowledged that Elijah could bring rain by building his 12 stones into an altar and praying to God, or that Moses could strike a stone and water would gush forth. These were acts of God, not of men or of stones. The Jews knew that they should not worship the stones or mystify them as the home of their god, but chose instead to associate them with specific historical moments when God revealed his power to the patriarch. By contrast, the early Greeks and other peoples set up stones, which they worshipped as gods. These unwrought stones were known as *megaliths*. Circles of these megaliths have also been found in England (Stonehenge) and Ireland (Newgrange).

Even today, stones may be used in a religious or ceremonial context. The famous Stone of Scone, situated in the coronation chair in Westminster Abbey since the thirteenth century, became a nationalistic symbol for the Scots. Before it was taken by Edward I from Scotland in 1296, 34 successive Scottish kings had been crowned at Scone Castle while sitting on this rectangle of red sandstone. Tradition has it that this 336-pound chuck of sandstone, the "Stone of Destiny," was Jacob's pillow, taken to serve as the pedestal of the Ark of the Temple, and later brought to Scotland. It became a symbol of Scotland's ancient heritage. On Christmas Eve, 1950, three college students from Glasgow broke into Westminster Abbey and stole the *Lia Fail*, the Stone of Scone, depositing it at Arbroath Abbey. It was taken back to Westminster in time for Elizabeth II's coronation, but finally ceremonially returned to Scotland in 2001, as a testimony of the new Scottish Parliament's convening for the first time in nearly 300 years.

Anglo-Saxon kings were usually anointed standing on a stone at Kingston-on-Thames. Swedish monarchs also stood on a stone to be installed. German emperors took their oath of office beside a stone pillar, which is now in front of the Church of St. Ambrosio in Milan. Apparently, all of these are traditions tied to Scripture: Abimelech was installed as king "beside the oak at the pillar at Shechem" (Judg. 9:6), and the priest Jehoiada crowned Joash while the king stood beside the pillar, "according to custom" (2 Kings 11:14; Theodor H. Gaster 1969, 490).

The sacred black stone of Mecca, which is regularly kissed by worshippers, is known as the *Ka'ba*. It is now broken into three parts and some fragments, which are bound together with a silver band. It is a black stone with red and yellow coloring, perhaps a meteor. The famous Aqsa Mosque on the Temple Mount in Jerusalem contains the stone that was taken from the Church of the Ascension on the Mount of Olives. It is thought to bear the imprint of Jesus's feet and to be the spot from which he ascended to **Heaven**. In the Dome of the Rock is the *Sakhra,* a rock reported to be the one from which the "Apostle of God" (Mohammed) set his foot when he ascended into Heaven. Pilgrims pace around this rock just as they do around the Ka'ba (G.S.P. Freeman-Grenville 1998, 38).

The tradition of the sacred stone continues in some modern Christian worship: If Roman Catholics do not have a proper altar for the Mass, they may instead use a natural stone, consecrated by the bishop. The natural or uncut stone retains a mystique, a beauty, and power untouched by human craft. *See also* Altar; Stonemasons.

Further Reading

Freeman-Grenville, G.S.P. *The Holy Land: A Pilgrim's Guide to Israel, Jordan and the Sinai*. New York: Continuum, 1998. Gaster, Theodor H. *Myth, Legend, and Custom in the Old Testament*. New York: Harper & Row, Publishers, 1969. Gunn, R. M. "The Stone of Scone/Destiny," http://www.members. aol.com/Skyelander/stone (accessed June 18, 2005). Herman, Arthur. *How the Scots Invented the Modern World*. New York: Three Rivers Press, 2001. Hirsch, Emil G. and Immanuel Benzinger. "Stone and Stone-Worship," http://www.jewishencyclopedia.com (accessed June 18, 2005). Schulte, A. J. "Altar Stone," http://www.newadvent.org (accessed June 18, 2005). Witcombe, Christopher L. C. E. "Sacred Places," http://www.witcombe.sbc. edu (accessed June 18, 2005).

𝔖tonemasons

(2 Sam. 5:11;1 Chron.14:1; 1 Kings 5:17–18, 6:36; 2 Kings 7:9, 12:12; Amos 7:8) Stone is everywhere in Israel. The landscape is littered with stone, from Galilee's black basalt to Jerusalem's white limestone. It is no wonder that ancient Hebrews used stones for **altars**, well-coverings, entrances to tombs, walls, and buildings. The greatest and most revered of the work of the masons is in Jerusalem, a city built on rock, where Solomon and Herod both built magnificent **temples**, as well as walls, **palaces**, porticoes, and public buildings of glistening white stone. The famous Western Wall is the revered relic of that later massive construction.

King David, who was forbidden to build the Temple, nonetheless brought stonemasons from Tyre to build him a palace, using a combination of cedar and stone (2 Sam. 5:11, 1 Chron. 14:1). In the scriptural references to the building of Solomon's Temple, we see again that the Israelite king used Hiram's workers, who knew how to "dress" the stone, preparing it for placement in the building in "courses" (1 Kings 5:17–18, 6:36). The writer was clearly amazed by these men's skill, noting that they cut the "blocks of high-grade stone ... to size and trimmed [them] with a saw on their inner and outer faces" (2 Kings 7:9). He also differentiated between the masons and the stonecutters (2 Kings 12:12). Masons build with stone, while the cutters shape it; these roles must complement one another perfectly to produce the beautifully crafted wall or building.

It is no wonder that the fall of these walls and the destruction of this Temple proved a powerful symbol of the destruction of Judah and the prophesy of renewal: "The bricks have fallen down, but we will build with dressed stone" (Isa. 9:10). Ezekiel mentions the stonework of the Temple in his vision of the great altar with "four tables of dressed stone for burnt offerings" (Ezek. 40:42).

The Temple Mount and the buildings on it remain a testimony to human creativity. The limestone used comes from mountains around Jerusalem with horizontal layering that varies between 18 inches and 5 feet thick. The stonecutter would first chisel the rock in such a way as to flatten the face of the rock. Then he would use a pickax to dig narrow channels four to six inches wide on all sides except the bottom of the stone he was quarrying. Next he would insert dry wooden beams, hammering them tightly into place, and then pour water over them. The wood would swell and the stone would separate from the lower rock layer. He would then square off the corners and prepare the stone for transportation. The smaller stones would be placed on wagons, but some of the stones in the Temple Mount weighed 50 tons or more. They were transported on large wooden rollers. The stonemasons left 12-inch projections in the blocks to allow ropes to be placed so that the stone could be pulled and lifted by the powerful oxen. Josephus tells us that 1,000 oxen were used for this work (Leen and Kathleen Ritmeyer 1998, 48–49).

The Jews' pride in Herod's magnificent reconstruction of the Temple Mount provided Jesus with a dramatic reference point for his prophesies of the destruction of the Temple by the **Romans** in 70 A.D. and of his own death and resurrection. Standing on the Temple Mount, he told his **disciples:** "Do you see all these things?" "I tell you the truth, not one stone here will be left on another; every one will be thrown down" (Mat 24:2). Later, the witnesses at his trial used his own symbolic words against him, interpreting them literally as threatening to damage the Temple: "I will destroy this temple that is made with hands, and within three days I will build another made without hands" (Mark 14:58).

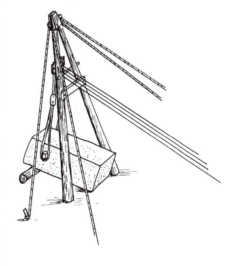

More frequent references in Scripture are to foundations and to cornerstones. The common practice was to dig down to living stone for the foundation of a construction to protect against shrinkage and erosion, a habit to which Jesus refers in his comment that a good mason "digged deep, and laid the foundations on a rock" (Luke 6:48). Builders would dig deep trenches and fill them with stone or lime, allowing this to settle below the surface of the ground. They would then set the cornerstone, which would determine the orientation for the rest of the construction. This was a broad, square stone that the mason would place in the spot where the two walls would meet. For private homes, much of the upper work would have been brick or wood. The carpenters and

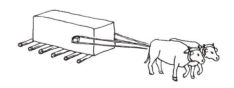

Machinery for lifting and moving stone, showing projections left on the stone to make it easier to handle.

the masons would have worked hand in hand to produce an integrated structure. Even in the great buildings of Solomon, the masons and carpenters shared the work, with the interior being primarily cedar.

When the entire structure was of stone, the labor was much more demanding. Oblong stones, laid in courses, formed the bulk of the walls. These had to be trimmed so that they fit tightly against one another. The masons of the Old Testament knew the method of alternating long and short stones so as to provide greater strength, economizing by constructing corners and supports of carefully dressed stone, and filling the space between with rubble. The excavators at Megiddo and Samaria found traces of red paint on the carefully dressed edges of the stone, apparently to ensure the correct alignment (E. W. Heaton 1956, 135). At the top corners, the mason would place thinner square blocks to hold the roof beams, which would be wooden.

For these tasks, the mason needed several tools. The measuring rod, a straight cane approximately 20 feet long, was used to measure wall spaces, especially between windows and doors. This leveling rod, reed, or line was strung between the corner stones to keep the construction straight. He also had a plumbline, a small inverted lead cone fastened by a cord to a cylindrical piece of wood made of the same diameter. He would hold this against the edge of the wall to make sure it was true and would stand over time.

The method for cutting stone into large blocks, using wood and water to break the limestone.

This is the image Amos used in God's testing of his people: "Behold I will set a plumbline in the midst of my people Israel" (Amos 7:8; Fred H. Wight 1953, 218).

Because stone was so heavy, it was costly to use for anything other than foundations and cornerstones in private homes. It was primarily restricted to public buildings. While the Israelites were in **Egypt**, they saw masons working with granite, sandstone, quartzite, and limestone, but their choices were more limited in Palestine. Most of the stone there was limestone, although the Galilee has quantities of basalt, a black volcanic rock. Probably the stones used in Solomon's Temple were quarried and dressed in Lebanon before shipment to Jerusalem. The limestone proved both beautiful and useful for the masons. While it remained underground, it was fairly easy to cut, and then could be laid in position quickly so that the blocks welded together before the hot dry air dried them out and turned the construction into a solid mass, much like concrete. They might be reinforced with a mortar made of clay mixed with crushed limestone or straw.

For this work in the quarry, the mason used many of the same tools as the **carpenter**. He could saw the limestone, trim it with a mallet and chisel, or a walling hammer. When quarrying large blocks of stone, like those used in the walls of the Temple Mount, wooden wedges were knocked into the stone with wooden hammers and then soaked until the stone cracked open with the force of expansion. Harder stone was shaped by repeated pounding with a large metal forge hammer, which Jeremiah used to describe the divine Word (Jer. 23:29, 50:23; D. J. Wiseman 1980, 126).

Masons' work grew more sophisticated over time, allowing historians to date ruins by the stone evidence. The earlier stones, used in altars or for boundary markers, were uncut. Later, masons cut shafts into the hillside, enlarging natural caves and making them into mausoleums and sealing the entrance way with great round stones that could be rolled away. They also cut silos and **cisterns**, which have been discovered at Lachish, Megiddo, and Gibeon. The famous water tunnel in Jerusalem has cut marks from the chisels of masons and miners. During the period of the monarchy, masons cut large stone pillar bases, and by Herod's day built the enormous and carefully crafted buildings: "By the Hellenistic period Herodian buildings at Jerusalem, Machpelah and other sites show the use of immense blocks of stone so carefully dressed as to be aligned without mortar, and it is still impossible to insert a knife blade between the joints" (D. J. Wiseman 1980, 126). Whether these master craftsmen were Israelites or foreign laborers, they had clearly developed significant skills. *See also* Carpenters, Carpentry.

Further Reading

Heaton, E. W. *Everyday Life in Old Testament Times.* New York: Charles Scribner's Sons, 1956. Ritmeyer, Leen and Kathleen. *Secrets of Jerusalem's Temple*

Mount. Washington, D.C.: Biblical Archaeology Society, 1998. Wight, Fred H. *Manners and Customs of Bible Lands.* Chicago: Moody Press, 1953. Wiseman, D.J. "Arts and Crafts," in *The Illustrated Bible Dictionary.* Sydney, Australia: Tyndale House Publishers, 1980.

Swine, Pigs

(Deut. 14:8; Lev. 11:7; Prov. 11:22; Matt. 7:6, 8:30–33; Luke 8:32–34, 15:15–16) According to Hebrew thought, the only creature lower than the **dog** was the pig. We are told not to give dogs what is sacred or to cast our pearls before swine (Matt 7:6). The writer of Proverbs found the pig physically repugnant and ridiculous when decorated: "Like a gold ring in a pig's snout is a beautiful woman who shows no discretion" (Prov. 11:22). When the Prodigal Son fell to his lowest possible depth in life, he was hired to feed pigs, and even "longed to fill his stomach with the pods that the pigs were eating" (Luke 15:15–16).

The term *pig* originally meant young swine, but has come to refer to the **animal** of any age and both sexes: the boar, the sow, or the piglet. Swine derived from wild boars, which ran through the forests and were known for their ferocity. Psalm 60:13 refers to them as the "swine of the woods." They were found in the thickets along the banks of the Jordan south of the Sea of Galilee, where these creatures still swarm (Emil G. Hirsh and I. M. Casanowicz 2004). They crush their prey, eating their fill, and then trample the rest.

They were apparently raised for **food** in **Egypt** and were known to the Israelites during the **Exodus,** although it is not clear that the Israelites ate their flesh before the prohibition in Mosaic **law.** Some scholars believe that the Egyptians also thought them unclean and unfit for human consumption.

The pig, the law asserts, "though it has a split hoof completely divided, does not chew the cud; it is unclean for you" (Lev.11:7). We find the additional admonition, "You are not to eat their meat or touch their carcasses" (Deut. 14:8). Some believe this rejection of pork was for sanitary purposes; the animal is especially subject to disease. As a scavenger, willing to eat anything, including excrement, the pig might pick up diseased material and carry infection or become infected. Also, the pig "is host of the tapeworm causing trichinosis; this passes one stage in the muscles of a pig and can be transmitted only by being eaten." These tapeworms can cause death in humans. Although thorough cooking can kill the worms, the primitive cooking techniques, with limited fuel, made this less likely. A complete ban seemed wiser than a strict set of cooking directions (G. S. Cansdale 1980, 55–56).

Pigs were also theologically suspect. Pig **blood** was sacrificed on Astarte's **altars,** and the animal itself came to be associated with her and her worshippers. Thus, one means of humiliating a Jew was forcing him to eat the flesh of swine, thus making him guilty of apostasy (Isa. 45:4). The final degradation of the nation by Antiochus IV Epiphanes was in sacrificing a pig on the altar of the **Temple** in Jerusalem. Josephus tells us that he "left the temple bare, and took away the golden **candlesticks**, and the golden altar, and table" and even the veils of the Temple. He emptied it of all its treasures and "built an **idol** altar upon God's Altar, slew swine upon it, and so offered a sacrifice neither according to the law, nor the Jewish religious worship in that country" (Josephus, *The Antiquities of the Jews,* 12:5:4). This final insult, horrifying Matthias and his heroic sons, triggered the Maccabean revolt.

Although it appears that this was a deliberate insult to the Jewish religion, it might have been a signal of a transformation of the Jewish worship into a **Roman** ceremony. The Romans considered pigs an ideal sacrifice, as is evidenced in depictions of them on the altar in the Roman Forum (Madeleine S. Miller and J. Lane Miller 1961, 712). When Antiochus sacrificed the swine, he also renamed the Temple in honor of Jupiter Hellenius.

Other nations left evidence in the form of pigs' bones, proving that they did raise pigs. Swine were bred for food and sacrificial offerings by **Canaanites** and Syrians, **Assyrians**, and **Philistines**. After all, swine were easy to breed, and breeders could grow rich easily. In addition to the succulent meat the pig provided for the table, its fat was used in embellishing cheeses, its bristles served as needles, and its excrement was used in tanning (Emil Hirsh and I. M. Casanowicz 2004). Nonetheless, some other cultures (including the Phoenicians and the Ethiopians) joined the Israelites in rejecting swine and their products for any purpose.

The best-known New Testament reference to pigs is the occasion of Jesus's driving the **demons** from the Gerasene demoniac into the herd of swine, which then raced over the cliff into the Sea of Galilee and were drowned (Matt. 8:30–33; Mark 5:11–16; Luke 8:32–34). The association of these creatures with demons signals the deep loathing with which they were viewed. *See also* Animals; Clean, Unclean; Law, Dietary.

Further Reading

Cansdale, George. *All the Animals of the Bible Lands.* Grand Rapids, Mich.: Zondervan Publishing House, 1970. Cansdale, George. "Animals," in *The Illustrated Bible Dictionary.* Sydney, Australia: Tyndale House Publishers, 1980. Hirsh, Emil G. and I. M. Casanowicz. "Swine," http://www. jewishencyclopedia.com (accessed June 18, 2004). Josephus, Flavius. *The Works of Josephus.* Peabody, Mass.: Hendrickson Publishers, Inc., 2001. Miller, Madeleine S. and J. Lane Miller. "Swine," in *Harper's Bible Dictionary.* New York: Harper and Row, 1961.

Synagogue

(Mark 1:21; Luke 7:5; John 6:59) Although no one knows quite when synagogues originated, many suspect that they developed during the **Babylonian** captivity in the sixth century B.C., when the Jews found themselves without their **Temple** and in need of places to study the **law** and to pray. They were forbidden to offer **sacrifices** anywhere but the Temple, but they still had other spiritual hungers. They wanted to meet to discuss the Torah (the first five books of the Bible) to fulfill the law of Moses. Thus, **sanctuaries** emerged where they could have instruction and **prayer** as a community. Some believe that Ezekiel may have inspired this development, beginning with gatherings in the **prophet**'s house (Ezek 8:1, 20:1–3; Madeleine S. Miller and J. Lane Miller 1961, 717).

After the return from captivity, Ezra and his successors reorganized Jewish religious life to include congregational **worship**, as well as the Temple ceremonies at Jerusalem. This led to the building of synagogues for assemblies of worshippers across the countryside. Psalm 74:8 refers to such a gathering place, but these were not limited to the old sanctuaries that had flourished in the years before the cult of the Temple developed. The Gospel writers record scenes of Jesus's teaching in the synagogues at Nazareth and Capernaum (Mark 1:21; Luke 7:5; John 6:59). There were others in Bethshean, Tiberias, Lydda, Maon, and Sepphoris, as well as various other places, a number of which have been excavated in recent years (Wilhelm Bacher, Lewis N. Dembitz 2004).

Early **Christians** often came from such synagogues as the Synagogue of the Freemen or Libertines (i.e., freed slaves) at Jerusalem (Acts 6:9), with which Paul is thought to have been associated. Some say there were as many as 394 synagogues in Jerusalem in 70 A.D., when Titus destroyed the city. Synagogues throughout the Roman Empire were used by the evangelists as places to preach the **Gospel** message. There are more than 50 references to such gatherings in the New Testament. Paul especially used these as hospitable centers for his missionary journeys, beginning in each city with the Jews and then reaching out to Gentiles. The 4 to 7 million Jews of the Diaspora built their synagogues in such far-flung places as **Egypt** and Rome (Madeleine S. Miller and J. Lane Miller 1961, 717).

The synagogue functioned as a little sanctuary where people in the neighborhood could gather to worship, and both children and adults could learn the law. It was also a social center helping to bind the Jews together in their community, discussing and solving problems. Here they could study the Scriptures, meet other Jews, celebrate weddings and births, lament persecution, and mourn the dead.

The officers of the synagogue, whose roles might be hereditary, were not **priests**, although they led the **Sabbath** services. The congregation was governed by elders who had the authority to exercise discipline and punish members by scourging them or excommunicating them. The chief officer was called the "ruler of the synagogue" (Mark 5:22; Acts 13:15, 18:8). He supervised the service, while an attendant (Luke 4:20) brought the scrolls of Scripture for reading and then replaced them in the **Ark**. He was also the person whose task it was to scourge offending members. The attendant instructed the children in reading the law. The dispenser of alms collected and distributed the alms. And an interpreter had the task of paraphrasing the law and the prophets in vernacular language to make them more understandable to the congregation.

The synagogue services involved **psalms**, the recitation of the Jewish creed, prayer, and a benediction. On certain prescribed days, portions of the law and the prophets were read, and sermons or interpretations might be preached. After a time of praise, the leader would close with the Aaronic blessing (Num. 6:24–26). The Mishnah (the **scribes'** expansion of the Torah) indicates that there should be five parts to the service:

1. The Shema was read (Deut. 6:4–9, 11:13–21; Num. 15:37–41).
2. Prayers were recited, including the 18 petitions and benedictions, the first reading "Blessed art Thou, the Lord our God."
3. The reading of the law followed this, with the entire Pentateuch read over a period of time—the central portion of the service.
4. The section of the prophets was explained, with exhortations drawn from it.
5. A benediction marked the conclusion of the service. (C. L. Feinberg 1980, 1502–1503). The early house churches of the Christians and their earliest pattern of services clearly derived from the order of worship in these synagogues.

The architecture of the synagogue buildings may be surmised from the numerous archaeological remains. In Palestine alone, there were three types:

1. The Galilean type, with monumental and richly decorated facades, facing toward Jerusalem, usually having three entrances
2. The basilican plan, used extensively in Byzantine churches, with modest exteriors and splendid interiors
3. The broadhouse synagogues found in a few locales of Palestine and cities of the Diaspora, with a shrine located along the long wall (Lee Levine 1993, 723)

Although there have been many designs over time, the essential components are an interior large enough to house the congregation, aisles that allow passage of the attendant, a space for a portable ark in which the scrolls of the law and the prophets are kept, "chief" seats for the religious and governing leaders of the synagogue (sometimes called the "Seat of Moses"), and a platform from which the reading and speaking might take place. Men and women were seated apart and still are in more orthodox synagogues. Decorations are limited, but might include the seven-branched **candlestick**, the ark in which the Torah scroll is kept, but little else.

The loss of the Temple and the absence of the solemn sacrifices associated with it were keenly felt by the Jews, especially on holy days. The synagogue, which provided a place for prayer and reading of the Torah became a substitute for it (C. L. Feinberg 1980, 1499). The tradition of the synagogue continues to the present with these centers often architecturally diverse and still functioning as houses of worship, sacred **meals**, and of study for the community of Jews they serve. *See also* History in the Bible; Sacrifice; Temple.

Further Reading

Bacher, Wilhelm and Lewis N. Dembitz. "Synagogue," http://www.jewishencyclopedia.com (accessed October 21, 2004). Feinberg, C. L. "Synagogue," in *The Illustrated Bible Encyclopedia*. Sydney, Australia: Tyndale House Publishers, 1980. Levine, Lee. "Synagogue," in *The Oxford Companion to the Bible*. New York: Oxford University Press, 1993. Miller, Madeleine S. and J. Lane Miller. "Synagogue," in *Harper's Bible Dictionary*. New York: Harper and Row, 1961.

T

Tabernacle

(Exod. 25:8, 26, 27, 35–38; Heb. 9:2–12; Rev. 22:3) "Let them make me a sanctuary that I may dwell among them," God commanded Moses (Exod. 25:8). This "Tabernacle," "Tent of Meeting" or "dwelling place" was a transitional stage between the **altars** the patriarchs had built in various places and the **Temple** that Solomon was to build in Jerusalem. It was a holy **sanctuary** set apart from the ordinary dwellings of the Hebrews. A **tent** among their tents, God's tabernacle marked his presence in their midst, provided a holy place for the **Ark of the Covenant**, a location for the other precious furniture of worship, and a gathering spot for the mandated times of worship—the **Sabbaths**, **festivals**, and ceremonies included in the Code of Holiness (outlined in the law of Moses). An enclosed space that had the altar, the basin, and the tent, with the Holy Place and the Most Holy Place, separated by a curtain, this construction, minutely detailed, was a guide to worship, as well as a place for it.

Fifty chapters in the Bible are devoted to the Tabernacle, mostly in Exodus, Leviticus, Numbers, and Deuteronomy. Four chapters in Hebrews also review and reinterpret these details of construction and explain their symbolism, pointing to the elements as "types" foreshadowing both Solomon's Temple and the eternal Temple. The precise dimensions of the building, the designs, and the materials are all included in the original plan, as well as the discussion of the construction. The materials range from the mundane **goats'** hair and tanned rams' skins the Hebrews used in constructing their own tents to the precious **gems** and gold, treasures dedicated to their God.

Combining details from the designs of **Egyptian** temples and of desert shrines common among the migratory peoples, the Hebrews built a portable shrine to serve them until they were settled in **Canaan**. The wooden frame covered with cloth hooked together with loops could easily be taken down, packed up, and moved as the Israelites changed their place of habitation. The whole arrangement was fitted with rings and carrying poles to make it portable. The tabernacle formed a continuing center for worship during a transitional time in Hebrew life.

The rectangular design, 100 cubits long and 50 cubits wide, allowed worshippers to move from the profane world to the most sacred space in a succession of visual images, starting with the wide entrance (30 cubits) to the entire enclosure. The first thing the worshipper would confront was the huge bronze altar with its "horns" at the corners (5 cubits square and 3 cubits high) on which the **animals** would be sacrificed in the flames. Next was the copper basin or laver, in which the **priest** would wash before entering the Holy Place, the first room of the covered area. Here, he would see the golden table holding the **Bread** of the Presence and the golden altar of

incense, designed somewhat like the bronze altar, with four horns. Nearby was the lampstand, or menorah, with seven **lamps** with six branches, minutely detailed, and looking like a stylized tree. The precious **metals** were used in the Holy Place, and the bronze was in the courtyard.

On the **Day of Atonement**, the High Priest, properly robed and properly prepared, was allowed to lift the embroidered curtain and enter the Holy of Holies, the final section of the Tabernacle, a 10-cubit square area that held the Ark of the Covenant, the repository of the most sacred objects of the faith, including the tablets of the **law**. Two **cherubim** with outspread wings ornamented the Mercy Seat or atonement cover, over the top of the Ark. It was here that God promised to meet and communicate with the representative of the community—reflected by the light—the glory of his presence, which illuminated this most sacred of rooms.

The design, which was patterned on the heavenly dwelling of God, reflects the worship practices required of the Hebrews and points to the more elaborate design of the Temple itself, which was to have much the same pattern and furnishings. *See also* Bread; Incense; Lamp; Metal: Copper and Bronze; Priest, High Priest; Sacrifice; Temple.

Further Reading
Alter, Robert. *The Five Books of Moses: A Translation and Commentary.* New York: W. W. Norton and Company, 2004. DeVaux, Roland. *Ancient Israel: Its Life and Institutions.* Grand Rapids, Mich.: William B. Eerdmans Publishing Company, 1961.

Tax Collector

The Greek word for publican or tax-collector (*telones*) means a collector of tax or customs on behalf of the Romans, a person employed by a tax farmer or contractor. "As early as 212 B.C., there existed in **Rome** a class of men . . . who undertook state contracts of various kinds . . . their work included the collection of tithes and various indirect taxes. The system was very open to abuse, and the publicans seem to have been prone to extortion and malpractice from the very beginning" (J. H. Harrop 1980,1520).

Jesus was frequently in the company of tax collectors or "publicans" and even called one of them to be a **disciple** (Matt. 18:17). Much to the horror of the community, he ate with tax collectors "and other sinners" (Mark 2:15). Matthew (or Levi), a tax collector whose customs office was on the road from Damascus to Acre, not far from Capernaum, proved to be one of Jesus's most faithful disciples. He welcomed Jesus and his followers to his house and followed him throughout his short ministry, writing one of the early **Gospels**, which seems to be aimed particularly at a Jewish audience.

The Jews resented tax collectors partially because they despised paying taxes to a gentile government, and partly because many of the officials were greedy and dishonest. As John the Baptist noted, when the publicans came to him for **baptism** asking what they should do, he responded: "Exact no more than that which is appointed you" (Luke 3:12, 13). A man like Matthew, although probably a local resident who knew the practices of his fellow countrymen, would also have had to violate the **Sabbath** to gather taxes from travelers on the road for the goods they were carrying. For this practice and for their constant contact with Gentiles, the publicans were considered ceremonially unclean by the strict Jews. The **rabbis** therefore taught that their pupils should not eat with such persons (J. H. Harrop 1980, 1520).

Zaccheus, another follower, was probably not an ordinary tax collector, but "rather a tax commissioner, who farmed out a whole district, and had other tax collectors under his jurisdiction. His conversion was so thorough that he agreed, 'If I have taken anything from any man by false accusation, I restore him fourfold' (Luke 19:8)" (Fred H. Wight 1953, 227). Zaccheus may have been like those tax gatherers mentioned by the Talmud who worked for Rome, governing Palestine and collecting the taxes as a state official:

> The Romans left to the governors or procurators the collection of the regular taxes, such as the land-tax and poll-tax, but leased the customs duties, the market tolls, and similar special imposts. The lessees were generally Roman knights; but there were among them Jews also.... The fact that they were helping the Romans in the exaction of the heavy taxes imposed upon the Jews, combined with the rapacity of some tax-collectors who, taking advantage of the indefiniteness of the tariffs, overcharged the taxpayer, rendered this class of officials hateful to the people. Hence the stringent Jewish legislation which classified the tax-collectors with robbers. Thus, for instance, it was forbidden to take payment in coin from the treasury of the tax-gatherer or to receive alms from it, because the money had been gained by robbery.... The tax-gatherer was ineligible to serve as **judge** or even as a witness.... If one member of a family was a tax-gatherer, all its members were liable to be considered as such for the purposes of testimony, because they would be likely to shield him. (Joseph Jacobs and Isaac Broydé 2005)

The practice of collecting taxes was much older than the Roman Empire. **Egypt**, under the Ptolemies, levied taxes on each city and annually leased the collecting of them to the highest bidder. This tax collector would then gather as much as he could, keeping those profits over and above the debt owed to the government. Historians tell us that those who failed to pay their taxes were beheaded and their possessions confiscated. With this kind of pressure, tax collectors could become quite wealthy (Jacobs and Broydé

2005). Although we have no scriptural records, most scholars assume that other parts of the Hellenistic Empire had similar practices. *See also* Gospel, Gospels; Measures; Taxes, Tithes, Tributes.

Further Reading

Harrop, J. H. "Tax Collector," in *The Illustrated Bible Dictionary.* Sydney, Australia: Tyndale House Publishers, 1980. Jacobs, Joseph and Isaac Broydé. "Tax-Gatherers," http://www.jewishencyclopedia.com (accessed January 17, 2005). Wight, Fred H. *Manners and Customs of Bible Lands.* Chicago: Moody Press, 1953.

𝔗𝔞𝔵𝔢𝔰, 𝔗𝔦𝔱𝔥𝔢𝔰, 𝔗𝔯𝔦𝔟𝔲𝔱𝔢𝔰

(Deut. 18:1–5; 1 Sam. 8:11–15, 10:27; Mark 12:17) A tithe is a tenth of money, land, or products that is paid to a religious group or to a monarch. A tax is a regular payment demanded by an authority or ruler. A tribute is the money paid by a state when it has been conquered to the conqueror. Unlike the money contributed freely by believers to God, these were demanded under threat of **punishment**—even death. During the period of the **Roman** dominance of Israel, there were reports of tax dodgers being beheaded.

Taxing, tithing, and demanding tribute are as old as civilization. Archaeologists digging among the remains at Ur, in modern Iraq, thought to be the birthplace of Abraham, have found evidence of a system of taxes that dates back to the second millennium B.C. "Taxes were paid in kind: every inhabitant of Ur paid in his own coin. Oil, cereals, fruit, wool and cattle made their way into vast warehouses, perishable articles went to the temple shops" (Werner Keller 1982, 17).

A Tryrian silver shekel (the coin preferred for payment of Temple tax) provided a source of revenue for "money changers in the Temple."

Tithes

Abraham, who gave a tenth "of all" the spoils (Gen. 14:20), set a precedent for the "tithe," which was the tenth reserved for God's work. Jacob followed this pattern, giving to God as well (Gen. 28:20–22). Under the law of Moses, this became a requirement of the Hebrews, obligatory that they give a tenth of the seed of the land, the fruit of their trees, and every tenth animal that passed under the rod (Lev. 27:30–33). This was to be used for a variety of purposes, finally determined by the rabbis to be of three kinds:

1. The tithe given to the Levites, who had no land of their own

2. The tithe taken to Jerusalem for the provision of the landowner and his family
3. The tithe to be given to the poor (Joseph Jacobs, M. Seligsohn, Wilhelm Bacher 2005)

The Levites themselves, who were given a tithe "for an inheritance" (Num. 28:21–26), were expected to give a tenth of the tithe to the priest (Deut. 14:22–29).

Because it was considered an undue burden to take the tithe to the Temple every year (usually on the eve of Passover), most landowners took their produce to the city every third year. In the meantime, they stored it at home for the use of the Levite, the stranger, the fatherless, and widows. Even so, the Temple became so full of tithed produce that the leaders were obliged to build special chambers for the abundant offerings (2 Chron. 31:6–12; Neh. 10:39, 13:12).

Even in the earliest days of tithing, occasional churlish people chose to hold back their contributions, apparently without punishment (1 Sam. 10:27), thus reinforcing the voluntary nature of these payments. In the premonarchical period, tithing was considered the mark of the good man, the appropriate response for God's bounty to him. Under the **kings**, however, as Samuel had warned (1 Sam. 8:11–15), taxes probably were required. King David's census (2 Sam. 24:1) was apparently planned to provide a basis for "a methodical distribution of the military burdens and taxes; but Solomon was the first monarch to systematize the furnishing of foodstuffs . . . , and to demand toll from merchants" as well as imposing an additional money-tax (Emil G. Hirsch and Caspar Levias, 2005). As this shifted from a religious to a governmental requirement, it became more like a tax than a voluntary contribution.

Taxation

The Egyptian system, probably established by Joseph, was somewhat different from the concept of the tithe. All of the land belonged to the pharaoh, except for the temples, and all the Egyptians were serfs of the crown. In Israel, the system of private property had been established from early times.

The king's levy of a "tithe," which was clearly a tax required of the people, was on the fields, the vineyards, and the herds, just as it was in neighboring communities. The kings had the right over the "first mowing of the meadows" (Amos 7:1), of pasturage, and of forced labor by the people. The king, in return for all the wheat, barley, oil, and livestock (Ezek. 45:13–16), assumed responsibility for all public sacrifices and oblations (Ezek. 45:17; deVaux 1961, 140–141).

King Solomon made enormous demands on his people, forcing them into servitude and taking their wealth for his great building programs. Once he had expanded the role of government, he was not inclined to reduce it again, nor were his successors, although their taxation was sometimes considered "voluntary" except in time of **war**. Illegal "taking" was nonetheless within the power of the king, even when he did not choose to exercise this regal theft.

The "poll tax," also known as the "capitation tax" was one levied on each individual. After the Exile and the building of the new Temple, this seems to have replaced tithing as the annual rabbinical tax. It was used for the maintenance of the Temple and the purchase of sacrifices, especially when the people had money rather than land (Ezek. 45:9–12; Neh. 10:33–34).

Any time that the rulers had a census (as in the case of King David or Caesar Augustus), the suspicion was that it was in preparation for a program of taxation (Gotthard Deutsch and M. Seligsohn 2005).

Tribute

In addition, levies were sometimes demanded of conquered peoples to pay tribute to foreign conquerors (2 Kings 15:19–20). This was usually required of one nation by another. Ancient "tribute lists" have been discovered that show the Egyptians demanded tribute from various cities all around the region. The Israelites also required tribute of Mesha, king of Moab. When he failed to provide the wool of 100,000 lambs and 100,000 rams, the Israelites invaded his country. Sennacherib set a per capita tax on the Jews, as did the Syrians, the Greeks, the Seleucids, and the Romans (Emil G. Hirsch, Caspar Levias 2005).

The post-exilic foreign rulers such as the **Persian** kings demanded a toll, although they exempted the **priests** and Levites (Ezra 7:24). Nehemiah notes that, "We have borrowed money for the king's tribute" (Neh. 5:4). Taxes became a particularly heavy burden under the Ptolemaic and Seleucidan kings, who farmed out the tax-collection business in a system called "tax farming" (Hirsch et al. 2005).

By New Testament times, the Roman Empire required the payment of regular taxes to Caesar, using Roman coin. Julius Caesar was considered lenient toward the Jews "and was even considerate with regard to the Sabbatical year" but "under Augustus conditions changed" (Hirsch, et al. 2005). Jesus was born at the time of a census by Caesar Augustus, who undoubtedly planned to use the information for more efficient taxation. Jesus paid taxes himself (Matt. 17:24–27) and gave advice on the correct attitude toward paying taxes—"Render to Caesar the things that are Caesar's" (Mark 12:17). During his ministry, Jesus had to respond to numerous questions regarding taxes. The Romans considered refusal to pay taxes as a rebellion "against the suzerainty of the Romans" and justification for execution.

Ironically, although the members of the **Church** of the New Testament lived under this system of taxes (Rom. 13:6–7), within the faith they also chose to return to the old voluntary system of contributions to the work of God, in some cases not limiting this to the tithe. In addition, they often collected money for those in need, even for a brief time holding all things in common. Many modern churches continue to encourage tithing, and many believers find tithing for the Lord a blessing. *See also* History in the Bible; Slavery, Slaves; Tax Collector.

Further Reading

Deutsch, Gotthard and M. Seligsohn. "Poll-tax," http://www.jewishencyclopedia. com (accessed June 21, 2005). DeVaux, Roland. *Ancient Israel: Its Life and Institutions*, trans. by John McHugh. Grand Rapids, Mich.: William B. Eerdmans Publishing Company, 1961. Hirsch, Emil G., Eduard Konig, Joseph Jacobs, and Schulim Ochser. "Taxation, " http://www.jewishencyclopedia. com (accessed January 11, 2005). Hirsch, Emil G. and Caspar Levias. "Mesha," http://www.jewishencyclopedia.com (accessed June 21, 2005). Jacobs, Joseph, M. Seligsohn, and Wilhelm Bacher. "Tithe," http://www. jewishencyclopedia.com (accessed June 21, 2005). Keller, Werner. *The Bible as History.* New York: Bantam Books, 1982.

Temple

(2 Sam. 7:1–7; 1 Chron. 22:1–19; 1 Kings 6:1–37; 2 Kings 24:10–13, 25:9–17; Ezra 1–3; Heb. 10:20) Solomon's Temple was the culmination of years of planning and the subject of centuries of veneration and idealization. The **Tabernacle**, which had traveled with the Israelites in the wilderness years and probably for sometime afterward, finally disappeared, leaving only the Ark of the Tabernacle and the elaborate plans for its construction. Because there are no further mentions of the Tabernacle, it seems likely that it was replaced by fixed sanctuaries, such as Shiloh, and then by the Temple.

The Ark was moved from place to place carried into battles, conquered by enemies, and fixed in sanctuaries. Once David consolidated his power and chose Mount Zion as the place for his city, he joyfully brought the Ark to that site. He also erected an **altar** on Zion to be the site of the future Temple. King David danced and sang before the Ark and priests offered sacrifices at the altar. He had anticipated building a permanent temple there, but was forbidden by God. Some believe this prohibition was a result of his sin with Bathsheba, others because of his bloody career as a **warrior**. For the time being, the Ark was laid to rest in its "holy place," under a specially prepared tent.

In establishing Jerusalem as the heir to the sanctuary of Shiloh and to the Tent in the desert, David signaled that the Hebrew people were no longer

Twelve Tribes, but a unified nation, worshipping one God in David's Holy City. The altar marked the place where the Temple would stand, based on the appearance of an angel near the threshing floor of Arunah the Jebusite. It was where Melchizedek brought Abraham bread and wine and blessed him (Gen. 14:18). Everything had come together to prepare for the work of Solomon.

Solomon's Temple

David had prepared the way, not only choosing the site, but preparing the plans and the inventory of furnishing, the materials for the gilding, and the gold ingots that were to be used in designing the sacred objects. He brought together the teams of workmen and set the classes and outlined the functions of the clergy (1 Chron. 22–28). The task of actually constructing the Temple, however, fell to David's son, King Solomon, a man of peace. The work consumed seven years of his reign, from the fourth to the eleventh years.

For the task, Solomon made an alliance with Hiram, King of Tyre, who was able to furnish him with skilled workers and with the famous cedar of Lebanon. Solomon also used large numbers of forced laborers from among his own people for carrying and "hewing" the heavy **stones** (1 Kings 5).

As planned, the Temple was built on the land on top of Mt. Moriah on the "threshing floor" that David had purchased from Arunah for 50 silver shekels (2 Sam. 24:34). Later legend tied the location to the altar where Abraham agreed to **sacrifice** his beloved son. Rabbinical legend also identified it with the location of Adam's birth and of the first altar, on which Cain and Abel offered their sacrifices (Joseph Jacobs, Judah David Eisenstein 2005).

According to the directions in 2 Chron. 4 and 2 Kings 7, as well as the memories of the exiled **prophet** Ezekiel, the Temple faced east, stood high, with walls and **gates**, and was surrounded by dependencies (buildings that housed the **priests**, the treasury, the **grain** storage, etc.) Solomon erected a large number of buildings on the stone foundations of the Temple Mount, including his own **palace**, the palace of the Pharaoh's daughter, the **throne**-room, the porch of pillars, and the **house** of the forest of Lebanon, apparently all designed by the Phoenician artisans. This magnificent "pile" of buildings was certainly more impressive than anything else the Hebrews had seen since settling in **Canaan**.

The Temple was three stories high, arranged with ledges so that it had the appearance of steps, like a ziggurat. The main sanctuary had windows with latticework to provide light, and a roof of wood. The interior was cedar, lined with gold. The floor was fir wood overlaid with **gold**, the doorposts of olive-wood, supporting folding doors of fir. On the doors were carvings of **cherubim**, palm trees, and flowers, which were overlaid with gold.

The building consisted of a series of worship areas, moving from the secular to the most sacred. The exterior courtyards provided sacred space for those who were not priests. At the front of the Temple, Solomon erected two bronze pillars, called "Jachin" and "Boaz," 18 cubits high, with capitals shaped like carved lilies. In front of the Temple (as in the case of the Tabernacle) stood a great brazen altar 20 cubits square and 10 cubits high. To the southeast, in front of the Temple, was the molten sea, a large laver 10 cubits across, ornamented with knobs and resting on the backs of 12 **oxen**. There were also smaller, portable lavers for ceremonial cleansing.

Inside the Temple, in the first Holy Place, were the gold table of showbread and the small golden altar for **incense**. The five **candlesticks** on each side of the altar of incense and the implements for care of the candles—tongs, basins, snuffers, and firepans—were also of gold. The Holy of Holies, the most sacred place, housed the **Ark of the Covenant**. There, the chest with its Mercy Seat was thought to be the location of the *Shekinah,* the Glory of God. Ezekiel especially noted the power of this cloud of light.

This majestic edifice was stripped of most of its treasures in later times and used for **tribute** to foreign powers, particularly by Tiglath-Pileser (2 Kings 16:17). Some later kings added to the construction, some desecrated it. In its long history, it mirrored the religious and political life of the nation. And finally, it was destroyed by Nebuchadnezzar in 597 B.C., the Temple treasury as well as the royal exchequer pillaged (2 Kings 24:13). Everything was carried away, "even the two great pillars and the Sea of Bronze, which was broken up so that the metal could be sent to Babylon.... Such was the end of the Temple which had been the pride of Israel" (Roland deVaux 1961, 322).

The Post-Exilic Temple

Ezekiel's Temple was a vision that probably reflected his memories of the buildings on the Temple Mount, as

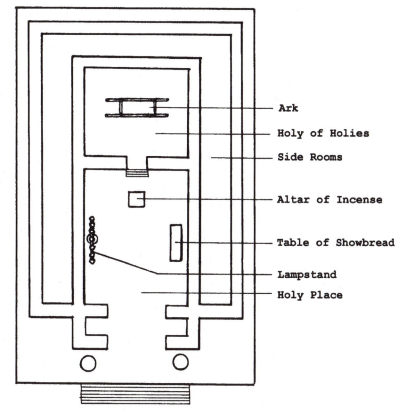

Temple floor plan for Solomon's Temple.

Ark

Holy of Holies

Side Rooms

Altar of Incense

Table of Showbread

Lampstand

Holy Place

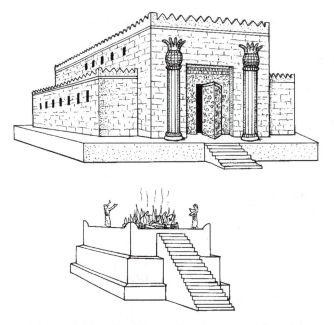

Solomon's Temple with the altar for the sacrifice of the animals, "burnt offerings" in front. The great pillars reflect Egyptian taste in architecture.

well has his hopes for a new Jerusalem (Ezek. 40:1–44, 9). His vision was influential in the later reconstructions of the Temple by Zerubbabel and Herod. This magnificent portrayal emphasized the holiness, purity, and spirituality of the Temple. He noted that it was to be a perfect square of sacred space, encircled by two walls, entered by gates guarded against foreigners. He did not detail the type of altar and assumed that there would be no Ark of the Covenant, but insisted that the glory of God would fill the sanctuary (Ezek. 44:4). His vision undoubtedly inspired much of the parallel portrayals of the City of God portrayed in Hebrews and Revelation. They too see the heavenly aspects of God's most holy place, but with no further need for sacrifices or rituals.

The Second Temple resulted from an edict of Cyrus in 538 B.C., allowing the Jews to return to Jerusalem and begin to rebuild the Temple at the expense of the royal exchequer. He returned many of the gold and **silver** furnishings taken by Nebuchadnezzar as well. Even in exile, the Jews had been saving for the rebuilding and refurnishing of the Temple, using the profits from their labor for this perennial dream. Although the exiles began immediately undertook their work on the second Temple, they were able to do little more than clear the rubble away from some of the old walls and complete some leveling before their labors were interrupted by neighboring Samaritans, who were opposed to the new construction.

In addition, the Jews' own preference for working on their own homes first made them less –than diligent to pursue the task. Zerubbabel was sent to supervise their work and the prophets Ezra and Zacharias encouraged them. The phrasing of the decree of Cyrus suggests that the new Temple was to follow the general plan of the older one, but with less elegance. Eventually the Jews had to raise money among themselves. Josephus recorded that, at the turn of the fourth century B.C., the Temple was a large building encircled by a wall with an altar of stones. Inside was an altar and a golden chandelier, the flame of which was kept continually alight (Roland deVaux 1961, 324). It was a much smaller building than Solomon's—60 cubits lower. Like Solomon's, it was finished in seven years.

This was the temple pillaged by Antiochus Epiphanes in 169 B.C. He desecrated the altar and took away the golden altar, the chandelier, the table of offerings, the veil, the gold plating, the precious vessels and treasures. He turned the building into a worship center for Zeus and slaughtered pigs on the altar, an act referred to as the "abomination of abominations." The Maccabean Rebellion followed this horror, and the country was finally swept into the great **Roman** Empire. When Pompey conquered Jerusalem 100 years later, he respected the sanctuary of the Temple and did not rob the treasury. Shortly thereafter, in 20–10 B.C., King Herod began to rebuild this Temple on the same spot, using the same design, carefully avoiding the demolition of the earlier structure, completing his work 10 years later. As a lover of ornate buildings, which he constructed fortresses at such sites as Masada and Caesarea. By refurbishing the Second Temple, he thought to curry favor with the Jews, who opposed having an Idumaean king.

His first project was the enormous enlargement of the Temple Mount itself, using gigantic stones, some of which still are in place in the famous Western Wall, known as the "Wailing Wall." He then followed the pattern of the earlier Temple, building a lavish new one with porticoes and stairs and courts. It was Herod's Temple that Jesus and his **disciples** knew. Mark records the wonder of the Disciples, who looked back at the Temple from across the valley, catching the glitter of the setting sun on the white limestone walls and the gold leaf embellishments: "Master, see what manner of stones and what buildings are here!"

Jesus's prophetic response must have struck them as frightening. As they studied the enormous stones and the solid construction, he asked: "Seest thou these great buildings? There shall not be left one stone upon another, that shall not be thrown down." He then spoke of the tribulations to come, probably referring to the destruction of Jerusalem, finishing with, "But when ye shall see the abomination of desolation, spoken by Daniel the prophet, standing where it ought not (let him that readeth understand), then let them that be in Judea flee to the mountains" (Mark 13:1–2, 14).

It was Herod's Temple to which the **Pharisees** thought Jesus meant literally when, using the Temple as an image of his body, he said that it could be destroyed and raised again in three days. It was the great curtain of this Second Temple, separating the Holy of Holies from the Holy Place (far too

The Second Temple layout with the main temple building in the complex, extra courtyards, and so forth. This was the design that Herod rebuilt and expanded.

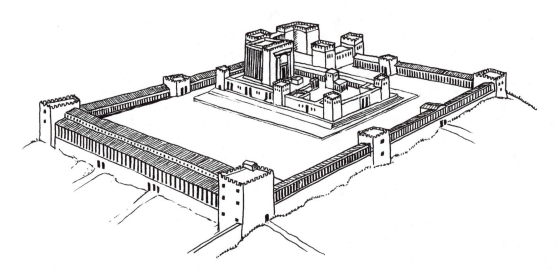

Herod's Temple, begun in 20 B.C. and completed in 62–64 A.D. The elaborate courtyard on the large foundation, the towers for protection, the covered walkways, and the numerous buildings made this one of the marvels of Jerusalem at the time, as noted by Jesus's disciples.

thick for human hands to rip) that was torn from top to bottom at the time of the **crucifixion**.

It was this Temple that was destroyed in 70 A.D., commemorated by the pictures on the Arch of Titus. By that time, Jewish nationalism had risen to a fever pitch. The Zealots stirred up passions all over the country, forcing the Romans to tramp down the rebellion, first in the Galilee and then in Jerusalem. They laid siege to the city, building ramps, using their engines of war, the catapults and battering rams. They cut down the trees around the city, crucified the thousands that tried to thwart them, starved the inhabitants, and finally took the city. In doing so, they destroyed the Antonia fortress and burned the Temple, or failed to keep the Jews from doing it. Thousands of citizens in Jerusalem died, perhaps a million. Many of the Christians escaped. Believing the warning that Jesus had given to his disciples, they fled to Pella, a city in Transjordan on the slopes of the Golan Heights, near Beth-sean. The contemporary historian Josephus calculated that 97,000 Jews were carried into captivity and slavery. In the year 71, Titus celebrated his great victory over Jerusalem with a procession through Rome that included 700 prisoners and the seven-branched candlestick and the table of the showbread from the Temple. They were placed in the Temple of Peace in Rome and pictured on Titus's triumphal arch.

Refusing to allow the Jews or the Christians to rebuild on Zion, Hadrian built a new Roman colony there, Aelia Capitolina. It had a race course, two baths, and a large theater. A statue of Jupiter was enthroned above the ruins of the Jewish Temple, and on the site of what is now the Holy Sepulcher was a shrine to the pagan goddess Venus. Another rebellion of the Jews in 132–135 ravaged the land, leaving almost nothing of the countryside Jesus knew, not a tombstone or a synagogue. Even the tree-covered landscape around Jerusalem and the Mount of Olives was laid bare, and all of the orchards were ruined.

Temple Imagery

Paul wrote to the Corinthians, following Christ's body imagery, "Know ye not that ye are the temple of God, and that the Spirit of God dwelleth in you? If any man defile the temple of God, him shall God destroy; for the temple of God is holy, which temple ye are" (1 Cor. 3:16–17). The author of Hebrews, following the beautiful vision of Ezekiel, interpreted the details of the Temple in Christian terms. There was no longer a need for a place of sacrifice, as the sacrifice of God's son atoned for all sins once and for all. Nor was there a need for a high priest; Christ was akin to Melchizadek, both king and priest. There was really no further need for the Temple itself now that humanity could hope for eternal life in the presence of God, dwelling in his Holy City.

In Revelation, John noted that he saw no Temple in the New Jerusalem "for the Lord God almighty and the Lamb are the temple of it. And the city had no need of the sun, neither of the moon, to shine in it: for the glory of God did lighten it, and the Lamb is the light thereof" (Rev. 21:22).

There are those, however, who yet believe there is yet to be a third Temple built on Zion in the last days. The continuing battles over the Temple Mount, the site of the original Temple, indicate that this place remains sacred to three of the great religions of the world. *See also* Altar; Candle, Candlestick; Sacrifice; Tabernacle.

Further Reading

DeVaux, Roland. *Ancient Israel: Its Life and Institutions.* Grand Rapids, Mich.: William B. Eerdmans Publishing Company, 1961. Jacobs, Joseph and Judah David Eisenstein. "Temple in Rabbinical Literature," http://www. jewishencyclopedia.com (accessed January 10, 2005). Josephus, Flavius. *The Works of Josephus.* Peabody, Mass.: Hendrickson Publishers, Inc., 2001.

Tents

Although Abraham came from Ur of the Chaldees, a land with well-built, two-storied **houses**, where the citizens had a rich knowledge of building construction, he spent the last of his life as a dweller in tents, or "houses of hair." So long as Abraham and his descendants remained herdsmen, moving from place to place to find good pastures, the **goat**-hair tent was the ideal dwelling. The black hair was available from the Hebrews' long-haired goats and woven by the women on looms. It was ideal for keeping out spring rains and winter winds. A very porous material, when it had been soaked by the rains and shrunk, the goat hair tent became waterproof. Raising the tent flaps allowed cool breezes in summer to blow through the tent, while providing both shade and shelter. If damaged, it could be patched, and the damaged section might be cut out and used as a mat or divider. The tent could also be rolled up by women and carried by donkeys to the next settlement with little trouble.

The typical tent was oblong in shape, a long canopy erected on poles and held in place with guy ropes and tent pegs. The women pitched the tent by spreading the top section smoothly on the ground, with the ropes straightened out. Then they drove pegs into the ground with a hammer. (It was one such peg that Jael used to kill Sisera, the leader of the Philistine forces. Jael hammered the peg into her guest's head as he slept in her family tent.) (Judg. 4:21). The women then got underneath the **cloth** and lifted it onto the nine poles, some of them seven feet high, arranged in three rows. When they were ready to break camp, it was again the women's job to take down and pack up the tents.

The main canopy of the tent could be enlarged easily, by the addition of more goat's-hair segments, as Isaiah suggests: "Enlarge the place of thy tent, and let them stretch forth the curtains of thine habitations; spare not: lengthen thy cords and strengthen thy stakes" (Isa. 54:2). Although there was little privacy in the tent, it could be divided by additional curtains, separating the men from the women, the sleeping quarters from the **cooking**

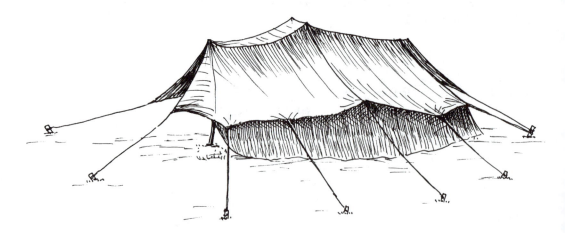

Nomadic tent, typical of the Hebrews from the time of Abraham. These tents, usually made of goats' hair, could be extended to include various "rooms" that were comfortable in winter and cool in summer.

area. Sometimes, the women might have a separate tent. In the story of Abraham, for example, Sarah did her cooking in another area, and she appeared to be in another compartment or another tent when she overheard the **angels** visiting with her husband (Gen. 18:10–15). Maidservants apparently also had tents separate from the rest of the family (Gen. 31:33).

The pilgrims settled in groves of **trees**, beside springs or **wells**, adjacent to good grazing lands. The clan's tents were often erected in a circular design for protection, with some of the **animals** bedded down in the middle. More fragile animals might be cared for next to the campfire or within the tent, a segment of the encampment away from the family. Next to the leader's tent might stand some emblem of his authority, such as **King** Saul's spear (1 Sam. 26:7). His tent was also larger than the others (Fred H. Wight 1953, 15).

This lifestyle was honored among the Jews even after they adopted more sedentary patterns. The Hebrew **Tabernacle** was a tent, the dwelling place of God, placed in the midst of them. Later, their houses and **palaces** were designed in much the same basic shape as the tents had been.

Even after the Promised Land was settled and civilized, certain of the main figures continued this migratory life. John the Baptist wandered about the countryside, as did Jesus, cooking over open fires. The **apostle** Paul learned the craft of tent-making as a boy, probably using goat's-hair cloth, and found this skill valuable as a way to support himself in his ministry. His native town, Tarsus, was in Cilicia, an area noted for its goat's-hair cloth (Madeleine S. Miller and J. Lane Miller 1961, 741). He was later joined by Priscilla and Aquilla, who shared this training. All of them had to purify themselves because their handling of goats' hair, and skins was considered a pollution (Num. 31:20).

Like modern bedouins, the tent-dwellers saw themselves as an independent folk, enjoying the open air and proud of their ways. Scripture prophesies that some of the sons of Ishmael would live in tent villages (Gen. 25:15). The flexibility and portability of the tent emphasized for the Israelites that they were sojourners in the land, reliant on God's grace for their lives. (Ps. 84:1–10; Jer. 4:20). Although they finally built cities, they always considered city-dwellers suspect, like the other descendants of Cain.

Long after they ceased to be migrants, they continued to remember their well-loved tents during the summer harvest seasons, when they built tent booths on their roof tops. The grass that grew on the sod roofs made the scenes all the more realistic. Even today, wealthy Arab families will camp in the desert in tents, apparently as a type of vacation and a means of remembering their tent-dwelling past. The **Festival** of the Booths, eight days of celebration that serves as the agricultural festival of thanksgiving (Lev. 23:39–44), also known as Sukkoth or the Feast of the Tabernacles, features the building of booths in the style of the old leafy structures made of branches used by farmers. This is one of the most joyful and popular of Jewish festivals. *See also* Festivals; Houses; Palaces.

Further Reading

Miller, Madeleine S. and J. Lane Miller. "Booths," "Booths, Feast of," "Tents," in *Harper's Bible Dictionary*. New York: Harper and Row, 1961. Wight, Fred Hartley. *Manners and Customs of Bible Lands*. Chicago: Moody Press, 1952.

Threshing, Threshing Floor

The Book of Ruth is a touching and humble story of a penniless woman, who had lost her husband and followed her widowed mother-in-law to a new country, where she was at first a gleaner in her kinsman's field. It provides a sketch of everyday life in ancient Bethlehem and in many other small villages. Naomi told her daughter-in-law Ruth that she should go to her kinsman, Boaz, whom she would find that night winnowing barley on the threshing floor. She went, after washing and perfuming herself and putting on her best clothes. Ruth found Boaz asleep, after he had eaten and drunk (Ruth 3:2–3). This daring act, which resulted in the kinsman redeeming both the widow and the land, is skillfully told and closely related to the activities of average people in the ancient world.

At the center of the town's activities was a the threshing floor, a circular space kept pounded down for the threshing of wheat and barley. It was from 30 to 50 feet in diameter, sometimes covered by "a tough, hard sward, the prettiest, and often the only, green plots about the village, and there the traveler delights to pitch his tent" (Fred H. Wight 1953, 181–182). The local farmers might also use the **winepress** area for this process, as did Gideon, to hide his **grain** from enemies (Judges 6:11). It was common to wait until the grain had been threshed and winnowed, and then for **Midianites** or other enemies to swoop down and steal the product of the year's labors.

The farmers would bring their sheaves to this central location, unless, like Boaz, they were wealthy enough to have their own private threshing floor. There, they would join the other men of the village in the work of threshing or pounding the stalks of grain to separate the chaff from the wheat. A rod, a staff, or flail—a short thick stick attached to the end of a wooden staff—might be used. Ruth used such an instrument to glean the ephah of barley she was allowed as a poor member of the community, according to the **law** of Moses (Ruth 2:17).

Sometimes **oxen** or other **animals** were led into the circle, using their hooves to pound the stalks, or they might drag a "sledge" around in a circle to help with the work. The sledge was made of two wooden planks fastened together, about three-by-six feet, in which were cut rows of square holes. Into these, the carpenter hammered sharp stones or bits of broken pottery or metal. On occasion the threshers must have used a kind of cart with wheels: Isaiah speaks of the "threshing cart" drawn by **horses** (Isa. 28:28) and also the sledge: "See, I will make you into a threshing sledge, new and

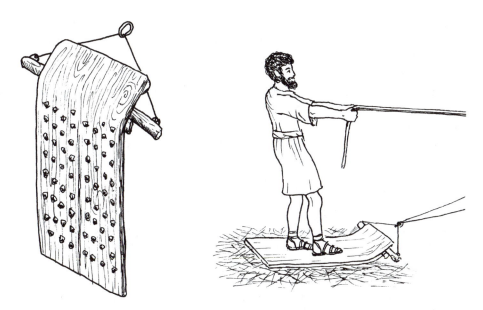

The farmer would stand on this sledge to weight it down while the oxen dragged it through the grain on the threshing floor to break it up and separate the wheat from the chaff.

sharp, with many teeth. You will thresh the mountains and crush them, and reduce the hills to chaff" (Isa. 41:15). The thresher might stand on the sledge or place a stool on it. He would guide the animals in a circle with one hand and use the **goad** in the other to shift the grain and encourage the oxen. As these heavy sledges moved over the stalks, the grain fell to the bottom and the straw remained on top, being gradually broken into many pieces by the hooves and the rocks. This straw was then used for animal fodder.

The oxen were not allowed to be muzzled threshing grain (Deut. 25). That is, they were allowed to eat of the grain and straw that they were trampling. They did wear a halter, a rope around the neck, to control their movements and to attach them to the sledge.

Next came the winnowing. The workers would use pitchforks to toss the grain into the air, letting the wind blow the chaff away from the grain, which fell back onto the floor. This was the source of the lovely image in Psalm 1, which pictures God winnowing the godly from the ungodly, who are "like the chaff that the wind driveth away." It was also Daniel's interpretation of Nebuchadnezzar's **dream** (Dan. 2:35). Proverbs notes that "A wise **king** winnows out the wicked; he drives the threshing wheel over them" (Prov. 20:26). The chaff that remained in the area was burned, suggesting something of the fate of the "ungodly." This is the source of Christ's image: "His winnowing fork is in his hand, and he will clear his threshing floor, gathering his wheat into the barn and burning up the chaff with unquenchable fire" (Matt. 3:12; Luke 3:17).

Finally came the sifting, with the use of a sieve to rid the grain of the final waste products. This was women's **work**, unlike the previous activities. The women would toss the grain in their sieves, blowing away any chaff that remained, and picking out small stones or dirt that may have been mixed with the corn. (Jesus used the image of sifting in speaking of Peter: "Simon, Simon, behold, Satan hath desired to have you, that he may sift you as wheat") (Luke 22:31).

The harvest that then remained was measured out and used for **food** or saved for seed, stored in the garner or urns. Excavators of Jericho found bits of millet, barley, and lentils that had been stored away 5,000 years ago in round clay bins (E.W. Heaton 1956, 102). The storage places were usually dry enough that the grain or lentils would keep indefinitely.

The process of pummeling the crops was so well known and brutal that it became a perfect image for **punishment**. Isaiah, for example, laments: "O my people, crushed on the threshing floor" (Isa. 21:10). And Micah proclaims, "Rise and thresh, O Daughter of Zion, for I will give you horns of iron; I will give you hoofs of **bronze** and you will break to pieces many nations" (Micah 4:13).

The threshing floor thus became a metaphor for the town itself. Arrival at a town was often described as reaching the "threshing floor" (Gen. 50:10; 2 Sam. 24:16; 1 Chronicles 13:9). This, of course, may be a result of its being an ideal campsite. When David was told to buy the threshing floor of Araunah the Jebusite (which most critics associate with Mt. Moriah) and to erect an altar there, it seems to indicate that David was taking control of the village. This was the spot where Abraham had offered Isaac to God as a sacrifice and where Solomon's **Temple** was eventually constructed (2 Chron. 3:1).

The threshing floor also served as the town center, a place where meetings were held: "Dressed in their royal robes, the king of Israel and Jehosaphat, king of Judah, were sitting on their **thrones** at the threshing floor by the entrance to the **gate** of Samaria, with all the **prophets** prophesying before them" (2 Chron. 18:9). *See also* Animals; Goad; Grain; Yoke.

Further Reading

Heaton, E. W. *Everyday Life in Old Testament Times*. New York: Charles Scribner's Sons, 1956. Wight, Fred H. *Manners and Customs in Bible Lands*. Chicago: Moody Press, 1953.

Throne

(1 Kings 10:18–20, 22:19; 2 Chron. 18:18; Ezek. 1:26, 10:1; Heb. 4:16, 8:1; Rev. 4:3–9, 22:3) A throne is the royal seat, or a seat of authority.

The original term comes from the Hebrew word "to cover," suggesting a canopied construction (R. J. McKelvey 1980, 1559). The term *cathedra* has also come to mean the seat of the bishop, placed in the building called a "cathedral." In all cases, the suggestion of the elevated seat is dignity and power.

In ancient history, the throne was simply a chair, sometimes on a platform, that raised the **king** above the rest of his **court**. By the time of Solomon, the throne was "inlaid with **ivory** and overlaid with fine **gold**" and "had six steps, and its back had a rounded top. On both sides of the seat were armrests, with a lion standing beside each of them. And twelve lions stood there on the one side and on the other upon the six steps: there was not the like made in any kingdom" (1 Kings 10:18–20). The careful attention to details of this construction suggests that Solomon was the first to have had such a lavish throne, impressing the chronicler. The gold and ivory testified to his power, the elevation pointed to his status, and the lions were probably symbols of Solomon's heritage, from the lion of Judah.

The **tent**-dwellers of Genesis had clearly been impressed by the throne they saw in **Egypt**, where the Pharaoh sat, holding his **scepter** and ordering his minions about (Gen. 41:40). They had also come to understand that their God was more powerful than the Pharaoh "who sits on the throne" (Exod. 11:5). Carrying the throne imagery with them into the wilderness, they began to speak of the "throne of God" (Exod. 17:16), portraying God as a king. With their theocracy, God was in fact their king until the selection of Saul as an earthly ruler.

Like the scepter, the throne quickly became a metaphor for the rule of a man or a dynasty, as in the "throne of David" (2 Sam. 3:10). To "sit on the Lord's throne, which he established," was to be the legitimate king (1 Kings 1:35, 37).

Solomon expanded the imagery somewhat by providing (in addition to his own elegant seat of power) a throne for his mother, Bathsheba, who had been instrumental in his coronation. He therefore allowed her to sit on a throne "at his right hand" (1 Kings 2:19), the position of influence. When he built the "throne hall, the Hall of Justice" or a "porch" as a place where he would **judge**, he had it covered with cedar from floor to ceiling, creating still another throne, the throne of judgment (1 Kings 7:7).

Prophets were inclined to focus more on the kingship of God than on the majesty of man, even men so powerful as Solomon. Micaiah's vision of the Lord, "sitting on his throne with all the host of heaven standing around him on his right and on his left" (1 Kings 22:19, 2 Chron. 18:18) became the repeated image. Isaiah had a parallel vision. "In the year that King Uzziah died, I saw the Lord seated on a throne, high and exalted, and the train of his robe filled the temple" (Isa. 6:1).

The Psalmist proclaimed that "the Lord reigns forever; he has established his throne for judgment" (Ps. 9:7), that he sits on "his heavenly throne"

(Ps 11:4); and that his throne "will last forever and ever; a scepter of justice will be the scepter of your kingdom" (Ps. 45:6); and that he reigns over the nations, seated on "his holy throne" (Ps. 47:8). Unlike the thrones made of gold and ivory, God's throne was founded on "righteousness and justice" and "love and faithfulness go before you" (Ps. 89:14); his throne was established "from all eternity" (Ps. 93:2) and is in **Heaven** (Ps. 103:19).

Isaiah mocked Lucifer's ill-fated plan to ascend into Heaven and raise his throne "above the stars of God: I will sit enthroned on the mount of assembly, on the utmost heights of the sacred mountain" (Isa. 1413). In his Messianic hope, he proclaimed that, "In love a throne will be established; in faithfulness a man will sit on it—one from the house of David—one who in judging seeks justice and speeds the cause of righteousness" (Isa. 16:5). Heaven will be his throne, "and the earth…my footstool" (Isa. 66:1). Ezekiel envisioned the majestic throne to be one of sapphire, with amazing figures of **cherubim** (Ezek. 1:26, 10:1). Daniel's imagery was very explicit when he saw the thrones set in place, "and the Ancient of Days took his seat. His clothing was as white as snow; the hair of his head was white like wool. His throne was flaming with fire, and its wheels were all ablaze" (Dan. 7:9).

Luke echoes the old prophets in his proclamation of Christ's birth, "He will be great and will be called the Son of the Most High. The Lord God will give him the throne of his father David" (Luke 1:32). Jesus expanded on this heavenly imagery of enthronement in his own **apocalyptic** pronouncement to his **disciples**, "I tell you the truth, at the renewal of all things, when the Son of Man sits on his glorious throne, you who have followed me will also sit on twelve thrones, judging the twelve **tribes of Israel**" (Matt. 19:28). Later he said, "When the Son of Man comes in his glory, and all the **angels** with him, he will sit on his throne in heavenly glory" (Matt. 25:31).

These prophetic images of the Last Judgment, with Christ enthroned at the right hand of God the Father, explain the message of Hebrews: "Let us then approach the throne of grace with confidence, so that we may receive mercy and find grace to help us in our time of need" (Heb. 4:16). And "We do have such a high priest, who sat down at the right hand of the throne of the Majesty in heaven" (Heb. 8:1).

By contrast, the Daughter of the Babylonians will "sit on the ground without a throne" (Isa. 47:1). Satan and Herod, the sinister forces of this world and the next, have their thrones, but they will be overcome (Rev. 2:13). In the Revelation of John, even the Earth and the Sky will flee before God's throne. This majestic throne "had the appearance of jasper and carnelian. A rainbow, resembling an emerald, encircled the throne. Surrounding the throne were twenty-four other thrones, and seated on them were the twenty-four elders. They were dressed in white and had **crowns** of gold on their heads. From the throne came flashes of lightning, rumblings and peals of thunder. Before the throne, seven **lamps** were blazing" (Rev. 4:3-5). Like the living creatures around Ezekiel's throne, this one had four living creatures, and they were covered with eyes, "in front and in back" (Rev. 4:6). Angels encircle the throne, singing, "To him who sits on the throne and to the Lamb be praise and honor and glory and power, forever and ever!" (Rev. 5:13). Then all the great multitude "from every nation, tribe, people and language" will come and stand before the throne, "wearing white robes and . . . holding palm branches in their hands" (Rev. 7:9). After describing the vision of the Last Judgment before the throne of God and of the Lamb, John announces: "no longer will there be any curse. The throne of God and of the Lamb will be in the city, and his servants will serve him" (Rev. 22:3). *See also* Apocalypse, Apocalyptic Literature; Crown; Kings.

Further Reading

Braun, Joseph. "Throne," http://www.newadvent.org (accessed February 7, 2005). Jacobs, Joseph and Judah David Eisenstein. "Throne," http://www.jewishencyclopedia.com (accessed February 7, 2005). McKelvey, R. J. "Throne," in *The Illustrated Bible Dictionary*. Sydney, Australia: Tyndale House Publishers, 1980.

Time

God separated the day from the night on the first day of **Creation**: He "called the light Day, and the darkness he called Night. And the evening and the morning were the first day" (Gen 1:5). This verse provides the double meaning of *day:* the lighted portion of the cycle of hours, and the full cycle. Later, a third meaning was added, a more general concept of a time, such as the "days of a man's life" or the "**Day of Judgment**." "To the ancient Hebrews a thousand years might, indeed, be as yesterday." Although there are rough approximations of time in much of the Old Testament, the Hebrews' history lived for them in the timeless present. Even their language has "no definite, clearly cut tenses like those common to the Greek and Latin languages. . . . The two forms of Hebrew verbs, the perfect and the imperfect, distinguish only between action which is completed and action which is still going on" (Mary Ellen Chase 1955, 34–35).

Measurement of Day and Night

For most of the Old Testament period, days were determined by the movement of the sun in a general way—when the sun was high, when the shadows fell long, or when it grew cool. The Israelites divided the period of daylight into 12 hours:

Sunrise	6:00 A.M.
first hour	7:00 A.M.
second hour	8:00 A.M.
third hour	9:00 A.M.
fourth hour	10:00 A.M.
fifth hour	11:00 A.M.
sixth hour	12:00 noon
seventh hour	1:00 P.M.
eighth hour	2:00 P.M.
ninth hour	3:00 P.M.
tenth hour	4:00 P.M.
eleventh hour	5:00 P.M.
twelfth hour:	6:00 P.M.

Without clocks or watches, or even sundials, the times were necessarily inexact. We know only that God walked with Adam in the Garden "in the cool of the day" (Gen. 3:8), which probably meant early evening. And Saul promised the men of Jabesh Gilead to help them "Tomorrow, by the time the sun is hot" (1 Sam. 11:9). Variations in the time of sunrise and sunset would change the timing as well.

"Horology," or the science of measuring time, was slow in coming to the Hebrews. In fact, there is no Hebrew word for *hour*, nor does Scripture mention *minutes* or *seconds* (Isidore Singer and Judah David Eisenstein 2005). The Book of Daniel, which was written partly in Aramaic rather than literary Hebrew, contains the only Old Testament reference to the concept of the *hour* (Mary Ellen Chase 1955, 33). In the New Testament, however, the term occurs frequently, probably because of the influence of the Romans and their concern for accurate measurements of both the individual days and the calendar.

The ancients' daytime hours began with sunrise and ran to sunset. The first use of a sun-dial, which Isaiah calls "the shadow of the degrees"(Isa. 38:8), was generally attributed to King Ahaz (ca. 739 B.C.). Some believe that this concept may have been imported from Assyria (Isaac Singer et al. 2005).

The night was measured from sunset to sunrise. The Hebrews did not have a means for subdividing the night, although the reference to "midnight" for the killing of the first-born in **Egypt** (Exod. 11:4) may indicate that they were aware of the "clepsydra" or water-clock, a device probably used by the

Egyptians. This was a device designed so that drops of water would fall at a fixed rate, allowing the calculation of the hours.

David also spoke of waking at "midnight" (Ps.119:62), leading some Jewish scholars to speculate that he had a harp hanging over his couch that he adjusted to the north wind (Isaac Singer et al. 2005).

When the **Romans** entered the Jewish world, they brought their own reckoning system, much like the modern, using the concept of "watches." The night was divided into three-hour "watches" to signal the changing of guards at the **gates** or on the city walls. The approximate times for these were:

first watch	6:00 P.M.
second watch	9:00 P.M.
third watch	midnight
fourth watch	3:00 A.M.

Weeks

The counting (but not naming) of the days of the first week of creation ended with **Sabbath** rest, when "God rested on the seventh day from all his work which he had made. And God blessed the seventh day and sanctified it" (Gen. 2:2–3). This separation of life into rotations of the sun, which were clustered into weeks of seven days, provided a basis for measuring time. The day, which was at first measured from sun up till sundown, later changed to sundown to sundown, providing guidance for celebration of the Sabbath.

The Old Testament concept of the days of the week coincided with the modern custom, with the "first" day being our *Sunday,* a term derived from pagan worship of the sun. *Monday* was named for the moon. The other days have been named for foreign gods, some Roman, some Nordic: *Tuesday* (Tiw), *Wednesday* (Woden), *Thursday* (Thor), *Friday* (Fria), and *Saturday* (Saturn). The Hebrew peoples were admonished in the Ten Commandments to honor the Sabbath or the seventh day, and keep it holy in commemoration of God's rest on the seventh day of creation. This holy day was changed in Christian

An Egyptian water clock, widely used in Isaiah's day.

calendars to honor the day of the Resurrection—Sunday, or the "Lord's Day"— thus making the first day of the week their "Sabbath" (See Acts 20:7; 1 Cor. 16:2; Rev. 1:10).

Months

The phases of the moon led to a structuring of days and weeks into months. Ancient peoples apparently determined early on that 12 cycles of the moon formed a year, the measurement to be determined partially by the appearance of the new or crescent moon and partially by the sun. Only four of these ancient names for months have survived in Scripture:

Ahib, the first month of spring, probably our March/April.
Ziw, the "month of bright flowers" was probably April/May.
Ethanim was the time when the early rains arrived in September/ October.
Bul was the time of the winter figs and plowing for the new planting, our October/November.

Notice the ties between seasons and harvest times. In the land of **Canaan**, spring brought harvest of barley and flax; summer started the dry season that lasted until September, when the early rains began. By December, there were heavy rains, even snow on high ground, gradually bringing new life to even barren countryside.

The problem with this lunar calendar was that, from time to time, it needed additional days, even months to be reconciled with the cycle of the seasons. The Israelites were apparently aware of the autumnal and vernal equinoxes (fall and spring), which they marked as the "going out of the year" (Exod. 23:16) and the "return of the year" (1 Kings 20:26). The Hebrews may have discovered the solar (sun-based) calendar during their sojourn in Egypt. Herodotus indicated that this calendar had 12 months, each with 30 days, plus 5 additional days (Herodotus 2, 4, quoted by F. F. Bruce 1980, 222).

In the earliest reckonings, the year began with autumn, the seventh month of Tishri. This was the beginning of the "sabbatical" year. After their time in Egypt, the Hebrews calculated the first month from the springtime, beginning with Nisan. These are the months of the Hebrew calendar as it appears in most of Scripture:

Nisan (or Ahib), March/April	springtime with rains, barley and flax harvest
Iyyar (or Ziv), April/May	dry season beginning
Sivan, May/June	dry season, early figs ripen
Tammuz, June/July	dry, grape harvest

Ab, July/August	dry, olive harvest
Elul, August/September	ending dry period, summer figs and dates harvested
Tishri (or Ehtanim), September/October	early rains
Marchesvan (or Bul), October/November	winter figs, plowing the land
Chislev, November/December	rainy season, planting crops
Tebeth, December/January	cold season
Shebat, January/February	cold but beginning of blossoms, almond trees
Adar, February/March	some spring rains, harvest of citrus fruits

The **festivals** and the pattern of life were determined by the cycles of nature, making springtime a time of joy in new life and fall a time of harvests and relief from the dry heat of the summer. The festivals by which the Jews commemorated major events in their history (such as the **Passover**) were replaced in the **Christian Church** year, with the celebrations marking events of the New **Covenant**. For Christians, Easter replaced Passover, **Pentecost** came 50 days later, and Christmas later took the place of pagan celebrations of the winter solstice. Some of these were later deemphasized by Protestant reformers, who saw the elevation of certain holy days ("holidays") as an unfortunate misunderstanding of a faith that celebrates every Lord's Day as a memorial of the Lord's death, resurrection, and promise of return.

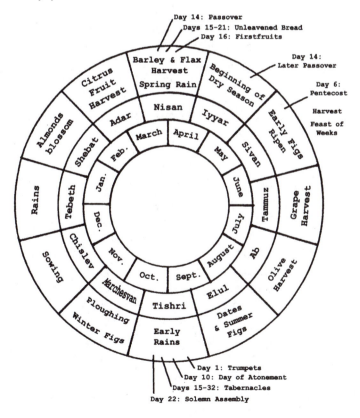

Months, seasons, and festivals.

621

Measurement of Historical Time

Determining days , months, and seasons was far easier than determining clusters of years. Eras were usually marked by the reign of a monarch or the activities of a foreign force, such as the "year of the kingdom of the **Greeks**" (1 Maccabees 1:10) or "the year that **King** Uzziah died" (Isaiah 6:1). The task of placing these indicators into some systematic chronology has been the work of myriad archaeologists, historians, and literary scholars for centuries. The wildly different dating of people and events in ancient history is easily explained by this lack of a uniform system. Because the New Testament cites numerous historical figures from Roman and Greek sources, it is easier for scholars to be somewhat more exact about the ministry of John the Baptist, the date of the **crucifixion** of Christ, or the years of the various Herods. But even here, the indicators are hard to discover because Scripture, by its very nature, usually deals with timeless ideas.

The measurement of larger blocks of years was eventually regularized, using the purported date of the birth of Christ as the point separating B.C. (before Christ) and A.D. (*anno Domini,* or "the year of the Lord"). (Christ's actual birth date is now considered, based on the details of the period in Roman history, to have been before 1 A.D.—perhaps 6 or 7 B.C.) This system, devised by Dionysius Exiguus, an abbot, continued under the Gregorian Calendar, created in 1582 under Pope Gregory XIII. It has always presented something of a problem for historians: There is no year zero, and there is a 33-year gap (the life of Christ) dividing the epochs. More recently, scholars concerned with the Christian bias implied in this nomenclature, have altered this terminology once again, preferring B.C.E. (before the common era) and C.E. (common era). The actual dates coincide with the older designations.

The concept of chronology (placing events and people in time) has been attributed to the Greeks. The Hebrews, however, believed that the story of their people and their relationships with God demanded a chronological narrative, beginning with the Creation itself. There were no dates provided for the whole story of the patriarchs, but the generations named and the ages of the people do help suggest a timeline for the Genesis years. The **Flood** narrative occurs in other cultures, but none of them can assign a specific date to the event. With the captivity in Egypt, historians had extrabiblical documents to help in the dating. The name of the Pharaoh, the use of iron chariots, and the building of pyramids all point to a time between 1492 B.C. and 1200 B.C. for the **Exodus**. The period of the **Judges** also lacks specificity regarding dates.

Not until the kings, specifically David, is there a real chronology in Scripture. Their reigns are dated in a curious way, not by their date of accession to the throne, but by Nisan, the beginning of the year in which they came to power (Emil G. Hirsch et al. 2005). Kings and Chronicles are full of details about chronology, using hundreds of chronological references.

Late in the monarchical period and afterward, other powers who conquered the Israelites, transporting them, returning them, invading them, and tormenting them, provide readers a stronger fix on chronology. The Israelites' interaction with other nations provide good sources for more accurate dating. The **Persians**, for example, dominated the Jews from around 537 B.C., allowing and even encouraging the rebuilding of the **Temple**. The invasion by Alexander the Great and the subsequent rule by the Ptolemies and the Seleucids, the conquest by the Romans, and the final destruction of Jerusalem and the Temple in 70 A.D. are fully documented by historians. The dates assigned to the life and death of Jesus are derived from references to Herod, Caesar Augustus, and Pontius Pilate. The persecutions mentioned in Revelation would appear to match those suffered under Domitian in 81–96 A.D.

The continuing study of the Bible and time, as it was measured in ancient Israel, relies on archaeological discoveries, historical research, and close scriptural analysis. Each year opens up paths to more exact details of chronology. *See also* Creation; Festivals; History in the Bible.

Further Reading

Bruce, F. F. "Calendar," in *The Illustrated Bible Dictionary*. Sydney, Australia: Tyndale House Publishers, 1980. Chase, Mary Ellen. *Life and Language in the Old Testament*. New York: W.W. Norton and Company, Inc. 1955. Gormley, Michael. "P.C. Scholars Take Christ out of B.C." Associated Press report, *The Washington Times*, April 25, 2005. Heaton, E. W. *Everyday Life in Old Testament Times*. New York: Charles Scribner's Sons, 1956. Hirsch, Emil G., Jules Oppert, J. Frederic McCurdy, Richard Gottheil, and Joseph Jacobs. "Chronology," http://www. jewishencyclopedia.com (accessed January 8, 2005). Keller, Werner. *The Bible as History*. New York: Bantam Books, 1982. Singer, Isidore and Judah David Eisenstein. "Horology," http://www. jewishencyclopedia.com (accessed January 7, 2005).

Tongues, Speaking in

(**Job 20:16; Ps. 137:6, 140:3; Acts 2:1–13, 10:10:44–46, 19:6; 1 Cor. 12–14**) *Tongues*, in Scripture, refers both to the part of the body and to language. The term was used for lip or mouth as well, as the instrument of speech. Thus the metaphor of a "sharp tongue" likened the tongue to a sword, emphasizing the tremendous influence speech has for good or ill.

In the story of the Tower of Babel (Gen. 11:1ff.), the "confusion of tongues" signified the alienation that resulted from the separation into different languages. The balance for this scene, in Acts 2, at the time of the Pentecost, "cloven tongues like as of fire" sat on the followers of Christ, who were "filled with the Holy Ghost." This spiritual gift, known as *glossolalia,* allowed people to speak in different languages and to understand one another.

This same phenomenon, possibly behind such passages as 1 Thessalonians 5:19 and Romans 12:11, later came to be described as ecstatic utterances, not necessarily related to any spoken language. This interpretation, some believe, came from the religious frenzy of the Greek mystery cults, which taught that the spirit of the god came into the person and spoke through him or her.

Speaking "in new tongues" was mentioned in Mark 16:17 (perhaps not a part of the original **Gospel**) as a sign of faith in Christ, accompanied by the outpouring of the Holy Spirit on the first Gentile converts. It came to be seen as a mark of the **Christian**, a sign of the worldwide reach of the Gospel. The debate whether the original "tongues" were known languages or ecstatic utterances continues in many churches. Paul noted that the interpretation of tongues was also a gift of believers (1 Cor. 14:13) and essential if members were speaking in unintelligible languages. He considered the gift of interpretation parallel with the gift of prophesy (1 Cor. 14:5). Without it, the tongues were of value only to the person speaking. Although he himself had this gift, he thought that the Corinthians overused it, and he discouraged its exercise in public.

Among modern charismatic **churches**, such as the Pentecostals, glossolalia is encouraged. Other churches see it as a gift that was limited to the early **apostles**, no longer necessary in Christian faith. *See also* Babel, Tower of; Pentecost or the Day of the First Fruits.

Further Reading

Miller, Madeleine S. and J. Lane. "Tongue," "Tongues of fire," "Tongues, Speaking with," in *Harper's Bible Dictionary.* New York: Harper and Row, Publishers, 1961. Putman, W. G. "Tongues, Gift of," in *The Illustrated Bible Dictionary,* 3 volumes. Sydney, Australia: Tyndale House Publishers, 1980.

Trade

During the biblical period, Israelites were not extensively involved in commerce except for a few exceptional periods. For the most part, they had a natural, self-sufficient economy. Each household provided its own food, tools, clothing, and housing. Most also had a few luxuries, such as gold, silver, iron, and **salt**. These were provided by traveling merchants, probably **Canaanites** or **Philistines**. In fact, the Hebrew word for *merchant* or *trader* was *Canaanite.* The Ishmaelites and the Phoenicians are named as merchants in the Old Testament stories (Gen. 37:25; Isa. 23; Ezek. 27:27). The good woman of Proverbs 31:24 probably had her dealings with

Canaanites when she was selling her wool. Hosea pictured the trader as one "in whose hands are false balances, he loves to oppress" (Hos. 12:8). Ezekiel also disparaged the commercial activities of Tyre in his great lament over the city (Ezek. 27:28–36). This low view of merchants in the ancient Israelite culture probably grew from the belief that Israel's real wealth was their land, which was theirs by conquest and inheritance.

The **Tribes of Israel** were "settled in the uplands of Palestine, and therefore were not touched by the streams of commerce which flowed by the two great caravan routes along the coast, through Tyre, Acco, and Gaza, to Egypt, and from South Arabia, through Petra on the east side of the Jordan, to Damascus" (Richard Gottheil, Joseph Jacobs et al. 2005). Abraham was thought to be a trader who had caravans traveling from Mesopotamia to **Egypt**. He probably followed this route as he made his epic journey from Haran to Palestine and then down into Egypt and back to Canaan. His descendants were more interested in local market places and barter with neighbors, needing few of the luxuries exchanged by the great merchants along the caravan routes.

In ancient times, the Hebrews had little to trade, chiefly their excess **animals** and the by-products of these animals, their agricultural products, and the work of their craftsmen. Their villages and towns had markets or bazaars, probably like modern farmers' markets, where **grains**, **wines**, oil, **pottery**, **tools**, textiles, dyes, and **leather** products were bought and sold (or bartered when coins were not available).

Before settling in Canaan, the Hebrews' interest in markets and trade (except for the selling of Joseph to Midianite or Ishmaelite slave traders) is not mentioned in Scripture. After the settlement of communities and the establishment of religious centers, markets appear to have prospered. Jerusalem, for example, had a "**Fish** Gate," which required regulation because so many merchants were trying to sell their fish on the **Sabbath**. (Salted fish was a great favorite for export.) Archaeologists assume that Damascus, Samaria, and Jerash were trading centers. Some villages were thought to specialize in certain products such as certain types of pottery or olive oil. Gradually the larger cities functioned as regional markets for village produce, allowing bazaars near (usually outside) the city **gate**.

Although the Israelites were not a merchant people like their neighbors, the Phoenicians, Aramaens, and the Canaanites (Prov. 31:24), they did become effective middlemen. "In the tenth century B.C., the Hebrews enriched themselves by transshipping merchandise—chariots and horses e.g.—between Egypt and Asia Minor" (Madeleine S. Miller and J. Lane Miller 1961, 771). Solomon worked out a trade agreement with Hiram of Tyre to allow Hiram to use Israel's port of Ezlon-geber in return for Hiram's furnishing of ships and sailors to bring luxury wares to Solomon (1 Kings 9, 10). Solomon himself was a larger exporter of wheat and oil, using these products to pay Hiram for the timber and the use of skilled workmen (1 Kings 5:25). His **horses** and **chariots** probably came from Egypt.

Major products for export from Israel included honey, balsam, wheat, and oil to Phoenicia (1 Kings 5:11; Ezra 3:7; Ezek. 28:17); spices, balm, myrrh, pistachio nuts, almonds, honey and oil to Egypt (Gen. 37:25; Hosea 12:1); and wool and sheep were sent to Moab as tribute (2 Kings 3:4). The Israelites imported timber from Phoenicia (1 Kings 5:11); corn, horses, and chariots from Egypt (Gen. 41:57); and gold, silver, spices, precious **stones**, **ivory**, peacocks, armor, and mules from Arabia, Ophir, and other Eastern countries. Inside the country, salt was sent from the Dead Sea to other regions, cattle and wool was shipped from pastures beyond the Jordan, and corn chiefly from the plain of Esdraelon to markets in Jerusalem and other cities (Zeph. 1:11; Richard Gottheil, Joseph Jacobs et al. 2005).

King Ahab obtained permission to set up a special street or bazaar in the market of Damascus, something like the one mentioned in Isaiah 2:6: a place where contracts were made with "sons of aliens." Much of the money in the treasury that was used for **tribute** to Sennacherib must also have derived from commerce. Much of the luxurious feminine apparel that shocked Isaiah (3:18–24) must have been imported.

The Old Testament portrays markets as gathering places of peddlers, hawkers, and merchants (Gen. 37:28; Prov. 31:24; Neh. 3:32, 13:20). The Gospels portray them as noisy places where laborers could be hired, political and religious issues discussed, and information exchanged (Matt. 11:10, 20:3; Mark 12:38). After the Exile in Babylon, the Jews were far more sophisticated and experienced traders. No longer an agricultural people, they had learned from their neighbors to engage in trade and finance. By Maccabean times, it appears to have become a custom to have markets in villages once a month, then twice a week, on Mondays and Thursdays. **Synagogue** services were scheduled to coincide with market days in the towns.

Merchants were generally despised (Hosea 12:7) as being people who cheated the unsuspecting and used the work of other people for their own profit. They were unregulated by Jewish **law** except for a few rules relating to weights and **measures**, loans to the poor, forgiveness of debts in the Sabbatical or Jubilee Year, and slave-trading (Lev. 19:35–36, 25:3, 44–45; Deut. 23:20, 15:2).

Unfortunately, this zeal for buying and selling did not stop with the marketplace. Jesus was horrified to see the vigorous exchanges of animals and **money** in the very precincts of the **Temple**, making his Father's house "a den of thieves" (Matt. 21:12). The reader has only to picture the oriental bazaar with the animals and the haggling over prices to imagine the scene that he found so outrageous.

The separation of the Jews from the land and from any opportunity to remain farmers or simple tradesmen pushed them increasingly into commerce. "In the Diaspora, Jewish exiles could not pursue traditional agrarian ways of life, the hallmark of the Israelite kingdom. There they moved into other vocations, such as commerce and banking, which did not require much real estate" (Philip J. King and Lawrence Stager 2001, 193). Aramaic archives from Elephantine Egypt, the home of a Jewish colony, reveal Jewish merchants and bankers as early as the fifth century B.C. When they returned from the Exile, their land had been taken by other families and they had forgotten their agrarian skills and lost their taste for the agrarian life. It was impossible for them to resume farming and herding like the "people of the land," a phrase that had earlier described them. The Jews turned to commerce and manufacturing.

In their later history, they developed a special aptitude for commerce in regions where they were excluded from trades. With the rise of Islam, commercial activity among the Jews exploded: In Europe, there was a rising demand for luxuries from Moslem lands, and at the same time, trade between Christians and Moslems was forbidden. This left an opening for the Jews, who were tolerated by both groups as intermediaries. "Within two centuries after the foundation of Islam, the Jews appear to have almost monopolized the trade between Europe and Asia" (Richard Gottheil, Joseph Jacobs et al. 2005). *See also* Measures; Money Changers; Transportation and Roads.

Further Reading

Blaiklock, E. M. "Trade and Commerce," in *The Illustrated Bible Dictionary*. Sydney, Australia: Tyndale House Publishers, 1980. Gottheil, Richard, Joseph Jacobs, Herman Rosenthal, and Friedman Janovsky. "Commerce," http://www.jewishencyclopedia.com (accessed June 28, 2005). King, Philip J. and Lawrence E. Stager. *Life in Biblical Israel*. Louisville, Ky.: Westminster John Knox Press, 2001. Miller, Madeleine S. and J. Lane Miller. "Trade and Transportation," in *Harper's Bible Dictionary*. New York: Harper and Row, Publishers, 1961.

Transportation and Roads

The Israelites were a traveling people—"in journeying often" as Paul said (2 Cor. 11:26). This Included "Abraham trekking from Ur to Haran and Canaan; Joseph being carried to Egypt by Midianite camel traders; Israel making the Exodus from Egypt; the Apostles, risking perils of land and sea to promote the Gospel." Both the Old and New Testaments contain hundreds of allusions to *roads* and *ways*. Prophets even gave practical hints for road improvement (Isa. 40:3; John 1:23). Malachi, thinking of the messengers who were sent out ahead of their lords to clear roads or highways of rubble that might impede their journey, was echoed by John the Baptist, who also came to "prepare the way" for Jesus (Mal. 3:1; Matt. 11:10; Madeleine S. Miller and J. Lane Miller 1961, 772).

Jesus was constantly on the road, back and forth between Galilee and Jerusalem, from Nazareth to Caparnaum, over to Caesarea and back to the Decapolis. Even the resurrected Christ met his **disciples** on the road to Emmaus.

Land Travel

The Hebrew words for *road* mean different things, but in general refer to "that which is trodden underfoot." This describes a surface packed down with traffic. One term for road is used only in poetry; another designates a major highway prepared by removing stones and by grading the rough surface, "to carry out road work," or "to cast up a highway." This is the word Isaiah uses regarding the Jews' return from Babylon in a procession. Isaiah was portraying the great road Yahweh would build from Babylon to Palestine: "In the wilderness prepare the way of Yahweh, make straight in the desert a highway for our God" (Isa.40:3). In doing so, he used two words for road, and another in a later section: "Go through, go through the gates; prepare ye the way of the people; cast up, cast up the highway, gather out the stones; lift up a standard for the people" (Isa. 62:10, 57:14 KJV; Philip J. King and Lawrence Stager 2001, 178).

Even in Genesis, travel had been over well-known roads, where the people walked, rode on their beasts of burden, or were carried in various vehicles. Abraham was thought by some to have been a trader who had caravans traveling from Mesopotamia to **Egypt**. He probably followed the famous caravan route as he made his epic journey from Haran to Palestine and then to Egypt. He and his family traveled with **donkeys** and **camels**, which carried their burdens. Because the rivers of Palestine were easily forded in many places, bridges and **boats** were unnecessary along the way. Nor did donkeys require wide or smooth roads for their paths. These sure-footed animals can walk over rocky terrain or up mountains with a steady gait. Except for the section of the journey over desert lands, camels would have been of little use.

By the fourth millennium B.C., wheeled vehicles were becoming common around the Mediterranean. Four-wheeled carts, two-wheeled chariots, and heavy wagons were available by the day of Joseph (Gen. 45). These were useful in flat country, but not on the narrow, rock-strewn roads of Palestine. Mules carried even the royalty through the rugged country. Both **animal** and human porters carried heavy burdens through the mountain terrain and over the rough roads (Matt. 11:28). **Horses** were less useful in Israel than donkeys and less suited as pack animals, although they became popular in Solomon's day, primarily for **warfare**.

The various conquering armies, with their horses and chariots, improved the roads, bringing their heavy equipment and returning with loads of booty and lines of prisoners. Finding the old roads too narrow and rocky for their purposes, they set about leveling and widening them. An **Egyptian** writer said that Palestinian roads were filled with "boulders and pebbles... overgrown with reeds, thorns and brambles" (G.G.G Garner 1980, 1583). The **Assyrians** used engineers to lay bridges and level tracks for their carts and siege engines. The Persians continued some road improvements, although mostly they paved only those roads around their own large

Covered carts with wooden wheels drawn by yoked oxen date from 3500 B.C. and may have been used occasionally by Hebrews. Jacob was probably carried to Egypt in such a cart.

cities. Many towns and villages had stone streets within the walls, but the roads between them were rarely more than worn paths. No one was responsible for clearing them of stones or fallen trees or for smoothing out rugged terrain. It was not until **Roman** times that roads were laid out with paving stones and properly maintained. To ensure their *Pax Romana* and communication through their official postal service, the Romans needed a means to reach all parts of their vast empire. The **epistles** that form such an important part of the New Testament, from Luke to Revelation, were a by-product of the new roads and the ease of communication and travel.

Roman highways were "well drained, and were curbed, often with travertine. They had wells at convenient intervals" and they were well maintained. The Romans cleared the ground carefully, put down a layer of rubble, then flat stones laid in lime, and covered with another layer of rubble. The top was paved with polygonal blocks of silex or balsaltic lava "neatly fitted into concrete, intersticed with balsatic stone." Sometimes, blocks of stone were used instead. Along the edges of busy streets, narrow, elevated footpaths, like modern sidewalks, kept pedestrian traffic separate. Milestones marked the distance from Rome (Madeleine S. Miller and J. Lane Miller 1961, 777). One excellent example of these roads, the Appian Way, is still visited by pilgrims. It ran from Rome to Capua and was the path that Paul took to the Appii Forum (Acts 28:15).

The primitive, difficult roads of the Old Testament had additional problems. Robbers and wild animals lurked by the side watching for prey. Travelers usually gathered into caravans for safety. The Romans made roads safer, policing them in search of brigands. Until the Romans ruled the sea, the ships were also unsafe for travelers. Pirates were common and brutal. For travelers, *Pax Romana* was a real blessing, in spite of the high price in taxes and loss of freedom.

Palestine was a crossroads of the ancient world, forming "a land bridge between Egypt and Mesopotamia, linking Africa, Asia, and Europe via military and trade routes" (Philip J. King and Lawrence Steger 2001, 176). The pattern of the routes was determined by topography, the chief routes lying in a north-south direction, with secondary roads running east-west. Judah was off the beaten path of international travelers. The great caravan trails of the Middle East still exist. They follow river beds, valleys, and smooth terrain. These were probably the roads that the Israelites followed in times of migration because of famine or hostile forces. Many of these eventually became major roadways and then highways and railroads.

The routes most often taken, like the Kings' Highway and the Via Maris (the Way of the Sea), were the most direct paths through numerous countries. The Way of the Sea was the coastal highway that went from Egypt to Phoenicia, Syria, and Mesopotamia, following the East Mediterranean Coast, turning inland at the Carmel Range, moving across the Plain of Jezreel at Megiddo, and then heading northward, along the west side of the Sea of Galilee, north to Damascus, and then across to Mesopotamia. It was also called the "Way of the Land of Philistines" and the "Way of Horus." This would have been the natural path for the Israelites fleeing Egypt to take, but they avoided the "Way of the Land of the Philistines" and took the King's Highway instead. This road passes through the Transjordanian Platea, close to the desert. It crosses **Edom**, **Moab**, **Ammon**, Gilead, and Bashan, and then continues north to Damascus (Num. 20:17).

Another north-south route "passed through the highlands of Samaria and Judah, running from Jerusalem to Bethlehem, Hebron, and points south" (Judg. 21:19; Philip J. King and Lawrence Stager 2001, 177). There were numerous east-west routes as well. Jesus undoubtedly took the standard roads from Nazareth down to the Sea of Galilee by way of Cana. Nazareth itself was situated at a crossroads of caravan routes that became military highways under the Roman rule. Because he walked most of the time, except when crossing the Sea of Galilee in a boat or riding a donkey into Jerusalem, Jesus would have avoided the main highways. He probably walked to Jerusalem along the shady path along the Jordan River.

Jerusalem was a center of commerce and religion, the intersection of highways to Mesopotamia, Cappadocia, Phrigia, Egypt, Libya, and upper Galilee. Paul used many of these roads in his numerous travels. His hometown, Tarsus, was another intersection of highways. He was converted on the road to Damascus, a city in which there is still a "Street called Straight." He is thought to have used the Egnatian Road that ran from Dyrrachium on the Adriatic across the country that is now Yugoslavia, Macedonia, and Thrace into Thessalonica, and various other cities, ending at Philippi and the Aegean Sea. These cities have become famous for their congregations that received the epistles from the **apostle**.

Sea Travel

Ancient Israel was, for much of history, a country with no navigable rivers or usable ports. The Song of Deborah does refer to Dan and Asher as "seafaring tribes" (Judg. 5:17), but they were probably economic wards on Canaanite or Philistine ships and at ports—seamen and dockworkers. Until New Testament times, the Jews showed almost no interest in the sea. One of the rare exceptions was the **prophet** Jonah, who sailed from Joppa, on a ship owned and managed by gentiles. He did not enjoy the voyage, which was cut short when he was thrown overboard, swallowed by a whale, and then cast up on the shore.

It was the **Phoenicians** and the **Philistines** who controlled the ports and sailed around the Mediterranean and beyond. An Egyptian relief (1182–1151) in Luxor shows a battle between Egyptians and "Sea People" that depicts the vessels: "The Sea People's crafts have gently curving hulls ending in nearly perpendicular posts capped with bird-head devices facing outboard. Raised castles are situated at both bow and stern" (Philip J. King and Lawrence Steger 2001, 179). These "hippos" ships were named by the Greeks for their resemblance to the head of a horse (Greek *hippos*). They had rigging that allowed them to tack in the wind, a crow's nest at the top of the mast, and a composite anchor for better anchorage, especially in sand. There were also "round" models and a "long " model with a pointed ram, used as a warship. The Phoenician ships were tall, with high masts and with upper and lower decks. Assyrian reliefs show them with two banks of oars, probably manned by slave labor.

Ezekiel compared the city of Tyre to a Tyrian merchant ship built with superior materials, using technical details for the kinds of timber used for hull, mast, oars, and benches: "They built for you the hull of juniper from Senir. They took cedar from Lebanon to make a mast over you. Of oaks of Bashan were made your oars. They made your benches of ivory (inlaid) in cypress from the island of Cypriotes. Byssus with embroidery from Egypt was to be your sail, to be (rigged) for you to the yard. Bluish-purple and reddish-purple from the coast of Cyprus were your canopy" (Ezek. 27:5–7). Scholars assume that the prophet either traveled to Tyre where he saw their naval forces or by some other means had detailed information about this seaport city and its ships.

Archaeologists have discovered that the ancient view of limited trading, close to shore, may be unfair to the Phoenicians. Two of their ships, which set sail from Phoenicia sometime between 750 and 700 B.C., have been discovered 50 kilometers west of the seaport of Ashkelon. They were heavily laden with amphoras, which were once filled with fine wines; each of them carried more than 12 tons of wine (Philip J. King and Lawrence Stager 2001, 182–183; 185). These "tubs" (as the Greeks called them) were found upright on the bottom of the Mediterranean with their bows heading west.

Solomon was the first king of Israel to build and use ships. Scripture tells us that he "built a fleet of ships at Ezion-Geber, which is near Elath on the shore of the Red Sea, in the land of Edom" (1 Kings 9:26). From there he and Hiram expanded their vast commercial activities to dominate trade in the Red Sea. This commercial fleet, called the "Ships of Tarshish" (heavy, seagoing merchantmen like those discovered at the bottom of the Mediterranean), was designed for long voyages. These were the ships that, once every three years, brought the amazing cargoes of gold, silvery, ivory, apes, and peacocks (1 Kings 10:22).

Sea travel, even after this time, was not a normal feature of Jewish life, although the people appreciated the advantages brought by the commercial ships that sailed the Mediterranean Sea. Even as late as the first century A.D., Paul took his missionary trips on cargo ships owned and operated by gentiles.

Imagery

For the Jew, unlike the Greek, sea imagery would always seem alien. If describing distance or activity, they spoke of a "day's journey" or "the way." (A day's journey was 27 to 37 kilometers.) The ancient Israelite thought in terms of the great routes through the country. He knew the perils of going "the way of the land of the Philistines" (Exod.13:17). He knew the dangers along the way, including the need for finding a safe place to spend the night and to water his animals. He walked to market when he needed to buy or sell his animals. He and his family walked to Jerusalem for the great **Passover festival**, singing the **Psalms** of ascent as they trudged up the mountainside. It is hardly surprising that Jesus described himself as "the way, the truth, the life" (John 14:6) and that the early Christians were known as people of "the Way" (Acts 19:23).

Paths, journeys, roads, and highways are constant reference points in Scripture. They represent the "way of the righteous" or the "way of the godly" (Psalm 1:6). The choice of life was between the straight or crooked way, the narrow path to salvation or the wide highway to damnation. The road a man took was to do the Lord's will, to preserve his family in time of drought, to return to his own country, to celebrate a festival, or to preach the Word. It was not simply for adventure.

The literary uses of the road imagery have thus been common. There were journeys into self, a way of seeing Dante's *Divine Comedy,* in which he travels deep into the center of Hell, up around Mount Purgatory, and finally into the Heavens to be blessed with the awesome experience of God. The pilgrimage that John Bunyan's Christian took helped him escape the City of Destruction and arrive at the City Beautiful. These classics have set the model for hundreds of stories about paths, roads, journeys throughout Western literature. *See also* Agriculture; Boats and Ships; Camel; Chariots; Donkey, Ass; Trade.

Further Reading

Garner, G. G. "Travel in Biblical Times," in *The Illustrated Bible Dictionary.* Sydney, Australia: Tyndale House Publishers, 1980. Jacobs, Joseph and the Executive Committee of the Editorial Board. "Roads," http://www.jewishencyclopedia. com (accessed June 27, 2005). King, Philip J. and Lawrence E. Stager. *Life in Biblical Israel.* Louisville, Ky.: Westminster John Knox Press, 2001. Miller, Madeleine S. and J. Lane Miller. "Trade and Transportation," in *Harper's Bible Dictionary.* New York: Harper and Row, 1961.

Trees

Trees were far more numerous in biblical times than they are in modern Israel. References suggest that there were forests and woodlands near the towns and cites and groves of trees in various spots in the desert lands. David's son, Absalom, died when his hair caught on the branches of trees in the woods. Jesus picked fruit from trees on his way into Jerusalem. **Olive** groves were everywhere. Wood and branches were used in building construction and in some of the **festival** celebrations. They were also used for tools, ships, and numerous farm implements. Trees, like **stones**, often marked the boundaries in fields, which were cultivated by the community and lacked fences.

Some of the loss of trees can be attributed to farming, some to overuse of the limited supply, and some to war. During wartime, enemy forces would cut down the trees and place them against the walls, setting fire to them. In his account of the fall of Jerusalem to the Romans in 70 A.D., Josephus tells of the massive numbers of trees used during the siege of the city, which left the valleys and the surrounding hills deforested.

Fruit Trees

Apples or Apricots, Peaches

Apples appear in some passages of Scripture (Prov. 25:11; Joel 1:12; Song of Sol. 2:3, 5), although it is not clear that the fruit involved is the one we know. Some believe that these may have been apricots, peaches, or other fruits. The "fruit" in the Garden of Eden is commonly thought to be an apple, but is not identified as such. (In Latin, the word for *apple* and the word for *evil* are identical—*malum.*) This may explain why the Tree of Knowledge was thought to be an apple tree (Gen. 3:3). Artists have traditionally pictured Eve biting into an apple as the **snake** writhes around the tree.

Citrus Fruit Trees

Oranges, lemons, and other citrus fruits flourish throughout the Mediterranean, but are not mentioned in Scripture.

Date Palms

Date palms grew wild in the tropical valley of the Jordan, down as far as the Egyptian border. Jericho was known as the "City of Palm Trees." They also grew on the fringes of the desert where they were watered by springs or other sources. Travelers such as the Israelites (Exod. 15:27) found them invaluable for both shade and fruit. The branches of the tree were taken to Jerusalem as part of the celebration of the **Passover** festival. "Palm Sunday" reflects this use of cut branches that were used to provide a royal welcome to Jesus as he rode into Jerusalem (John 12:13).

Among the Romans, the palm frond was a symbol of victory, a meaning carried over into Christian symbolism. Martyrs were often depicted with a palm, and Christ was shown bearing the palm branch, symbolizing victory over death.

The date palm is a tall, slender tree with a tuft of feather-like leaves; it flourishes in the hot Jordan Valley. Jericho was known as "the city of date palms." Many household gardens had date palms, with families enjoying the tasty fruit it produced. Branches (or leaves) from this tree were strewn in Jesus's path on Palm Sunday, at his triumphal entry into Jerusalem (John 12:13) as symbols of victory.

Fig Trees

The fig was another common and much cherished tree. It bore fruit three times a year. The early figs ripened near the end of May and were called "hasty fruit" (Isa. 28:4; Nahum 3:12). They were considered a delicacy because they came before most other fruits. The regular harvest arrived around August, and there were even a few "winter figs" that appeared late in the fall.

The fruit of the fig tree and the leaves usually come at the same time, unlike most other fruit trees. Thus, when a tree breaks out into full leaf, it is a sign that summer is near (Matt. 24:32). When Jesus cursed the barren fig tree, he was noting that it was giving a false impression that it was bearing fruit. This appears to be a warning against those who pretend to be what they are not (Mark 11:13–14, 20–21).

Figs are a delightful food, good fresh or dried. They are nutritious and sweet. They could be packed away in pottery jars or "matted" together in cakes (1 Sam. 25:18), kept and enjoyed all year round. They were also abundant, with trees so plentiful in Israel that the fruit was exported to the neighboring regions. The prophet Amos was a cultivator of "sycamore" fruit (Amos 7:14), probably a form of fig that was smaller and less palatable. These grew wild along the highways. It was on such a tree that Zacchaeus climbed to see Jesus when he was on his way to Jericho (Luke 19:4; Arthur W. Klinck 1947, 40).

The fig leaf is usually pictured as the first clothing, which Adam and Eve sewed together to make themselves aprons. As a result, some suggest that the fig, rather than the apple, was the original tree of temptation in the Garden of Eden. Because of this, it has become a symbol for lust, and its many seeds make it an image of fertility. For many years, nude statues in the classical mode had the genitalia of the figures covered by fig leaves, probably as a reference to the original "aprons" in Genesis 3:7.

The sycamore fig was a sturdy little tree with a short trunk and widely spreading branches that grew in Egypt and the lowlands of Palestine. Egyptians used its timber for coffins and other objects. The figs are edible, as we know from Amos 7:14, when the prophet identifies himself as a dresser or tender of the fruit—one who cuts the top of each fig to ensure its ripening as clean, insect-free fruit. Zacchaeus climbed a sycamore to see Jesus pass (Luke 19:4).

Olive trees, when very old, had gnarled trunks. (Some say that there is a twist in the trunk every year of the tree's life.) They can live for up to 2,000 years.

Olive Trees

The most popular and productive of the food-producing trees were the olives. Apparently Palestine has an ideal climate and soil for these trees, which grew in abundance and were used for a variety of products, many of which became some of Israel's chief exports.

Pomegranates

The pomegranate tree is like a hawthorn or a thorn apple tree, but taller with somewhat larger fruit than the apple. The juice is sweet and tangy, the seeds reddish-purple. The Song of Solomon speaks of the spiced wine made from its juice (Song of Sol. 8:2). The shape of the fruit became part of the design of the brass pillars in Solomon's Temple (2 Kings 25:17), probably indicating its symbolism. In pagan art it symbolized the return of spring and the rejuvenation of the earth probably because of its many seeds, indicating fertility. In Christian art, it represented the hope of immortality and of the resurrection (George Ferguson 1966, 37).

The **law** of Moses forbade the cutting down of fruit-bearing and useful trees, even during time of war. They were not to be used in building defenses, probably in hopes that the slow-growing and productive trees would survive the immediate horrors and provide a food source for the survivors (Deut. 20:19–20). The Romans had no respect for this law, nor did most of the other invaders.

Nut and Other Trees

Acacia Trees

Also known as *shittah*, the acacia was a tree that grew in desert wadis of the Sinai and the Jordan Valley. This hard wood was used for the **Ark** and for portions of the **Tabernacle** (Exod. 25).

Algum Trees

This coniferous tree (mentioned in 2 Chron. 9:10–11) is also called the *Cilician fir* or the *evergreen cypress.*

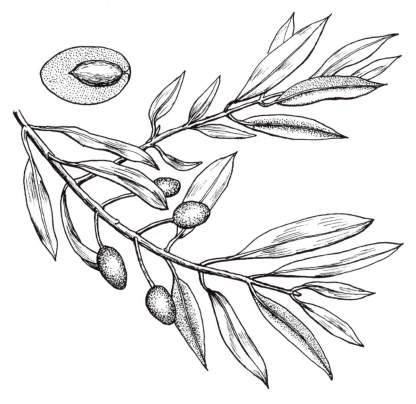

Almond Trees

The almond tree is among the first to blossom in the spring. Almond trees have been plentiful throughout the recorded history of the Near East (Gen. 43:11; Exod. 25:33; Eccles. 12:5).

Olive trees (*Olea europaea*) were among the most popular and productive in Israel, a source of food, oil, light, and exports.

Almug Trees

This tree, thought to be a native of India, was imported into Judah with gold from Ophir (1 Kings 10:11–12). Some believe it to be a Lebanese tree.

Cedar Trees

The famous cedars of Lebanon, which Solomon used in the building of his Temple, were giant evergreens. Solomon also used these in the construction of chariots. These cedars were sometimes as high as 40 meters, spectacular for their stature, the very image of majesty.

These stately trees became the image used by Ezekiel as the sign of the Messiah and his Kingdom: "I will also take of the highest branch of the high cedar … and will plant it upon an high mountain" (Ezek. 17:22; George Ferguson 1966, 29). The cedar became a symbol of Christ,

Pomegranate flower bud from the small tree or bush that produced this prized tree with its bright red blossoms and apple-shaped fruit.

based on both the Messiah tradition and on the quote from the Song of Solomon (5:15): "his countenance is as Lebanon, excellent as cedars."

Cypress Trees

These evergreen trees provide excellent timber and have often been planted in cemeteries, thereby making them symbols of mourning and death.

Ebony Tree

This is a reddish black tree that grows in the drier parts of tropical Africa. It was used in **Egypt** for fine furniture, scepters, and **idols**.

Holm Tree

The wood of this tree was used for making heathen idols. It was an evergreen holm oak, probably imported to Israel.

Oak Trees

Oak trees were once plentiful in Palestine, covering parts of the Plain of Sharon. They were usually considered sacred, marking some of the most significant moments and places in Bible history: Rebekah's nurse was buried under an oak (Gen. 35:8); Absalom caught his hair in the boughs of a great oak (2 Sam. 18:9); the oaks of Bashan were proverbial for their wood (Isa. 2:13; Ezek. 27:6). There are references also to acorns and the pods or "husks" of the carob tree, which were used to fatten herds of pigs raised by the Gentiles in Palestine. This was the food the Prodigal Son found himself forced to share (Luke 15:16, 8:32; Arthur W. Klinck 1947, 41–42). The term *terebinth*, which is sometimes translated as *oak*, usually refers to any large tree (Roland deVaux 1961, 279).

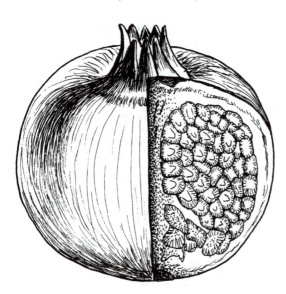

Pomegranate fruit was widely viewed as a fertility symbol because of the vast number of seeds it contained. It was a common design in decorations, including the high priest's robe (Exod. 28:33), Solomon's Temple pillars, and the silver shekel of Jerusalem.

Pine Trees

Pine trees grew in the hills of Palestine. They are tall, slender trees with needles rather than leaves and soft, pliable timber.

Plane Trees

This large deciduous tree grew in rocky stream beds in northern Palestine. It is sometimes called a "chestnut" in translations, although chestnut trees are not native to the region.

Acacia trees flourish in the desert, making them an appropriate source of wood for constructing the Tabernacle or the Tent of Meeting, which traveled with them in their wilderness years.

Poplar Trees

Otherwise known as the *balsam* or *mulberry* tree, this tree provided rods for Jacob when he was deceiving Laban (Gen. 30:37). It is a tall tree with rustling leaves (2 Sam. 5:23–24, 1 Chron. 14:14–15) and is like the willow in that it grows beside streams, where its branches easily take root.

Sycamine Trees

Known also as *black mulberry* or *sycamore,* this is a small sturdy tree with blood-red, edible fruits (F. N. Hepper 1980, 1592).

Tamarisk Trees

This is a soft-wooded tree that grows in desert wadis. It has numerous slender branchletts and scalelike leaves with small tassels of pink or white flowers. Abraham planted a tamarisk tree around Beer-sheba (Gen. 21:33).

Terebinth Tree

This is the small tree that grows in the hills of Palestine, providing turpentine (Isa. 6:13). The large Atlantic terebinth resembles an oak, has a similar name, and may have been confused with it in the Old Testament.

The almond tree blooms in Israel as early as January, marking the awakening of the fruit trees in the region. Its blossoms are "pink-flushed white," so beautiful that they have inspired ornamental work (Exod. 25:33–34). Aaron's amazing rod that broke forth in buds is thought to have been a cutting from the almond tree (Num. 17:1–11).

Walnut Trees

Walnut trees are common throughout Palestine. The walnuts, mixed with almonds, dried raisins, and figs, were used at meals. They were also carried by shepherds and other travelers for their lunch.

Willow Trees

The Jews lamented their captivity by singing the sad psalm, "By the waters of Babylon we sat down and wept," adding that they hung their harps on the willow trees (Ps. 137:2). The weeping aspect of the willow, leaning its branches over toward the water, makes it a perfect symbol for their mourning. In Christian iconography, the tree's ability to flourish and remain whole no matter how many branches are cut off has made it a symbol of the Gospel of Christ, which "remains intact, no matter how widely it is distributed among the peoples of the world" (George Ferguson 1966, 40).

The cedar of Lebanon was a large, spreading coniferous tree with durable wood, much prized for building. David's house, Solomon's Temple, and the Second Temple were all built of the wood from this tree (2 Sam. 5:11; 1 Kings 5:6–10; Ezra 3:7).

Sacred Trees

In the Mideast, certain trees have traditionally been considered sacred. In Mesopotamian portrayals, they are usually related to fertility gods and are symbols of fertility. Astarte's tree, for example, was the cypress. This ancient tradition is related to worship in "high places." Deuteronomy condemns this fertility worship in groves of trees (12:2), which was so appealing during most of Israel's history (Roland deVaux 1961, 477–478).

Certain trees were associated with different figures in Scripture: the Palm-tree of Deborah, the Oak near Shechem where Jacob buried his family's idols (Gen. 33:4); and the Oak of Mambre, where Abraham set up an altar (Gen. 18:4, 8). Abraham also planted an oak or tamarik tree by the sacred well at Beer-sheba (Gen. 21:33).

It was natural that trees have played an important part in Christian symbolism, standing for both life and death. From the trees in the Garden of Eden (the Tree of Life and the Tree of Knowledge), to the trees in the Garden of

Gethsemane, and the tree (or cross) on which Christ was crucified, trees have proven powerful images in Scripture. *See also* Gardens; Olives, Olive Oil, Olive Trees.

Further Reading

Bacher, Wilhelm and Judah David Eisenstein. "Trees, Laws Concerning," http://www.jewishencyclopedia.com (accessed June 25, 2005). Burton, George A. and the Executive Committee, "Tree Worship," http://www.jewishencyclopedia.com (accessed June 25, 2005). DeVaux, Roland. *Ancient Israel: Its Life and Institutions*, trans. by John McHugh. Grand Rapids, Mich.: William B. Eerdmans Publishing Company, 1961. Ferguson, George. *Signs and Symbols in Christian Art*. New York: Oxford University Press, 1966. Hepper, F. N. "Trees," in *The Illustrated Bible Dictionary*, 3 volumes. Sydney, Australia: Tyndale House Publishers, 1980. Klinck, Arthur W. *Home Life in Bible Times*. St. Louis, Mo.: Concordia Publishing House, 1947.

Trial by Ordeal

In the absence of clear evidence such as eye witnesses, trials often had to be determined by "ordeals." Using various forms of tests of truthfulness, the court appealed to God for adjudication. "Ordeal by words," which included **curses**, **blessings**, and **oaths**, called for divine judgment. This was considered the most serious of "ordeals." Divine will was also thought to be revealed by the casting of lots, used to determine the identity of criminals (Josh. 7:13–26; 1 Sam. 14:38), for election of **king** (1 Sam 10:19), and for obtaining decisions in civil cases (Prov. 18:18). The casting of lots was the special privilege of the high **priest**, who wore "breastpiece of judgment" with its oracular set of the **Urim and Thummim** (Exod. 28:15, 30; Prov. 16:33). Among laity, drawing of lots (like drawing straws) was sometimes used for distribution of the land (Num. 26:55, 33:54).

The person undergoing ordeal touched a divine object or "drew near to God." That is, he might approach or touch a sanctuary so that the curse would fall on him, or he (or she) might touch the scroll or the laver or at least phylacteries (Ze'ev W. Falk 2001, 55–56). Note that this parallels our idea of swearing to tell the truth, "by Almighty God," with our right hand on the Bible. Some people will say (probably in jest), "Let lightening strike me if what I say is not the truth!"

The Assyro-**Babylonian** river ordeal does not seem to have existed among the Hebrews, but there are some references to "ordeals by water." A wife suspected of adultery was examined by the "water of bitterness," that is, a mixture of water from a sacred spring, dust from the sanctuary, and the ink in which the curse was written (Num. 5:22). A similar procedure was followed with regard to those guilty of making the golden calf (Exod. 32:20). They were forced to drink the water into which the calf statue had been ground.

A number of these trials by ordeal continued into the eighteenth century in many Western countries, especially among ecclesiastical courts. Trial by water was frequently used in connection with testing for **witchcraft** all over Europe, England, and America during colonial times. Subsequent revisions in American law, especially after the excesses of the Salem Witch Trials, eliminated numerous of the old forms of evidence, including Trial by Ordeal. *See also* Court Officials; Punishments; Trials, Courts; Urim and Thummim, Casting of Lots; Witchcraft, Witches.

Further Reading
Falk, Ze'ev W. *Hebrew Law in Biblical Times.* Provo, Utah: Brigham Young University Press, 2001.

Trials, Courts

A trial is a testing of an argument between two parties to determine what is true and just, ending with a decision that will rectify the wrong that was supposedly committed. The first trial recorded in Scripture was that of Adam and Eve. Shortly after **Creation**, God gave Adam a single **law:** "And the Lord God commanded the man, saying, Of every **tree** of the **garden** they mayest freely eat: But of the tree of the knowledge of good and evil, thou shalt not eat of it: for in the day that thou eatest thereof thou shalt surely die" (Gen. 2:16–17). When the first couple broke this law, God charged them with the disobedience, listened to their perjured defense, and pronounced judgment on them, thereby revealing himself to be a God of justice. The second instance follows with the murder of Abel by Cain (Gen. 4), tracking the same pattern of violation, lies in the defense, and judgment on the murderer. The concept of justice—of laws, trials, and penalties—lies deep in Hebrew thought. God, the ultimate father of humankind, established the rules of life, gave the law to his chosen people, and continues to adjudicate the breaches in that law, and set the appropriate punishment. The only escape from this pattern of sin and judgment is through the grace of God, provided (according to Christian thought) by the redemptive sacrifice of Jesus Christ.

Trials in the Old Testament
The story of the Bible follows this paradigm, even as the numbers of people grew and the laws and the violations of the law multiplied. In the

family or the tribe, the father was the final word on matters requiring a decision between disputing parties. This remained true as the family became a clan and the clan grew in numbers to become a nation. It was the pattern as late as Moses, who had the additional advantage of having God-given law to use for guidance, which he transcribed and provided for his people. His father-in-law noted that Moses was overburdened by trying to adjudicate every matter and recommended that he allow others assume part of the task of judging. Moses did assign **judges** to help him govern the **Tribes of Israel**. After the Israelites crossed the Jordan into Israel and settled the land, they chose judges from their midst. These men and women were charismatic individuals, often military leaders such as Gideon, Deborah, and Samson. Later, as cities grew, the village or city's assembly of elders convened in the **gate** of the city to judge crimes and settle disputes in the community.

The **priests** and the **king** served as the supreme court, the higher authorities called on only when the local courts could not determine the justice of a case. Although local clergy do not appear to have been part of local courts, they may have formed special tribunals in the sanctuary (Deut. 17:9, 19:17, 21:5, 33:10) for judging theological transgressions.

Some scholars speculate that priests may have originally been content to deal with purely religious matters, but later involved themselves in civil cases, "especially where the matter had to be submitted for divine decision" (Ze'ev W. Falk 2001, 47). Examples of religious crimes would include blasphemy or breaking the **Sabbath**. Cases where the evidence was unclear and there were no witnesses might call for **trial by ordeal** or the casting of lots, in which case, the priest would be essential to the proceedings as God's representative. The swearing of **oaths** and pronouncing of **curses** were also considered calls for divine intervention. The goal of the Hebrew trial was to reconcile the culprit with the community, forcing him or her to confess, make restitution, suffer punishment, and thereby find **atonement**.

In the Old Testament, we see a variety of trials and hearings: the blasphemer (Lev. 24:10–23), the Sabbath-breaker (Num. 15:32–36), the daughters of Zelephoehad claiming their inheritance (Num. 27:1–11), the trial of Achhan (Josh. 7:1–26), the civil case between Boaz and his kinsman at the town gate (Ruth 4:1–12), the trial of Ahimelech (1 Sam. 22:6–23), the petition of the woman of Tekoa (2 Sam. 14:4–11), the petition of the two harlots before King Solomon (1 Kings 21:1–16); the trial of Naboth (1 Kings 21:1–16), the trial of Micah the Morasthite (Jer. 26:18–19, Micah 3:12), the trial of Uriah ben Shemaiah (Jer. 26:20–23), the trial of Jeremiah (Jer. 26:1–24), and the trial of Susanna (Dan. 13:1–64).

One of the most interesting of the Old Testament examples is the trial of Job, with God sitting in judgment. The irony in this case is that Job cannot determine that he has in fact broken any of God's laws. Much of the language of the book is judicial, with charges brought by accusers, protests of innocence, swearing of oaths, seeking a redeemer, and the final judgment by and reconciliation with God.

Trials in the New Testament

In the New Testament, we again see a long succession of legal activities, this time within the overlay of more complex Jewish and **Roman** judicial structures. The concept of the law as administered by the Romans was clearly different from that of the Hebrews: the king or Caesar, from whom the law derived, could order a man to be executed without cause. Herod the Great, appointed king by Rome, was apparently endowed with such authority, even allowing him to order the slaughter of the innocents and permitting another King Herod to demand the beheading of John the Baptist.

The twists and turns of the trial of Jesus (Mark 14–15) reveal the complex interplay of courts: the **Sanhedrin**, the Roman governor of Judea, and Herod Antipas the Tetrarch of Galilee. Each hopes to shift the responsibility for the decision to another: the high priest's servants captured Jesus in the garden and took him to Caiphus, the high priest, for examination. The **scribes** and elders examined Jesus, summoned witnesses against him, but "found none" (Matt. 26:60). Jesus offered no defense, acknowledging that he was indeed "Christ, the Son of God" (Matt. 26:63). The Jewish court found him guilty of **blasphemy**, spat in his face, "buffeted him; and others smote him with the palms of their hands" (Matt. 26:67).

They then sought to put him to death. The Jewish authorities could have ordered him stoned to death (as we see later in the trial of Stephen), but they apparently preferred to have him crucified, a death only the Romans could inflict. They therefore took him to Pontius Pilate, the Roman governor of Judea, charging Jesus with treason against Rome. Pilate examined Jesus, asking him if he was "King of the Jews," but found no fault in him. Discovering that he was a Galilean, Pilate evaded judgment by referring him to the jurisdiction of Herod, who quickly returned Jesus to Pilate, probably arguing that the alleged crime occurred in Jerusalem. Pilate then offered to appease the crowd by punishing Jesus before releasing him. When the angry crowd clamored for Jesus's death, the Roman administrator proposed using the custom of freeing a prisoner during the **festival**, hoping the mob would choose Jesus, but bowed to their will when they called for the release of Barabbas instead. The **crucifixion** itself was a Roman punishment, usually reserved for the worst of the criminals, and considered especially humiliating. Jesus hung on the cross between two thieves.

The Book of Acts is full of arrests and trials, echoing this double system of justice, with the Jews handling theological concerns and the Romans judging the civil and criminal matters. The first antagonists of the young **Church** were King Herod and some powerful members of the Sanhedrin, who examined Peter and John, threatened them, and released them (Acts 4).

Shortly thereafter, the Jewish tribunal arrested them and put them in a public jail for false teaching, from which they were miraculously released (Acts 5:17ff). Then the Sanhedrin brought blasphemy charges against Stephen, using false witnesses, found him guilty, and sentenced him to death by stoning (Acts 6:8ff). (Saul, later Paul, was the investigator and the arresting officer in this case.) Then Herod Agrippa, having ordered James' death (Acts 12:1), seized Peter and imprisoned him, planning for a public trial. Once again Peter escaped miraculously. Herod died before the trial was to begin, thereby rendering the case null and void.

Paul, a Roman citizen as well as a Jew, made sophisticated use of both systems of law. He was charged with disturbing the peace when he drove the **demons** from a slave girl (Acts 16:19–21). On the basis of this accusation, he was flogged and put in prison with his feet in stocks, although subsequently the magistrate ordered his release. This was the first occasion when Paul used his Roman citizenship to demand a public apology (Acts 16:37). In other legal cases, Jason posted a bond for defying Caesar's decrees (Acts 17:7); Gallio refused to interfere with the Jews and their theological disputes, insisting that they were making charges that were not crimes in Roman courts (Acts 18:12). The city clerk of Ephesus refused to accept charges against Paul, noting that he did no harm to Artemis, had not robbed her **temples** (Acts 19:35–46).

In Jerusalem, the theological courts once again tried to stop Paul, this time with false charges that he had violated the Temple (Acts 21:27). The Romans took him prisoner, thereby saving him from the crowd, and the commander ordered him taken to the barracks, flogged, and questioned (Acts 22:22–24). At that point, he once again announced he was a Roman citizen, innocent, but in chains (Acts 22:29). The Romans acknowledged that there was no charge against him that merited death, but kept him imprisoned in Caesarea for a series of trials under different governors: Antipastis, Felix, Festus, and King Agrippa. Imprisoned without due process, he appealed to Caesar, thereby forcing the authorities to take him to Rome for trial. This appeal allowed any Roman citizen to be heard in Caesar's court in Rome, the highest court in the empire. His speeches before the Roman authorities, recorded in some detail in Acts, provide good evidence of the justice system administered by the Romans in their far-flung provinces in the first century A.D. By and large, Paul seems to have admired the fairness of the Roman courts (Acts 24:10, Rom. 13:4), which contrasted with the Sanhedrin's corruption of justice. Ironically, the blending of theology and law, which had been at the heart of Judaic law, now had become a tool for tyranny.

Generally, cases were referred to authorities in accordance with their concerns, whether sacred or secular, against God or man. As late as the Renaissance, much of Europe continued this division between clerical courts and civil ones. In England, for example, the decision to try a person in an ecclesiastical court might be made on the basis of literacy. It was assumed that only clerics could read and write. The administrative authority with appropriate jurisdiction would hear the charge or petition.

The rules of the court involved many elements that continue to serve as bedrock of American jurisprudence, although with some obvious differences: the party with the grievance was expected to appear in person, along with the defendant before the bench, bringing along any witnesses. At least two witnesses were expected to testify. The role of the witness was considered extremely serious. In fact, if their testimony resulted in death by stoning, the witnesses were called upon later to "cast the first stone." The plaintiff might also bring to the court material evidence of the crime.

The court would also examine the accused, listen to oaths and prayers that reinforced his case, and render judgment according to the law. How the priests or elders "arrived at their verdict we do not know. They may have used some form of ritual divination ... or trial by ordeal" (Num. 5:11–31), "but whatever their means, the result was held to be the binding verdict of God himself" (E. W. Heaton 1956, 169). Even today, the court's decision is final. No one can be tried twice for the same crime, or face "double jeopardy."

One of the unusual aspects of jurisprudence was the consideration of intent. Like many modern courts, the Israelites tried to determine whether there was premeditation or simply a moment of uncontrollable passion when the guilty act was performed. Obviously, planning and executing a murder were more serious than an accident or spontaneous response. On the other hand, insanity was no defense.

Punishment would be administered according to the powers and practices of the time. In short, it was an evolving system, blending with the requirements of circumstances, calling on the law of Moses when possible, but bending to the dictates of the Medes and Persians (Dan. 6:8, 15) where necessary. *See also* Court Officials; Judges; Law; Punishments; Trial by Ordeal; Urim and Thummim, Casting of Lots.

Further Reading

DeVaux, Roland. *Ancient Israel: Its Life and Institutions.* Grand Rapids, Mich.: William B. Eerdmans Publishing Company, 1961. Falk, Ze'ev W. *Hebrew Law in Biblical Times.* Provo, Utah: Brigham Young University Press, 2001. Heaton, E. W. *Everyday Life in Old Testament Times.* New York: Charles Scribner's Sons, 1956.

Tribes of Israel

(**Gen 48:8–20**) When the sons of Jacob migrated to **Egypt** to avoid the famine in their own land, they traveled as families. These 12 sons multiplied in Egypt, even under the persecution of the Pharaoh, so that they numbered thousands by the time of the **Exodus**, emerging not as families but as tribes.

These tribes, named after their first leaders, are often clustered by the wives and concubines of Jacob:

Leah bore Reuben, Simeon, Levi, Judah, Issachar, and Zebulum.
Rachel bore Joseph and Benjamin.
Zilpah bore Gad and Asher.
Bilhah bore Dan and Naphtali.

When Jacob met Joseph's sons, Ephraim and Manasseh, he divided Joseph's portion between them, changing the number of the tribes from 12 to 13 (Gen. 48:8–20). The decision at the time when the land was divided among the tribes was to set aside the tribe of Levi for the role of **priests**. This meant that they were scattered among the other tribes and had no land of their own. Therefore, the other tribes were expected to provide for them.

Called *Israelites* because of their common ancestor, Jacob/Israel, the tribes were held together by blood relations and their devotion to Jehovah, when they settled in **Canaan**. They soon diluted the pure stock: they intermarried, took **slaves**, and accepted strangers into their midst, straining the old blood ties as they grew in numbers. Some of the original tribes grew weaker and some proliferated; Reuben and Simeon weakened and Judah absorbed their remnants (Josh. 19:1–9; Judg.1:3). When they united under the monarchy, they were known simply as "Israel," no longer as "tribes."

With the death of Solomon and the division of the kingdom, the southern region became known as *Judah,* and the northern as *Israel.* It was the northern tribes that were first carried off into captivity by the **Assyrians**, leaving Judah to survive another hundred years. Only Judah and Levi (or Benjamin) returned from exile, but these tribes had probably been joined by remnants of other tribes as well.

The mystery of the 10 "lost tribes" has excited scholars and believers throughout history. A large number of biblical prophesies relate to this group that were transported to Assyria and placed in Halah and Habor, on the stream of Gozan, and in the towns of Media. Groups in Arabia, India, and Abyssinia trace their lineage and customs to this group, as do the priests in Japan, and students of the American Indians, and Mormons. There are even those who believe that the British and the Teutons are descendants of the Ten Lost Tribes (Joseph Jacobs and the Executive Committee of the Editorial Board 2004).

The tribal structure was a bridge between the clan and the monarchy, based on blood relationships and kinship ties. Except for stories in Joshua and Judges, we know little of the life and activities of the tribes themselves.

They appear to have had a loose confederation that occasionally would unite against a common enemy. Gradually, the terminology of *tribes* seems to have been related to the land assigned the group rather than to the group itself. "the tribe was not the basic social or economic unit in Israel in either pre-monarchic or later times; the basic units were the family and the village, which were bound together by local agricultural and other common concerns." The tribe "was a much looser unit whose main function was apparently in a period before the monarchy, to provide a militia in times of danger" (R. N. Whybray 1993, 779). This function disappeared with the monarchy, leaving the tribes as nothing more than a form of genealogical identification. In the New Testament, it was essential that Jesus be placed in the tribe of Judah, a descendant of **King** David, making the point that he was the "great high priest" without being a member of the tribe of Levi. Within the **Christian** community, however, Paul clearly stated that "In Christ, there is neither Jew nor Greek," rendering moot the whole concern for tribal heritage (Gal. 3:28). The bloodline was no longer the key to a man's value. His faith, not his tribe, became the central fact of his life. *See also* Creation; Holy Spirit, Holy Ghost; Pentecost or the Day of the First Fruits.

The approximate assigned locations in Israel of the Twelve Tribes.

Further Reading

Jacobs, Joseph and the Executive Committee of the Editorial Board. "Tribes Lost Ten," http://www.jewishencyclopedia.com (accessed December 12, 2004).

Whybray, R. N. "Tribes of Israel, in *The Oxford Companion to the Bible*. New York: Oxford University Press, 1993.

U

Unclean. *See* Clean, Unclean

Urim and Thummim, Casting of Lots

(Exod. 28:30) The casting of lots for determining God's will was a common practice in ancient times. It was a popular form of divination, often using the sacred lots blessed and cast by the **priest** or sacred soothsayer. In Hebrew tradition, the Urim and Thummim, possibly pebbles or pieces of wood, were carried in a pouch under the priest's breastplate (Exod. 28:30). They might be used to make decisions in trials or courts where there were disputes that could not be resolved by other means. No pictures or examples have been discovered to reveal whether they were stone or wood, or whether they had peculiar markings or shapes.

All through the Old Testament, the casting of lots was a part of both sacred and pagan practice. One of the earliest ceremonial practices was in the selection of the scapegoat: two **goats** were designated to have lots cast for them, one to become the scapegoat and one "for the Lord" (Lev. 16:8, 21–22). The one "on whom the Lord's lot fell" was a sin offering, the other was sent into the wilderness.

Among the ancient Hebrews, casting lots became a pragmatic means for dividing up the territory among the tribes (Josh.18:8). The brothers of the descendants of Aaron also cast lots for their duties in the presence of David, other celebrities, heads of families, and priests (1 Chron. 24:31). The priests, in turn, divided up the duties of the year's worship activities by lot (Neh.10:34), requiring some of the families to bring contributions of wood for burning at set times. Even the decision on which **gate** of David's city was to belong to which family was decided by lot (1 Chron. 26:13).

Later, after their return from the **Babylonian** captivity, the Jews determined which people of which families from which **tribes** were to dwell in Jerusalem by selecting 1 of every 10 to live in the holy city (Neh. 121:1). Apparently, this allowed an impartial means for determining divisions of duties and honors, thereby avoiding argument.

Even among the pagan folk around them, lots were seen as a valid means for making divinely blessed choices, as in the case of the Persians, who "cast Pur, that is, the lot to consume" their enemies and "to destroy them" (Esther 9:24f). The sailors on Jonah's ship determined the person responsible for the rough seas by casting lots (Jonah 1:7).

In some cases, lots are tied to the consulting of omens, as in the prediction that the King of Babylon would stand at the fork of a road and "seek an omen.... He will cast lots with arrows, he will consult his **idols**, he will examine the liver" (Ezek. 21:21). Here, Ezekiel was describing some common devices for divination, studying the entrails of **animals**, for example, and basing one's faith on idols.

Joel told of inhumane uses of the practice: "They cast lots for my people and traded boys for prostitutes" (Joel 3:3); and Obadiah, lamented, "On the day you stood aloof while strangers carried off his wealth and foreigners entered his gates and cast lots for Jerusalem, you were like one of them" (Obad. 1:11).

In the New Testament, the **Roman** soldiers cast lots for Jesus's garments at the foot of the cross (Luke 23:34). Later, when the **Disciples** were faced with the need to select a replacement for Judas Iscariot, they chose Matthias by lot (Acts 1:26). Some scholars speculate that, although lots were not mentioned after this point in the New Testament, the practice may have continued to be in use for some time afterward.

In some **Christian** traditions, for example, it became a custom to determine **church** leadership by the casting of lots. And some believers still hold to the idea that God will act through the **Holy Spirit** to provide guidance through random opening of Scripture and reading of individual verses.

The pagan uses of drawing lots—drawing straws, casting dice—has become a standard part of decision making. Many athletic activities begin with the flip of a coin. In most cases, this is seen as "luck" rather than divine intervention. *See also* Blessing; Curse; Witchcraft, Witches.

Vineyards

Isaiah's famous "Song of the Vineyard" describes beautifully the Israelite's love of his carefully cultivated field in which he nurtured his grape vines:

> Now will I sing to my wellbeloved a song of my beloved touching his vineyard. My wellbeloved hath a vineyard in a very fruitful hill:
>
> And he fenced it, and gathered the stones thereof, and planted it with the choicest vine, and built a tower in the midst of it, and also made a **winepress** therein:
>
> and he looked that it should bring forth grapes, and it brought forth wild grapes.... I will tell you what I will do to my vineyard: I will take away the hedge thereof, and it shall be eaten up; and break down the wall thereof, and it shall be trodden down: And I will lay it waste: it shall not be pruned, nor digged; but there shall come up briers and thorns:
>
> I will also command the clouds that they rain no rain upon it. (Isaiah 5:1–6)

Isaiah's song provides a rich analysis for understanding the problems confronted by the vine-dresser. The **prophet** drew on the everyday life of the peasants and farmers of Palestine. Much of the rocky hillsides of the region lend themselves to viticulture, or the growing of grape vines. By digging and gathering the stones, the workmen could build terraces, like stair steps, up the mountains, preferably on the rainy side. They had to cultivate the rocky soil by hand, with mattocks rather than **plows**, working deep into the soil, before planting slips of grape vines, and covering the roots with mulch and fertilizer. Sometimes the farmer would put rocks back around the roots to help retain moisture and provide condensation during the night.

Because wild grapes have stronger roots and stems than cultivated ones, the general practice was to graft the cultivated variety into the stem of the wild one. On occasion, as Isaiah noted, the "choicest vine" fails to produce anything but the "wild grapes" (Isaiah 5:4–5). In this case, the farmer must "lay waste" to it, as it has no value.

When the good vine begins to grow, the farmer must prune it and brace the main vines to keep them off the ground. He must also weed the surrounding area to keep the thorns and briers from choking out the good plant. (These vines that he trimmed off might serve as the material for making baskets.) To keep **animals**, such as foxes, from attacking the "tender grapes" (as noted in the Song of Solomon), the farmer would hedge the vineyard in, often with a **stone** wall. This would have a single

Vineyard showing grapes and tower for the watchman. The upper terrace shows olive trees growing with the grapes. The watchtower was a combination of living space and lookout for enemies and predators, like "the little foxes," which might attack the crop.

gate and would be protected against thieves by a watchman who lodged during the harvest season in the **watchtower** erected in the midst of the vineyard.

Grapes, raisins, **wine**—all products of the vineyard—were staples in the Hebrew household. Usually the vineyard, except for smaller ones that formed a part of kitchen **gardens**, were shared by a whole village. Only a **king** or a wealthy landowner could afford his own extensive vineyard. An indication of the abundance of life during Solomon's lifetime was that Judah and Israel, "from Dan to Beersheba, lived in safety, each man under his own vine and fig **tree**" (1 Kings 4:25).

At harvest time, the village men would join in harvesting the grapes, cutting them off with sickles, and carrying them on poles and in baskets to the winepress. The rich imagery of Scripture reveals some of the practices of the harvest, endowing it with fuller meaning. Revelation, for example, described the Last Days in this imagery: "Take your sharp sickle and gather the clusters of grapes from the earth's vine, because its grapes are ripe" (Rev. 14:18).

Another example would be in the harvesting: as in the harvest of **grain**, the laborers were forbidden to pick the vines clean, leaving some of the grapes that fell to the ground or those clusters that were difficult to pull off the vine for the gleaners—"the alien, the fatherless and the widow" (Deut. 24:21).

Jeremiah used the gleaner imagery for God's thoroughness in judgment of his people: "Let them glean the remnant of Israel as thoroughly as a vine; pass your hand over the branches again, like one gathering grapes" (Jer. 6:9). Here we see God as a laborer in the field, going back over each branch to pick the last of the grapes or the last of his children.

After the harvest, the grapes would be put into the press, where they might be pounded with the bare feet of the villagers. Jeremiah mentions that the people shouted as they jumped about in the ripe grapes (Jer 25:30). The juice would run down a trough into containers, from which it was transferred to wineskins. Joel found sinister meaning in these scenes of abundance, "Come, trample the grapes, for the winepress is full and the vats overflow—so great is their wickedness" (Joel 3:13). This foreshadows the great image of the "grapes of wrath" in Revelation: "The angel swung his sickle on the earth, gathered its grapes and threw them into the great winepress of God's wrath (Rev .14:18–19).

Some of the harvest would be retained and dried in the sun, producing raisins, a staple of the diet for the remainder of the year. The workers were encouraged to eat as many of the grapes as they wanted, enjoying the sweet fruit, and rendering this a time of festivity. In the days of the **Judges**, the festivities led also to the spirit of political rebellion: "And they [the men of Shechem] went out into the fields, and gathered their vineyards, and trod the grapes, and made merry, and went into the house of their god, and did eat and drink, and cursed Abimelech" (Judges 9:27).

If the soil was bad, the stock poor, or the rainfall insufficient, the grapes might prove sour. This is the basis of the chilling prophesy, "The fathers have eaten sour grapes, and the children's teeth are set on edge" (Jer. 31:29). Some of the most painful imagery in Scripture depicts God's people without any harvest of grapes: "no cluster of grapes to eat" (Micah 7:1), and "no grapes on the vines" (Hab. 3:17). Isaiah warned: "The new wine dries up and the vine withers; all the merrymakers groan" (Isa. 24:7).

Vineyards were recorded as far back as Noah's day (Gen 9:20). They flourished in **Egypt**, and Moses gave to the Israelites **laws** concerning them: a **sabbatical** for the land (Exod. 23:11) and provision for the gleaners (Lev. 19:10). King Ahab and his wicked wife, Jezebel, coveted the vineyard of their neighbor, Naboth, (1 Kings 21:1–2) and killed him for it.

As is evident from the previously cited examples, vine imagery is abundant in Scripture: Joseph was described as a "fruitful vine near a spring, whose branches climb over a wall" (Gen. 49:22). The Psalmist called the fecund wife a "fruitful vine" (Ps.128:3). Proverbs pictured the good wife as one who buys a field and plants a vineyard (Prov. 31:16). It was Ezekiel who saw the flourishing vineyard, "planted in good soil by abundant water so that it would produce branches, bear fruit and become a splendid vine" (Ezek 17:8). Jesus told the **parable** of the landowner with the evil renters

(Matt. 21:33–40; Mark 12:1–9; Luke 20:9–16). Again, he drew on this rich vineyard imagery when he announced, "I am the vine; you are the branches. If a man remains in me and I in him, he will bear much fruit; apart from me you can do nothing" (John 15:5). *See also* Wine; Wine-press, Wine-making.

Visions. *See* Dreams

War, Warfare: General

(Gen. 14:1–17, Rev. 12:7–9) Scripture is bracketed by two cosmic wars. In the first, the epic Battle of the **Angels**, Satan challenged God and was cast out of **Heaven** with all his legions (Rev.12:7–9). In the final great battle of Armageddon, the cataclysmic clash of forces will mark the end of time (Rev. 19:11–15). In between, men have fought one another in a series of skirmishes, battles, and wars. These often engaged or were led by God's people, who served as participants, victims, and victors. The pivotal location of Palestine, between Mesopotamia and **Egypt**, made it the natural pathway for the great armies of the ancient world.

In the Old Testament

As individuals and as a **tribe**, Abraham's children and grandchildren and all the generations that followed had their **blood** feuds with various enemies. The first documented war in Scripture occurred when Abram's nephew Lot, as well as the other residents from Sodom and Gomorrah, was vanquished and taken captive by the nearby **kings** (along with their wealth as booty). Abram gathered his **warriors** (probably his **shepherds** and other manservants, his relatives and "confederates") and led them north to Dan, where he confronted and fought the Elamatic king Chedorlaomer and his five allies. They were slaughtered, the captives freed, and their booty recovered, although Abram refrained from taking the spoils of war for himself (Gen. 14:1–17).

Centuries later (ca.1000 B.C.), when Israel became a nation after the **Exodus**, the **law** of Moses established certain rules of warfare (Deut. 20), but was silent regarding the right to wage war. Although the commandment "Thou shalt not kill" was included, the people appear to have assumed that battle was required for survival.

> With Yahve leading her into battle, Israel need not fear. Those who have built houses but have not dedicated them are to be exempted from military draft; also those who have planted vineyards, but have not enjoyed the fruit; also those who have become betrothed but have not consummated the marriage; and those who are fainthearted and fearful. A city that surrenders to Israel is to pay tribute and its inhabitants are to be enslaved. (Samuel Sandmel 1978, 409–410)

The chapters follow with details regarding those taken prisoner, the execution of men who offer resistance, the preservation of fruit trees during a siege, etc.

These rules appear to describe a "Holy War," that is a war required by God. It was a religious action. The best example is the war to punish the Amalekites for their ancient atrocity (their efforts to exterminate the Israelites during the Exodus). During the period of the Tribal Confederacy, the call to serve in war was a test of loyalty to God. This was part of the covenant (Judg. 5:2, 9). The warriors consecrated themselves and agreed to certain disciplines: abstinence from sexual intercourse, for example (1 Sam. 21:4, 5; 2 Sam. 11:11). In the fighting, Yahweh himself was the military leader. With great cries and ferocity, the Israelites would attack the enemy with the "terror of God," hoping the enemy would flee in "panic and confusion" (Bernard W. Anderson 1966, 134–135). The spoils of such a war were to be given to God, to be totally consumed in a holocaust. When Saul acted out of mercy or rationality to save one man and some livestock, he was accused of a great sin. He was acting disloyally to God, who required the total **sacrifice**. This failure of King Saul proved the turning point in his life, leading to the loss of his crown and his power.

The leaders who came after Moses, such as Joshua and the **judges**, were warriors who led their people in taking the promised land from the **Canaanites** and then in protecting their settlements from the **Philistines** and others who threatened them. Later, it was the kings, who were the warriors, gradually growing from David's band of brigands to Solomon's standing armies, fully equipped and battle-ready. Warfare had become a habit, apparently a regular activity of the springtime (2 Sam. 11:1).

In the years of the divided kingdom, the kings bought off or fought off numerous adversaries until the end of the kingdom of Judah and the fall of Jerusalem in 586 B.C. From that time on, the wars involved other nations, with the Jews serving largely as a pawn in a much larger game. Skirmishes by the Maccabees and others, rebellions from time to time, and acts of courage marked the later days, but never real warfare. The **Zealots** dreamed of rebellion, but never achieved their goals. The **Essenes** envisioned a final battle between the forces of darkness and the Sons of Light, perhaps prefiguring the **apocalyptic** vision of John in his great revelation.

In the Old Testament, war was considered service to God; therefore most wars were Holy Wars. Jehovah was considered the war god, who required his people to fight for him. Through **prayers** and the casting of lots, the people came to an understanding of the need for battle. The **Ark of the Covenant** was often carried by the army, and a **priest** went along with the warriors. Prayer was constant during battles; God's hand was apparent to the Hebrews. God directed Moses to lift his arms in prayer or told Joshua to select certain soldiers and send the others home. It was assumed that God himself was leading the army, giving them victory, and that they were fighting to preserve the promise he had made to his people.

If the people fell short of victory, fell victim to sieges or slaughters, were taken into captivity, or suffered the other outrages visited on the defeated, the prophets interpreted this as a sign of God's displeasure, resulting from their disobedience (Amos 2:14–18; Isa. 1–5, 9:8–10:22, 14:28–23:18; Micah 1–3; 6:9:16; Jer. 1:11–16, etc.). The prophetic books are full of admonitions, warnings, and **lamentations** concerning their sinful conduct. In some cases, the Jews cried out that their enemies were more evil than they: they worshipped pagan deities, performed grotesque acts of cruelty, and yet prospered. The prophets were then compelled to explain the over-arching plan of God, that he sometimes used evil men to work for the good of his people. "Isaiah and Micha, the eighth-century B.C. prophets of Judah, agreed with Amos and Hosea that Assyria was the 'rod' of God's anger (Isa. 10:5)" (Buckner B. Trawick 1970, 168).

The prophets also provided hope for the crestfallen Jews, telling them that they were still God's people. Even though he punished them, he would redeem them and forgive them. Even though they continually deserted him, he remained the God of compassion (Hosea 13:14; Isa. 10:20–27).

The Psalms are full of war imagery, often calling for God to visit his wrath on Israel's enemies or thanking him for a victory. Psalm 20 appears to be a battle hymn and Psalm 21 an expression of gratitude for victory. Luther derived his powerful hymn "A Mighty Fortress Is Our God" from Psalm 46; another battle song. Psalm 68, interpreted as a battle march, was a favorite of the Crusaders, the Huguenots, Savonarola, and Oliver Cromwell. Psalm 74 laments the ruin of Jerusalem, possibly at the time of the Babylonian captivity.

Psalm 83 is subtitled "A prayer for the destruction of Israel's enemies" and actually names them: Edom, the Ishmaelites, Moab, and the Hagarenes. Such "imprecatory" Psalms are particularly violent, in the style of Deborah's War Song or Moses's and Miriam's victory song. The singers saw their God as a vengeful god of war (Nahum 2:13). C.S. Lewis describes these as "cursings" (in Psalms 58:9, 10, for example), songs in which the Psalmist calls on God to bring his vengeance on the enemy in full measure. The assumption is that the enemy of Israel is the enemy of God, deserving of divine wrath. Some of the more historical Psalms delight in the power of God to smite the enemies of his people, revealing his hand in their special history.

Lewis notes that a corrective to this natural inclination to hate the enemy exists within the Hebrew scripture itself, in Leviticus 19:17, 18: "Thou shalt not hate thy brother in thine heart ... thou shalt not avenge or bear any grudge against the children of thy people, but thou shalt love thy neighbour as thyself" (C.S. Lewis 1958, 26). In addition, the law protected the livestock of the enemies as well as the neighbors of the Israelites (Lev. 23:4, 5). And Proverbs offered powerful advice to the warrior or the person with malice in his or her heart: "Rejoice not when thine enemy falleth, and let not thine heart be glad when he stumbleth" (Prov. 24:17), and "If thine enemy hunger, give him bread" (Prov. 25:21).

The strong sense of God's people striving to prevail amid a host of adversaries is constant throughout the Old Testament. It is hardly surprising that the Jews dreamed of the "great **day of the Lord**," when Jehovah would finally bring his full power to bear on the enemies who tormented Israel throughout the centuries (Zeph. 1:14–16). The longed-for **Messiah** was to be, in many people's visions, a leader who would be a strong warrior in the mode of King David, once again bringing victory and peace to his people. Others (such as Isaiah) saw the coming Messiah as a "Prince of Peace." The dream was that eventually a time would come when God's people could "beat their swords into plowshares and their spears into pruning hooks; nation shall not lift up sword against nation; neither shall they learn war any more" (Isa. 2:4).

In the New Testament

In the New Testament, Christ's recorded statements regarding war were more nuanced. Although he said he brought not peace but a sword, this did not appear to mean warfare in a physical sense. The angel who proclaimed Jesus's birth heralded "Peace on earth, good will toward men." And when Peter raised his sword against the soldiers who took Jesus prisoner in the Garden of Gethsamene, Jesus rebuked him (Matt. 26:51–53). It was not, therefore, considered a Christian principle to spread faith by the sword (although many Christians have sought to do this very thing). Peter himself was later to urge his readers to "abstain from the desires of the flesh that wage war against the soul" and to submit to "every human institution"— whether emperor or governor (1 Pet. 2:11–14). He acknowledged that submission to unjust powers could result in pain, imprisonment, or even death, but saw this as a victory, the Christian's way of following Christ's suffering example.

Among the early Christians, "warfare" was usually interpreted as a spiritual battle. Like the **prophets**, these people dreamed of a time when "nation shall not lift up sword against nation, neither shall they learn war any more (Isa. 2:4; Mic. 4:3). This tradition continues in a pacifistic portion of the Christian world, which refuses to participate in battles, even for self-preservation, preferring martyrdom to violence.

On the other hand, much of the Christian world developed a philosophy based on St. Augustine's thinking of a "just war," one that is in service of God and humans, not for the acquisition of land or booty but for the protection of God's people and the faith. This, in turn, made possible the response of the Crusades, a series of wars against the "Infidels" who had taken over the Holy Land. The image of the Christian soldier, marching to war, has proven powerful, often using the imagery of the "grapes of wrath" as the warriors see themselves as God's servants, willing to die in the service of "King Jesus." *See also* War, Methods of; War, Weapons of.

Further Reading

Anderson, Bernard. *Understanding the Old Testament.* Englewood Cliffs, N.J.: Prentice-Hall, Inc., 1966. Lewis, C. S. *Reflections on the Psalms.* New York: Harcourt, Brace and World, 1958. Sandmel, Samuel. *The Hebrew Scriptures: An Introduction to Their Literature and Religious Ideas.* New York, Oxford University Press, 1978. Trawick, Buckner B. *The Bible as Literature: The Old Testament and the Apocrypha.* New York: Harper and Row, 1970.

War, Methods of

(Deut. 20:10 ff) Warfare, although fierce and barbaric, was fought in ancient days by a ritual that was almost legalistic in its attention to detail. For example, it was customary to fight in the springtime, when the weather allowed such activity. The Hebrews were expressly forbidden to attack an army without first demanding their surrender (Deut. 20:10ff.). As a matter of custom, **kings** expected a declaration of war, although they did not always honor this practice.

Before undertaking battle, the people were expected to pray to God to make sure they would be successful. The supposition is that the **priest** would consult the **Urim and Thummim** (Judg. 7:13:1) to determine whether this battle was blessed by God. Sometimes **dreams** or prophesies were signs, and Saul even tried to find help from a witch. Israelites began wars with burnt offerings and fasting to sanctify the fighting.

Signals for the beginning of battle might be runners sent to the different **Tribes of Israel**, banners placed on the tops of high mountains, or even more violent signs such as the case of the outraged Levite who cut his murdered concubine into 12 parts and sent them to each of the other Tribes of Israel (Judg. 19:29ff.) At the first sign of danger from an approaching enemy, a trumpet or warhorn was sounded or messengers were sent out to alert the people (Judg. 3:27; 1 Sam. 13:3; Judg. 6:35, 7:24).

Volunteers would assemble carrying their own arms, usually clubs, swords, and slings. When the group was large enough, they divided into "corps" for both marching and camping: a vanguard, the main body, two flanks, and a rearguard (Roland deVaux 1961, 217). The attacking forces, during the monarchy, divided into infantry, cavalry, and charioteers. There is no evidence, however, that the

A Judean spearman (with a leather shield, with bronze around the rim and boss), dating from the time of Sennacherib.

A Judean archer, taken captive and serving in Sennacherib's Assyrian army.

Israelites used cavalry to any extent or horse-drawn **chariots**.

In offensive actions, they would send out scouts and spies to help with the strategy for the battle, preferring to use the smallest possible force to accomplish their goal. Their favorite device, probably because of their limited numbers and primitive weapons, was the raid—a fast hit-and-run action. "By skilful use of daring attacks, bold tricks and ambushes, these small groups of troops, under the firm control of good leaders, succeeded in worsting enemy forces which were superior in numbers and weapons" (Roland deVaux 1961, 217).

Sometimes, the proposal for single combat replaced total warfare. "Champions" would be selected by both sides to settle the dispute. David's confrontation with Goliath is the most famous example of this practice.

The pitched battle followed a prescribed pattern: As the warriors approached the enemy, they would let out a fierce battle cry, which itself had a religious significance (Judg. 7:18, 20). The preference was for dividing the army, attacking from several directions at once, and enticing powerful enemies out of their fortified positions. Deborah used the strength of her adversary against him, tricking Sisera into bringing his iron chariots into the valley at the time of spring rains, when the clumsy mechanisms would be mired in the wet soil and the armies overwhelmed by the flooding waters. Ambushes at night or early in the morning, or night marches, were also used to throw the adversary off balance. Most of Israel's enemies were too large and powerful, too well equipped with heavy artillery for hand-to-hand combat. Scripture is full of shrewd devices used by wily warriors in the service of their people.

In defensive wars, the townspeople planned not only for the attack by a powerful enemy, but also for survival in case of a prolonged siege. They built their walls and fortified their **gates**. They strengthened their ramparts, gathered their stones, and sharpened their arrowheads. They planned for water supplies, bringing water in to fill **cisterns** or digging tunnels to springs, knowing that one of the first points of attack by invaders was the source of water. The townspeople stocked up their food supplies. And they waited.

The great armies of the threatening neighbors came with their massive equipment and their well-equipped armies, building great ramps, battering down the walls, setting fires at the gates, and flinging torches into the town.

The Israelites fought back with simple spears and clubs and stones, with flaming brands, and sometimes with bows and arrows. Cut off from outside suppliers, the townspeople's food supplies ran short and the prices escalated. Sieges might last for years, until the people finally collapsed from starvation. (The miraculous attack on Jericho lasted only seven days, but the siege of Jerusalem by the Babylonians lasted for two years.) Only in the case of Sennacherib's army, which was destroyed by the **angel** of death, did the invaders leave without a treaty or a bribe or total devastation. The most famous of these sieges was at Masada, which ended horribly for the Jews who fought off the **Romans** until every Jew was dead. The Jewish historian Josephus described the final days of Jerusalem (in 70 A.D.) after a prolonged siege by the Romans, in graphic, gory detail.

A battering ram used by Assyrians (detail from Sennacherib's famous relief) shows the elaborate machinery that was used in attacking fortresses and walled towns, such as Lachish (701 B.C.).

The chief method of attack began with throwing up a bank of rubble and soil outside the walls, providing a place from which archers might shoot their arrows to better effect. The **Assyrians**, who had hosts of slingers who hurled stones and firebrands, archers, and giant machines, were particularly vicious foes. They would build ramps to provide them access, pile all the trees they could find at the gates, and set fire to them. They would use catapults, or ballistic machines, to hurl stones into the city and against the wall. They would use slingers and archers to kill those on the tops of the walls. And they would use battering rams, enormous machines, that would be pushed up the ramps against the walls until they broke under the force. The famous bas relief of the capture of Lachish vividly portrays the slaughter they wrought. When Sennacherib invaded Palestine in 701 B.C., he bragged that he shut up King Hezekiah "the Jew, who did not submit to my **yoke**" like a "caged **bird**" (E. W. Heaton 1956, 156). The Assyrian monarchs entertained themselves by "arranging a ghastly human circus, in which the chief men of the community were brought on to the scene, either in cages or in chains, and then tortured, blinded, or burnt alive. One Assyrian king boasted that he had erected a human column of writhing agony" (E. W. Heaton 1956, 161). Noted for his barbaric treatment of prisoners, Ashurbanipal boasted that he flayed all of those who rebelled against him, "taking their skins and covering the pillars of his temple." One king recorded: "Monuments I erected I used human bodies after I severed their heads and limbs"(Robert T. Boyd 1969, 144). Victors in battle would cut off the hands of the people they had killed, giving the severed limbs to the **scribes** for an accurate count of their victims.

The Israelites were also believers in the scorched earth policy. Elisha instructed his forces, "And ye shall smite every fenced city, and every choice city, and shall fell every good tree, and stop all fountains of water, and mar every good piece of land with stones" (2 Kings 3:19). The invaders would strip the city of all valuables, burn the houses, and leave only rubble and ashes in their wake. The defeated men who survived the battle were usually slaughtered and the women and children taken captive.

The claim of booty (all the possessions of the defeated enemy) was a great motivation for the warriors. This was probably their only source of pay for their work. Among the Hebrews, this booty was divided, often with the leader and sometimes with the **Levites**. War was a prime source of **slaves** for ancient peoples. On occasions, such as "Holy War," the Israelites would observe a "ban"—the whole city or country, the people and possessions, would be set apart for God and no Israelite was permitted anything in it (Josh. 7; 1 Sam. 15). Limited bans, as in the case of Jericho (Josh. 6:18–24), allowed some of the booty to go to the priests for the service of God.

The rules for siege warfare are found in Deuteronomy 20:10–20: If the city lay in foreign territory, it must first be offered peace terms; if it then opened its gates, the populations would be subjected to forced labor; if it refused, it should be "invested," the men put to the sword, and everything else, people and property alike, considered spoils of war (Roland deVaux 1961, 237).

When a nation was defeated, the losing **king** might sue for peace and pay a ransom. There are some examples of treaties of peace in the Old Testament. The king of Ammon proposed that the people of Jabesh-gilead have the right eye of every inhabitant be put out (1 Sam. 11:2). King Hezekiah made the error of showing Sennacherib the treasures of the **Temple**, only to regret his foolishness when the **gold** and **gems** were then demanded as tribute (2 Kings 18:14). Often the king was killed and his body hung on a tree (Josh. 10:26).

Conquered peoples were sometimes taken captive and stripped of their property; sometimes they were slaughtered. In some cases, not even the cattle were left alive. Psalm 137 pictures even the children being dashed against rocks. Ten thousand Edomite captives were hurled from a cliff (2 Chron. 25:12). And David mutilated many Philistines by circumcising them (and taking their foreskins as evidence of the action) before of perhaps after killing them. Kindness to the enemy, allowing the men to survive, often resulted in a later renewal of violence, with the additional incentive of revenge. Slaughter or transportation of the remnants of the defeated enemy risked no such second acts to the drama.

After the town had been looted, it was usually burned to the ground. Only orchards were to be saved. The Chaldean forces were particularly savage: they razed to the ground the fortifications of Jerusalem and every town in Judah (2 Kings 25:10). Even the walls of Jerusalem were not rebuilt until the days of the Return, and others not until the Hellenistic period (Roland deVaux 1961, 231).

"The victors generally returned home in triumphal processions and celebrated their victories with songs and festivals" (M. Seligsohn 2004). The victory song of Moses and Miriam and the song of Deborah are barbaric celebrations of the bloody battles against their enemies. The chants of "Saul killed his thousands and David his tens of thousands" seem to be the same kind of national celebrations. Many of the Psalms are celebrations of the long history of wars fought and won, with God's help. *See also* Chariots; Slavery, Slaves; War, Warfare: General; War, Weapons of.

Further Reading

Boyd, Robert T. *Tells, Tombs and Treasure: A Pictorial Guide to Biblical Archaeology.* New York: Bonanza Books, 1969. DeVaux, Roland. *Ancient Israel: Its Life and Institutions.* Grand Rapids, Mich.: William B. Eerdmans Publishing Company, 1961. Heaton, E. W. *Everyday Life in Old Testament Times.* New York: Charles Scribner's Sons, 1956. Seligsohn, M. "War," http://www.jewishencyclopedia.com (accessed June 10, 2004).

War, Weapons of

As citizen-soldiers, the Israelites tended to use the weapons close at hand. The shepherd's rod and crook made useful clubs and spears, the knives used for pruning vines could be turned into swords. David used the slingshot, the traditional tool of the rural man and boy. With time and need, more effective instruments of warfare emerged. **Metal** tips on spears gave them greater force. Metallurgy improved, allowing for longer swords.

In his battle with Goliath, David was offered Saul's armor, but refused it, preferring to fight in the manner he knew best, without cumbersome covering. The usual defensive armor was simple enough: a breastplate, which was probably a **leather** vest to shield against blows; a helmet, probably

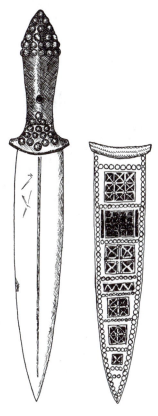

A dagger and sheath found at the Royal Graves at Ur (2600 B.C.). The elaborate design and precious metals with inlay suggest a ceremonial rather than a functional use for this weapon.

"Khopesh" sword, that was standard in all armies of the Near East during the period of the Judges of Israel. There were no efforts to make them a work of art.

with leather earflaps; and a small round shield or buckler. Larger, oblong shields that covered the whole body might be carried by a servant, but were too cumbersome for a single warrior. Goliath was thought to have had such a massive shield. The shields and bucklers were usually made of leather that had been stretched on wooden frames. Later, more valuable ones were made of metal. It is these that have survived to be unearthed by archaeologists.

One of the earliest, most primitive, and effective weapons was the slingshot like the one that David would have used to fight Goliath. Shepherds used these simple leather weapons to shoot stones at wild animals attacking their sheep.

When Saul was killed in battle, his shield was displayed in the temple of Ashtaroth as a victory trophy. Arms were stored in armories in David's era, when the army was larger and more professional. In fact, the term *armory* is used regarding the Tower of David, which was built on the walls of Jerusalem to "hang a thousand bucklers, all shields of mighty men" (Song of Sol. 4:4). Other buildings for the storage of arms are mentioned in 1 Kings 10:17, where Solomon was said to keep "five hundred golden shields" (Morris Jastrow Jr. and Frederick de Sola Mendes 2004).

The first helmets were probably made of **cloth**, wood, or leather. Later they were made of bronze. The officer's helmet was made of bronze, the most popular metal before **iron**. Chronicles notes that Uzziah outfitted all his troops with helmets and coats of mail (2 Chron. 26:14). If the helmets were designed like those of the **Assyrians**, they were high and pointed, with ear pieces and crests

The coat of armor or breastplate was made of plates of leather or bronze fastened together (1 Kings 22:344). Bronze greaves protected the legs from the knee to the ankle, but the feet were shod in leather sandals, not Assyrian high-laced boots (E.W. Heaton 1956, 147 The belt supported a sheath in which the warrior kept his sword or long knife, usually on the left side.

These are the items listed by Paul in his letter to the Ephesians: "Put on the whole armor of God, that ye may be able to stand against the wiles of the devil.... Stand therefore, having your loins girt about with truth, and having on the breastplate of righteousness; And your feet shod with the preparation of the gospel of peace; Above all, taking the shield of faith, wherewith ye shall be able to quench all the fiery darts of the wicked. And take the helmet of salvation, and the sword of the spirit, which is the word of God" (Eph. 6:11–17; William Sanford LaSor 1993, 794). Offensive weapons included a war club, which men used in hand-to-hand combat. With this, they would bash in heads. The sword or dagger would slash, cut, or stab the enemy. (Many of the surviving pictures of the time show severed heads—sometimes stacked in great piles). Usually having a double edge, the sword was used for hacking, not for the fancy sword-play of later years. The battle-axe was held much the same way. The spear and lance were thrusting and throwing weapons, The spear had a bronze or iron head attached to a wooden shaft. The lance was lighter and shorter, more useful in hand-to-hand fighting.

Warriors with bows and arrows and shield-bearer. Such shields were much heavier and more effective than the small round shields that warriors would carry in one hand while wielding a sword with the other.

The best and simplest of the offensive weapons remained the slingshot, with its river stones for flinging by the "slinger." This was a cloth or leather strip with a "hollow" into which a stone was placed. The strings were held in such a way that the stone could be whirled around the head to build up power, then one end of the strip released and the stone would sail to its destination (William Sanford LaSur 1993, 794). In a rocky terrain like Israel's, this ammunition was always available in abundance, convenient to use as a weapon—and quite deadly.

Later, the bow and arrow became popular as well. The wooden bow was strung with durable string made of gut or hide (a process called "treading the bow"). The arrows were made of reeds, having either flint or metal tips. They apparently had the owner's name on them, allowing the archers to mark who had credit for the kill. Because metal was valuable, this may also have also allowed the owner to retrieve the arrow after the battle.

The great engines of war, "invented by cunning man" were rarely used by the Israelites, although they were certainly used against them and their fortress cities. **Chariots** were used only briefly in Israel's history, apparently providing less flexibility than fighting on foot—their traditional manner. Although the Israelites understood catapults and battering rams, they had little use for them. It was usually the enemy who had chariots of iron, catapults and other siege weapons, which they brought against the cities of Palestine. After the early days of the **Judges**, when Israelites were conquering **Canaan**, their wars were usually defensive. They had no use for attack machinery. *See also* History in the Bible; Metal: Copper and Bronze; Metal: Iron; War, Warfare: General; Warriors.

Further Reading

Heaton, E. W. *Everyday Life in Old Testament Times.* New York: Charles Scribner's Sons, 1956. Jastrow, Morris, Jr. and Frederick de Sola Mendes. "Armory," http://www. jewishencyclopedia.com (accessed November 12, 2004). LaSur, William Sanford. "Weapons," in *The Oxford Companion to the Bible.* New York: Oxford University Press, 1993.

Warriors

(Num. 1:45–50, 26:2; 1 Sam. 14:52, 21:4–5, 26:28; Acts 10:1–2) In the early days of the Old Testament, there was no distinction between warriors and the rest of the people. Every adult male over age 20 was expected to join in fighting for his tribe or his country. There were no stable military organizations so long as the Israelites lived a semi-nomadic life (Roland deVaux 1961, 214). Abraham's warriors were apparently man servants, herdsmen, and relatives. As Scripture says of his fight against the kings who took Lot captive, "he armed his trained servants, born in his own house, three hundred and eighteen, and pursued them unto Dan" (Gen. 14:14).

When the family of Jacob sought vengeance against Shechem, they invaded the town with all the tribe's young men and slaughtered all their adversaries, "rescued" Dinah and spoiled the city "because they had defiled their sister. They took their **sheep**, and their **oxen**, and their asses, and that which was in the city , and that which was in the field, And all their wealth, and all their little ones, and their wives took they captive, and spoiled even all that was in the house" (Gen. 34:26–29).

Later, when the family had increased in numbers during the centuries they sojourned in **Egypt**, Joshua and Gideon found they fought better by selecting out the brightest, the best, the most alert, and the most motivated of the warriors. These fighters retained membership in their own tribes and probably returned to their mundane chores once the fighting was done. Deborah cursed those tribes who would not join in the battle against Israel's common enemy (Judg. 5:23). Charismatic leaders gathered their kinsmen and servants, plotted their strategy, and fought quick battles.

Deuteronomic law forbade certain men from joining the battle: whosoever had betrothed a wife and had not taken her, or had built a house and had not dedicated it, or had planted a vineyard and had not eaten of it, or who was fearful and faint-hearted. Such folks were instructed to return to their homes (Deut. 20:5–9). Others, at least in the premonarchical period of the **Judges**, fought their battles. Then the warriors returned to their **vineyards** and herds, using their weapons for more peaceable purposes.

Some of these judges may have acted as a kind of "champion" (a single warrior who represented the entire group in his battle) as in the case of David and Goliath. David himself had handpicked men whose daring feats were noted in Scripture (2 Sam. 5:21, 21:15). Special companies of carefully selected men were later led by Ishbaal (2 Sam. 23:8–12) and Abishai (2 Sam. 23:18). These were young warriors who proved outstanding in their valor. They sometimes formed the loyal band surrounding the **king**. The "royal bodyguard" that protected the early kings, Saul and David, were referred to as "youngsters" or "cadets." They apparently acted as squires or armor-bearers, being well born and separate from either the old veterans or the young recruits (Roland deVaux 1961, 220–221).

Saul also had "runners," an early version of special forces, who could carry out the king's orders for revenge or could protect the king in times of great peril. Later these men were responsible for guarding the **palace** in Jerusalem, which had a special room for the "runners" and a "Runners **Gate**" (1 Kings 14:27–28; 2 Kings 11:4, 6, 11, 19). These later references indicate that their numbers increased over time.

The professional army, men who dedicated their lives to **warfare** or protection of the king and Israel, appeared in the reign of David, who used mercenaries in the capture of Jerusalem (2 Sam. 5:6) and the defeat of the Philistines (2 Sam. 5:21, 21:15). These professional fighters were distinct from the volunteers and recruits who traditionally served only in times of emergency.

Because war was considered a sacred obligation, David's census (his process for mustering the Israelite army for war) was seen as a violation of the Hebrews' requirement of seeking God's will before planning war. By taking this upon himself, he provoked God's anger (2 Sam. 24:1–9).

DeVaux notes the distinctions between the household troops and the rest of Israel during the **Ammonite** War. The regular soldiers of Ammon, Israel, and Judah slept in **tents**, but the guards slept in the open country (2 Sam. 11:11); the attacks were launched by the guards, and the contingents of Israel and Judah were held in reserve until the final assault. The professional soldiers launched the offensive, and then the national army came up to provide support and chase the enemy (1 Kings 20:15–20; Roland deVaux 1961, 221).

The Israelites came to believe that the war-**chariots**, which the Israelites had seen in Egypt and confronted in **Canaan**, were essential for successful warfare. By 1500 B.C., most of her neighbors were using chariotry in battle. Traditional charioteers were men who were skilled in breeding **horses** and in making light but strong two-wheeled chariots. David had the chariot horses his forces captured hamstrung, keeping only 100 of them (2 Sam.10:18, 8:4). He subsequently seems to have built up a small chariot force for his own use.

His sons clearly enjoyed the thrill that came from driving chariots. When Absalom was plotting to usurp the throne, he drove through the streets with his chariots and runners going before him (2 Sam. 15:1, 1 Kings 1:5). With his long hair blowing in the wind, he must have been quite dashing.

It was the far more lavish Solomon who built up the war-chariots of Israel. These quickly overshadowed the mercenary foot soldiers. Solomon apparently bought the horses in Cilicia (famous for breeding fine horses) and the chariots in Egypt (where the craftsmen were more skilled in metallurgy). Archaeologists have discovered places where the horses were quartered and the chariots housed, "chariot towns" such as Gezer and Megiddo. Many were also kept in Jerusalem. The stables at Megiddo could hold 450 horses (Roland deVaux 1961, 222–223). Chariots required a three-man team: the charioteer, the combatant, and the "third" who was probably the armor bearer.

Later kings occasionally used mounted troops: 2,000 Israelites chariots were said to have taken part in the battle of Qarqar; the Armaen wars weakened this branch of the military, but some chariots were later used by Samaria (2 Kings 7:13, 10:2). Mounted cavalry without chariots, which had been the principal fighting force of certain peoples, such as the Scythians, appeared about 1000 B.C. in the Near East. Among Israelites, however, "horseman" usually means a chariot team or the men who rode in chariots, not horseback riders (Roland deVaux 1961, 224).

The camp of soldiers was considered a holy place, where God was present. That explains the **priest** and the **Ark of the Covenant**. Nothing unclean was allowed in it, including nocturnal emissions or human excrement (Deut. 20:4, 23:14). The warrior was to refrain from sexual intercourse (1 Sam. 21:4–5). Uriah the **Hittite** (the husband of Bathsheba) interpreted this **law** to mean he must remain "clean," even when he was on furlough and even though his king allowed him to go to his wife—in fact, encouraged it. David's cynical abuse of this good man's virtues, including his loyalty to his **oaths** and his valor in battle led to his wife's seduction and his own death and to the prophet Nathan's strong condemnation of the callous king.

While they were serving, Jewish soldiers had certain privileges: they were allowed to take wood without incurring the charge of robbery, they might eat fruit they found even if it had not been properly tithed, and they were not required to wash their hands. They were also allowed to eat any **food** they found in the houses of gentiles (M. Seligsohn 2005).

As the kingdom grew, the kings found they needed larger armies for more ambitious purposes; they began conscription of young men and even payment of foreign mercenaries. David, for example, employed **Philistine** soldiers (2 Sam. 15:18), much to the displeasure of his fellow countrymen. In times of emergency, this regular army was supplemented by recruits, who were enlisted by a recruiting officer and a **scribe** (2 Chron. 26:11). Some believe that this unpopular policy declined and disappeared by the end of the seventh century B.C. **Fortresses** were manned by private citizens who were called up for a period of regular service (E.W. Heaton 1956, 145–146).

In addition to the commander-in-chief (usually the king), the officers included subordinate leaders, like Joab, the general whom David commanded to place a yet lower officer, Uriah, in the forefront of the battle so that he would be killed. This ranking of officers, with members of the royal family at the top, indicates more regular warfare and larger forces.

In her later days, when Israel became vassal to one great power after another, the defense of the local fort or garrison was probably the major function of the military. Only during the rebellion of the Maccabees do we see a real resurgence of warfare, and this was more a kind of guerrilla war against occupying forces. The warrior-hero, Judas Maccabeaus, became once again the old fashioned revered figure typical of David's day or the period of the Judges.

For the most part, the references in the New Testament to soldiers are to **Roman** officers, including the centurion, "a man under orders" who believed in Jesus's authority and followed his commands. Pontius Pilate had barracks of soldiers at hand to put down rebellions and take prisoners. At the Crucifixion, Jesus's garments were divided among the Roman soldiers. Ironically, the image of the warrior became a portrait of the Christian in battle against the forces of Satan, and eventually Christ himself was portrayed in Revelation as a warrior riding forth to a final cosmic victory. As in the War of the Sons of Light and the Sons of Darkness, a description of which was found among the Dead Sea Scrolls (William Sanford LaSor 1993, 792), the world was expected to end with a great final battle, in which the Messiah would be the victor. The one who is called "Faithful and True" would come with the armies of **Heaven** to smite the nations (Rev.19:11–15). *See also* War, Warfare: General; War, Methods of; War, Weapons of.

Further Reading

DeVaux, Roland. *Ancient Israel: Its Life and Institutions.* Grand Rapids, Mich.: William B. Eerdmans Publishing Company, 1961. Heaton, E. W. *Everyday Life in Old Testament Times.* New York: Charles Scribner's Sons, 1956. LaSor, William Sanford. "War," *The Oxford Companion to the Bible.* New York: Oxford University Press, 1993. Seligsohn, M. "War," http://www.jewishencyclopedia.com (accessed January 11, 2005).

Washing of feet

(1 Sam. 25:40–41; Luke 7:36–38, 44; John 13:5; 1 Tim. 5:10) For most moderns from Europe or America, the foot-washing ritual of hospitality seems quite alien. It was and is a common practice in the Arab world and was used among the biblical Israelites. For a weary traveler who wore sandals and walked long distances in the dust, it was a real courtesy. As most people removed their shoes at the door to the tent or house and went barefoot, it was also an aid to the housewife. It protected the mats, rugs, or divans from accumulated filth.

Among the Israelites, after bowing, greeting, and kissing, it was the first duty of the host to offer a guest water for washing his feet (Gen. 18:4, 19:2, etc.) To abstain for a length of time from washing them was a sign of deep **mourning** (2 Sam. 19:24). A servant might assist the guest by pouring the water over his feet, rubbing the feet with his hands, and wiping them with a napkin (Fred H. Wight 1953, 75).

Within the family, this was a service that the wife was expected to render to her husband—along with preparing his drink and bed no matter how many maids she had— (Emil G. Hirsch, Welhelm Nowack, and Solomon Schechter 2004).

In religious rituals, **priests** were expected to wash their hands and feet when they entered the **Tabernacle** or approached the **altar** of burnt offerings. No one was allowed to approach the **king** or prince without such preparation, and therefore no one should approach God without appropriate cleansing. This was a portion of the very detailed **Law** of Purity (Lev.11–16).

Jesus, realizing that this was the humble gesture of the gracious host or servant, gladly took the basin and towel and washed his **disciples**' feet. At another time, the zealous gesture of the sinful "woman in the city" who brought an alabaster box of ointment, and stood at his feet "weeping, and began to wash his feet with tears, and did wipe them with the hairs of her head and kissed his feet, and anointed them with the ointment" was for Jesus a model of faithful behavior. He rebuked Simon by saying, "Seest thou this woman? I entered into thine house, thou gavest me no water for my feet: but she hath washed my feet with tears, and wiped them with the hairs of her head" (Luke 7:36–38, 44).

Paul recommended that the widow wash the saints' feet (1 Tim. 5:10), a sign of the Christian obligation to be hospitable to fellow believers and of her own

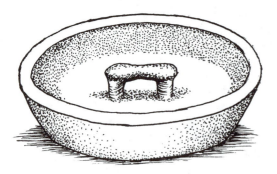

Basin used in ancient Israel for the purpose of washing feet.

humility and diligence. In some **churches** today, the ritual of foot-washing continues, with much the same meaning of mutual service. *See also* Bath, Bathing; Hospitality.

Further Reading

Hirsch, Emil G., Welhelm Nowack, and Solomon Schechter. "Feet, Washing of," http://jewishencyclopedia.com (accessed June 14, 2004). Wight, Fred Hartley. *Manners and Customs of Bible Lands.* Chicago: Moody Press, 1953.

Watchtower

(Isa. 5:2; Matt. 2133; Mark 12:1) A watchtower was any high building that allowed the watchman to survey the countryside for signs of trouble. It could be anything from a simple booth covered with sheltering branches to an elaborate round stone building, like a truncated windmill, having a spiral staircase running around the outside wall. The building might be topped by branches or even have trees growing on the flat thatched roof.

It generally stood near the **gate** of the **vineyard**, where a watchman could keep guard against foxes, jackals, and other **animals** that loved the fresh grapes. The more mature harvest was threatened by thieves who might invade the vineyard and steal the grapes. The watchtower usually served as the watchman's shelter for the duration of the harvest. Both Isaiah and Jesus refer to the building of such watchtowers (Isa. 5:2; Matt. 21:33; Mark 12:1).

This model of the agricultural tower was replicated in the towers that protected cities and **palaces** in later times: Shechem (Judg. 9:49), Peniel (Judg. 8:17), Hananel (Neh. 3:1), and Jerusalem (Neh. 3:25). "The Israelites secretly did things against the Lord their God that were not right. From watchtower to fortified city they built themselves high places in all their towns" (2 Kings 17:9). They trusted these watchtowers, not God, to protect themselves against the **Philistines**. Isaiah later told the people that, "The fortress will be abandoned, the noisy city deserted; citadel and watchtower will become a wasteland forever, a delight of **donkeys**, a pasture for flocks" (Isa. 32:14).

These tent-dwellers viewed the construction of tall buildings as a dangerous and prideful activity. The first tower recorded in Scripture (actually a ziggurat)—the **Tower of Babel**—proved a **curse** to God's people, scattering them rather than protecting them (Gen. 11:4). Much later the construction of the tower of Siloam proved tragic, with the tower falling on the people (Luke 13:4). Towers, symbols of human strength through arms, often proved a sad delusion for humankind. Enemies found devious means to undermine, burn, invade, and demolish such constructions throughout history. *See also* Fortifications, Fortified Cities, Fortresses; Palaces; Vineyards.

Further Reading

Keller, Werner. *The Bible as History*. New York: Bantam Books, 1982.

Waters

(Gen. 1:2, 6, 9) Water was one of the first elements at the **Creation**, even before light. "And the earth was without form, and void; and darkness was upon the face of the deep. And the Spirit of God moved upon the face of the waters" (Gen. 1:2). The "Great Deep" covered the earth at this point: "And God said, Let there be a firmament in the midst of the waters, and let it divide the waters from the waters" (Gen. 1:6). Finally, he said, "Let the waters under the heaven be gathered together unto one place, and let the dry land appear: and it was so" (Gen 1:9). Later, he filled the seas with abundant life as he did the land. These statements established for the Hebrews their concept of the "waters"—those above the earth that brought rain and dew, those below the earth that provided drinking water and irrigation.

The destructive power of water is portrayed in the story of the **Great Flood** and the parting of the Red Sea. The story of Jonah revealed it also as a transforming image, sometimes seen as the **resurrection** from the dead. The nourishing power of water is revealed in the patriarchs' digging of **wells**, the references to springs and **cisterns**, Hezekiah's tunnel to protect Jerusalem in a time of siege, the changing of water into **wine** at Cana, and the living waters we find in Revelation. Water was already the symbol of life before it became the symbol of new life in **baptism**. In a land as arid as Israel, water has always been a precious commodity, treasured by the people.

"Waters above the Earth"

The ancient Hebrews accepted the idea that there were waters "above the earth" for the very simple reason that they saw rain, snow, and hail come from above. They assumed that there was a great reservoir of water above the firmament that God released from time to time through the windows of Heaven. They especially relied on the rains to provide life for themselves, their animals, and their harvests.

The winter rains are essential to life in the Near East. They come after the long dry summer, from June to September. Beginning in mid-September, the rains revive the vegetation and reinvigorate the land. Rain blows in from the Mediterranean for two or three days at a time, allowing intervals for ploughing, planting, and harvesting. This pattern of frequent rainfall continues until late March, when the drier weather sets in. Sometimes, there is also the "later rain," which comes in April.

On their return from captivity, the Hebrews were relieved to discover that the Promised Land did not require the laborious artificial irrigation of Egypt. When the rains came in their seasons, the harvests followed, as a gift of God (Deut. 11:11, 11:13; Lev. 26:4). The Hebrews also saw the denial of such rains as a sign of God's judgment on them; he allowed it to fall in some places and not in others (Deut. 11:17; Amos 4:7).

In addition to the welcome rains, the dew is important to much of the coastal region of Palestine. The moisture that comes in during the day from the Mediterranean is cooled at night and falls as dew. In some areas, this is so heavy that it provides a quarter of the moisture of the region (Pat Alexander 1987, 4). On cloudless nights during the summer, the westerly winds sweep across the sea and deposit moisture in the form of a mistlike fine spray on the crops, refreshing the vegetation (Kaufmann Kohler and Emil G. Hirsch 2005).

There are numerous biblical references to this dew: the Psalmist speaks of "the dew of Hermon that cometh down upon the mountains of Zion" (Ps. 133:2). It was one of the tests that Gideon required of the Lord to prove the validity of his message—that the dew appear on the fleece one day and not on the ground, reversing the pattern the second day (Judg. 6:36–40). In response for this demand for proof, the dew provided a bowl full of water when wrung out of the wet fleece.

The gentle, reviving power of the dew was to become a symbol of God's grace. It was also, like rain, a source of fertility and regeneration, making it an image of the **resurrection**. As Isaiah says, " A dew of herbs is thy dew, and the earth shall cast off the spirits of the dead" (Isa. 26:19). In much of rabbinical literature, the "dew of resurrection" became a staple concept.

"Waters under the Earth"

There are two lakes that dominate the geography of Palestine: Galilee in the north and the Dead Sea in the South. Only Ganesaret or Galilee has water that can be used for drinking and for crops. Between these "seas" is the Jordan River, the only river of any size that flows all year long. Fed by springs in the north, it was so important that it became the boundary, the indicator of land holdings, with Transjordan only occasionally part of Israel. Other rivers tend to be seasonal, overflowing during the rainy season and drying up entirely during the summer. As the population grew, in order to have **agriculture** beyond the Jordan valley, farmers were forced to irrigate their crops, using canals and later aqueducts (during the time of the **Roman** occupation).

Springs also provided fresh water in a thirsty land. Abraham and Isaac dug wells for water supply. Wells were so important that cities were sometimes

The famous Pool of Siloam, a principal source of water for Jerusalem, where Jesus sent the blind man to wash and be healed (John 9:7–11).

built adjacent to them; they were the stopping places for caravans and the meeting place for the neighborhood. They are mentioned throughout the Old Testament as prize assets, even of **kings**. The patriarchs also had springs. The artificially constructed hollow that allows spring water or underground water to collect was called a "well of living water" (Gen. 26:19). Jacob's well, mentioned in the Gospels, would be such an example (John 4:2). It was 23 meters deep and 2 1/2 meters in diameter (Emil G. Hirsch, Immanuel Benzinger, Schulim Ochser 2005).

In Jerusalem, every house of any significance had its own cistern. Cisterns were bottle-shaped constructions, like chambers, hewn out of rock or built up with walls of considerable size that were used for the collecting of rainwater. Unlike open pools, they, like the wells, were wholly covered. Even the hole at the top that allowed the visitor to draw the water up in **leather** buckets was tightly closed with a large stone so as to prevent anyone from using it without permission (Emil G. Hirsch et al. 2005, Exod. 2:16, Isa. 40:15, Gen. 29:3, etc.)

The different sources of water, the quality of the water, and its accessibility became the key to many events and exchanges in Scripture. Much of the imagery of the **Psalms** and **Proverbs**, of Job and the **prophets**, and of Jesus and his **disciples** focused on water, often separating the concept of "living waters" from "still waters" (running streams or springs as opposed to ponds). The prophets saw the force of water in their prophesies of justice pouring down like a mighty river. Storm stilled the storm in the lake of Galilee, and Peter walked—briefly—on the water of that same lake, the same one where he and his fellows made their livelihood by fishing.

The sea or ocean is the most rarely mentioned form of water. The Israelites escaped from Egypt, not on ships, but by the parting of the Red Sea. The Hebrews were not a seafaring people, like the Phoenicians and the **Greeks**; they viewed the sea with considerable respect and even fear. Jonah's experience was well known, and Paul always risked shipwreck on his journeys. The Mediterranean Sea was turbulent much of the year. Only in summer was it comparatively safe to sail in the small ships that were available. Until late in Bible history, the sea as a mode of travel to distant places was of little interest to the Israelites.

Water was also of great use as a sign of hospitality (drinking, washing feet); it was used for purification, and for baptism. "Thirsting for water" became an image of the soul's thirst for God. Jesus offered the woman at the well true satisfaction for her thirst and promised blessedness to those who "hunger and thirst after righteousness." When Jesus died, water and **blood** flowed from his side. And the promise of Revelation was that the Lamb would lead his people to the springs of living water. The good news of Revelation is that the believers will hear these words, "Come! Whoever is thirsty, let him come; and whoever wishes, let him take the free gift of the water of life" (Rev. 22:17). *See also* Baptism; Bath, Bathing; Clean, Unclean; Cosmology; Hospitality; Resurrection; Washing of Feet.

Further Reading

Alexander, Pat. "Environment of the Bible," in *Eerdmans' Family Encyclopedia of the Bible*. Grand Rapids, Mich.: William B. Eerdmans Publishing Company, 1978. Hirsch, Emil G., Immanuel Benzinger, and Schulim Ochser. "Well," http://www.jewishencyclopedia.com (accessed January 3, 2005). Kohler, Kaufmann and Emil G. Hirsch. "Dew, " http://www.jewishencyclopedia.com (accessed January 5, 2005).

Weather

In biblical times, the Hebrews lived most of their lives out of doors. They may have slept in **tents** and **houses**, but they cooked, tended to their **animals**, fished and fought, and even worshipped outside. Obviously the weather was a real concern, yet the word for *weather* appears only three times in Scripture: a reference in Job to the fair weather coming from the north, a reference in Proverbs regarding a garment for protection from the cold, and a single New Testament reference to the red at night (or a red sunset) promising a fair day to follow (Job 37:22; Prov. 25:20; Matt. 16:2).

The *seasons* were the more common reference. The famous quotation in Ecclesiastes 3 tells us that "For everything there is a season." Other Scripture reinforces this, with references to the rainy season, the season for harvesting, the dry season, the season for figs, etc. The hot dry climate of the region was relieved for half of the year with a rainy season, bringing a time of fruitfulness and plenty. The Israelites did not need weather reports to know that the winter rains were coming.

These seasons were so much a part of the peoples' lives that they formed much of the background of their thought. Just as there were seasons of rain and drought, so there were human seasons of joy and sorrow. Just as plants were planted, flourished, and were harvested, so human lives were marked by **birth, marriage,** children, and **death**. The natural rhythms of an agricultural people can be easily traced all through Scripture. They attributed this comforting repetition and harmony to the ongoing sovereignty of a benevolent deity, who used these seasons to bless (and sometimes to **curse**) them. Their **festivals**, which marked these seasons in their calendar, also reinforced their religious beliefs.

They closely observed the signs of weather: clouds, winds, dew, and rain. And they adjusted their **prayers** to reflect their concerns. Sometimes they were forced from the land into alien territories by droughts that disrupted the expected rhythms. Details of clouds, wind, dew, and rain are common in Scripture, revealing both their worldview and their everyday lives. (See Waters for a discussion of dew and rain.)

Clouds

In rabbinical literature, clouds were thought to hang from the firmament, racing across the **heavens**, sometimes carrying **water** and sometimes not. The waters that were said to be above the firmament came through the multiple "windows" into a receptacle formed by the clouds, which broke them into drops, acting like a giant sieve. They were considered "grinders," grinding the water into individual rain drops (Joseph Jacobs, Gerson B. Levi, Solomon Schechter, and Kaufmann Kohler 2005.) The climatic conditions of Palestine led people to speculate on these clouds. During the rainless season, May to October, there was not a cloud in the heavens (1 Sam.12:17, 18). On those occasions when a cloud did appear, it was driven quickly across the sky, leading the poetic writers to note that enemies might "come up as clouds," (Isa. 19:1, 9:8). Job complains that his happiness passed away like a cloud (Job 30:15). On occasion, great clouds gather, and the heavens pour out tremendous rain storms, swelling rivers (as in the case of Deborah's battle). This too took on figurative shape with Isaiah, who noted God's words: "I have blotted out, as a thick cloud, thy transgressions" (Isa. 44:22). Because the clouds most often brought life-giving rain, they might symbolize God's favor (Prov.16:15). Or the black clouds might signify misfortune (Ezek. 30:18) or a curse (Job 3:5).

In the Mediterranean climate of **Canaan** or modern Israel, the summer can be so hot and dry that plants cease to grow for weeks or even months. Most of the rain falls between October and April and rarely in other seasons. The rainfall decreases as one goes south or inland, and the rain varies from year to year in each region. For most farmers, the hills have proven to be the best land, as well as the Jordan Valley and the Valley of Esdraelon. In the springtime, even the desert breaks into life, revealing multiple wildflowers among the rocks. The dews that sweep in from the ocean provide a second natural source of moisture. Hosea mentions these dew clouds, which revive dried vegetation as yet another sign of God's favor (Hos. 14:5).

Clouds gradually took on additional symbolism because of bits of religious history. When God chose to appear to his saints, he sometimes appeared in clouds. Both Isaiah and the Psalmist picture the clouds as God's **chariots** (Isa.19:1; Ps. 54:3). When God appeared to Moses on Mount Sinai, he came in clouds and thunder and lightening (Exod. 19:16). And when God protected his people in their flight from the Pharaoh, he covered them with a pillar of cloud by day and a pillar of fire by night (Exod. 13:21). It is therefore not surprising that the *Shekinah,* the glory of God that accompanied the **Ark** and covered the mercy-seat (Lev. 16:2; 1 Kings 8:10; 2 Chron. 5:13, 14), appears to have been a bright cloud.

The New Testament is also full of cloud references, often echoing the tone of Daniel 7:13, which, in his **Messianic** vision, spoke of the cloud of divine glory that carried the Son of Man. Thus Matthew 24:30 and others speak of the "son of the cloud." John's Revelation proclaimed, "Behold, he cometh with clouds; and every eye shall see him" (Rev. 1:7). This introduced the **vision** of the Son of Man.

Wind

The ancient Hebrews realized that the clouds were driven by winds. In Job's great experience when he confronted God, he heard that, "The tempest comes out from its chamber, the cold from the driving winds," and later God asked him, "What is the way to the place where the lightning is dispersed, or the place where the east winds are scattered over the earth?"(Job 37:9, 38:24). Jeremiah spoke of the "four winds" (49:36), when he used the imagery of God's wrath, "scattering" the people to the winds as a means of inflicting punishment (Ezek. 5:10, 12). Ezekiel also used the four winds in his message from God: "This is what the Sovereign Lord says: Come from the four winds, O breath, and breathe into these slain, that they may live" (Ezek. 37:9). Daniel told of a vision of the "four winds of heaven churning up the great sea" (Dan. 7:2). In the great **apocalyptic** vision in Matthew, Jesus echoed and expanded this image of the four winds: "And he will send his **angels** with a loud trumpet call, and they will gather his elect from the four winds, from one end of heaven to the other" (Matt. 24:31). In Mark we see that the four winds represent the "ends of the heavens" (Mark 13:27), apparently the source of these mysterious forces. Revelation repeated and expanded the wind imagery, noting, "After this I saw four angels standing at the four corners of the earth, holding back the four winds of the earth to prevent any wind from blowing on the land or on the sea or on any tree" (Rev. 7:1).

The Psalmist spoke of winds as God's messengers, like all of nature, "lightning and hail, snow and clouds, stormy winds ... do his bidding" (Ps. 104:4,

148:8). Matthew recorded that the winds, rebuked by Jesus, did his bidding, causing the men to exclaim, "What kind of man is this? Even the winds and waves obey him!" (Matt. 8:26; Luke 8:25). From the earliest scenes in Genesis, the winds were portrayed as God's tools for **blessing** or cursing humans. The waters receded after the **Great Flood** when God "sent a wind over the earth" (Gen. 8:1). It is clear in Joseph's interpretations of the Pharaoh's **dreams** that the east wind could be cruel and scorching, ruining the crops (Gen. 41:6, 23). In the experience of the plagues, the west wind "caught up the **locusts** and carried them into the Red Sea" (Exod. 10:19), establishing that winds could bring either blessings or curses. It was the east wind that turned the sea into dry land and divided the waters for the Israelites to escape the Egyptian captivity (Exod. 14:21).

Another wind blew quail in from the sea so that the wanderers would be furnished with food (Num. 11:31). Later in Scripture, we learn that the south wind was hot and sweltering (Job 37:17); this also seems to be called "the desert wind." As Luke recorded, "And when the south wind blows, you say, 'It's going to be hot,' and it is" (Luke 12:55). The north wind, on the other hand, brought rain (Prov. 25:23) and relief. Both Jonah and Paul experienced the force of violent storms at sea, when their ships were in great danger.

Ecclesiastes suggests that the wind goes round and round, returning from the corners of the earth, noting that much of human life is as empty as chasing the wind—an image for the empty life. Isaiah repeats this in his image of the false pregnancy, when the labor pains result in the birth of the wind—not salvation as hoped (Isa. 26:18).

Although the wind often accompanied the human experience of the Lord's presence, as in the case of Elijah (1 Kings 19:11), and the believers at the **Pentecost** (Acts 2), Scripture is clear that "the Lord was not in the wind." The wind was simply one of his creations, a tool for communicating his will, holding it in his "storehouses" (Ps. 135:7). Human frailty in the face of God's mighty power is expressed by Job's images: "How often are they like straw before the wind, like chaff swept away by a gale" (21:18); or "Terrors overwhelm me; my dignity is driven away as by the wind, my safety vanishes like a cloud" (30:22). Eventually, Job acknowledged that it was God who "established the force of the wind and measured out the waters" (Job 28:25). Like Job, the Psalmist portrayed God in all his majesty, mounted on **cherubim** and soaring "on the wings of the wind" (Ps.18:10).

The mysterious imagery of the wind is repeated in portrayals of the **Holy Spirit** in the New Testament. As John notes (3:8), "The wind blows wherever it pleases. You hear its sound, but you cannot tell where it comes from or where it is going. So it is with everyone born of the Spirit." This is echoed in the coming of the Spirit at Pentecost: "Suddenly a sound like the blowing of a violent wind came from heaven and filled the whole house where they were sitting" (Acts 2:2). *See also* Festivals; Time; Waters.

Further Reading

Gower, Ralph. *The New Manners and Customs of Bible Times.* Chicago: Moody Press, 1987. Jacobs, Joseph, Gerson B. Levi, Solomon Schechter, and Kaufmann Kohler. "Cloud," http://www.jewishencyclopedia.com (accessed February 2, 2005).

Weddings

(Gen. 1:28, 2:23–24; Song of Sol.; Matt. 22:2, 25:1–13; John 2:1–11; Rev. 19:7–8, 21:2) As in modern times, weddings in the ancient world were occasions for celebration. They were not religious ceremonies in ancient Israel because marriage was considered a civil contract (Roland de Vaux 1961, 33).

Preliminaries

The young couple were forbidden to be alone together before the ceremony. They were allowed to meet and talk, with chaperones at a discreet distance, to determine if they found one another physically attractive. Most of the preliminaries to the ceremony were involved with the drawing up of their legal contract. The rabbi might be involved as a friend of the family, but often another third party served in matchmaking (*shidduch*) for the young people, negotiating for the two families the terms of the agreement, including the **dowry**. When the two families had met and decided to agree to the marriage, they had a small reception, known as a *vort,* at which they signed the contract.

Copies of marriage contracts (which are probably like those used in ancient Israel) have been discovered in the Jewish colony at Elephantine, dating from the fifth century B.C. Earlier contracts were probably somewhat less formal. The formula in these indicates that the husband would attest, "She is my wife and I am her **husband**, from this day for ever." The wife made no declaration (Roland de Vaux 1961, 33). Ezekiel indicated it was a covenantal agreement, much like that between God and Israel: "Yea, I plighted my troth to you and entered into a **covenant** with you, says the Lord God, and you became mine" (Ezek. 16:8).

At the signing and witnessing of the *ketuvah,* or marriage contract, which in traditional Jewish weddings was written in Aramaic, the husband's obligations to his wife were explicitly drawn up, including plans in case he should divorce or predecease her. This legally binding agreement was often written as an illuminated manuscript and became a work of art, to be framed and displayed in the home (Rabbi Mordechai Becher 2005). This legal process was followed by eating and drinking, toasting the couple with the traditional exclamation *lehaims* ("to life!) Some orthodox Jews continue this practice today.

The Importance of Marriage

No matter what the wife's circumstances, men were expected to marry before they were 20 years old, although the patriarchs often waited until they were much older. Propagation of the human species was the first positive commandment in the Bible: "Be fruitful and multiply" (Gen. 1:28). Realizing that the family was the central unit of the culture, vital to the continuation of their faith as well as their family, the Hebrews encouraged their sons to avoid marrying in haste or marrying women unworthy of them. Because the mother was destined to be the prime influence in the early days of the children's lives, her faith was considered significant to the faith of the whole family. This concern with the purity of the line and the continuation of the faith made the family's role in the arrangements, including the selection of the spouse and the betrothal documents, essential. Picking a good wife who was faithful, hard-working, and loving was significant for the young man and for his continuing family circle.

Women of different faith backgrounds were considered especially problematic. Esau's choice of wives from Ishmael's family line annoyed his mother and intensified his alienation from the family. Later, King Solomon's marriage to women from foreign countries and pagan religions was to cause difficulties for his country. After the return from Exile, the leaders discovered that many of the Jews had intermarried with Samaritans and others. Ezra sternly forbade the practice and required that the offenders divorce their wives and put aside their children from these inappropriate marriages (Ezra 10). In the Christian era, Paul was concerned about Christ's followers marrying non-Christians, being "unequally yoked" (1 Cor. 7:10–16).

Proverbs explains the perils of the quarrelsome wife (21:9, 19; 25:24) and the blessings of a good one (12:4). The Song of Solomon triumphantly proclaims the delights of the happy marriage, based on true love and sexual pleasure. The whole book is a celebration of the wedding day, with the songs and delights of the experience.

Despite these customs, many of the marriage arrangements in Scripture were forced or casual, with little of the formal protocol the Jewish community applied to the appropriate choice of a lifetime partner. In time of **war**, women who were conquered in battle might become wives of the **warriors** (Judg. 21:20–23). And in times of peace, **slave** women might serve as either concubines or wives. It is doubtful that elaborate weddings and festivities marked these less formal relationships.

The Wedding Ceremony

The wedding itself was (and is) a time for dressing up, gathering together with friends and relations, eating, drinking, and rejoicing. It marked the moment when a new family unit was being formed. The Song of Solomon portrays much of the splendor of the bridal activities (at least the royal ones). In it, the couple's obvious delight in one another is convincing proof that even an arranged marriage was not just a commercial transaction.

Wedding garments were often lavish, with the bride and groom dressed like a **king** and queen. Jeremiah described the bridal attire (2:32), and Isaiah described the bridegroom (61:10). The bride was bathed and her hair braided with precious stones (Ps. 45:14–15; Isa. 61:10; Ezek.16:11–12). Like modern brides, she was surrounded by friends or "companions," like modern bridesmaids. The groom also dressed in his finest clothes and jewels (Isa. 61:10) and was accompanied by groomsmen.

The bride in Revelation "made herself ready" by a ritual bath and dressing in clean white linen (Rev. 19:7–8), but most brides must have enjoyed all possible colors and fabrics. The bride would be veiled (a sign of modesty), which worked to confuse Jacob when he thought he was marrying one daughter and actually was wedded to another. In modern Jewish ceremonies, the groom veils the bride, perhaps to make sure that he does not repeat Jacob's error. The ornate and often almost opaque veil was often decorated with coins, which were also part of the dowry.

In the evening of the wedding day, these groups formed a procession. The bridegroom set out from his home to get his bride. At the bride's home or some prearranged place, the groups would meet for the ceremony. The *chuppah* or canopy is a decorated piece of cloth held aloft as a symbolic home for the new couple. Modern Jews frequently include the canopy for the event. In Jewish ceremonies, this is the place where the rabbi or family member recites a blessing over **wine**, praising God for marriage and the family. The groom takes a plain gold (representing the "bride's price") ring and puts it on his bride's finger, reciting in the presence of two witnesses: "Behold you are sanctified to me with this ring, according to the **Law** of Moses and Israel." This is followed by the reading of the marriage contract and the *sheva brachos,* or seven blessings, each involving a cup of wine. A final glass of wine is shared by the bride and groom, after which the groom breaks a glass by stamping on it, symbolizing the destruction of Jerusalem, keeping this sorrow in their hearts even in the midst of joy.

Later, probably when the couple arrived at their wedding chamber, the veil was "taken off and laid on the shoulder of the bridegroom, and the declaration was made, 'The government shall be upon his shoulder'" (Ralph Gower 1987, 66).

The Post-Wedding Activities

After the ceremony, the two groups of friends, as well as those who were invited to the wedding feast, would form a procession from the bride's home to the couple's new home. This is the first time the bride and groom have been alone together. In modern weddings, this time usually involves a private **meal**, after which they go to the banquet for the guests, introduced for the first time as a married couple.

The invitation to the feast is brilliantly pictured in Jesus's **parable**, where the guests are called to come and celebrate. They carried oil **lamps** to light the way down dark passageways. Jesus gave us a famous picture of the "foolish virgins" who failed to keep their lamps burning so that they could join the celebrations when the bridegroom came to take his bride through the streets to the marriage celebration (Matt. 25:1–13). The bridegroom's friends who came along with him placed on the groom's head a **crown** or diadem for the occasion (Isa. 61:10). They sang and played their tambourines as they danced through the streets. The Song of Solomon records some of the wedding songs they might have sung.

It is hard to reconstruct the wedding activities in the ancient world. The actual ceremony was probably the entry of the woman into the husband's **house** or **tent**. The bride and groom would enter under a canopy when they arrived at the house. Then they would preside over the wedding feast, leaving to consummate their marriage. As we see in Isaac's marriage to Rebekah, a woman he had never seen, when she entered his tent (i.e., married him), he was "delighted with her."

For her entry into the bridal chamber, the bride was usually joined by a cluster of her friends, who took her to the sleeping area, singing love songs. The *prothalamion* was the processional song they sang; the *epithalamium* was the song of the bridal chamber.

There was often an extended time of dancing and drinking at the home of either the bridegroom or the bride's parents. In the case of Samson's tragic wedding, the great feast at his bride's home lasted for seven days (Judg. 14:12). Sometimes **feasts** went on for two weeks. The wedding feast at Cana, which was the occasion for the first of Jesus's **miracles**, took place at the bridegroom's house (Matt. 22:2; John 2:1–11) and involved the lavish flow of wine.

Although the marriage was consummated the first night, the guests remained, celebrating the display of the bloodstained linen that provided evidence of the bride's virginity. These linens were preserved in case her husband should ever choose to libel her as not having been a virgin at the time of her wedding (Deut. 22:13–21). The physical nature of the songs in Song of Solomon testifies to the sensual nature of the celebration, which was the community's tribute to the sexual union and the hope for children. The scene at Cana suggests that the guests stayed until the wine ran out, with the worst wine being served last. One estimate is that the guests at Cana drank 120 gallons of wine before the "ruler of the feast" discovered the excellent new wine Jesus provided (John 2:6–10). And the picture of Samson's wedding feast implies that riddles and jokes may have served for entertainment.

Later Traditions

In Jewish weddings after the destruction of the Temple in 70 A.D., painful elements were introduced to the ceremony in memory of that bitterness. In addition to breaking a glass, they also sang songs lamenting their sorrow at Zion's loss. There were also customs in various places of showering the bridal couple with wheat and coins, or with rice, or other signs of wealth and fertility. In some places, "nuts and flowers were strewn in the path of the pair, and they were showered with barley" (Cyrus Adler and M. Grunwald 2005). Up until the fourteenth century, the presence of a rabbi was not required at a wedding, although he might be invited to speak at the feast. The ceremonies were often in the home or the **synagogue**.

In **Christian** tradition, the weddings took on a more religious nature, primarily because of New Testament references to the **Church** as the Bride of Christ. They were not only performed in churches by a **priest**, but also came to be considered a sacrament of the Roman Catholic Church. The Protestant Reformation stripped weddings to their sacramental nature, making the wedding a secular ceremony, with many weddings being performed in homes, even with a justice of the peace rather than a minister administering the vows. Protestant clergy do perform wedding services, although they often restrict their services to marriages between believers, and often refuse to perform marriage ceremonies for people who have been divorced for unbiblical causes.

Since the nineteenth century, American weddings have taken on a royal flavor, with elegant wedding dresses, long trains, many attendants, and beautiful music—all in a magnificent setting of a cathedral or large church. In the late twentieth century, this practice was rejected by many young people who preferred a simple ceremony, sometimes the vows are written by the participants and are performed in an outdoor setting. In large cities, people with less wealth or time choose to go to a justice of the peace for a quick, no-frills wedding.

In much of Scripture, marriage took on allegorical interpretations: the marriage covenant became a metaphor for Israel's relationship with God. Jeremiah spoke of Israel as God's bride (2:1–3, 7:34); Hosea's marriage to a prostitute was seen as a metaphor for God's alliance with the fallen Israel. In the New Testament, marriage became the image of Christ's union with his Church (Rev. 19:7–8, 21:2). One of the final and most impressive images in Scripture is the wedding feast of the Lamb:

> Let us be glad and rejoice, and give honor to him; for the marriage of the Lamb is come, and his wife hath made herself ready. And to her was granted that she should be arrayed in fine linen, clean and white: for the fine linen is the righteousness of the saints, And he saith unto me, Write, Blessed are they which are called unto the marriage supper of the lamb. (Rev. 19:7–9)

The vision ends with the famous invitation: "And the Sprit and the bride say, Come. And let him that heareth say, Come. And let him that is athirst come" (Rev. 22:17). *See also* Betrothal; Covenant; Husband and Wife; Marriage.

Further Reading

Adler, Cyrus and M. Grunwald. "Marriage Ceremonies," http://www. jewishencyclopedia.com (accessed February 8, 2005). Becher, Mordechai. "The Jewish Wedding Ceremony," (Ohr Somayach) http://www.ohr.edu (accessed May 27, 2005). DeVaux, Roland. *Ancient Israel: Its Life and Institutions.* Grand Rapids, Mich.: William B. Eerdmans Publishing Company, 1961. Gower, Ralph. *The New Manners and Customs of Bible Times.* Chicago: Moody Press, 1987. LeGall, Dom Robert. *Symbols of Catholicism.* New York: Assouline Publishing, 2000.

Wells

Wells in the ancient world were much like those in the modern one—shafts dug deep into the earth to reach the water that lies below the surface. They differed from springs, natural bursts of living water that might

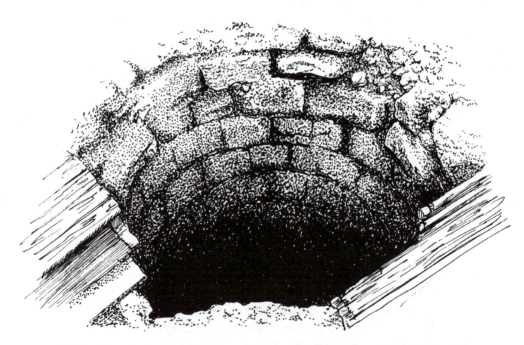

Well at Beer-sheba, showing the method used in bracing up the well's interior against contamination and collapse.

flow all year or dry up in certain seasons, in that they required drawing the water to the surface. They also differed from **cisterns**, which collected rain water into lined reservoirs that sometimes covered as much as an acre of land (A. C. Cotter 2005).

Wells, by contrast, were thought to contain "troubled waters" and required considerable effort to extract water from the earth. They were so important that they became the gathering places for caravans, settlers, and finally cities. "To the wells, the **shepherd** of the sun-baked hillside would lead his flock of **sheep** and **goats** out of the thirsty stretches of rock and prickly shrubs. Long caravans, legions of soldiers, and solitary wayfarers would hasten to wells toward sunset to refresh their weary limbs and forget the blazing heat of noon" (A. C. Cotter 2005). It was also to the wells that the young women, usually the older girls of the family, would go to gossip and replenish their supply of **water** for the family. One of their main jobs outside of the home was fetching water from the local well or spring at the beginning or the end of the day.

The man who dug the well had the right to name it and to use it. Abraham, for example, dug a well in Beer-sheba (Gen. 21:30), and his son Isaac was best known for his restoration of wells that his father had dug (which had been filled up by Philistines) (Gen. 26:16–22). The owner of the well also reserved the right to refuse its use to others, although this was considered an unfriendly act that might lead to battles. The King of Edom, for instance, refused to allow the **Israelites** to drink from his wells, despite their offer to compensate him for the privilege (Num. 20:19). The owner usually covered his well or cistern with a stone to prevent **animals** and waste from polluting the waters, which were accessed by dropping a **leather** bucket (with a rope attached) into the depths and drawing up the water to the surface. By helping a young woman remove this stone so that she could water her sheep, Moses won the affection of Zipporah, who later became his wife. Earlier, when Rebekah

Well showing women drawing and carrying water and man with skin filled with water. It was usually women's work to draw the water and supply the household. They would draw the water up in a leather bucket and pour it into a pottery jar or an animal skin to carry it. A heavy stone often was placed over the mouth of the well to protect the water when no one was using it.

drew water for a stranger's **camels**, she displayed remarkable generosity and hospitality (Gen. 24:11, 13).

Jesus was also met by a generous Samaritan woman when he stopped for a drink and a conversation at Jacob's well. He used the opportunity to offer her in return "living water." When she worried that the well was deep, not a source for living water, he responded, "Whosoever drinketh of this water shall thirst again: But whosoever drinketh of the water that I shall give him shall never thirst; but the water that I shall give him shall be in him a well of water springing up into everlasting life" (John 4:10–14). Like many of the prophets, Jesus saw the springs as signs of God's grace, bringing new life to the dry earth. The well and its water served him as a lively means of communicating with a woman thirsty for something more than water. *See also* Cistern; Weather.

Further Reading

Cotter, A. C. "Wells in Scripture," http://www.newadvent.org (accessed February 9, 2005). Gower, Ralph. *The New Manners and Customs of Bible Times*. Chicago: Moody Press, 1987. Hirsch, Emil G., Immanuel Benzinger, and Schulim Ochser. "Well," http://www.jewishencyclopedia.com (accessed February 10, 2005).

Wine

Wine, "which cheereth God and man" (Judg. 9:13) was the drink of choice all through ancient times. Solomon advised, "Go, eat your **food** with gladness, and drink your wine with a joyful heart, for it is now that God favors what you do" (Eccles. 9:7). And later he noted that, "A **feast** is made for laughter, and wine makes life merry," but cynically added, "but money is the answer for everything" (Eccles.10:19). Isaiah warned that wine makes a man think better of himself than he should, laughing at: "those who are heroes at drinking wine and champions at mixing drinks" (Isa. 5:22). From the planting of the **vineyards** to the harvesting of the grapes and the dancing in the **winepresses**, the details of viticulture are everywhere in the ideas and images of Scripture, from Genesis to Revelation.

Wine was identified and judged in ancient days as it is today by its color, its place of origin, and its age, or "vintage." The wine from Sodom was the poorest kind, probably growing out of the land adjacent to the Dead Sea (Deut. 32:32); Samaria, a more fertile land, was the center of vineyards for the Israelites (Emil G. Hirsch and Judah David Eisenstein 2005). The red wine of Samaria was preferred over the white wine of Lebanon (Hos. 14:7, Ps. 75:9; Jer. 31:5; Mic. 1:6).

The so-called new wine was strong and fresh. This was the wine left in the vat for a period, later to be bottled for the regular 40-day fermentation period. It was fermented naturally in the hot near-eastern sun. Apparently this had a powerful effect on the drinker: the believers at **Pentecost**, overcome with the **Holy Spirit**, were accused of being drunk on "new wine" (Acts 2:13).

The "ordinary" wine was the current vintage, aged for the usual 40 days or more. "Old wine" was from the previous year; and the "very old wine" was the third year's vintage. This more potent older wine was called "strong drink." It was the wine against which the wise men of Proverbs and others warned: "Wine is a mocker and beer a brawler; whoever is led astray by them is not wise" (Prov. 20:1); "whoever loves wine and oil will never be rich" (Prov. 21:17). Isaiah pronounced against those (including **priests** and **prophets**) who "stagger from beer and are befuddled with wine" (Isa. 28:7).

As a readily available and tasty drink, grape juice appeared in many popular and useful variations: sweetened, unfermented grape juice; spiced wine; and diluted wine, not to mention vinegar. One **rabbi** asserted that fermented wine, if it was to be considered wine at all, must be strong enough to take one-third water and retain its taste (Emil Hirsh and Eisenstein 2005). Other variants of wine included a sweet syrup made of grapes, wine dregs, and vinegar; old wine mixed with clear water and balsam (used after bathing); caper-wine, (an ingredient in sacred incense); a blend of wine with honey and pepper; smoked or fumigated sweet grapes transformed into a drink; and a sauce of oil and garum to which oil was added. Ancient people even found a way to use wine as an emetic, taken before a meal.

Like people of other ancient cultures, the Israelites welcomed guests with **bread** and wine (Gen 14.:18). It was the sign of **hospitality**, like the **washing of feet** and the **anointing** with oil. Jesus's participation in the **wedding** at Cana (John 2:10) indicates the love of wine and the manner of its dispersal, beginning with the better vintage and ending with the poorer. The wine was poured slowly from a large stone vessel with a rim and a strainer to avoid stirring the dregs at the bottom. The vessel served as a kind of cooler. It might also be poured from an earthen pitcher into a drinking vessel. If it were to be mixed with water, a large mixing bowl was used for that purpose. The wine was drunk from a small bowl or a cup. Foreign dignitaries, such as those who hosted Esther and Daniel, were more likely to use goblets of gold and silver (Esther 1:7; Dan. 5:2).

Wine has had a long-standing role in religious rituals. Melchizedek greeted Abraham with bread and wine (Gen. 14:18). Mosaic **law** listed wine among the "first fruits" to be brought to the Lord, and mandated a "quarter of a hin" of wine for drink offerings (Exod. 29:40; Lev. 23:13). Libations were to be made from specific grapes, grown in isolated places in the vineyards, and stored in precise ways. The drinking and drink offerings were a regular part of **festivals**, especially the **Passover**. It was, in fact, at such a celebration that Jesus and his **disciples** shared a cup at the **Last**

Supper (Matt .26:27; Luke 22:17–20; Mark 14:23). The words of the institution of the Last Supper, which we find in 1 Corinthians, make explicit that the wine represents Christ's **blood**, spilled for sinners (1 Cor.11:26). The worshipper is to "Drink this cup in remembrance of me."

In some cases, the priests were forbidden to drink wine, as a sign of abstemiousness, an understandable practice in view of the abuse of wine recorded by the prophets. **Nazirites** took a vow to abstain from strong drink, as seen in the cases of Samuel and Samson.

Wine also served medicinal purposes, as a stimulant, a help the digestion, and cure many of the pains of aging (Emil G. Hirsch and Eisenstein 2005). Paul advised Timothy to have a little wine "for the stomach's sake" (1 Tim. 5:23). It undoubtedly served to sterilize the drinking water when mixed in bowls and drunk by the entire family. The **parable** of the Good Samaritan, in which the Samaritan bound up the poor man's wounds, "pouring in oil and wine" (Luke 10:34), indicates that wine was used to sterilize wounds long before anyone understood the nature of germs and infections.

It was also a part of **mourning**: "Give strong drink unto him that is ready to perish, and wine unto those that be of heavy hearts" (Prov. 31:6). The meal of consolation involved 10 cups of wine: three before the meals, three between the courses, and four after the grace. Unfortunately, this therapeutic practice expanded to an additional four cups, resulting in general drunkenness that required a change in the practice (Emil G. Hirsch and Judah Eisenstein 2005).

It was also an important part of weddings, with the ceremony itself marked by drinking wine and smashing the goblet. The wedding feast involved an extravagant use of wine over a prolonged period of days, celebrating the nuptials and the beginning of the new family.

Wine-bibbing, the abuse of wine, was acknowledged as a problem throughout Scripture. It is associated with loose women, the careless indulgence of the flesh, and debauchery. Thus, the Ephesians were admonished not to get drunk on wine (Eph. 5:18), and Timothy was warned that **church** leaders must not be given to overindulgence in strong drink (1 Tim. 3:8).

Given the ambivalent attitude toward wine all through Scripture—its sacred purpose and its carnal abuse—it is not surprising that the imagery flows in two streams. On the one hand, God blessed his people with fruitful vineyards and vats overflowing with wine. It is the very image of graciousness, sharing, love, and sympathy. On the other hand, according to the prophet Jeremiah, the whore of **Babylon**, with a gold cup in her hand, made the whole earth drunk. "The nations drank her wine; therefore they have now gone mad" (Jer. 51:7). In John's Revelation, once again Babylon the Great has received "the cup filled with the wine of the fury of his wrath" because "with her the **kings** of the earth committed adultery and the inhabitants of the earth were intoxicated with the wine of her adulteries" (Rev 16:19, 17:2).

Wine, which often stands in the place of **blood** imagery, is one of the richest images in all of Scripture. It could stand for life or death, joy or sorrow, celebration or lamentation. *See also* Cures, Medicine; Vineyards; Weddings; Winepress, Wine-making.

Further Reading

Coogan, Michael D. "Wine," in *The Oxford Companion to the Bible.* New York: Oxford University Press, 1993. Hirsch, Emil G. and Judah David Eisenstein. "Wine," http://www.jewishencyclopedia.com (accessed January 12, 2005).

Winepress, Wine-making

When the harvesters had gathered the ripe grapes in baskets, they took them to the winepress, which was usually located in the midst of the **vineyard**. The press was sometimes a pit dug in the earth, lined with stones and mortar. This could also be used as a **threshing** floor. Gideon, for example, was "threshing wheat in a winepress" (Judg. 6:11). Preferably, it was hewn out of solid rock, usually limestone. The vat had a channel on one side, allowing the juice from the grapes to flow down to a trough on the lower level (E.W. Heaton 1956, 105). Isaiah spoke of the rock-hewn winepress: "he cut out a winepress as well" (Isa. 5:2).

The fermentation process took about six weeks. Sometimes the wine was allowed to stand in the vat, but more often it was drawn off into earthenware jars. It was allowed to ferment for 40 days, during which the skins and stalks settled into muddy deposit at the bottom. The "new **wine**" had to be separated from the "lees" by gently pouring it into other containers and straining it. Too much handling could turn it into vinegar. After the appropriate time, the wine was sealed in jars with wax or pitch or tied into wineskins. The jars kept the wine cool for the family's use. Wine was a daily drink for the family, often mixed liberally with water.

The wineskins might be reused, but it was considered preferable to use new wineskins for new wine, which was very strong. A dried-up skin would burst with the pressure of the fermentation (Luke 5:37; Matt. 9:17). The people of Gibeon used old wineskins to trick Gideon into believing that the delegation was from a distant country, using cracked and mended skins as evidence of their long travels (Josh. 9:4–13). This ruse worked, preserving their lives.

Treading grapes on the **Sabbath** was strictly forbidden. Nehemiah warned against the harvesting, treading, and selling that he saw as clear violations of the **law** of Moses (Neh. 13:15). The law was liberal in allowing activity to be joyful: the workers could eat of the grapes, sing and dance as they pounded on the grapes with their bare feet. Their shouts of joy are mentioned several times in Scripture. Jeremiah uses this custom to prophesy sad times ahead: "And joy and gladness is taken from the plentiful field, . . . and I have caused wine to fail from the winepresses: none shall tread with shouting; their shouting shall be no shouting" (Jer. 48:33). From the time the fruit ripened in July until September, whole families would camp out in the vineyards. It was a grand **festival** time for Israel, as it was in much of the ancient world. This was most famous in Greece, where the Great Dionysia resulted in the production of wild parties and powerful drama.

The picture of abundance in Hebrew prophesy is a winepress that is full and vats that overflow (Joel 3:13). Ironically, as in the case of Joel, this is also the portrayal of wickedness and of God's fury with man's iniquities: "The lord . . . has summoned an army against me to crush my young men. In his winepress the Lord has trampled the Virgin Daughter of Judah" (Lam.1:15).

Those who trampled the grapes and shouted with delight stained their clothing with the dark red juice of the grapes, leading Isaiah to comment on the blood imagery implied, "I have trodden the winepress alone; from the nations no one was with me. I trampled them in my anger and trod them down in my wrath; their blood splattered my garments, and I stained all my clothing" (Isa. 62:2–3).

This bloodlike wine permeates the imagery in Revelation. Here we see "he that sat on the cloud thrust his sickle on the earth; and the earth was reaped." And another **angel** "thrust in his sickle into the earth, and gathered the vine of the earth, and cast it into the great winepress of the wrath of God. And the winepress was trodden without the city, and blood came out of the winepress, even unto the horse bridles, by the space of a thousand and six hundred furlongs" (Rev. 14:14, 19–20). Finally, in this fearful **apocalyptic vision**, John saw the rider of the white **horse** who "shall rule them with a rod of iron: and he treadeth the winepress of the fierceness and wrath of Almighty God" (Rev. 19:16).

In American culture, this image echoes in "The Battle Hymn of the Republic," sung during the Civil War and repeated in later conflicts where the wrath of God has appeared to be "trampling out the vintage where the grapes of wrath are stored." *See also* Festivals; Pots and Pottery; Vineyards; Wine.

Further Reading

Heaton, E. W. *Everyday Life in Old Testament Times.* New York: Charles Scribner's Sons, 1956.

Witchcraft, Witches

(Exod. 22:18; Deut. 18:10; 1 Sam. 28:7–8) A witch is a person (usually a woman) who practices witchcraft: dabbling in the occult arts, **magic** and sorcery; casting spells; calling on the spirit world; reading the future in tea leaves or animal entrails. (The masculine form of the term is *wizard*.)

Although the term *witchcraft* is used rarely in Scripture, this occult practice is grouped with all forms of divination and magic, both black and white. *Black magic* is usually seen as evil, with a combination of alliance with evil spirits, casting of spells, and **curses**. *White magic* is more benign, again using the occult, but for good purposes: to undo curses or spells cast on people.

Scripture forbids witchcraft a number of times: In Deuteronomy 18:10, we are told, "Let no one be found among you who ... practices divination or sorcery, interprets omens, engages in witchcraft." The penalty for witches is quite clear: "Thou shalt not suffer a witch to live" (Exod. 22:18).

Despite this prohibition, King Saul sought out the witch of Endor in hopes of having her call forth the spirit of the dead **prophet** Samuel. He obviously knew the extent of his iniquity in consulting a woman "that hath a familiar spirit" who functioned as a medium. He "disguised himself" and went "by night" (1 Sam. 28:7–8). The woman protested that witches and wizards have been "cut off ... out of the land" and assumed that he was setting a snare for her, "to cause me to die" (1 Sam. 28:9). At his insistence, the woman did call forth the spirit of Samuel, or at least convinced Saul that she had by describing him and pointing to him. The old prophet listened impatiently to Saul's litany of complaints about his life, noting that the errant **king** deserved his pathetic condition. Furthermore, "the Lord will also deliver **Israel** with thee into the hand of the **Philistines**: and tomorrow shalt thou and thy sons be with me" (1 Sam. 28:19). This prediction of defeat and death caused Saul to swoon. The witch revived him, reminded him that this was all his idea, not hers, and offered him **bread** to give him strength. Interestingly, the bread she made for him was unleavened. In all of this, it was Saul, not the woman doing his bidding, who was the transgressor.

Occult practices continued with later kings, especially encouraged by Solomon's tolerance of the diverse faiths among his host of wives. The prophets mentioned witchcraft occasionally (Mic. 5:12; Nah. 3:4), relating it to casting spells, sorceries, and **idolatry**. The evil king Manasseh (2 Kings 21:3, 5; 2 Chron. 33:3, 5) "used enchantments, and used witchcraft, and dealt with a familiar spirit and with wizards: he wrought much evil in the sight of the Lord, to provoke him to anger" (2 Chron. 33:6). Manesseh is often portrayed as representing the low point in Judah's pre-exilic history: he introduced the abomination of Moloch worship in the Hinnom Valley (Deut. 18:10). During the reign of Manesseh, these **altars** in "high places" again flourished, and it was this king who "caused his children to pass through the fire of the valley of the son of Hinnom; also he.... used enchantments, and used witchcraft, and dealt with a familiar spirit, and with wizards: he wrought much evil in the sight of the Lord" (2 Chron 33:6).

Consultation with mediums and familiar sprits, witches, and wizards continued into New Testament days, being explicitly forbidden by Paul in his epistle to the Galatians, when he listed these along with other problems such as idolatry, hatred, discord, jealousy, fits of rage, selfish ambition, dissensions, and factions (Gal. 5:20). Increasingly, the terminology of *harlot* replaced *witch* as the female embodiment of apostasy. Thus, in Revelation, we hear about the whore of Babylon, not the witch of Endor.

The medieval world developed a fascination with necromancy, leading the Renaissance **churches** to strike out against the practice of witchcraft with a special fury. In Europe there was a witch craze, based on a book by two priests who identified the marks of witches. Hundreds of women and some men were tortured and killed during the next two centuries, spilling over into the New World, culminating in America with the Salem witch trials in 1692. Subsequent to this brief frenzy of witch hunting, the colonists altered their laws to remove many of the subjective tests that had been used to determine the guilt of witches.

The modern revival of *wicca,* the practice of witchcraft, has been tied to the rise of feminism. At the same time, a playful use of the imagery of "familiars" (black cats or yellow birds), deliberately gothic settings, and a popularization of the celebration of Halloween have created a flourishing industry of novels and films dealing with putative witchcraft and wizardry, for example, *The Wizard of Oz* and the Harry Potter books.

The reason for the development of witchcraft, according to some scholars, was the exclusion of women from much of religious ritual in Judaism. Women therefore found powerful roles in the **temple** cults of the eastern religions and of their neighbors. Jezebel, with her coterie of pagan priests and her worship of **Asherah**, became the embodiment of the practice of witchcraft.

Another speculation by modern feminists involves the practice of medicine. Because women, as mothers and wives, often doctored the sick members of the household, they developed some remedies passed on to other women by oral tradition. Over the centuries, they discovered cures involving herbs and other natural medicines that were not understood by men. This secret knowledge came to be considered dangerous and idolatrous, linking the wise old midwives and healers to the occult. This tie to natural healing has led to the celebration of "Mother Earth," now known as worship of "the Great Goddess."

As defined by some of the practitioners, modern witches are seeking to reconstruct "an old religion in a new format, gradually working out a theology that owes more to ancient Indo-European models than to the 'reverse Christianity' associated with the idea of Satanism." The points of difference between this worship and Christianity are:

1. The female principal is deified, seen as equal to, or greater than the male.

2. Body and soul are seen as one and the same.
3. Nature is sacred, not to be abused or dominated by humans.
4. The individual will has intrinsic value, not to be dominated by the will of a deity.
5. Time is circular and repetitive, involving a pattern from birth to decay to rebirth.
6. Original sin does not exist, nor is there any clear separation of "good" and "evil."
7. Sexuality, spontaneity, humor, and play activities belong in ritual, representing the positive force of life (Margaret Walker 1983, 1090).

In this listing, it is clear that many modern churches have adopted some aspects of the Goddess religion and that many of the ideas permeate modern thought and life. *See also* Idols, Idolatry; Illness; Magic.

Further Reading
Kitchen, K. A. "Witches," in *The Illustrated Bible Dictionary*. Sydney, Australia: Tyndale House Publishers, 1980. Russell, Jeffrey Burton. "Witches," in *Biblical Tradition in English Literature*. Grand Rapids, Mich.: William B. Eerdmans Publishing Company, 1992. Walker, Barbara G. *The Woman's Encyclopedia of Myths and Secrets*. San Francisco: HarperSanFrancisco, 1983.

Work: Men's

Men in Scripture are usually pictured at work. All through the history of the Hebrews, the simple chores of life were handled by all classes of men. This is reinforced by God's making a **shepherd** Israel's **king** and a **carpenter** the **Messiah**. The apostle Paul was a **tent**-maker, and the chief of the disciples, Peter, was a **fisherman**. Mundane chores of the **Temple**, like cleaning the **animal** waste, was handled by Levites, chosen by God for his service.

Men could move across ranks quickly: Joseph went from **slave** to viceroy to the Pharaoh. Moses moved from a courtier in the halls of **palaces** to a shepherd in Midian to a **prophet** in the wilderness and a leader of his young nation. Class and wealth were undoubtedly important, but most of those with wealth are presented as flawed people with troubled lives. Like the "Rich Young Ruler," they found it difficult to enter **Heaven** with their obsessive attention to all their possessions keeping them firmly earthbound.

In the early days of the Hebrews, the men were most often the shepherds, minding their flocks, leading them from pasture to pasture, protecting the sheepfolds from intrusion of predators, both human and animal. Some scholars believe that Abraham, however, was not a simple shepherd but a prosperous merchant who had a thriving caravan business. That would have explained his vast number of servants and animals. His manservants seem to have cared for the animals, feeding and watering them, packing the loads they carried, and leading them along the way. When **camels** became a regular part of caravans, they often formed long lines led by a handful of men skilled in managing caravans.

When they had settled on the land, these men were also expected to serve as soldiers in defense of Abraham's property, expected to fight his **wars** for him, including the one that he undertook for his nephew Lot. In the second millennium B.C., **warriors** were simply the men of the clan who were healthy and brave enough to fight. They were not professional mercenaries.

Later patriarchal families probably settled long enough in certain pastures to allow the men to become farmers on a small scale, hunters of animals in the wilderness, as well as herdsmen for the **sheep, goats**, and **oxen**. They dug the **wells** and built the **cisterns**, and protected them from enemies. They also built the rude stone **altars** and hauled the lambs and bullocks to them for slaughter. Before the role of **priest** was clearly differentiated from the rest of the men, the patriarch served as the one who performed the **sacrifice**.

The Hebrews entered **Egypt** as herdsmen, but eventually were drafted into the Egyptian work force as slave labor, only to leave as herdsmen once again. In captivity, they were the **brick** makers, producing the materials used in the building of the great pyramids. They were forced to make the bricks without straw or find the filler for themselves. They also must have been involved in the heavy labor of pulling **stones** up long ramps and other tasks at the construction sites. Few of the Israelites would have known the lavish lifestyle and easy labor of a Joseph or Moses, who belonged to the ruling class. They instead worked long days under the lash of cruel overseers and returned to their rude huts at night.

Later, after the **Exodus** and the sojourn in the desert, as they settled at last in the land of **Canaan**, the men again mingled their shepherding, fighting, and building activities. One whole tribe, the Levites, was dedicated to the priesthood, to the maintenance of the **Tabernacle**, and later to the Temple, to keeping the rituals and preserving the sacred spaces. The tools they used and kept in shape indicate that they raked the ashes, scooped up the remains of the altar offering, and carried out the waste. The very fact that one gate in Jerusalem was named the "Dung Gate" suggests the heavy lifting involved in keeping the Temple looking beautiful when hundreds of animals were penned, slaughtered, and sacrificed there. Only a few of the Levites were priests, and only one (or two) could be the High Priest. Other holy men were **scribes, rabbis**, or lawyers—people who studied the **law**, taught it, and loved it.

Average men built simple huts to house their families or continued to live the life of nomads dwelling in tents. Some planted **vineyards** and fields of

grain. They tilled the soil and harvested the crops, carrying their first-fruits to the altars where priests performed the ceremonies. Some became bakers for the community, building ovens and providing a central place for the provision of **bread**. Some became carpenters, helping others build their houses. It is clear from the surviving artifacts that there were **jewelers**, iron-workers, dyers, fullers, **potters**, etc. The growth of villages into cities allowed men to differentiate their work, some specializing in crafts that require years of training to perfect.

Some became professional warriors, or leaders in battle, some became **judges**, and some became prophets during this phase of Jewish history. The first two of Israel's kings in the new monarchy started out as shepherds, slept in **caves**, hunted in the fields, fought in the battles with their men, and lived much like their fellow Israelites.

It was Solomon who endowed the kingship with pomp and circumstance, inviting laborers from other countries to help design and build his massive works, recruiting his countrymen more often as common laborers. His soldiers now learned to drive **horses** and fight with **iron** weapons, becoming a professional force. Israel now had port cities and needed sailors to sail larger ships, not just the little **boats** used by the simple fishermen who went out on the Sea of Galilee. His palace staff would have included all the specialists: the butcher, the baker, and the candlestick maker. He had **musicians** at court and scholars, keepers of his vast harem, **tax collectors** for his burdensome levies, a variety of priests and priestesses for the many religions of his wives and concubines. Certainly his court would have hired jewelry-makers and goldsmiths, artisans in **ivory** and stone, architects and **stonemasons**, singers and dancers. His urbane cities now had merchants in larger number, storekeepers with a variety of wares, some of which were manufactured in this land, and many imported from vast distances, from all regions of the known world.

When the Jews were taken into captivity in Babylon, they longed for their fields and flowers, the life close to the land, their tiny villages, and open countryside. Yet these farmers and small-town laborers quickly learned that they could thrive by the use of their wits, becoming counselors to monarchs, wise men in the palace, merchants in the towns, and craftsmen working with wood or **leather**.

Although they learned to adapt to the culture and the land where they were held, a remnant returned eagerly to their own country and to Jerusalem, where once again they were builders, quarrying the stone and fitting it together in the massive walls that made them feel safe and into houses, in which they would rebuild their families.

They continued to serve as builders in Herod's day and again found themselves subservient to an alien force, this time the **Romans**. Some of them served as tax collectors or soldiers who themselves served at the pleasure of the conqueror. They were also shepherds, carpenters, and fishermen.

Men's work, in ancient times as in modern, was as varied as the times and situation required. One Bible commentary (*The Word in Life Study Bible*) lists 350 different jobs men and women performed according to the record in Scripture. *See also* Carpenters, Carpentry; Fishermen, Fishing; Kings; Priest, High Priest; Rabbi; Scribes.

Further Reading

Tischler, Nancy M. *Men and Women in the Bible*. Westport, Conn.: Greenwood Press, 2002.

Work: Women's

Women in the Bible are typically pictured performing household chores: **cooking** or serving **meals**, suckling and protecting their children. As seen in the descriptions of the home and **family**, these were time-consuming and important tasks. The woman was often the teacher of the faith and of the customs for the young children, keeping the family firmly in the tradition.

In Ancient Israel

Among the wives of the Patriarchs, we see women at the **well**, drawing the water for their family and for strangers in need. They were undoubtedly the ones who also washed the **clothes** at the nearest stream, laid them out to dry, and carried them home, probably in baskets on their heads. They must certainly have been an integral part in the chores of the nomadic life of the tent-dwellers—cording the **goats'** hair for the fabric, weaving it. The young woman Moses married seemed to be tending the sheep, probably work undertaken by daughters when the family had no sons.

Whenever they stopped for the night, the women drove the pegs in the ground, fixed the poles in place, placed the tent over them, raised the tent, and tightened the ropes. They put the cooking utensils and the furnishings in place, and when they were ready to move, their chores must have involved the packing and clearing and the loading of the **animals**.

It is hard for a modern woman to imagine how difficult the life of a woman would be without running water, fixed shelter, refrigeration, and washing machines. These women would gather the food, grind the meal, cook the **bread** and meat, serve it, and clean the pots.

In **Egypt**, we see midwives who delivered the Hebrew babies and refused to honor the edict of the Pharaoh. When Moses was a child, his young sister Miriam watched over him, negotiated his adoption by the Egyptian princess, took him home to her mother, and probably spent many years quietly teaching him about the Israelites, his secret family. When Moses fled to

Midian, he met his future bride first as a shepherdess trying to water her animals, but unable to remove the heavy **stone** cover from the well. We later see her as a traditional member of the family, but it is she who has the background in the faith and advises Moses that their son must be **circumcised**. In the **Exodus**, we see Moses's sister, Miriam, proclaimed a prophetess; she was also a poet who led the women in **song** and **dance**; and she was an advisor to her brother Moses when he became a man and a leader of his people.

Later, when the Lord provided the **law** to Moses, the description of the **Tabernacle** detailed much that was to be women's work: the baking of the shewbread, the preparation of the tent, the needlework involved in the embroidered hangings, and the serving of the sacred meal. Although women were excluded from the priesthood, they had tasks connected with worship. Hannah, the mother of Samuel, for example, continued to provide her son with garments even when he had gone to live with Eli, the old **priest**, at Shiloh. A wife and mother was also a seamstress. In the New Testament, Dorcas was apparently a talented seamstress, celebrated for her many gifts to others (Acts 9:36).

Prostitutes

That the law of Moses is so clear about prostitution suggests that this was already a common profession for women, perhaps one of the few ways a single woman could survive. Certainly in pagan fertility cults, temple prostitutes were a standard part of the worship practices. But we see traces of prostitution among the Hebrews as well, as in the case of Judah, who was tricked by his daughter-in-law, Tamar. She dressed like a prostitute to trick him into doing his duty: "And she put her widow's garments off from her, and covered her with a veil, and wrapped herself, and sat in an open place.... When Judah saw her, he thought her to be a harlot; because she had covered her face" (Gen. 38:13 -15). This passage indicates that prostitutes were recognized by their placement and their clothing. (It also indicates that a widow had a prescribed code of dress that identified her status.) A footnote to this passage asserts that the word *zonah* indicates a common harlot, but a later reference to a *hagedeshah* suggests that Judah thought the woman to be a **Canaanite** temple prostitute (KJV, 77)

Later, it was Rahab, possibly a prostitute or perhaps just an innkeeper, which Hebrews apparently considered the same thing, who helped the Israelites at the siege of Jericho. Still later, Solomon described in some detail the "strange" and tantalizing woman who lures the man to his ruin (Prov. 2:16–22, 5:3–8, 6:24ff). Samson also discovered the temptations of prostitutes, especially among the **Philistines**. The prophet Hosea married a prostitute, possibly a temple prostitute named Gomer, who became for him a symbol of Israel's infidelity to God.

Other Roles for Women

By the time of the **Judges**, women had a greater variety of tasks. Deborah was both a wife and a judge; she was invited to join the soldiers in battle. Jael, pretending to be a generous hostess, offering shade and curds, demonstrated her prowess at tent-building (as well as murder) by using a tent peg to kill her enemy. This suggests that the tent-dwelling existence and chores continued for men and women, perhaps in this case as an auxiliary to warriors who had to fight in fields far from home.

Ruth, on the other hand, was the more traditional woman, accepting her primary mission to be a wife and mother. When she found neither role available, she became a gleaner, picking up the last scraps of grain from the fields, apparently at some considerable risk to her own safety because the **agricultural** workers harassed defenseless women. The Book of Ruth is full of words connected with women and their work.

The widow is clearly seen as pitiful, having no protector. The mother is the woman most blessed, having both a husband to care for her and a child to guarantee her future security. A childless widow, without men to support her, travailing in the fields, was the most pitiful of all creatures. Later, in the apocryphal Book of Judith, we see that a wealthy and prestigious widow, like Judith, however, might have considerable power, feeling an obligation to fight her village's battles for them through the use of feminine wiles.

Among the monarchs, women served as queens and as consorts, usually wielding their power through weak or smitten husbands or through their sons, for example, Jezebel or Bathsheba. During the time of Exile, Esther was chosen to be part of the harem of a foreign monarch, where her main work was to remain beautiful to please her master. Women were not usually the primary rulers, like the Queen of Sheba, but had authority and persuasive devices at hand that they could use.

Gleaning in the fields, a task performed often by women, most notably Ruth. The poor and widowed were allotted the last of the grain, which they were free to "glean" after the laborers had harvested most of the grain.

Upper-class women in **Roman** times had considerable power, if not authority. Herodias used her daughter Salome's erotic dance to pressure her husband, Herod, to behead John the Baptist. The tradition of music and dancing suggests that this was work that women might be assigned, although it was not discussed in Scripture.

The most impressive tribute to the multifaceted life of women in the Old Testament is in Proverbs describing the "virtuous woman":

The heart of her husband doth safely trust in her, so he shall have no need of spoil.

She will do him good and not evil all the days of her life.

She seeketh wool, and flax, and worketh willingly with her hands.

She is like the merchants' ships; she bringeth her food from afar.

She riseth also while it is yet night, and giveth meat to her household, and a portion to her maidens.

She considereth a field, and buyeth it: with the fruit of her hands she planteth a vineyard.

She girdeth her loins with strength, and strengtheneth her arms.

She perceiveth that her merchandise is good: her candle goeth not out by night.

She layeth her hands to the spindle, and her hands hold the distaff.

She stretcheth out her hand to the poor; yea, she reacheth forth her hands to the needy.

She is not afraid of the snow for her household: for all her household are clothed with scarlet.

She maketh herself coverings of tapestry; her clothing is silk and purple. . . .

She looketh well to the ways of her household, and eateth not the bread of idleness. (Prov. 31:10–31)

This prosperous woman was clearly a partner with her husband, keeping the household running smoothly, overseeing the servants in the manufacture of **cloth**, buying and selling in the marketplace, planting a **vineyard** with her own hands. She was a philanthropist and an advisor, a hard-working, smart business woman.

The New Testament describes other women with business skills: Lydia, for example, was a dyer of purple, with a household of workers. Priscilla appeared to be a partner with her husband in the tent-making industry, which they invite Paul to share. There were more single women in Roman times, largely because monogamy had become more customary. Some women seem to have had their own private means, as in the cases of Mary and Martha, and Mary Magdalene. The women who were present at the **Crucifixion** may have helped in the preparation of the body for entombment. Later they became **church** workers and evangelists working faithfully in the new churches.

Paul apparently met a number of professional women on his travels, some in curious lines of work. One was a diviner who followed Paul, crying out that he was from God. She was the **slave** of a magician (Acts 13:6–12). Wherever Paul went on his missionary journeys, he found women who invited him to their homes and lent him support. Some of these, like Lydia, had maidservants in their homes to perform the rituals of **hospitality**.

Actually, whether in the earliest days among the tent-dwellers, or among the sophisticated city-dwellers in **Greek** and Roman times, the women would have baked the bread, churned the milk, spun the thread, woven the cloth, made the clothes, served the meals, minded the children, and kept the flame of their homemade candles and of the faith burning. *See also* Cooking, Cooking Utensils; Cloth; Clothing; Meals; Tents; Witchcraft, Witches.

Further Reading

Tischler, Nancy M. *Legacy of Eve: Women of the Bible*. Atlanta: John Knox Press, 1977.

Writing and Reading

Bits and pieces of clay tablets, papyrus, and vellum have helped archaeologists piece together the history of writing. These scholars now realize that writing has its roots deep in prehistory, perhaps going back to the ninth millennium B.C. In fact, some believe that the "mark" God put on Cain after he had slain his brother was a sign that protected him from others—a pictorial symbol. At first such picture-symbols were reduced to a few marks and then were stylized to wedge-shaped signs that represented both syllables and ideas. Using symbols for plants, animals, birds, fish, and men, scribes could use this primitive cuneiform, and later hieroglyphics, to communicate over great distances.

The earliest writing actually discovered and studied by archaeologists dates from approximately 3100 B.C. It was found at Uruk on the Euphrates River. Parallel examples have been found in the Nile Valley. These were in cuneiform and hieroglyphics, which flourished for the next three millennia (Philip J. King and Lawrence E. Stager 2001, 300). The alphabet, which was essential for narrative accounts, was invented by the **Canaanites** in the second millennium B.C.

For the first phase of its usage, writing was used almost exclusively for accounting: lists of merchandise and land donations. Signs on tokens (small clay coins with inscriptions) are among the first evidence of these transactions. In Ur, **scribes** began to use writing for other purposes, such as recording the names of the dead on gold, silver, and lapis lazuli bowls, statues, and seals to ensure the survival of the person after death. By 2000 B.C., records

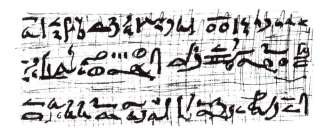

Egyptian writing on papyrus from the "dream manual."

of historical events—the celebration of victories—represented the "gateway to literature.... writing was used for historical, religious, legal, scholarly and literary texts" (Schmandt-Besserat 2004). By then, various peoples were experimenting with alphabets, and literacy had become one of the hallmarks of culture (D. J. Wiseman, K. A. Kitchen, and A. R. Millard 1980, 1657–1671).

Inscriptions from Canaanite artifacts suggest that, although literacy was still very limited, there were schools for scribes for "the elite ... namely, scribes versed in international languages of the day," as is evidenced by a multilingual cuneiform text from Ashkelon, dating from about the thirteenth century B.C. (Philip King and Lawrence Stager 2001, 303).

Although writing is not mentioned in Scripture before the time of the **Exodus**, when Moses transcribed the **law**, Abraham's background in Ur would indicate that he might have been literate and perhaps taught his children and grandchildren this skill. Moses may well have learned to read and write from the royal scribes in the courts of **Egypt**. Someone else must have taught him Hebrew script, as well as Egyptian. He is credited with writing the five books of the Pentateuch, including the words Jehovah spoke to him, the record of the Exodus, and the commandments handed down on Sinai.

Joshua apparently could write as well, as is evidenced by his writing a copy of the commandments when he renewed his people's **covenant** with God (Josh. 8:32). Samuel wrote the charter of the kingship of Saul (1 Sam 10:25), and David wrote his hasty letter to order the death of his mistress's husband (2 Sam.11:14). Solomon wrote numerous letters to Hiram of Tyre about the details of the **Temple** that he proposed building (2 Chron. 35:4), perhaps using a scribe.

Most of the **prophets** wrote down their prophesies after delivering them orally. There is evidence of literacy with Isaiah (1 Chron. 26:22; Isa. 8:1) and likelihood of this ability with Hosea (8:12) and Malachi (3:16). Although Jeremiah dictated his letters to an amanuensis named Baruch, he may well have also been literate as well (Jer. 30:2).

Many leaders throughout history used the services of scribes to do their writing for them. Ezra

Aramaic writing on papyrus, fifth century B.C.

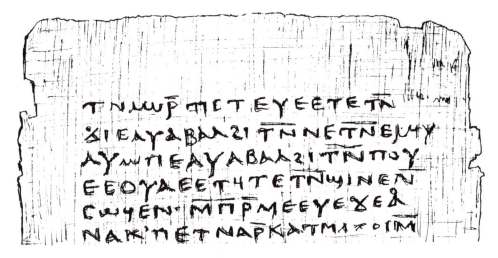

Coptic writing on papyrus, part of John's Gospel.

was a scribe himself (8:34), and Nehemiah wrote down the covenant to argue against the enemies of his people (Neh. 9:38). We also know that Daniel and other Jews of the **Babylonian** captivity could read and probably could write as well, although the skills were not invariably linked (Dan. 5:24).

Jesus referred frequently to writings of the Old Testament, which he had probably studied as a young boy. He wrote at least one time in public, with a stick in the sand, suggesting that he who is without sin should cast the first stone at the woman taken in adultery.

Talmudic scholars note that there were schools that taught reading and writing in the days before the destruction of the Second Temple, thereby making literacy more common than the 10 percent estimated among non-Hebrews in the first century A.D. Scholars believe that some of those who heard Jesus's words were literate and made contemporary records of his "sayings." It was, after all, an expectation in Jewish society that men should be able to read the scriptures (Alan Millard 2003, 16).

Paul and the other **apostles** were clearly literate, communicating frequently in writing through the **epistles** they exchanged. The vast majority of the New Testament books are letters addressed to various members of the faith community.

The importance of writing, especially as an element of preserving and transmitting sacred Scripture, grew over time. The monks of the medieval period laboriously transcribed the words in beautiful illuminated manuscripts. The later Protestant reformers translated those words and made them available, especially after the invention of the printing press, to multitudes of people in the increasingly literate world of the Renaissance. In the

United States, one of the main reasons for the establishment of schools was to teach children to read and write so that they could read the Bible. Today, the Bible remains a best seller, with translations into every language and with formats to match most any taste. *See also* Scribes; Writing Materials.

Further Reading

King, Philip J. and Lawrence E. Stager. *Life in Biblical Israel.* Louisville, Ky.: Westminster John Knox Press, 2001. Millard, Alan. "Writing," in *Biblical Archaeology Review* (November/December 2003). Schmandt-Besserat, Denise. "How Writing Came About," http:biblicalarchaeology.org (accessed March 20, 2004). Wiseman, D. J., K. A. Kitchen, and A. R. Millard. "Writing," in *The Illustrated Bible Dictionary.* Sydney, Australia: Tyndale House Publishers, 1980.

Writing Materials

Early peoples used almost any surface for their writing: **stone**, wooden writing-boards, **ivory** treated to hold a wax surface, clay tablets, baked tiles, papyrus, or **leather** (or parchment). They even used ostraca (singular *ostracon*), which were bits of broken pottery. Originally in Mesopotamia, merchants made marks on *bullae,* or wads of clay, to send brief and simple messages over long distances. **Scribes** later wrote in cuneiform script on clay tablets, using reeds with wedge-shaped tips. A trimmed reed or brush might also be used on ostraca, marking with a natural form of ink.

Archaeologists have uncovered a variety of writing materials, including the following, many of which are on display in museums, such as the Archaeological Museum at the University of Pennsylvania.

Clay was readily accessible and easy to handle and therefore was the most common writing material. It could be rolled out in a tablet, on which a scribe could make incisions with a reed. When dried or baked, the marks became permanent. It also could molded into a small balls or *bullae* (in which a seal impression was made). These were useful for sealing documents and might also serve as a form of currency. They were sometimes marked with the number of objects included in the shipment, serving as a primitive form of packing inventory.

A number of bullae have been discovered in Jerusalem and other places, apparently used to seal documents written on papyrus or leather. After the scribe completed writing the document, he rolled and secured it with a string, applying a glob of soft clay to the knot and then pressing a seal to it. When the recipient opened the document, he could tell if anyone had tampered with it by the broken bullae or the mutilated seal. Many of these have been preserved by the intense fire that destroyed the scrolls. The heat baked

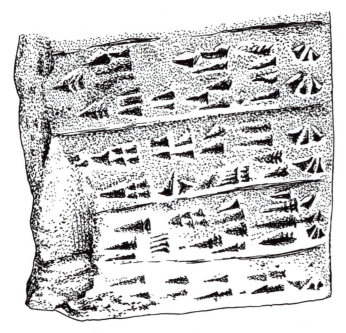

Clay tablet written in Ugaritic cuneiform from fourteenth century B.C., Syria.

and preserved these seals, thousands of which have survived.

Clay was regularly used for **pottery**, both baked and unbaked. The pots broke easily, and the bits of broken pots provided potsherds or *ostraca*, which were the scrap paper of the time, useful for writing notes in ink. After they had served their purpose, they could be discarded.

Wood might also be used. Yahweh ordered Ezekiel to write on a "piece of wood," which was perhaps wooden writing board (Ezek. 37:16). Apparently the wood was coated with wax, often formed into books with the leaves fastened together in some manner. In **Assyrian** reliefs, scribes were pictured taking head counts on such wooden tablets. Because wood decays quickly, evidence of this form of writing materials has not survived except in art.

(In some cases, *ivory* might be substituted for wood. For example, archaeologists have discovered one book of omens, containing 12 ivory leaves with **gold** hinges, prepared for Sargon II of Assyria, and recovered from a well at Nimrud (Philip J. King and Lawrence E. Stager 2001, 308). This would have been an expensive way to communicate, probably limited to royalty on special occasions.

Stone was the preferred material for official decrees, which were often scratched or chiseled in stone so that they might be made public and permanent (John L. White 1993, 432–433). Numerous of these lapidary inscriptions have survived, including the Moabite Stone, a basalt stela with an inscription that commemorates a victory of the king of Moab over Israel. This stone and others have proven valuable to historians who are seeking to understand the written form of the languages.

For more extensive writing rather than terse inscriptions, "it was customary to coat rough stone surfaces of stelae or walls with plaster before writing on them in ink" (Philip J. King and Lawrence E. Stager 2001, 304). This is probably what was intended by the command in Deut. 27:3: "you shall write on them all the words of this **law**." To have inscribed the extensive laws outlined in the books of Moses with a mallet and chisel would have been enormously time-consuming. A discovery of a an ink inscription on a once-plastered wall at a **temple** in the Jordan Valley dating about 700 B.C. testifies to the continuing use of this method for transcribing important documents.

Metal, like stone, might be incised, probably with a stylus, a tool with a pointed **iron** tip, as Jeremiah noted: "The sin of Judah is written with an iron stylus; with an adamant point it is engraved on the tablet of their hearts, an on the horns of their **altars**" (Jer. 17:1). The Qumran Caves included among their finds the "Copper Scroll"—two copper sheets engraved in Hebrew. Some speculate that precious sacred documents were often copied onto copper, which was more permanent than vellum or papyrus. Bronze arrowheads have also been discovered in the Judean hills, inscribed with the names of their owners. Metal bowls or pitchers might also have inscriptions, especially commemorative citations, scratched with a stylus. Although metal survives over time better than wood, it is also valuable and is often melted down to be used for other purposes, especially in time of war. Only a few of these examples of writing have survived.

Parchment and *vellum* (skins) were used for important correspondence. For the documents of the faith, this was the primary material. The Dead Sea Scrolls, for example, were written in ink on tanned leather. Various skins might be prepared for this purpose including sheep, goat, and calf. The leather was stripped of all hair and other matter, cleaned thoroughly, and treated so that it would remain pliable. These were the Hebrews' favorite writing surface during Old Testament times.

Cyperus papyrus, the basic material for the earliest paper, is made from the stems of this water plant.

Papyrus, which came into use during the Persian and Greco-Roman eras, was lighter and more useful for personal correspondence. It was the preferred material in **Egypt**, being especially valuable in a dry climate. Although not mentioned in the Bible, it was apparently used for Hebrew documents as early as the seventh century B.C. The jars of papyrus scrolls found at Qumran, near the Dead Sea, contain a letter and a list of names, legal and administrative documents, and bits of Scripture. These discoveries are remarkable because the material is perishable and discoveries of papyrus documents are rare.

The ink used on the plaster, parchment, or papyrus was either black or red. Baruch, Jeremiah's amanuensis, said that Jeremiah dictated the words to him, "and I wrote them with ink on the scroll" (Jer. 36:18). The black ink was charcoal mixed with gum, oil, and other materials. The red was derived from red ocher or iron oxide and gum. The stylus, which functioned as a brush, was a reed, cut at an angle to come to a point, much like a quill pen.

The documents could be of varying size: tiny clay balls, larger tablets of clay, small or large wooden writing boards, and papyrus or vellum scrolls of great length. After biblical times, the early book form became increasingly popular. This was the *codex*, a number of papyrus or parchment sheets collected and folded, fastened together at one edge, and sometimes protected by covers. They might be enclosed by an envelope, stamped with the wax seal of the sender. *See also* Scribes; Writing and Reading.

Further Reading

King, Philip J. and Lawrence E. Stager. *Life in Biblical Israel*. Louisville, Ky.: Westminster John Knox Press, 2001. White, John L. "Letter-writing in Antiquity," in *The Oxford Companion to the Bible*. New York: Oxford University Press, 1993. Wiseman, D. J., K. A. Kitchen, and A. R. Millard. "Writing," in *The Illustrated Bible Dictionary*. Sydney, Australia: Tyndale House Publishers, 1980.

Yoke

The yoke, which the Hebrews probably discovered first in **Egypt,** was a simple brace that held **animals** together for hard labor. Usually **oxen** or **donkeys** were yoked together with a stick of wood, from which were suspended ropes that fit around their necks. This then was attached to another stick that held the **plow.** When the farmer pressed down on the plow, and the oxen pulled forward, the plow would dig into the earth.

In later years, yokes were made of heavier wood and finally were even of **iron.** The early design was simple and light, but too easy to break. Even in this case, the animal's head was forced to a lowered position, and he was pressed to conform to the movements of his partner. Behind him, the farmer held the **goad** to urge him forward, and the plow pulled against the earth to make his movements laborious. It is not surprising that animals fought this device.

It was important to the animal's comfort and efficiency that he not be "unequally yoked," meaning matched with a different species. Thus, an ox was not to be yoked with a donkey (Deut. 22:10). This particular mismatch became the source of Paul's image of the union between a Christian and a non-Christian, using the yoke as an apt metaphor for **marriage.** As he says, "For what do righteousness and wickedness have in common?" (2 Cor. 6:14). Earlier, the Psalmist had considered the inappropriate yoking of a whole people to an alien god, the **Baal** of Peor.

Oxen, which were either male or female (but castrated if male), were yoked in pairs, as were donkeys. Some historians even believe that **camels** may have been yoked for plowing. The term *yoke* referred to two animals. Thus, when Job, at the latter end of his life, had a "thousand yoke of oxen," he actually had two thousand oxen (Job 42:12).

The prophet Jeremiah, under inspiration from God, made bonds and yokes and put them on his own neck. He also sent them to various **kings** in the region with the commandment that they were to "put their neck under the yoke of the king of **Babylon**" (Jer. 27). The yokes were to symbolize submission to this tyrant, who had already stripped the **Temple** of many of its treasures. False **prophets** argued that Judah and her neighbors should throw off Babylon's yoke, even enticing Jeremiah to let Hananiah the prophet take the yoke off his neck and break it. But God's firm response was: "Thou has

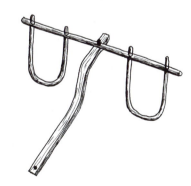

Two types of yokes, one heavier than the other, for donkeys or oxen working together to pull plows or chariots.

Yoke with ropes rather than wood around animals' necks, a type probably used by many farmers.

broken the yokes of wood; but thou shalt make for them yokes of iron" (Jer. 28:13). This signified that the harsher burden would follow their feckless rebellion. Jeremiah used a series of vivid images to enforce his prophetic utterances. The yoke as a metaphor for submission was one of his best, and wearing the gear designed for animals reinforced the humiliation of submission.

Because the most common use of the term *yoke* is for oppression, "breaking the yoke" means breaking free of bondage. Jesus's use of the imagery is unique in Scripture: "Take my yoke upon you and learn from me, for I am gentle and humble in heart, and you will find rest for your souls. For my yoke is easy and my burden is light" (Matt. 11:29–30). His command for a willing submission to an "easy yoke" contrasts with the "yoke of slavery" that the Jewish Christians tried to force on their gentile converts (Gal. 5:1; 1 Tim. 6:1). Peter insists, commenting on the insistence that **Christian** converts must first follow Jewish practices: "Now then, why do you try to test God by putting on the necks of the **disciples** a yoke that neither we nor our fathers have been able to bear?" (Acts 15:10). *See also* Agriculture; Animals; Goad; Plow.

Zealots

The Zealots were a part-political, part-religious group who arose during the time when Judea was controlled by the Hellenists and subsequently the **Romans**. Their goal was to defend the **law** and the national life of the Jewish people against idolatrous Rome. This aggressive and fanatical war party operated between the time of Herod until the fall of Jerusalem and the defeat at Masada. "The members of this party bore also the name *Sicarii*, from their custom of going about with daggers (*sicæ*) hidden beneath their cloaks, with which they would stab any one found committing a sacrilegious act or anything provoking anti-Jewish feeling"(Kaufman Kohler 2005). Josephus, the Jewish historian of the period, notes that the name *zealots* came from "Jesus the son of Gamala, and Ananus the son of Ananus, when they were at their assemblies, bitterly reproached the people for their sloth, and excited them against the zealots; for that was the name they went by, as if they were zealous in good undertakings, and were not rather zealous in the worst actions, and extravagant in them beyond the example of others" (Josephus, *Wars* 4:3:9).

The original group arose under the leadership of Judas the Galilean and was an organized band considered "robbers" by the historian Josephus. They rebelled against King Herod, largely because he was an Idumean. Their preferred method for dealing with problems was assassination. The original targets were: "Whoever steals the libation cup (Num. 4:7) or curses one with the aid of the Holy Name, ... or has sexual intercourse with a Syrian [heathen] woman]" (Kaufmann Kohler 2005). These are all acts that were not causes for criminal procedure, but were nonetheless offensive to those of the faith (or those who were "zealous" for God). Examples include Phineas, who killed Zimri for his relations with a Midianitish woman (Num. 25:11–14); Levi, who slew the men of Shechem for raping his sister Dinah (Gen. 34); and Judith, who beheaded her conqueror and would-be seducer (in the apocryphal Book of Judith).

The Maccabean revolt against the Hellenizing influences and atrocities reinforced this extreme view of purity and righteousness against enemies of God, encouraging acts of violence. In that period, Phineas came to be regarded as the ideal type of priestly zealot. Their basis for attacks against foreign rulers was that they had no **king** but God. Calling Herod "king" was especially repellent to these true believers, as he was not even a Jew. In addition, when Rome controlled the region, their cultural practices were an offence to the Zealots: their gymnasia, their arenas, their graven images, and their celebration of numerous religions were all abominations.

Recent scholars (notably Richard A. Horsley) have determined that this was not a single band of **warriors** with a coherent strategy, but a ragtag coalition of popular groups seeking the overthrow of Rome, notably the "dagger" people, who were urban terrorists, those seeking a messianic savior, and followers of popular kings. All were outraged by the colonial situation, which brought to Palestine great debt, unemployment, social division, crime, banditry, and finally revolt (J. Andrew Overman 1993, 826). The Zealots were not simple "robbers" as stated by Josephus, but religious purists who rejected foreign control. They plotted the murder of Herod, hiding their daggers beneath their cloaks. Although their plot was discovered, they had won such enthusiastic support from the people that the spy who revealed their plans was torn apart by the crowd.

This party, also known as *Nationalists* or *Caanites,* appeared in guerilla bands that "traversed Galilee under the leadership of Ezekias, whom Herod executed. But the Nationalist party was not destroyed, only held in check, during his iron reign.... During the civil war which followed the accession of Archelaus ... the standard of the Nationalists was again raised in Galilee. Judas, the son of Ezekias, took possession of the city of Sepphoris, and armed his followers from the royal arsenal there" (Alfred Edersheim 2004, 167). This same Galilean family provided leaders and martyrs to this movement for some years, with the final one, Eleazar, dying at Masada along with the whole Nationalist cause.

Because this band was active in the region of the Galilee during his entire lifetime, Jesus of Nazareth would have known some of them. Simon the Zealot, also known as Simon the Canaanite (Luke 4:15, Acts 1:13), may have been a member of this group, and it is suspected that Judas Iscariot was also a member. Judas appears to have dreamed that Jesus would be an earthly ruler, the messianic hope, overthrowing the despised Roman Empire. Some believe that Jesus preached the Sermon on the Mount (Matthew 5) as an attack on the Zealots' advocacy of armed resistance and the violent overthrow of the government. The Zealots' principle of refusing to pay **taxes** to the Romans was directly contradicted by Jesus's admonition to "render unto Caesar that which is Caesar's." He made it clear to his **disciples** that his kingdom was "not of this world."

It is possible that Barabbas, whom the mob sought to free in place of Jesus, was part of this terrorist group. When these ardent patriots found themselves ruled by usurpers, they fled with their wives and children to the **caves** and fortresses of Galilee to fight and die for their convictions and for their freedom.

There was a brief moment in history when the Zealots seem to have triumphed, 66 A.D., the time of the First Jewish Revolt against Rome. At that point, led by John of Gishala, a large number of citizens rebelled against the Romans; they seized both Jerusalem and the ancient **fortress** at Masada. The "patriots of Jerusalem celebrated the year 66 as the year of Israel's deliverance from Rome, and commemorated it with coins bearing the names of Eleazar the **priest** and Simon the prince" (Kaufmann Kohler 2005).

But they were soon to see reversals. "The year 67 saw the beginning of the great **war** with the Roman legions, first under Vespasian and then under Titus; and Galilee was at the outset chosen as the seat of war" (Kaufmann Kohler 2005). The rebellion ended with the destruction of the **Temple** and the city in 70 A.D. The people were reduced to slavery, the treasures carried off to Rome. The Zealot leader Eleazar ben Jair made his last stand at Masada, where he and his followers fought off the Romans during a prolonged siege. At the end, the last of the rebels committed suicide rather than serving these idolatrous foreigners. In his final speech, Eleazar said that it was a "privilege to die for the principle that none but God is the true Ruler of mankind, and that rather than yield to Rome, which is **slavery**, men should slay their wives and children and themselves, since their souls will live forever" (Kaufmann Kohler 2005). *See also* History in the Bible; War, Warfare: General; Warriors.

Further Reading

Edersheim, Alfred. *The Life and Times of Jesus the Messiah.* Peabody, Mass.: Hendrickson Publishers, Inc., 2004. Josephus, Flavius. *The Works of Josephus.* Peabody, Mass.: Hendrickson Publishers, Inc., 2001. Kohler, Kaufmann. "Zealots," http://www.jewishencyclopedia.com (accessed February 11, 2005). Overman, J. Andrew. "Zealots," in *The Oxford Companion to the Bible.* New York: Oxford University Press, 1993.

Selected Bibliography

Bibles and Apocryphal Materials

Alter, Robert. *The Five Books of Moses: A Translation and Commentary*. New York: W.W. Norton and Company, 2004.

Barnstone, Willis, ed. *The Other Bible*. San Francisco: HarperSanFrancisco, 1989.

The Holy Bible (1611 King James Version). Philadelphia: A.J. Holman Company, 1947.

The King James Study Bible. Nashville: Thomas Nelson Publishers, 1988.

Meeks, Wayne A., ed. *HarperCollins Study Bible*. New York: HarperCollins Publishers, Inc., 1989.

Miller, Robert J., ed. *The Complete Gospels*. San Francisco: Harper Collins Publisher, 1994.

The New English Bible. Oxford: Oxford University Press, 1970.

The New International Version Study Bible. Grand Rapids, Mich.: Zondervan Publishing House, 1995.

Sproul, R.C., gen. ed. *Reformation Study Bible* (English Standard Version). Orlando: Ligonier Ministries, 2005.

The Word in Life Study Bible. Nashville: Thomas Nelson Publishers, 1993.

Commentaries, Dictionaries, and Encyclopedias

Alexander, Pat, ed. *Eerdmans' Family Encyclopedia of the Bible*. Grand Rapids, Mich.: Wm. B. Eerdmans Publishing Co., 1978.

Davidson, Gustav. *A Dictionary of Angels, including the Fallen Angels*. New York: The Free Press, 1967.

Douglas, J.D., ed. *The Illustrated Bible Dictionary*, 3 volumes. Sydney, Australia: Tyndale House Publishers, 1980.

Henry, Matthew. *Matthew Henry's Commentary in One Volume*. Grand Rapids, Mich.: Zondervan Publishing House, 1961.

Holman, C. Hugh. *A Handbook to Literature*, 3rd edition. New York: The Odyssey Press, 1972.

Jeffrey, David Lyle, ed. *A Dictionary of the Biblical Tradition in English Literature*. Grand Rapids, Mich.: William B. Eerdmans Publishing Company, 1992.

Metzger, Bruce M., and Michael D. Coogan, eds. *The Oxford Companion to the Bible*. New York: Oxford University Press, 1993.

Miller, Madeleine S., and J. Lane Miller. *Harper's Bible Dictionary*. New York: Harper and Row, 1961.

Walker, Barbara G. *The Woman's Encyclopedia of Myths and Secrets*. San Francisco: HarperSanFrancisco, 1983.

Web Sites

Official Web site for the *Catholic Encyclopedia*, http://www.newadvent.org (accessed December 23, 2004).

http://www.everythingjewish.com (accessed May 11, 2005).

Official Web site for *The Jewish Encyclopedia*, http://www.jewishencyclopedia.com (accessed December 23, 2004).

Web site for *The Oxford English Dictionary*, http://www.oed.com (accessed December 23, 2004).

Resource Books

Albright, William Foxwell. *Yahweh and the Gods of Canaan*. Garden City, N.Y.: Doubleday & Company, Inc., 1969.

Anderson, Bernard. *Understanding the Old Testament*. Englewood Cliffs, N.J.: Prentice-Hall, Inc., 1966.

Boyd, Robert T. *Tells, Tombs and Treasure: A Pictorial Guide to Biblical Archaeology*. New York: Bonanza Books, 1969.

Bulfinch, Thomas. *Mythology*. New York: The Modern Library, n.d.

Cansdale, George. *All the Animals of the Bible Lands*. Grand Rapids, Mich.: Zondervan Publishing House, 1970.

Chase, Mary Ellen. *The Bible and the Common Reader*. New York: The Macmillan Company, 1945.

Chase, Mary Ellen. *Life and Language in the Old Testament*. New York: W.W. Norton and Company, Inc. 1955.

Darom, David. *Animals of the Bible*. Herzliam Israel: Palphot Ltd., n.d.

DeVaux, Roland. *Ancient Israel: Its Life and Institutions*. Trans by John McHugh. Grand Rapids, Mich.: William B. Eerdmans Publishing Company, 1961.

Edersheim, Alfred. *The Life and Times of Jesus the Messiah*. Peabody, Mass.: Hendrickson Publishers Inc., 2004.

Eusebius. *Eusebius' Ecclesiastical History*. Trans., C.F. Cruse. Peabody, Mass.: Hendrickson Publishers, 2000.

Fagan, Brian. *Eyewitness to Discovery*. Oxford: Oxford University Press, 1996.

Falk, Ze'ev W. *Hebrew Law in Biblical Times*. Provo, Utah: Brigham Young University Press, 2001.

Ferguson, George. *Signs and Symbols in Christian Art*. New York: Oxford University Press, 1966.

Figgis, John. *The Divine Right of Kings*. Gloucester, Mass.: P. Smith, 1970.

Finkelstein, Israel, and Neil Asher Silberman. *The Bible Unearthed: Archaeology's New Vision of Ancient Israel and the Origin of its Sacred Texts*. New York: Simon and Schuster, 2001.

Freeman-Grenville, G.S.P. *The Holy Land: A Pilgrim's Guide to Israel, Jordan and the Sinai*. New York: Continuum, 1998.

Gaster, Theodor H. *Myth, Legend, and Custom in the Old Testament*. New York: Harper & Row, 1969.

Gillespie, George. *Aaron's Rod Blossoming*. London: Richard Whitaker, 1670.

Glueck, Nelson. *The Other Side of Jordan*. Winona Lake, Ind.: Eisenbraums, Inc., 1970.

Gower, Ralph. *The New Manners and Customs of Bible Times*. Chicago: Moody Press, 1987.

Graves, Robert, *The Greek Myths*, 2 volumes. Baltimore, Md.: Penguin Books, 1955.

Graves, Robert, and Raphael Patai. *Hebrew Myths: The Book of Genesis*. New York: McGraw-Hill Book Company, 1964.

Hamilton, Edith. *Spokesmen for God: The Great Teachers of the Old Testament*. New York: W. W. Norton and Company, Inc., 1936.

Hare, Harold W. *The Archaeology of the Jerusalem Area*. Grand Rapids, Mich.: Baker Book House, 1987.

Heaton, E. W. *Everyday Life in Old Testament Times*. New York: Charles Scribner's Sons, 1956.

Holtz, Barry W., ed. *Back to the Sources: Reading the Classic Jewish Texts*. New York: Simon and Schuster, 1992.

Jenkins, Philip. *Hidden Gospels: How the Search for Jesus Lost Its Way*. New York: Oxford University Press, 2001.

Josephus, Flavius. *The Works of Josephus*. Peabody Mass.: Hendrickson Publishers, Inc., 2001.

Keller, Werner. *The Bible as History*. New York: Bantam Books, 1982.

King, Philip J., and Lawrence E. Stager. *Life in Biblical Israel*. Louisville, Ky.: Westminster John Knox Press, 2001.

Klinck, Arthur W. *Home Life in Bible Times*. St. Louis, Mo.: Concordia Publishing House, 1947.

Latourette, Kenneth Scott. *A History of Christianity*. New York: Harper and Row, 1953.

LeGall, Dom Robert. *Symbols of Catholicism*. New York: Assouline Publishing, 2000.

Lewis, C.S. *Reflections on the Psalms*. New York: Harcourt, Brace and World, 1958.

Morey, Charles Rufus. *Christian Art*. New York: Longmans, Green, 1935.

Negev, Avraham. *The Archaeological Encyclopedia of the Holy Land*, rev. ed. New York: Thomas Nelson Publishers, 1986.

Osborne, Harold, ed. *The Oxford Companion to Art*. Oxford: The Oxford Press, 1970.

Platt, Rutherford H. Jr., ed. *The Forgotten Books of Eden*. New York: The New American Library, 1974.

Pleins, David J. *When the Great Abyss Opened: Classic and Contemporary Readings of Noah's Flood*. New York: Oxford University Press, 2003.

Ritmeyer, Leen and Kathleen. *Secrets of Jerusalem's Temple Mount*. Washington, DC: Biblical Archaeology Society, 1998.

Ryken, Leland, and Tremper Longman III, eds. *A Complete Literary Guilde to the Bible*. Grand Rapids, Mich.: Zondervan Publishing House, 1993.

Sandmel, Samuel. *The Hebrew Scriptures: An Introduction to Their Literature and Religious Ideas*. New York: Oxford University Press, 1978.

Seel, Thomas Allen. *A Theology of Music for Worship Derived from the Book of Revelation*. London: The Scarecrow Press, Inc., 1995.

Segal, Alan F. *Life after Death: A History of the Afterlife in Western Religion*. New York: Doubleday, 2004.

Sheler, Jeffery L. *Is the Bible True? How Modern Debates and Discoveries Affirm the Essence of the Scriptures*. San Francisco: HarperSanFrancisco and Zondervan Publishing House, 1989.

Smith, Mark S. *The Early History of God: Yahweh and the Other Deities in Ancient Israel*. Grand Rapids, Mich.: William B. Eerdmans Publishing Company, 2002.

Smith, William Robertson. *Lectures on the Religion of the Semites*. Sheffield, England: Sheffield Academic Press, 1995.

Sproul, Barbara C. *Primal Myths: Creating the World*. New York: Harper and Row, 1979.

Squire, Russel. *Church Music: Musical and Hymnological Developments in Western Christianity*. Bloomington, Minn.: Bethany Press, 1962.

Tischler, Nancy M. *Legacy of Eve: Women of the Bible*. Atlanta: John Knox Press, 1977.

Tischler, Nancy M. *Men and Women of the Bible*. Westport, Conn.: Greenwood Press, 2002.

Trawick, Buckner B. *The Bible as Literature: The New Testament*. New York: Harper and Row, 1968.

Trawick, Buckner B. *The Bible as Literature: The Old Testament and the Apocrypha*. New York: Harper and Row, 1970.

Volbach, Wolfgang F., and Max Hirmer. *Early Christian Art*. New York: Abrams, 1961.

Werner, Eric. *The Sacred Bridge: The Interdependence of Liturgy and Music in Synagogue and Church during the First Millennium*. New York: Ktav Publishing House Inc., 1984.

White, L. Michael. *From Jesus to Christianity*. San Francisco: HarperSanFrancisco, 2004.

Wight, Fred Hartley. *Manners and Customs of Bible Lands*. Chicago: Moody Press, 1953.

Wilson-Dickson, Andrew. *The Story of Christian Music: From Gregorian Chant to Black Gospel*. Minneapolis: Fortress Press, 1992.

Woolley, C. Leonard. *The Sumerians*. New York: W.W. Norton & Company, 1965.

Wright, George Ernest. *Biblical Archaeology.* Philadelphia: The Westminster Press, 1957.

Wright, George Ernest, ed. *Great People of the Bible and How They Lived.* Pleasant-ville, N.Y.: The Reader's Digest Association Inc., 1974.

Wright, George Ernest. *The Westminster Historical Atlas to the Bible,* Philadelphia: The Westminster Press, 1956.

Index

About the Author

NANCY M. TISCHLER is Professor Emerita of English and the Humanities at the Pennsylvania State University. Her previous books include *Men and Women of the Bible* (2003) and *Student Companion to Tennessee Williams* (2000), both available from Greenwood Press.